Kiwis *in* CONFLICT

Kiwis *in* CONFLICT

200 YEARS *of* NEW ZEALANDERS AT WAR

Chris Pugsley
with **Laurie Barber, Buddy Mikaere,
Nigel Prickett and Rose Young**

David Bateman
in association with

TAMAKI PAENGA HIRA
AUCKLAND MUSEUM

Half-title:
Some of the 7000 New Zealanders who served with the Royal Navy during the Second World War.
JORDAN COLLECTION, AIM

Opposite title page:
In the Switch Trench on the Somme, 15 September 1916. BRITISH OFFICIAL PHOTOGRAPH, AIM

Page 7:
A V company patrol moving in the Horseshoe (a company defensive position located eight
kilometres south east of the Australian Task Force base at Nui Dat), Phuoc Tuy Province 1967. NZ
DEFENCE OFFICIAL PHOTOGRAPH, AIM

Page 8:
A New Zealand soldier holding a captured German MP40 Schmeisser submachine gun. QEII ARMY
MEMORIAL MUSEUM

Publisher's note: All photographs and artefacts within the collection of Auckland War Memorial
Museum Tamaki Paenga Hira are noted with the letters AIM.

Originally published in 1996 as *Scars on the Heart* by David Bateman Ltd,
30 Tarndale Grove, Albany, Auckland, New Zealand in association with Auckland War Memorial
Museum.

This new edition published in 2008.

Copyright © Auckland Museum, Chris Pugsley, Laurie Barber,
Buddy Mikaere, Nigel Prickett, Rose Young, 1996, 2008
Copyright © David Bateman Ltd, 1996, 2008

ISBN 978-1-86953-708-1

Cover design Shelley Watson/Sublime design
Bookdesign by Chris O'Brien/Pages Literary Pursuits
Printed in China through Colorcraft Ltd, HK

CONTENTS

Part Four: The Second World War 1939–1945

Chris Pugsley

Part Five: Searching for Security

Chris Pugsley

FOREWORD

In his foreword to the first edition of this remarkable book, Dr T L Rodney Wilson, Director of Auckland War Memorial Museum from 1994 to 2007, noted that the Museum was 'unique among Australasian museums, being both a comprehensive museum of Human History and Natural History, and a War Memorial'. The evolution of Auckland's museum into a War Memorial was the achievement of Thomas Frederick Cheeseman (1845–1923), the Museum's curator. It was Cheeseman's vision and acumen that convinced the people of Auckland and the New Zealand Government to fund the building of a War Memorial Museum in the Auckland Domain, completed in 1929. In fact, the Museum's association with armed conflict goes back to its foundation in 1852, during the hiatus in hostilities between Maori and Pakeha following the conclusion of the 1845–46 Northern War, and before the commencement of the Waikato War of 1863–64. John Smith, the founder, stated in his announcement in the *New Zealander* in October 1852 that the Museum would collect, among other things, 'Weapons, clothing, implements etc., etc., of New Zealand, and the Islands of the Pacific'.

Auckland Museum's first home was a humble cottage in Grafton Road, virtually under the ramparts of the heavily fortified Albert Barracks, and its first official patron was Lieutenant-Governor Colonel R H Wynyard, the military commander of the tiny garrison town. Many of the great examples of Maori taonga or ancestral treasures that came into the Museum's collections in the late 19th century arrived as a result of the displacement of Maori communities and property caused by the fighting. In this context Cheeseman's reinvention of Auckland Museum as a War Memorial seems less of an adroit political manoeuvre than a conscious realisation of political reality, locating the human and natural history stories of New Zealand within the heritage of conflict and resolution between its constituent peoples.

Scars on the Heart, the war-themed gallery installation on which this book is based, was conceived to complement and honour the 12,143 names inscribed in stone on the walls of Auckland War Memorial Museum's Halls of Memory. These record men and women, enlisted for service from the Province of Auckland, who gave their lives that others may live in freedom: 7297 in World War I, 4702 in World War II, 41 in Korea, 66 in Malaya/Borneo, and 37 in Vietnam. *Scars on the Heart* seeks to honour the sacrifices of all New Zealand in wartime. It has been assembled from primary sources – the immediate personal impressions of New Zealanders at war at home and abroad, as recorded in the collections of Auckland War Memorial Museum. Since *Scars on the Heart*, the title of the original edition of this book, was first published, these collections of letters, diaries, photographs, medals and memorabilia have grown considerably, as New Zealanders have been increasingly concerned to preserve the memory of the sacrifices made by their kinsmen and women. The impact of war on the day-to-day detail of personal lives is perhaps the insight that strikes home most keenly in this wonderful volume. The authors, under the energetic guidance of Dr Chris Pugsley, have ensured that these stories are told as much as possible through the personal accounts of men and women who served. Let them never be forgotten.

Dr Vanda Vitali
Director
Auckland War Memorial Museum

ACKNOWLEDGEMENTS

That *Scars on the Heart* exists is due to the vision of Rodney Wilson, the Director of the Auckland Museum. He drew together a team of historians and experts in late 1994 to discuss the re-design of the War Memorial Floor of the Auckland Museum. From these meetings came the concept and themes for the permanent exhibition on the impact of war on New Zealand society over the last two centuries, appropriately titled 'Scars on the Heart'. This book is the written work of some of the members of that team: Laurie Barber, Buddy Mikaere, Nigel Prickett, Rose Young and Chris Pugsley. Equally valuable insights and advice came from other members who, though not directly involved in the writing, played a vital role in the exhibition, and as its themes and structure are integral to the exhibition so they are as much co-contributors to this book as those listed as authors. Rodney Wilson, Judith Binney, Gillian Chaplin, Peter Hughes, Gordon Maitland, Katrina Stamp and Richard Wolfe have all shaped this work. Rodney Wilson, in particular, always saw the bigger picture both in design and story terms while we occasionally got lost in the trees. Jenny Cave had the enthusiasm and drive to get the concept for the book off the ground, and Michael Evans continued a benign but influential overview.

Indeed one should name all the museum staff who have laboured on 'Scars on the Heart' over the last two years. Each one owns a piece of their exhibition and of this publication: Rose Young and her equally hard-working and dedicated history curatorial slaves: Myfanwy Eaves, Chris Arvidson, Debbie Dunsford, Ramola Prasad, Grant Philpott and all. Merv Beach and his team of weapons enthusiasts. Richard Wolfe and his display staff: Geoffery Logan, Angus Mackenzie and Natalie Guy. Julia Gresson and her conservators: Merv Hutchinson, Janet Clougherty, Annette McKone, Stephen Brookbanks, Gaynor Duff, Nel Rol and David Wise to name but a few.

The invaluable Library staff, first under Peter Hughes, and then, in turn, under Gordon Maitland and Janice Chong, who found manuscripts, references and photographs on demand, and who also put up with the singing: Jacqui Eathorne, Jeny Curnow, Richard Head, Maureen Sole, Sandy Sparks, Heather Stone, Cecelia Street, Eddie Sun, and especially Barbara Spiers who kept track of all the photographs and illustrations. In addition there are the many library volunteers who have assisted with xeroxing and in sorting material. Katrina Stamp and her educational team: Wendy Johnstone, Sarah Ross, Florence Hassell, and Angela Farrell. The receptionists: Sharron Prouse, Chris Whitman and Maureen Hoeft. All of the attendants, with particular thanks to John Clarke. The night staff, and the unsung heroes of finance branch.

Krzysztof Pfeiffer has taken the wonderful photos of the exhibition objects, coloured images, and produced the detailed images of the New Zealand, Anglo-Boer and First World War campaigns. Nikki Payne deserves equal thanks for her fine photography and printing of the hundreds of images from the Second World War and post-war periods. Tracy Wray did not want to be mentioned but is a hard-working member of Krzysztof's band. The visual excellence of the photography in both the exhibition and the book is their achievement.

Then there are the many others: Kai Hawkins and his team at Design FX, Brian O'Flaherty, Scott Elliffe, Jenny Ball, Priscilla Thompson, Barbara Russell, Chris Crump's gang, Frances Carswell's sandwich team, Mere Whaanga, Oliver Stead, Tony Rasmussen, Andrew Carr, Louis Le Vaillant, Angela Lassig, Tania Walters, Kimi, Sharon Sweeney Lauder, Antoinette Nielson, Judy Wong, John Wilson, David Wilkie, Rob Robson and Noel Lane. These and the many others who worked on the project and work in the Auckland Museum have made the last two years of 'Scars on the Heart' such an exhilarating and enjoyable experience.

This work is dedicated to all of the staff of the Auckland Museum and to the institution which they serve.

The writers would like to acknowledge the sources, references and individuals quoted in the text. In turn I would like to thank Laurie Barber, Buddy Mikaere, Nigel Prickett and Rose Young. Each of their chapters is worthy of a book, and each has presented a uniquely personal view of a period in our history. There are many stories that could not be given justice within the space I gave them, and any shortcomings or omissions are my own as editor.

Special thanks are due to Marion Minson, Joan McCracken, and the staff of the Alexander Turnbull Library; Major Colin Hodgkinson, Windsor Jones, and Dolores Ho of the Queen Elizabeth II Army Memorial Museum, and the Kippenberger Memorial Library of that institution. Frank Stark, Bronwyn Taylor and staff of the New Zealand Film Archive, Wellington, Carolyn Carr and the staff of the Defence Library, Headquarters New Zealand Defence Force. Lieutenant Commander Peter Dennerly and his staff at the Royal New Zealand Navy Museum, Devonport. Tim Ryan, Richard Stowers, Malcolm Thomas, Lawrence Watt, Alwyn Owen, John Crawford Assistant Director History of Headquarters New Zealand Defence Force, Jock Vennell and Judith Martin of the *New Zealand Defence Quarterly* and the many others who have given time and advice to answer all our queries.

Chris O'Brien designed the layout, Geoffrey Cox did the maps, and Natalie Guy the diagrams and charts. All have our appreciation, but special thanks are due to Tracey Borgfeldt our editor at David Bateman Ltd who unsuccessfully battled with me to produce to deadline, yet still managed by threats and cajoling to get this work out of us. This book is her achievement.

Chris Pugsley

PART 1

New Zealand Wars

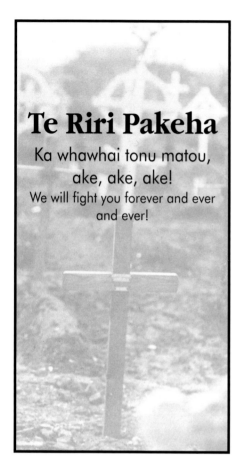

Te Riri Pakeha

Ka whawhai tonu matou, ake, ake, ake!

We will fight you forever and ever and ever!

Mate atu he toa, whanau mai he toa — One warrior dies another is born
AD1100–1769

We are a warrior people. It was fighting that brought us here over a thousand years ago when our islands in the eastern Pacific Ocean, Te Moana nui a Kiwa, became too crowded. In this new empty land, we lived peaceably until we gathered our numbers again, and now we have the strength, we fight. We fight for possession of the best hunting and fishing grounds and the warm, fertile valleys and coastal plains where our kumara can flourish.

We hold the lands our ancestors lived on through force of arms.

> *A man took possession of territory by the strength of his arm, and rested his claim on his conquests. 'Na Tenei,' he would say, stretching out his arm — 'by this I obtained it'.*
>
> Rev. Thomas Buddle[1]

We jealously guard our mana, our honour, and insults are avenged with blood. As a result, we whirl in an endless cycle of revenge.

We also fight for love.

> *He wahine, he whenua, ngaro ai te tangata.*
> *Because of women and land, men die.*

But we are looking upon this fighting world, where the best warriors are marked by alertness and swift reflexes in the wielding of hand weapons, differently now. Ships have arrived no tawhiti noa, from the far distance, and there is much that is new to think about.

Ka huri te ao — The world changes
1769–1840

Since 1769, when Captain Cook came on the first of his three visits, we have obtained new weapons. Steel blades for axes, patiti, and guns, pu. Weapons of thrilling power.

Muskets have changed the way we fight. Hand-to-hand combat has given way to dealing death from a distance. Chiefs measure their power by the number of guns their followers carry. We work long hours to accumulate trade goods; timber, dressed flax, meat (from the pigs we now own), fish and potatoes. We do it to purchase fire power.

Formerly our fighting was small-scale skirmishing and feuding. Now there is slaughter of thousands as tribes who have guns take their revenge on those who have not yet been able to trade for them.

> *When we ask the chiefs, when their wars with each other will terminate? they reply, never, because it is the custom of every tribe who loses a man to*

Previous page:
Meremere from Whangamarino Redoubt, 1863. Charles Heaphy.
ALEXANDER TURNBULL LIBRARY

never be content without a satisfaction and death of another...

George Clarke, missionary[2]

Hongi Hika of Ngapuhi has been quickest among us to take advantage of the new. He visited England in 1820 and met King George IV. The King gave Hongi many gifts which, except for a suit of armour, he traded for guns in Sydney. When Hongi returned to this country, he mounted a reign of terror. In 1823 Hongi dragged his war canoes across country to raid Te Arawa at Rotorua. Te Arawa, with one gun, faced Hongi's soldiers, with their hundreds. Te Arawa is said to have lost many people.

But those who live by the sword die by it, as the Pakeha say, and Hongi died of a gunshot wound in 1829.

Now warfare is changing again, because everyone has guns. But the old fierce joy in war has not changed.

[the warriors] were engaged in preparation, rubbing up their muskets, decorating their heads with feathers and tying around their waists shawls and handkerchiefs of various colours... some few of the leading men had a mantle of scarlet cloth trimmed with dogs' hair, others had splendid native mats: thus equipped with two or three cartridge boxes each, and here and there a sabre they now prepare for their haka or dance, accompanied with horrid yells and screeches, throwing their bodies into frightful attitudes, distorting their countenances, turn their tongues nearly to the back of their heads, and their eyes rolled inside out, each jumping as high as his strength would allow him, tossing up the same time the stock of his musket. To display the brass, which is kept perfectly bright...

From the diary of Henry Williams, missionary[3]

Because everyone now carries a gun, caution rules; we sit behind bushes and take potshots at each other! The fighting even stops when the arms dealers' schooners sail in to replenish our supplies.

Tuesday 13 March 1832
A schooner arrived and anchored at some distance. Sent the boat to the pa to enquire the loss, answer 4 killed and 3 mortally wounded. Could not learn what the Ngapuhi had suffered. The firing did not cease until dusk. A boat came alongside from the Ngapuhi and informed us that 1 was killed and some wounded. The European who came in the boat expressed his intention of supplying Ngapuhi with arms and ammunition as much as they required on trust.

From the diary of Henry Williams, missionary[4]

Wednesday 14 March 1832
Calm, clear night. The natives in the Pa pouring forth bitter cries and lamentations, bewailing their loss, and a gun occ'ly fired, adding to the solemnity of the scene. At break of day two canoes came from Ngapuhi alongside the Fairy *for some great guns and small arms ammunition etc. etc, the pa opened fire upon them but the shot fell short. The natives seemed to scowl upon us, knowing that we disapproved of their proceedings.*

From the diary of Henry Williams, missionary[5]

What we need is a way to exit from this unproductive war without any stain on our dignity. We have found one in the teaching of missionaries, whom we have hitherto tended to ignore. The Atua of the missionaries requires peace. So we are getting baptised as Christians, in order not to have to pursue revenge.

Te Hokowhitu a Tu — The Warriors of the War God
(The Northern Wars) 1840–1850

On 6 February 1840, at Waitangi, we Maori sign a Treaty which cedes control of our country to the Pakeha. In exchange, we are promised protection from foreigners, equal citizenship, and a guarantee that our lands and possessions will remain ours.

It is now four years after the signing and one of us, the Bay of Islands Chief Hone Heke, has found cause to regret it. The government has not stopped the sale of our lands, and its move to Auckland from the first capital at Kororareka, or Russell, has meant that Heke and the other northern chiefs have suffered a huge decline in trade and revenue.

Heke's protest has been to cut down the flagpole at Kororareka four times. Kororareka burns and although we are blamed, the fire might have been started accidentally by residents rushing to get out. The government is scared. There are more of us than them. They have brought in troops from Australia.

Heke and his cousin Kawiti are our leaders in the fighting which the Pakeha call 'Heke's war'. Waka Nene and his brother Patuone, among others, are fighting on the Pakeha side for here is a chance to settle some old scores. At Puketutu we meet a British bayonet charge and experience exploding rockets for the first time. Although many of us are killed, we drive the British soldiers into the wet night. As they retreat, we look on them with contempt because they leave their dead in the fields for us to bury.

Later at Ohaewai, the British say 'We'll soon deal to Johnny Heke!' and lob gas-filled canisters ineffectually into Heke's pa. But Heke wins handily when the troops charge into a killing ground and fall in rows before the fire power of his muskets and carronade loaded with chain.

the Soldiers fell on this side and that like so many sticks thrown down
Rihara Kou of Ngapuhi[6]

The British military command have taken Heke and the genius of Kawiti too lightly and pay the price. Waka Nene describes his Ohaewai ally, Colonel Despard, the British commander as 'he tangata kuware', 'a stupid person'.

WAR IN THE NORTH, 1845–46

1. **March 1845:** Hone Heke cuts down the flagpole and sacks Kororareka.
2. **May 1845:** Battle at Puketutu ends without clear victor.
3. **June 1845:** Tamati Waka Nene defeats Heke at Ahuahu.
4. **1 July 1845:** Kawiti defeats troops at Ohaeawai.
5. **January 1846:** No clear winner at Ruapekapeka but the war is ended.

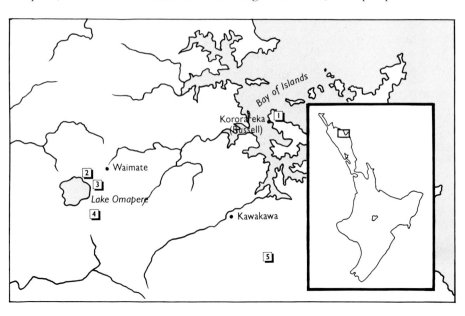

* * * * *

Ruapekapeka is our fighting pa high on the Bay of Islands hills with a clear view around it, now that we have chopped down the forest. We have watched the Pakeha and their Maori friends, over one and a half thousand in all, drag their heavy guns from the sea; through the swamps and bush and up steep hills to fire on us. We defend from the safety of our bomb-proof shelters and we hold our lines. We look to God to help and protect us. We have been fighting since the first day of the new year, 1846.

* * * * *

On the morning of Sunday 11 January 1846 while most of us attend morning service in the rear of our fort, or take a rest from the almost continuous shelling in the rear trenches, the Pakeha attack, and get into the pa. We continue the fight from the forest but outnumbered and with our many wounded we withdraw.

After the battle Kawiti says:

> *I have stood five successive engagements with the soldiers belonging to the greatest white nation in the world, the soldiers that we have been told would fight until every man was killed. But I am perfectly satisfied they are men, not gods and had they nothing but muskets, the same as ourselves, I should be in my pa at the present time.*[7]

This is the end of Heke's war. The government has issued a proclamation of peace and Ngapuhi are returning to their homes.

Tamati Waka Nene fought alongside the British authorities in the Northern War — very much in pursuit of his own aims. AIM

Ka po te ao — The world turns dark (The slide into civil war) 1850–1860

With all the Pakeha coming to settle in Auckland city, this has been a time for opportunity and prosperity for many of us who have supplied the town with food and building materials.

These new immigrants are beginning to outnumber us! And with the protection of numbers, many of them act as if they own the country. Few Pakeha now bother to learn to speak our language, and in fact it's only our land they want — especially the lands on the outskirts of the fledgling settlement of New Plymouth in Taranaki and closer to Auckland, the rich Waikato plains. We are being pushed to the margins.

We realise that for Pakeha, wealth is calculated not in people but in economic power, which is based on the productivity of the land. If sales of our land do not stop, Maori face a future in which we will be dependent on the Pakeha for our livelihood.

In order to avoid a future of dependency, we have put our lands under the mana of a king chosen from our own people.

It is now 1859. Governor Browne has agreed to buy land in Waitara, Taranaki, offered by Te Teira. The land is not Te Teira's to sell, by our customary law. It is clear to us that the implications of this are of the most serious kind: no land will ever be safe from purchase. We are resisting the surveying of the disputed land by building a fort there, and the government has sent soldiers and guns to fight us.

When we signed the Treaty of Waitangi in 1840 the Governor said that we and the Pakeha were one people. Maori are citizens equal with Pakeha.

Today is 17 March 1860. Some exult, but today is a day of great sadness. Our fellow citizens have come to battle against us and we fear that a bitter, bloody civil war has begun.

* * * * *

Haere hei kai ma nga manu Go as food for the birds
Potatau Te Wherowhero, the first Maori King[8]

Some of us, from Ngati Maniapoto, from Ngati Haua, from Ngati Raukawa, from Waikato itself, march south to the Taranaki fighting. The warning of our king, Potatau, rings in our ears.

On the morning of 6 November 1860, many of us meet our fate at a place called Mahoetahi. You can go there yet and see our final resting place. Our memorial reads:

He whakamaharatanga i nga Rangatira toa o Waikato, a Wetini Taiporutu ma, I hinga ki konei

In remembrance of the warrior chiefs of Waikato, of Wetini Taiporutu and his comrades, who fell here

British troops stand guard over the house of King Potatau Te Wherowhero at Ngaruawahia. NICHOLL ALBUM, ALEXANDER TURNBULL LIBRARY

Riria! Riria! — Fight on! Fight on! (The war in the Waikato and the Bay of Plenty) 1863–1865

It is now 1863. The fighting continues in Taranaki. Here, Pakeha Auckland seethes with rumours of attack by Waikato, and our people who were living quietly on the southern borders of Auckland have been cleared out, as if they were dangerous rebels! We are told it is because we will not swear an oath to the Queen and give up our arms.

Sir George Grey, who has been recalled as Governor, says that he will not destroy our king, but will dig around him until he falls of his own accord. We have been pondering the Governor's meaning as we watch the troops build a road south toward us. Pakeha call it the Great South Road. It is no ordinary road, but a chain in width with a metal surface, wide and strong enough to carry gun carriages and ammunition carts.

We say, if you carry the road past the Mangatawhiri stream we will know you mean war.

The road has come to the stream. The Pakeha have built what they call a warehouse beside it. It has blockholes for firing out of, and looks just like a military barracks.

* * * * *

On 12 July 1863 the troops cross the Mangatawhiri and we Waikato, the King Movement tribes, and our allies, are at war.

Tamihana Tarapipipi Te Waharoa — William Thompson, 'The King-maker'

Wiremu Tamihana was a King Movement leader (Pakeha call him 'The King-maker'), a committed Christian and a hereditary chief of Ngati Haua. His story of the war is our story.

Tamihana saw what the consequences of war would be, given the disparity of numbers, equipment and organisation between us and the Empire. He had tried to stop his kinsman Wetini Taiporutu from going to fight in Taranaki in 1860 and arranged the brief truce between the government and Taranaki in 1861. He also wanted to stop the slide towards the civil war in the Waikato. He said:

> *I wish to understand the case, but do not see it. They [the Pakeha] have forsaken the right way, they have become deranged. But let us not take up arms in an unrighteous cause... I do not forget some of the Kings of Judah who engaged in unrighteous war, how they perished in their sin. Therefore I hesitate, and say let us see our way.*[9]

After troops invaded the Waikato, Tamihana gritted his teeth and said:

> *While the governor holds his weapon I hold mine. I am not willing to go to war but let me have a just cause.*

At Rangiriri, along the line lying between the river and Lake Waikare, we Waikato Maori, Tamihana among us, have made a determined stand. We have built a central redoubt supported by a line of double trenches. These defences are garrisoned by about five hundred men. We face a force of over 1400 supported by artillery and, floating untouchable on the river, six gunboats.

Wiremu Tamihana Tarapipipi Te Waharoa saw clearly the consequences of war with the Pakeha, given the disparity in numbers, equipment and organisation of the two sides. AIM

We fight bravely and throw the British troops back time after time, but the shelling takes its toll. The trenches are breached. With the redoubt almost surrounded, Tamihana and some of the other leaders slip away in the night, taking the wounded with them.

At dawn, a white flag is raised so that terms can be negotiated. Some of us ask the British for more powder so that we can continue the fight. The soldiers refuse. But under the white flag, the troops are soon pouring into our trenches shaking hands with us, pleased that the fighting has ended. In the confusion we are told we are now prisoners and that they we should give up our weapons. The ignoring of the usual conventions of war is irritating, but it is the deaths of some of the women and children inside the Rangiriri redoubt which most upsets Tamihana who has returned with reinforcements who are now not needed.

In an effort to stop further slaughter, Tamihana has sent his greenstone mere to General Cameron and a message that he wishes to negotiate peace. Both mere and message are ignored.

The deaths at Rangiriri lead to an understanding that the innocent should be moved to a safe place although that place is not named. We Maori think that Rangiaowhia village is to be the safe haven for these noncombatants. But war comes to this undefended kainga on the morning of 21 February 1864, its sound borne on the hooves of the cavalry and the crash of weapons.

The raupō houses of the village are full of fearful women, crying children and men too old to fight. More of them crowd into the churches to shelter from the rifle fire. The troops surround the houses and fire into them. The fire is returned by those of us with weapons and the commanding soldier goes down, mortally wounded. The Pakeha troops are incensed. The houses are set on fire, whether deliberately or from the fireflash of musket powder is not known. An old man trying to surrender holds his empty hands up. 'Spare him! spare him!' command the officers but shot after shot crashes out and he falls down dead. The soldiers are beyond control and loot the village. Tamihana, who has been leading a successful action nearby, is grief stricken. Later he writes:

> *Three of the laws of England were at that time broken by the laws of New Zealand; for this New Zealand law*
>
> *1. Ambuscades; that is to say, secret attacks.*
> *2. Killing women and children.*
> *3. Burning people alive with fire.*
>
> *When I found that English people adopted that mode of action, I called to the Maori and enjoined them not to return again to those practices. 'Leave it to be for England to take up the putrefactions of my ancestors, viz killing women and children, and burning people alive in their sleeping houses.' O friends, because of this did I fully consent to the fighting; because of my women and children having been burnt alive in the fire which was suffered, rather than the edge of the sword, to consume their flesh. I would not have regarded it had it been only the men.*[10]

Nearby at Orakau, on 31 March 1864, three hundred of us stand again against the Pakeha. Maori soldiers from many of the tribes are with us in a battle which lasts three days and which earns us the admiration of the British General, Cameron. The Pakeha call upon us to surrender and we stand to give this famous reply:

> *Ka whawhai tonu matou, ake, ake ake...*
> *We will fight you forever and ever and ever.*

On the afternoon of the third day, out of water and ammunition, we decide to run. Ringed by troops and artillery Orakau has now become a trap. Placing the women and children in the middle, we break for a freedom which many do not make. In the deserted pa, in the swamps or amongst the scrub, unarmed women or the wounded get little sympathy, their lives end with a bayonet thrust.

Most distressing is the killing of a widow, bayoneted as she brushes the dirt from her dead husband's face for one last look. The cavalry ride down the survivors like animals and the pursuit that marks the end of the battle leaves

Rewi Maniapoto was in command of Maori fighters at Orakau, where the pa held out for two days against over-whelming British numbers in the best known battle of the New Zealand Wars. Rewi and part of his force escaped south of Puniu River on the third day. There was to be no more fighting in the Waikato. AIM

over one hundred and sixty dead. Most of those left alive are wounded. It is the end of the Waikato war.

Rangiaowhia and Orakau break Tamihana. On 27 May 1865, at his birthplace of Tamahere, he is finally permitted to lay down his taiaha and surrender. A mean-spirited General Carey accepts his surrender with these words:

> *You caused your people to go to war. You have now ended it by making peace.*[11]

When Tamihana died on 27 December 1866 most of his lands and those of his people were either sold or under the control of Pakeha.

> *There is something very sad in the death of this patriotic chief; a man who possessed such an influence for good, should thus have been ignored by the Government, when by his aid, had he been admitted to our councils, a permanent good feeling might have been established between the two races.*
>
> Rev. Richard Taylor, missionary[12]

Pukehinahina

Now, in 1864, the fighting has shifted to the Bay of Plenty, to Tauranga. The British have now invaded this land and many of us hurry home from the Waikato to defend our homes here.

We build a fort, flimsy above ground but with strong hidden earthworks. The Pakeha call it 'the Gate Pa', but we know it as Pukehinahina. The British call on us to surrender but we refuse. Our chief jokes:

> *E kore au e whakaae kia hoatu aku pu; engari ka aea atu koe a ka parakuihi au ki Te Papa...*
> *I cannot give up my guns but if you wish I shall have breakfast with you in Te Papa...*[13]

Our handful fight a great battle with the British and win. They panic before our guns and run. They will remember this day, 29 April 1864, as their heaviest defeat.

At Pukehinahina we fight under a set of written rules, through which we aim to stay true to our Christian beliefs in the midst of war.

> *1. Do not kill Pakehas left wounded but leave the wounded to live whether they are Maori or Pakeha.*
> *2. Neither work by stealth.*
> *3. Let the fight be a fair fight.*
> *4. Let our wounded be cared for.*
> *5. The soldier who flees, being carried away by his fears, and goes to the house of the priest with his gun (even though carrying arms) will be saved; I will not go there.*
>
> Rawiri Puhiraki, Ngai Te Rangi chief, and Henare Taratoa, Christian, of Ngati Raukawa[14]

The British wounded lie dying on the night battleground, crying out in their pain and fear. Men and women at the risk of being shot creep about the Pukehinahina killing fields to find them and give them water.

At the next battle, at Te Ranga, the British take their revenge. Our pa is only half completed when they come in overpowering force. Rawiri and Henare are both shot and bayoneted at Te Ranga. When they turn over Henare's body they find our rules pinned to his shirt. In his pocket is the text for the day:

**Waikato War 1863–1864:
Maori Roll of Honour**

July, 1863
Koheroa, Martin's Farm, Great South Road: 30 killed

August
Williamson's Clearing: 3 killed

September
Camerontown (Lower Waikato): 7 killed
Kakaramea, Hill's Clearing: 6 killed
Pukekohe East, Burtt's Farm: 40 killed

17–18 September
Wairoa South stockade and Otau: 8 killed

October
Titi Hill, Mauku: 20 killed

November
Rangiriri: 50 killed

December
Wairoa ranges: 8 killed

February, 1864
Waiari: 40 killed
Rangiaowhia: 12 killed
Hairini: 25 killed

March–2 April
Orakau: 160 killed

For their 'rebellion', taking arms to defend their homes against the invading army of the government, Waikato Maori are punished by the confiscation of over 1 million acres of their best land.

THE WAIKATO WAR, 1863–64

1. **1862-63:** Troops upgrade Great South Road to the Waikato.
2. **July 1863:** Troops cross Mangatawhiri Stream to invade the Waikato.
3. **July 1863:** Koheroa — first battle of the war.
4. **July-December 1863:** Maori attacks and ambushes in south Auckland.
5. **October 1863:** Maori evacuate Meremere defences.
6. **November 1863:** Crucial battle at Rangiriri opens way to the Waikato.
7. **December 1863:** Troops occupy Ngaruawahia.
8. **January 1864:** Troops advance up Waipa River.
9. **February 1864:** Troops occupy Te Awamutu and Rangiaowhia.
10. **March-April 1864:** Battle of Orakau ends Waikato War.
11. **April 1864:** Troops defeated at Gate Pa.
12. **June 1864:** Maori forces defeated at Te Ranga.

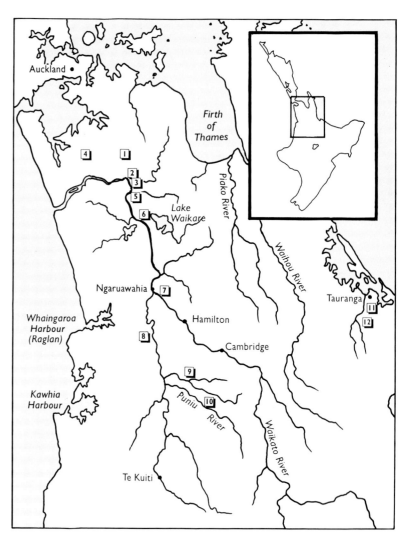

If thine enemy hunger, feed him. If he thirst, give him drink.

Our punishment for our 'rebellion'? The Governor says he will take a quarter of our best lands; his officials take half and, with time, most of the rest.

The settlers write in newspapers that we want to drive the Pakeha into the sea and return to our old warrior ways. The settlers reason is clouded by fear and ignorance. We are fighting for the ideals of justice both we and they believe in. We are fighting to keep the equality we were promised in 1840.

Nga tau o nga mamae — Years of despair (The Prophet's wars)

When war broke out in 1860 we felt betrayed. Pakeha said, take our religion and our form of government, develop the economy and learn to read and write and you will be citizens of the greatest empire of the world.

We tried to do all that. But when the Pakeha brought in a professional army to back up a faulty purchase of land, nothing of what we had been told seemed true any more. Pakeha seemed to intend to make our country theirs alone. The only thing we were expected to contribute was the land.

Outnumbered, outgunned, unable to trust the law, betrayed, we turned to religion.

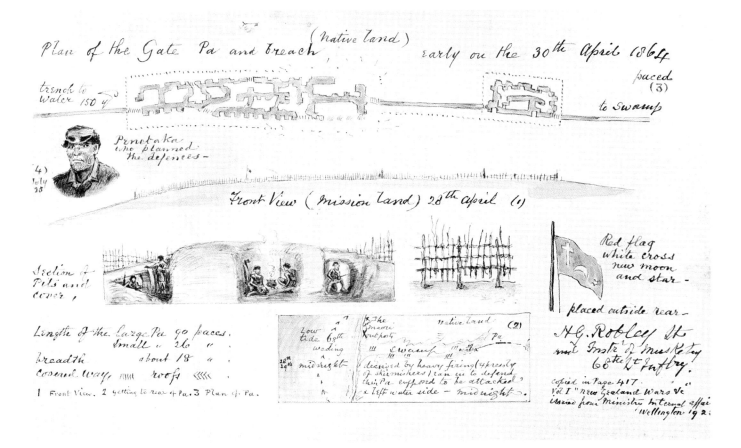

Plan of the Gate Pa and breach, (native land) early on the 30th April 1864

trench to water 150 y'

paced (3)

to swamp

Penetaka who planned the defences —

(4) July 28

Front View (mission land) 28th April (1)

Section of Pits and cover,

Length of the Large Pa 90 paces.
Small " 20 "
breadth about 18 "
covered way. [illegible] roofs [illegible].

1 Front View. 2 getting to rear of Pa. 3 Plan of Pa.

Low tide 68th Maori outposts native land (2)
[illegible] Swamp Pa
wading
18th 20th midnight deceived by heavy firing (expressly of skirmishers) ran in to defend their Pa supposed to be attacked
& left water side — midnight.

Red flag white cross new moon and star —

placed outside rear —

H.G. Robley Lt and Instr. of Musketry 68th Lt Inftry.

copied in Page 417.
Vol I "New Zealand Wars &c"
issued from Ministry Internal affair
Wellington 192[?].

The ingenious design of Pukehinahina (Gate Pa) enabled its Maori defenders to survive a massive bombardment with only light casualties and made their victory possible over vastly greater British forces. H G ROBLEY, AIM

Lay preacher Henare Taratoa is credited with drawing up the rules of engagement at Pukehinahina. Later he was killed at Te Ranga, where the rules were found pinned to his shirt. In his pocket was a text from the Bible: If thine enemy hunger, feed him. If he thirsts, give him drink. H G ROBLEY, AIM

23

Kereopa Te Rau was an early follower of the prophet Te Ua Haumene, and a fierce opponent of the government after his family was killed at Rangiaowhia in 1864. On 2 March 1865 he played a major part in killing the missionary Carl Volkner at Opotiki, and then swallowed the dead man's eyes, hence his name 'Kaikaru'. Kereopa led Hauhau in several fights before he joined the guerilla leader Te Kooti. In 1871 he was captured by Ropata Wahawaha. He was tried for murder and hanged in Napier in 1872. AIM

Ropata Wahawaha of Ngati Porou fought alongside Pakeha against Hauhau and Te Kooti in the East Coast, Poverty Bay and Urewera districts. A ruthless and implacable fighter, he personally killed many Hauhau including unarmed prisoners. He is shown wearing his New Zealand Cross and War Medal. For his services he was also awarded a sword of honour by Queen Victoria. AIM

In October 1862, The Archangel Gabriel called Te Ua Haumene, a teacher of the Bible in Taranaki, to be a prophet of the Lord. The angel told him that God had restored the covenant he made in Abraham, and Israel (Maoridom) were his people. He said that the book of Revelation, which prophesies the end, will be fulfilled in this generation: after this present time of tribulation, the righteous will dwell in New Canaan (New Zealand) in peace and unimaginable plenty.

For many of us this is a biblical message of hope and inspiration. In its services of worship, believers walk in prayer around huge masts. They speak in tongues and prophesy as Te Hau gives them utterance, and they believe that the future will hold every good thing that they have dreamed of possessing.

The Pai Marire, good and peaceful, faith has spread north to us, especially among soldiers. The Hauhau believe they have spiritual protection from the bullets, and this makes them persistent and reckless fighters. At Te Morere, Sentry Hill, and on Moutoa Island, we fight with the fearlessness of the zealot. Many of us are taken prisoner and the Governor has placed us on his island, Kawau, a military prison camp.

Under the faith we have taken the fight to many parts of the island now. Mt Eden has its share of Hauhau prisoners too, and in 1866 the Te Whakatohea chief Mokomoko, Horomona Poropiti (Solomon the Prophet) and others are hung for the killing of Carl Volkner the missionary at Opotiki.

* * * * *

Te Ua Haumene the prophet is also a prisoner and lives in the Governor's House on Kawau Island. His energy is drained by his captivity and the Governor lets him go home to die in October 1866. But new prophets have arisen everywhere to take his place.

Te Kooti Arikirangi has been a Hauhau prisoner, transported to the Chatham Islands. He has led a daring escape in July 1866 by capturing a visiting ship and sailing 600 kilometres back to New Zealand. Since landing on the mainland, he has conducted a guerilla campaign against anyone he regards as his enemy, Maori and Pakeha.

The campaign has taken Te Kooti and his small army through most of the central North Island, including the Waikato at Tapapa. At Tapapa Te Kooti shows his fearlessness. On a January morning in 1870 he ghosts out of the fog, turning on the soldiers chasing him in a dawn attack. To confuse his enemy he has his soldiers carry a British flag and one of his lieutenants, Peka Makarini, blows contrary orders on a captured bugle.

This has been a different war to the earlier imperial set piece engagements. The government troops are settlers and Maori, and much of the fighting has been between us and our relations. It finally peters out in 1872 when Te Kooti takes refuge in the King Country.

Since then we have kept the peace, and made peaceful protest our tikanga, our policy, and our mana. We have kept the peace regardless of the provocation.

But old injustices continue to bite, the enduring one being the loss of our lands for which we have fought through the century. Te Kooti said before he died in 1893 the canoe for us to paddle now is the law. We are now organising so that we have kotahitanga, political unity, and take our grievances not to the battlefield but to the courts of law. We do not, and will not, cease to seek justice.

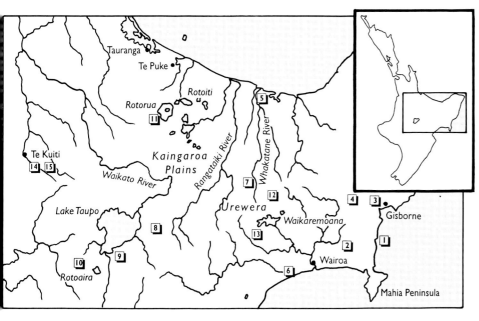

1. **10 July 1868**: Te Kooti Arikirangi lands at Whareongaonga after escaping with 300 followers from exile on the Chatham Islands.
2. **July-August 1868**: Fights off pursuit.
3. **10 November 1868**: Raids Matawhero, Poverty Bay.
4. **December 1868-January 1869**: Escapes from Ngatapa but many followers killed.
5. **9 March 1869**: Raids Whakatane.
6. **10 April 1869**: Raids Mohaka.
7. **April-May 1869**: Whitmore invades the Urewera.
8. **7 June 1869**: Te Kooti surprises militia at Opepe.
9. **25 September 1869**: Defeated by Ngati Kahungunu at Te Ponanga.
10. **3 October 1869**: Defeated at Te Porere.
11. **7 February 1870**: Driven from Rotorua.
12. **1870-1872**: Evades pursuit in the Urewera.
13. **February 1872**: Last shots fired at Mangaone.
14. **May 1872**: Reaches sanctuary in the King Country.
15. **1883**: Receives a formal pardon.

The land will remain forever to produce food, and after you have cut down the old trees to build houses, the saplings will continue growing, and in after years will become larger trees; while the payment I ask for will soon come to an end. The blankets will wear out, the axes will be broken after cutting down a few trees, and the iron pots will be cracked by the heat of the fire.

Te Waharoa of Ngati Haua [15]

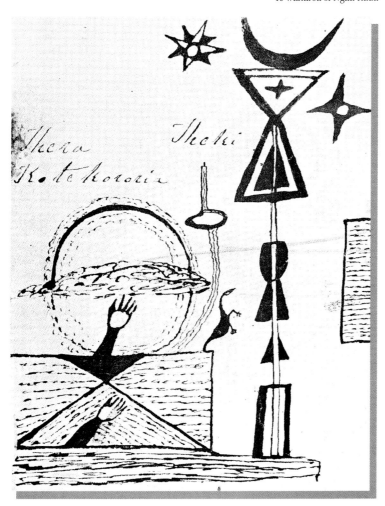

Aporo's book of dreams. Drawings by this Hauhau mystic show how in later years the faith leaned heavily towards the supernatural for the deliverance of Maori from the nightmare that the wars had created. ALEXANDER TURNBULL LIBRARY

The Settlers' Story

The 19th-century New Zealand Wars were fought between European settlers backed by the British Army and indigenous Maori tribes. The struggle changed this country from a Maori land to a predominantly European one.

In the 1840s fighting took place in the Bay of Islands (1845–6), Wellington (1846) and Wanganui (1847) districts. In 1860 war began in Taranaki where there was to be intermittent conflict for a decade. Also in the 1860s there was fighting in the Bay of Plenty, Wanganui and East Coast districts, and in the Waikato where the decisive campaign took place in the years 1863–4. The pursuit of Te Kooti, which extended over four years (1868–72) in a wide area of the central and eastern North Island, is generally considered to signal the end of the New Zealand Wars.

Reasons for the 19th-century fighting are not hard to find. At issue was the law and government which would prevail in New Zealand. While the transfer of vast areas of land from Maori to Pakeha is in many ways the most obvious result of the New Zealand Wars — and certainly the best remembered, hence the often used name 'Land Wars' — it must not be forgotten that the critical issue was one of power.

The settlers arrive

It was not until the late 18th century that Captain Cook put New Zealand firmly on the world map and Europeans began to settle here, to lay the foundation for the conflict which was to follow.

At first there were only a few missionaries, traders, sealers and whalers who were accommodated in an essentially Maori environment. This was to change in 1840 when Maori chiefs signed the Treaty of Waitangi to give sovereignty to the British Crown. At the same time tribes were guaranteed possession of their lands, forests and fisheries, and were given the rights and privileges of British subjects.

With a British governor and administration now in place there followed a rapid increase in European population, soon to put pressure on those very Maori possessions which the Treaty guaranteed. In 1840 the Pakeha population was about 2000; by 1858 60,000 settlers outnumbered the native Maori.

Almost all the newcomers were British. We came here to escape rural unemployment and the often miserable conditions in new industrial towns, and the inequalities of wealth and opportunity in our distant homeland. Professional men and the younger sons of county squires hoped for opportunities they were denied in crowded England; working men longed to give their families a better life. Some wished to recreate England in the south Pacific; many came to leave all that behind.

> *The aim of this company is not confined to mere emigration... Its object is to transplant English society... our laws, customs, associations, habits, manners, feelings — everything of England, in short, but the soil.*
>
> New Zealand Company, Twenty-third Report, 1847[1]

At the heart of the newcomers' hopes for a new life was land. Many English settlers saw Maori land as essentially unused, and argued that our creation of wealth by the development of farms and roads and towns would benefit both races. But Maori tribes were growing sensitive to the threat posed by our rapidly growing numbers, and the loss not just of land but of independence as well. A warning of where this might lead was the 1843 killing of 22 Nelson settlers who were attempting to enforce a survey of land at Wairau.

The means of war

The 19th-century British Empire depended on military power. The Royal Navy controlled the seas, the lifeline of empire, as no nation has done since; and the British Army was a formidable fighting machine, experienced in war. The Napoleonic and Crimean wars were fought against major European powers, and there were numerous imperial and colonial campaigns around the world. In New Zealand the British Army bore the brunt of major campaigns until the mid-1860s.

The building block of the army was the regiment, 14 of which served here. They came mostly from barracks in England, Ireland and Australia, but also from India (the 43rd, 57th and 70th), Ceylon (50th) and Burma (68th). The 58th, 65th, 96th and 99th took part in campaigns in the 1840s (the 80th returned to Australia shortly before fighting commenced). The critical struggle of the early 1860s saw the 12th, 14th, 18th, 40th, 43rd, 50th, 57th, 65th, 68th and 70th Regiments in action. Royal Artillery and Royal Engineers also played important roles. In early 1864 British troops here peaked at more than 11,000 men.

Most of a soldier's life was spent in barracks where there was drill and weapons training, route marches and exercises. In distant New Zealand the English mail from loved ones took forever to arrive — the reply to a letter could take six months or more. Many soldiers had a wife and family with them; for others public houses helped overcome the boredom. Harsh discipline included floggings on the 'triangle' for a range of offences. Officers generally purchased their commissions so that there was a great gulf between the wealthy officer caste and enlisted men.

Archaeologist Reg Nichol's 1979 excavations carried out at the site of Albert Barracks in central Auckland tell something of the soldier's life. Fragments of china, and glass and stoneware bottles were common. Clay pipe pieces speak of the smoking habit popular among soldiers. Spoon and knife handles are cut with owner's names. Popular games are represented by dice, marbles and a domino and chess piece. And military badges, shako plates and brass and pewter buttons tell of the regiments and other units for whom the barracks were home between 1848 and 1871.

Alongside regular troops were naval contingents drawn from Royal Navy vessels which were in port. Settler forces included a variety of local militia and volunteer corps, 'Forest Ranger' and 'Bushranger' units, military settlers, and from 1867 the Armed Constabulary. When most of the British troops left in 1866 prosecution of the war was taken up entirely by local forces. Nor can it be forgotten that throughout the wars there were Maori who fought alongside us, either tribally organised and led, or incorporated in colonial units such as the Armed Constabulary.

Great, indeed, was the fear of the Maori when they heard of these soldiers, for all the pakeha agreed in saying that they would attack any one their chief ordered them to attack, no matter whether there was any just cause or not; that they would fight furiously till the last man was killed, and that nothing could make them run away.

told to F E Maning by an old chief of the Ngapuhi tribe[2]

The 58th Regiment on parade at Albert Barracks, Auckland, in 1858, the year they left New Zealand. ALEXANDER TURNBULL LIBRARY

'The Old Black Cuffs'

The 58th (Rutlandshire) Regiment was in New Zealand from 1845 to 1858, taking part in the Northern War, and afterwards serving for many years as garrison in Auckland where it played an important part in the official and social life of the young capital.

I called to see Sister Mary, she had one little child named John Thomas after Father & myself. I kissed her & the baby & took my farewell leaving her in tears. Shortly after, I met poor Father, he gave me 'Good Morning' & asked where I was going. I told him on business connected with the Brewery. 'How is it you are walking?' I said, 'It was such a fine morning I preferred walking to riding & I am not going far. Good bye Father'. I shook hands & that was the last I saw of my dear old Father.

John Mitchell of Stamford, Lincolnshire, leaves home to enlist in the 58th Regiment at Northampton, 1841. He rose to Quartermaster Sergeant before he was discharged in Auckland in 1853 and settled in New Zealand.[3]

The Northern War 1845–1846

War came first in the Bay of Islands district. For British settlers the issue was clear: the Treaty of Waitangi gave sovereignty to the Crown, and so the authority of the colonial government must be upheld.

Removal of the capital to Auckland had adversely affected shipping and economic activity in the Bay of Islands, at a time when control of that activity was itself slipping from chiefs' hands to a new colonial bureaucracy. For many Maori a galling symbol of the loss of chiefly power was the British flag flying on Maiki Hill above Kororareka. For British settlers, on the other hand, it represented sovereignty and reassurance.

Foremost among disaffected chiefs was Hone Heke Pokai of Ngapuhi who in July 1844 chopped down the Maiki Hill flagpole. Heke repeated this act of defiance twice more before 11 March 1845 when he and Kawiti led war-parties to Kororareka to fell the symbol of British authority for a fourth time. This time they went on to sack the town. The European population evacuated to ships anchored in the bay. So began the Northern War.

The destruction of Kororareka caused panic, not just in the north but also in Auckland when refugees arrived there from the Bay of Islands. The courage failed even of missionary Henry Williams, who had lived in New Zealand since 1823: 'It may be said it is only Kororareka that is gone; but Kororareka was the right arm, and it is my opinion that in three months there will not be an Englishman outside Auckland.'[4] There were some Aucklanders who sold their property and shipped out as quickly as possible. An earthwork redoubt named Fort Ligar was begun on the ridge west of the town where the casino now stands.

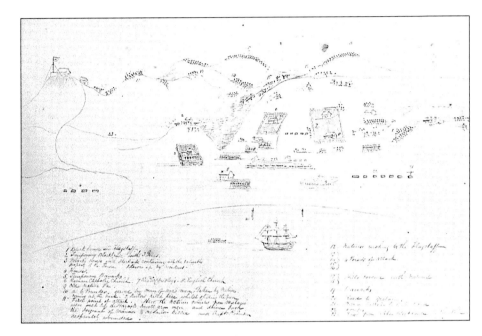

War began in the Bay of Islands on 11 March 1845 when for the fourth time Hone Heke chopped down the flagpole on Maiki Hill above Kororareka. Heke and the Kawakawa chief Kawiti went on to sack the town. The European community took to ships in the bay. WILLIAM BAMBRIDGE, ALEXANDER TURNBULL LIBRARY

Sir,
By my letter of the 6th instant, I reported to you that 'Hone Heke' with a party of rude young men, armed, had arrived at Russell, and committed several depredations on the inhabitants, at the same time using very threatening language, and thereby causing much alarm.

… I regret… to inform you, that early this morning, a portion of his tribe proceeded to the signal-station, and… have cut down the staff erected there.

H T Kemp, Protector of Aborigines, Russell, 8 July 1844[5]

As to the proximate cause which led to the destruction of Kororarika, we hesitate not to affirm that its fate was occasioned and hastened by the blind, mistaken policy of our Governor and his advisers, who, in direct opposition to common sense, obstinately persisted in re-erecting, and endeavouring to maintain the Flag-staff, before the proper time had arrived, by the acquisition of a sufficient force, for that purpose.

Editorial, *The Southern Cross*, 29 March 1845

In the war which followed British troops and significant Maori forces were ranged against sections of the Ngapuhi and Ngati Hine tribes under Heke and Kawiti. The alliance of colonial government and Maori suited the different ambitions of both parties. Among Maori allies leading men included Tamati Waka Nene and Te Taonui, who were to secure the only clear military success for the government when they defeated Heke at Ahu Ahu early in June 1845, wounding him in the process.

Following the disaster at Kororareka Lieutenant Colonel Hulme was sent from Auckland with 300 troops plus a naval contingent and some local volunteers. On arrival he destroyed a coastal pa and seized its chief, Pomare. But thereafter British strategy consisted of a series of expeditions into the interior where pa had been built to invite attack. So it was hoped that a decisive blow might be struck, but such a strategy by definition gave the initiative to the enemy.

Puketutu

The first expedition was in early May 1845 when Hulme set off for Lake Omapere where Heke was reportedly building a pa. The troops made heavy weather of the march inland, taking four days to travel only a few miles by cart road and bush track. The two sides met on 8 May 1845 at Puketutu.

The only British artillery consisted of Congreve rockets in the hands of a naval contingent, with which an ineffectual fire was opened up on the stockade. When troops were ordered forward they came under fire from the Maori position. Kawiti then led 300 men into the fight from bush outside the pa, and when the soldiers turned to deal with him, Heke led his men from the pa to attack them in the rear.

Late in the afternoon Hulme called off the attack, leaving the enemy in control of the battlefield — with British dead and probably some wounded as well. But our troops had the better of the close fighting — a lesson well taken by Maori who did not try again to tackle British troops on open ground.

> *A number of the red tribe... came at our people with a rush with their bayonets fixed on their muskets, yelling horribly, grinding their teeth, and cursing. Down went Kawiti's choicest warriors; the ground was strewn with them. Alas, it was a fatal mistake. We never tried that move again. Once was quite enough. But it was wrong of the red tribe to curse us. We were doing no harm; we were merely fighting them.*
>
> Maori warrior describing the bayonet charge on Kawiti's force at Puketutu[6]

Ohaeawai

In early June Colonel Henry Despard arrived in New Zealand from Sydney with two companies of his 99th Regiment. Thus there was a larger force available for the next expedition inland. The objective was a new fortification at Ohaeawai, which had been reworked by Kawiti on the site of an older pa belonging to the chief Pene Taui. The troops arrived before the pa on 23 June to secure victory which had eluded them at Puketutu.

Ohaeawai had been strengthened to withstand artillery fire, and to give maximum protection to the garrison which Kawiti well understood was likely to be greatly outnumbered by an attacking force. During a bombardment defenders were to stay in underground bunkers. When an assault was made they manned the firing trench behind a double stockade line, poking their guns through the timbers of the inner line and firing beneath the outer line which was supported above the ground by heavy posts.

A week's bombardment of the Ohaeawai defences had little effect. Even a 32-pounder ordered up from the bay — the biggest gun yet in action in New Zealand — failed to create an effective breach. Sorties by the pa garrison added to the discomfort of our troops.

The frustrated Despard then overruled the caution expressed by Waka Nene and Pakeha civilians and decided to storm the pa. An assault party of 220 men was drawn from the 58th and 99th Regiments, plus some seamen and Auckland Militia with scaling ladders. At 3 o'clock in the afternoon of 1 July they charged forward, soon to come under heavy fire at short range. Few men penetrated the outer stockade and those who did were even more exposed to enemy fire. Soon the 'Retire' was sounded, the retreating force suffering more casualties before they were out of range. In a few minutes half the assault force were casualties — 40 killed and 70 wounded.

Ohaeawai was the first of three severe rebuffs suffered in New Zealand by our regular troops attempting to storm Maori positions. The others were at Puketakauere, Taranaki, on 27 June 1860, and Gate Pa, Tauranga, 29 April 1864. Ten days after the assault Ohaeawai was found to be abandoned and was destroyed. The troops retired to Waimate.

> The whole front of the pa flashed fire, and in a moment we were in the one-sided fight — gun-flashes from the foot of the stockade and from loopholes higher up, smoke half-hiding the pa from us, yells and cheers, and men falling all round. A man was shot in front of me and another was hit behind me. Not a single Maori could we see. They were all safely hidden in their trenches and pits, poking the muzzles of their guns under the foot of the outer palisade. What could we do? We tore at the fence, firing through it, thrusting our bayonets in, or trying to pull a part of it down, but it was a hopeless business.
>
> Corporal Free, 58th Regiment[7]

Ruapekapeka

When it became clear that FitzRoy had not only blundered into war but seemed incapable of bringing it to a satisfactory conclusion he was recalled and a new governor appointed. George Grey arrived in Auckland in November 1845 and promptly prepared for another march inland. This time there were more than 1100 men, including a small naval contingent, Auckland volunteers and some East India Company artillerymen, plus several hundred Maori.

The objective was a new pa, Ruapekapeka, again built by Kawiti, high on a ridge south of Kawakawa. On the last day of 1845, three weeks after they set out, British forces set up camp in front of the pa and got the guns in position. After a long bombardment, on the morning of 11 January the pa was found to be empty and quickly occupied. There was fighting in the bush beyond the fortification — where most of our casualties were to occur — but it was again an unsatisfactory business.

Heke and Kawiti then met Tamati Waka Nene to agree on peace, with which Grey had no choice but to go along. Neither side emerged the winner but nothing was to be gained by continued fighting. Grey, who was nothing if not political, claimed success in a war in which the major government purpose seems to have been little more than to show who was in charge. For many settlers, however, the victory needed for confidence to be restored was distinctly lacking.

> I cannot discover that the rebels have any single grievance to complain of which would in any degree extenuate their present conduct... I believe that it arises solely from an irrational contempt of the power of Great Britain, accompanied by a desire upon the part of many of their Chiefs to gain influence and renown, and from a wish upon the part of their followers to share in the plunder and excitement which result from a successful rebellion on their part.
>
> Governor George Grey, writing to Lord Stanley 8 December 1845[8]

Two nations or one — Waikato, 1863–1864

The 1850s was without fighting between European and Maori. But at the same time the underlying conflict of interests became more acute as Maori initiatives to set up alternative political structures and organise opposition to land sales threatened the hopes and ambitions of the new settlers. Many North Island tribes united under the Waikato chief Te Wherowhero who was chosen the first Maori king in 1858, taking the name Potatau.

The spark which ignited the decisive campaigns of the sixties came from Taranaki. Here an isolated English settlement found itself unable to obtain more land. When Governor Gore Browne accepted an offer of land by a chief who it seems was not entitled to sell, he soon had to send troops to protect the survey. Local Te Atiawa quickly responded and in early 1860 our government again found itself embroiled in war, and with people who felt strongly that the law should be on their side.

> *It is a curious but an important feature of the present war, that the Natives regard themselves as fighting in support of law and order, in opposition to the illegal conduct of Governor Browne; and there can be no doubt that they are right in this view of the subject. The universal complaint heard from them is, all minor matters are regularly adjudicated on; but a man's land, which he has inherited from his remote ancestors, is taken away at the caprice of the Governor, or even by a subordinate land-agent.*
>
> Octavius Hadfield, Archdeacon of Kapiti, 1861[9]

Governor Grey, about 1864. AIM

The First Taranaki War of 1860–1 was inconclusive, and it was in a replay of his first appointment that Grey returned in September 1861 for his second term as governor, this time to resolve the issues left open by Browne. Grey soon identified the Waikato tribes under the Maori King as the strength of resistance to British government in New Zealand, especially as Kingite forces had travelled south to take part in the fighting in Taranaki. Auckland settlers who wanted access to rich Waikato lands had their own reasons for wanting to break the strength of the Maori King.

> *Two suns cannot shine in one sky, two kings cannot reign in one dominion and two races cannot avoid collision when living in one country under different laws and yielding obedience to distinct authorities.*
>
> Harriet Louisa Gore Browne[10]

Grey ordered the Great South Road extended from Auckland to the boundary of Waikato Maori land, and he prepared British troops and local forces for war. Of the Maori King — now Tawhiao, after the death of Potatau — he said, 'I shall not fight against him with the sword, but I shall dig around him till he falls of his own accord.' But it was to be the sword.

Invasion

In the winter of 1863 there was renewed fighting in Taranaki. Grey alleged Kingite involvement in the outbreak, and also a 'determined and bloodthirsty' plan to attack Auckland. On 9 July 1863 Maori living north of the frontier were told to take an oath of allegiance to Queen Victoria or retire south to the Waikato. On 12 July General Cameron ordered the 14th Regiment across the Mangatawhiri Stream into Maori territory. So began the critical struggle of the New Zealand Wars.

NOTICE

To the natives of Mangere, Pukaki, Ihumatao, Te Kirikiri, Patumahoe, Pokeno, and Tuakau.

All persons of the native race living in the Manukau district and the Waikato frontier are hereby required immediately to take the oath of allegiance to Her Majesty the Queen, and to give up their arms to an officer appointed by Government for that purpose. Natives who comply with this order will be protected.

Natives refusing to do so are hereby warned forthwith to leave the district aforesaid, and retire to Waikato beyond Mangatawhiri.

In case of their not complying with this order they will be ejected.

Auckland, July 9, 1863.   By his Excellency's order.[11]

The Ihumatau natives... were good neighbours and very much respected by the settlers around; nearly all their houses and fences have been destroyed; their church gutted, the bell, sashes, door and Communion Tables stolen and the floor even torn up and taken away; and their land is to be occupied by Mr. Russell's brother-in-law.

Letter by 'A Settler', *New Zealander*, 18 February 1864

... the other day a Captain of foot was steaming gaily down [the Waikato] on pleasure bent, and in the course of conversation at the little cabin dinner table gave it as his opinion that 'the Colonists were a greedy rapacious set,' that Russell (the War Minister) was the worst of the gang, and that nothing would be done till he was hung etc. etc.

'Perhaps Sir, you are not aware that I am Mr Russell,' said a quiet gentleman at table.

Lieutenant Colonel E A Williams, Royal Artillery[12]

By August our troops had reached Whangamarino where guns were placed to bombard Maori defences at Meremere situated on the ridge above the present power station. Meanwhile Maori forces struck at the Great South Road and settler farms to tie down troops behind the army. Not until the end of October was Cameron able to get past enemy defences at Meremere by using gunboats on the river. Meremere was then abandoned by the King's followers and an earthwork redoubt thrown up by troops in the middle of the old Maori trenches.

Garrison duty behind the advancing front is described by James Bodell, who enlisted in a British regiment in 1847 aged 16 and later lived in Australia before volunteering for service in the Waikato regiments.[13] Soon he was one of 100 men holding a post at Martin's Farm, on the Great South Road south of Drury. For Bodell life consisted of patrols, picket duty and getting drunk at every opportunity. A bootmaker who got into the post's rum ration, then topped it up with water in which he had been soaking shoe leather, received 50 lashes and two months' imprisonment — and no sympathy from Bodell whatsoever.

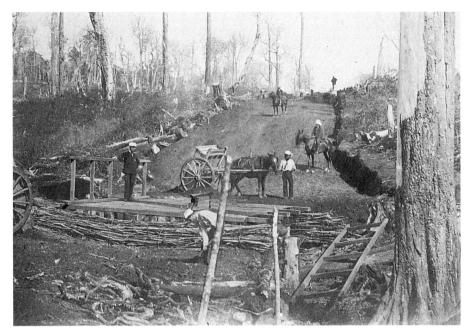

Before the war British troops pushed the Great South Road to the boundary of Maori land near Pokeno. The photograph, 'Deviation made by the Royal Artillery through Williamson's Clearing; road to Waikato', is from the album of Royal Engineer Lieutenant John Urquhart.
ALEXANDER TURNBULL LIBRARY

Photographer D M Beere shows the troops' invasion road to the Waikato. Behind the partly abandoned camp of the Naval Brigade is a small earthwork and stockade fort at the crossing place over the Mangatawhiri Stream. On the other side of the river a road climbs the hill to the 14th Regiment redoubt. AIM

The 65th (2nd Yorkshire North Riding) was the longest serving British regiment in New Zealand, arriving in 1846 and later playing an important part in fighting in Taranaki and Waikato in the early 1860s. Maori knew them as the 'Hickety Pips'; 1150 stayed on here after the war. From left are: Bugler Austin, Company Sergeant-Major William Acheson, Private Tobin, Lance-Corporal Lennox, and Sergeants Feltham and Russell. ALEXANDER TURNBULL LIBRARY

To those who judge merely by the rules of common sense — which, thank Heaven, is after all the ultimate court of appeal among Englishmen in such matters — the case stands plainly as follows: — The natives of Waikato and Taranaki have set up another king, and have systematically defied our authority; they have gone further, and have without provocation deliberately begun a war against her Majesty's troops, and her Majesty's authority; they are, therefore, clearly rebels, and open and dangerous rebels too.

Editorial, *The Daily Southern Cross,* 10 July 1863

... it is quite useless the soldiers going to the Waikato unless settlers are to follow... One thousand navvies will accomplish more than a regiment of soldiers; and ten thousand settlers on the Waikato will make the next treaty of peace a permanent one...

Letter to the editor from Joseph Newman, *The Daily Southern Cross,* 14 July 1863

It is not to be wondered at therefore that the treaty of Waitangi was found to be worth just whatever the Maori autographs appended to it might sell for, so soon as any collision of interests arose between the races... We have to maintain first our right to be here at all; and secondly, our right to impose our laws and customs on the Maoris. The first point... depends simply on the fact that there was room for us, and land only waiting for the application of our industry. But the question as to our right to make a foreign race submit to us, and to our law, seems to admit of more discussion...

The offence of the Maori consists, not so much in rejecting our law as in maintaining utter anarchy. His rebellion is against the laws of nature, of progress, and of civilisation; and it is in vindication of these laws that we are called upon to reduce him to submission and obedience.

Editorial, *The Daily Southern Cross,* 14 September 1863

Rangiriri

The decisive battle for Waikato took place at Rangiriri where the King's forces threw up a defensive line from the river across a narrow strip of land to Lake Waikare. On 20 November 1863 General Cameron had the advantage of almost 1500 men and artillery. The Maori force may have numbered 500, dug in behind strong earthworks.

'Naval attack at Rangiriri.' Charles Heaphy shows seamen with cutlasses and revolvers making a third assault on the centre of the Maori defences as unsuccessfully as the infantry and Royal Artillery before them. ALEXANDER TURNBULL LIBRARY

As at Meremere, Cameron landed troops from river boats behind the Maori line, but although our troops drove the enemy from some of the earthworks, repeated assaults on the central strongpoint were unsuccessful before night fell. The troops then bivouacked for the night, 'disgusted and disheartened' according to Lieutenant James Boulton of the 12th Regiment.

On the morning of the 21st a white flag flew above the Maori position. The troops went in — to the surprise of the defenders, who wished only to negotiate — and the battle was over. Forty-seven defenders are known to have been killed or died later and 183 Maori prisoners were taken. Two British officers and 35 men were killed and 93 injured, and in the weeks following four more officers and six men died of wounds.

Among the wounded was Captain Henry Mercer, shot through the mouth while leading a small party of artillerymen in an assault on the Maori strongpoint. He took shelter with a score of other men, many of them dead or wounded, who were unable to move back because of enemy fire. It was here that Assistant Surgeon William Temple and Lieutenant Arthur Pickard earned VCs for dashing across open ground to bring assistance. Mercer died a few days later, able only by writing to communicate with his wife who joined him. The township of Mercer is named after him.

Rangiriri was not, however, the victory Cameron sought, or, indeed, that Auckland settlers had wished for. Failure to take the Maori strongpoint, heavy British casualties, and the escape of many of the enemy during the night made the result less than decisive. Nonetheless, the way had been opened to the Waikato heartland and two weeks later Cameron entered the headquarters of King Tawhiao at Ngaruawahia.

Te Awamutu

In January 1864 British troops pressed forward by way of the Waipa River. The objective was rich agricultural land about Te Awamutu and Rangiaowhia which had played an important part in provisioning the Maori war effort. Cameron also hoped that any determined Maori defence of the district would enable him at last to effectively destroy the Kingite army.

Before Te Awamutu the greatest defensive line thrown up by either side in the New Zealand Wars barred Cameron's advance from Te Rore on the Waipa River. The Maori strongpoints of Paterangi, Pikopiko, Rangiatea and Manga-pukatea repeated the strategy of Meremere and Rangiriri. The aim was to draw our forces into an assault on a well-entrenched position and so impose casualties and a military defeat that would halt our advance.

But Cameron slipped past the Paterangi line on the night of 20 February and next day was at Rangiaowhia where a handful of defenders put up a brief fight before the troops withdrew to Te Awamutu. On the 22nd troops went out to Hairini on the Rangiaowhia road where defences had been hastily thrown up by Kingite forces pulled back from Paterangi. The line was rushed by men of the 50th Regiment and Forest Rangers, but it was another insubstantial fight which did not give the decision sought by Cameron.

Surveyor, artist and explorer Major Charles Heaphy of the Auckland Rifle Volunteers wears his Victoria Cross won at Waiari near Te Awamutu for aiding a wounded soldier under heavy fire, 11 February 1864. He was the first volunteer soldier in the Empire to be given the VC.

AIM

The first expression of that man's face, his attitude on receiving the first bullets is now as vivid before my mind's eye as when my heart first sickened over that sight. When the first shots struck him he smiled a sort of sad and disappointed smile; then bowing his head, staggering already — he wrapped his blanket over his face and received his death bullets without a groan, dropped quietly on the ground!

Gustavus von Tempsky at Rangiaowhia, 21 February 1864[14]

Orakau

At the end of March 1864 Kingite forces could be seen fortifying a low hill at Orakau, east of Te Awamutu, where fighters from a number of tribes were under the overall command of Ngati Maniapoto chief Rewi Maniapoto. The ensuing battle was to become the best known of all incidents of the New Zealand Wars.

Troops were quickly marched out to attack before the pa was completed. The first assault was by Forest Rangers and the 18th Royal Irish in the morning of 31 March. Over the next two days the garrison turned back all attacks, but without food, water and ammunition they could not continue the fight. Early in the afternoon of 2 April an appeal for surrender was met with the famous defiance, 'Ka whawhai tonu matou, ake ake ake!'.

Shortly after, the garrison broke out through British lines, survivors making their way south of the Puniu River. Despite the breakout, however, Rewi's force now suffered most of its casualties as Colonial Defence Force and Royal Artillery troopers ran them down in a rare opportunity for cavalry in the New Zealand Wars. The 40th Regiment endured some criticism for allowing the breakout in its section of the cordon. Once again Cameron was denied a decisive blow.

The district was now held by an occupation army, and Kingite forces retired south. So ended fighting in the Waikato. Soon much of the fertile land which had recently been fought over was in the hands of European farmers protected by Armed Constabulary and militia forces at frontier posts.

Gate Pa

Fighting was over in the Waikato but dramatic events were soon to turn attention to Tauranga. Early in 1864 Colonel Greer was sent to the Bay of Plenty harbour under orders to block the movement of enemy men and supplies to the seat of war. A base was established at Te Papa close to an old mission station, near the end of the point of land today taken up by the city of Tauranga.

The local Ngai Te Rangi tribe responded to Greer's presence by inviting an attack on their pa. When this failed they moved closer and threw up another fortification at Pukehinahina, just three miles from the British camp. This could hardly be ignored. Cameron by now was in Auckland and at once decided to go to Tauranga in person with more troops. It was a classic challenge and response of the New Zealand Wars.

On the evening of 28 April a small group of officers from among the assembled British force enjoyed dinner at the Te Papa mission house of Archdeacon and Mrs Brown. They were Captain Hamilton of the *Esk* and Commander Hay of *Harrier*, Assistant Surgeon Manley of the Royal Artillery, and from the 43rd Regiment its commanding officer Lieutenant Colonel H. J. Booth, Captains Glover, Mure, Hamilton and Utterton and Lieutenant Langlands. In 24 hours all but one would be dead.

On the morning of 29 April Cameron opened up with the most intense artillery bombardment ever to be employed against a Maori position, having at his disposal not just mortars and cannon, but five Armstrong guns including two 40-pounders and a massive 110-pounder. By mid-afternoon a breach in the defences was considered large enough for a storming party.

The assault force comprised 150 each of 43rd Light Infantry and seamen and marines drawn from vessels including the *Curacao, Miranda, Esk* and *Harrier*. At first the attack went well and quickly reached the interior of the pa, but losses were heavy among the officers and when the garrison fought

Captain J C F Hamilton of HMS *Esk* was among 31 British dead and 80 wounded at Gate Pa. His sword and medals are held in the Waikato Museum, in the city named after him. ALEXANDER TURNBULL LIBRARY

The 43rd Regiment and Naval Brigade assault on Gate Pa at first went well, before being thrown back with heavy casualties. H G ROBLEY, MUSEUM OF NZ

back from the maze of rifle pits and bunkers our men broke and fled, a third of them killed or wounded.

News of Gate Pa was greeted with consternation in Auckland. Here was a British army of almost 1700 men routed by 200 lightly armed Maori. Seven officers of the 43rd were killed, the four captains who had dined at the mission the night before lying close together near the breach. Manley received the Victoria Cross for attempting to save the life of the mortally injured Commander Hay and then returning to the pa to look for more wounded men.

As well as the two senior officers, the Royal Navy lost Lieutenant Charles Hill. Hill had survived the wreck of the *Orpheus* on Manukau Bar, 7 February 1863, still New Zealand's worst maritime disaster, in which three-quarters of the ship's 250-strong complement lost their lives. He was subsequently posted to the *Curacao*, a year to the day before losing his life in the distant country which had so nearly claimed it before.

> *The Pah from the outside looks the most insignificant place.*
> Lieutenant Spencer Nicholl, 43rd Regiment, before the attack on Gate Pa.[15]

> *Lieutenant-Colonel Booth and Commander Hay, who led into the work, fell mortally wounded. Captain Hamilton was shot dead on top of the parapet while in the act of encouraging his men to advance, and in a few minutes almost every officer of the column was either killed or wounded. Up to this moment the men, so nobly led by their officers, fought gallantly, and appeared to have carried the position, when suddenly they gave way and fell back from the work to the nearest cover.*
> General Cameron to Sir George Grey, 5 May 1864[16]

Te Ranga

Cameron now withdrew to Auckland with much of his force, leaving a garrison at Tauranga patrolling nearby countryside to prevent another pa from being erected in the vicinity. This was to have its reward on 21 June when Colonel Greer at the head of 600 men came across the enemy digging rifle pits at Te Ranga, a few miles inland of Gate Pa.

Greer called for assistance and drove the enemy from their uncompleted

General Cameron (at gun carriage wheel) with members of his staff and Royal Artillery, on the morning of the attack on Gate Pa, 29 April 1864. ALEXANDER TURNBULL LIBRARY

position; and so the 43rd and 68th were able to gain some revenge for Gate Pa. The troops lost 52 killed and wounded, but Maori losses were considerable, including 108 buried next day in the rifle pits and 15 who died of wounds. A month later many Ngai Te Rangi came into Te Papa to make peace; in a few weeks most of the remainder followed suit.

* * * * *

In the end the Waikato War was won, not on the battlefield, but by taking the land. European settlers now set about creating the mosaic of prosperous farms and towns which today we think of as characterising this part of New Zealand. Dispossessed Waikato tribes withdrew into the 'King Country' south of Puniu River. At the frontier the Armed Constabulary were to remain on patrol until the King Country was opened to the Main Trunk Railway in the early 1880s.

The bush campaigns

In the 1860s European settlers poured in, attracted by goldfields and the prospect of land. Only ten years after overtaking Maori numbers in 1858 four out of every five New Zealanders were Pakeha. By the end of the century Maori numbers were to be less than six per cent of the total. The shift to European use of the land was even faster. Between 1858 and 1867 the fenced area increased from 235,000 to 3,455,000 acres; at the same time sheep numbers grew from 1,523,000 to 8,418,000. In 1860, at the beginning of the decade of war, our settlements were scattered around the North Island coast and Maori tribes held the heartland, now it was Maori who were pushed to the edges of Pakeha land.

New technologies improved our advantage in waging war. It must not be forgotten that in the 1840s weapons technology was fairly evenly balanced, if we except European possession of artillery. Maori may even have enjoyed an advantage in reloading speed, especially with their use of double-barrelled shotguns. In the 1850s and 1860s, however, development of the rifled musket, followed by new breech-loading guns, vastly increased the rate of fire, accuracy and reliability of weapons which were available to Pakeha forces. Thus were the means of war tilted in our favour.

Nonetheless, the New Zealand Wars were about to enter a new phase. Fighting now shifted to the great bushed areas of the east and central North Island where small forces could carry on a guerilla struggle. At the same time, in 1868 and early 1869, the south Taranaki leader Titokowaru drove farmers and military forces back on the town of Wanganui before his support was to collapse. With British troops now largely gone our few trained units were on the move between the east and west coasts to deal with one crisis then another.

The escape of Te Kooti

The crisis on the east coast began on 10 July 1868 with the Maori prophet and guerilla leader Te Kooti Arikirangi landing at Whareongaonga south of Poverty Bay, having escaped with 300 followers from exile on the Chatham Islands. In the next four years he was to spread the flames of war from Gisborne and Mohaka on the east coast, to Whakatane and Rotorua, and south of Lake Taupo in the central North Island.

Te Kooti had been arrested as a spy in 1866. He experienced visions when ill during his imprisonment, and in the Chathams soon became spiritual leader of the exiles. On 4 July he led prisoners to overcome the guard and seize a visiting vessel, the *Rifleman*. On the beach at Whareongaonga Te Kooti taught his followers a new way of prayer which included raising the hand to God. From this gesture a new religion, the Ringatu, or 'upraised hand', took its name.

> *Upon looking back at this extraordinary episode in the history of New Zealand, it is difficult to say whether one's wonder is excited more by the precision, rapidity, and completeness with which the enterprise was planned and executed, or by the moderation shown in the hour of victory by a gang of barbarous fanatics who in a moment found their former masters bound at their feet, and their lives entirely at their mercy.*
>
> G S Cooper reports to the government on Te Kooti's escape from Chatham Island[17]

Poverty Bay

Te Kooti now made his way inland beating off pursuing forces in several running fights. His first idea was to go to the King Country, but this the Maori king, Tawhiao, would not allow. On 10 November 1868 Te Kooti struck at Matawhero near Gisborne killing about 70 Pakeha and Maori. His reasons seem to have included the settling of old scores including the sale of land in which he held an interest, and resentment at unjust imprisonment.

Among the victims was Major Reginald Biggs who was involved in Te Kooti's imprisonment in 1866. When the escaped prisoners landed at Whareongaonga, Biggs was in command of local militia forces and set out in pursuit. Te Kooti later claimed that he would not have attacked Poverty Bay if he had been left alone. Whatever the truth, Biggs was a prime target and was killed along with his family and household.

The 'Poverty Bay massacre' not surprisingly frightened many isolated Pakeha and Maori communities which could be reached from the great forest of the Urewera country and its surrounding ranges and river valleys. It was central to the European community's perception of Te Kooti as a dangerous murderer, and it stiffened government resolve to pursue Te Kooti for however long was needed.

MASSACRE AT POVERTY BAY
BURNING OF THE SETTLEMENT
THIRTY-FIVE PERSONS KILLED
TWENTY MISSING
FURTHER ATTACKS THREATENED

*There is no use mincing the matter at all in such cases — we are dealing
with savages of the very worst sort... To such men the achievement of the
other night — the surprise, the massacre in cold blood, the torture and
barbarous treatment of the helpless — are all matters of congratulation.*
The Daily Southern Cross, 14 November 1868

*Many of the atrocities perpetrated on the women and children are too
shocking for description: suffice it to say that nothing more horrible has
taken place since the Indian Mutiny of 1857...*
Governor Bowen reports to London[18]

Ngatapa

Te Kooti turned inland and occupied a hilltop — an ancient fortified pa — at
Ngatapa, a powerful position but lacking in water and without an easy escape
route. An attack on Ngatapa early in December was called off without success,
but at the end of December a bigger force of Ngati Porou and Armed Constabulary returned to lay siege.

After several days of probing each other's weaknesses, early on the morning of 5 January Te Kooti's force lowered itself over the cliff and escaped.
They were, however, chased by Ngati Porou and about 130 men brought
back and shot. Te Kooti himself travelled west through the mountains to seek
help from Tuhoe.

In March and April 1869 Te Kooti led raids on the Whakatane and Mohaka
districts by which he gained recruits and improved his stock of weapons and
ammunition. Striking quickly at two widely separated localities he also added
to fear in the Pakeha community. In response Colonel George Whitmore
directed an invasion of the Urewera country by three columns including
European and Maori forces. Whitmore failed to take Te Kooti but did destroy
the food supplies of his Tuhoe hosts.

Captain Gilbert Mair (left) with some of his
Arawa Flying Column at Lake Rotokakahi
(Green Lake) near Rotorua, 1870. Part of
Te Kooti's flag 'Te Wepu' (The Whip),
which was taken in the fight at Rotorua on
7 February 1870, can be seen at the right.
The kilts made bush travel easier.
D L MUNDY, AIM

Te Porere

Te Kooti then moved on looking for allies among King Country Maori and the Ngati Tuwharetoa of Taupo. At Opepe near Taupo he surprised a party of colonial cavalry, killing nine without loss to his force. At the end of September, however, he was defeated at Te Ponanga south of Lake Taupo by Ngati Kahungunu and Arawa, his failure ending any chance of King Movement support.

Te Kooti went on to build a pa at Te Porere near the bush edge beneath Mount Ruapehu. There his force of about 200 was attacked on 4 October by more than 500 Maori and Pakeha, who stormed the pa and drove the defenders into the bush. Te Porere was the last fight from a prepared position in the New Zealand Wars. Te Kooti fled to the King Country.

The pursuit of Te Kooti continued until 1872 with many skirmishes taking place, but never again did he attempt more than raids, ambushes and the evasion of pursuing forces. In May 1872 he again sought refuge in the King Country where he lived under Tawhiao's protection until pardoned by the government in 1883.

> *I was the first to fire, killing a big fellow who was shot in the mouth. The enemy fired a volley from end to end of the line, while I and my men lay flat. By practice I had learned to fire twenty to thirty shots per minute, particularly if I stuffed my mouth full of cartridges... All at once a middle-aged man sprang up shouting 'Kokiri!' [Charge!] He fired both barrels of his double-barrelled gun. I fired point-blank and he fell face-forward; his lower jaw was blown away.*
>
> Captain Gilbert Mair describes an incident in the hunt for Te Kooti[19]

The shaping of New Zealand

The 1845–6 campaign in the Bay of Islands district, the Waikato War of 1863–4, and the pursuit of Te Kooti from the July 1868 landing on the beach at Whareongaonga to his May 1872 retreat to the King Country are three chapters in one struggle. All are to be seen against the background of European settlement of this country.

Ambitions of the government in the first war were strictly limited, and in fact none too clear. Any hope that Heke's 'rude young men' would be taught a lesson was clearly not fulfilled; but there was not to be another war in the north.

The Waikato conflict, on the other hand, had very clear government objectives which were largely shared by the settler community. There must be an end to the King Movement's state within a state, and to its support for Maori in arms elsewhere in the North Island. To achieve this, as Auckland settler Joseph Newman wrote to *The Daily Southern Cross*, '... ten thousand settlers on the Waikato will make the next treaty of peace a permanent one...'[20] The confiscation of land was to win the war and secure the peace.

Newman's words had an interesting echo in 1870 when Colonial Treasurer Julius Vogel proposed a programme of borrowing in order to finance increased immigration and public works. Vogel argued that besides economic benefits this would bring fighting to an end. New immigrants and the opening up of the country by public works would, 'do more to put an end to hostilities and to confirm peaceful relations, than an army of ten thousand men.'[21]

The campaigns in pursuit of Te Kooti took place beyond the frontier of

European settlement. Memories of Poverty Bay were too vivid for settlers in some districts to relax before he was brought to account, but the important work of making farms and towns in the rich lowlands could now be pushed forward. The pursuit of Te Kooti's dwindling force is one of the remarkable stories of our history, but the shape of New Zealand's future meanwhile was being decided elsewhere.

Conflict between Maori and Pakeha over the issues which had led to war did not end in 1872. In Taranaki a considerable military campaign took place in 1880–1 to disperse the followers of Te Whiti and Tohu at Parihaka. That there was no fighting was a decision of the Maori leadership. Demonstrations of police and military strength have continued into the present century, as at Maungapohatu in 1916 when two supporters of Rua Kenana were shot dead, and at Bastion Point, Auckland, in 1978. In one form or another the struggle between Maori and newcomers in this country may be with us a long time yet.

PART 2

Fighting the Empire's War

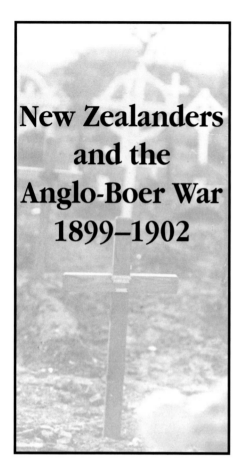

New Zealanders and the Anglo-Boer War 1899–1902

When you've shouted 'Rule Britannia,' when you've sung 'God Save the
*   Queen,'*
When you've finished killing Kruger with your mouth,
Will you kindly drop a shilling in my little tambourine
For a gentleman in khaki ordered South?
He's an absent-minded beggar and his weaknesses are great —
But we and Paul must take him as we find him —
He is out on active service, wiping something off a slate —
And he's left a lot o' little things behind him!
Duke's son — cook's son — son of a hundred kings —
(Fifty thousand horse and foot going to Table Bay!)
Each of 'em doing his country's work (and who's to look after their things?)
Pass the hat for your credit's sake, and pay — pay — pay!

Rudyard Kipling[1]

When Britain and her Empire went to war with two land-locked Lilliputian Afrikaaner republics the world joked about an elephant declaring war on the ants. In October 1899 few pundits expected that the British Empire's war with the Afrikaaners of the Transvaal Republic and the Orange Free State would be a hard-fought affair, unresolved until 1902. Fewer still envisaged that Britain would need to call for help to the white Anglo-Saxon colonies of Empire, and recruit 16,000 Australians, 6000 Canadians and 6500 New Zealanders to fight beside 450,000 British Regular and County Regiment 'Tommies': and this half million to crush a fighting force of 87,000 Afrikaaner farmers (Boers)![2]

The truth is that the second Anglo-Boer War forced a demanding learning curve on the British War Office and its generals. Their opponents dictated a war of movement; of ambush, abandonment of fixed lines of communication, division of forces, and of total war. Imperial generals could no longer rely on set-piece battles, Napoleonic drills and cavalry. It was to be a war of mounted infantry, dismounted to fight; of marksmen, guerilla raids and ambush, of machine guns and barbed wire; of cultural bitterness, and scorched earth. It was no 'gentlemen's war'! The fighting ended with the 'bitter-enders' joining the 'hands-uppers' in surrender, in the Peace of Vereeniging, signed on 30 May 1902; but Boer resentment and British attempts to anglicise the Afrikaaner by repressing their culture lingered long after, to create a culturally resistant group that was eventually to gain political dominance and control the affairs of South Africa in the mid-20th century.

'Shouting "Rule Britannia"'

This was New Zealand's first overseas war, and New Zealanders responded with hysterical delight to Britain's invitation to the conflict. New Zealanders took for granted that if Mother said that the Boers must be brought into line, then Mother must be right. Colonial New Zealanders proudly called themselves 'sons and daughters of Empire'; and children of immigrants, who had never set foot in Great Britain, called their parents' home 'the Motherland'. The turn of the century was a time when patriotic imperialists abounded. Audiences roared approval at the finalé of Gilbert and Sullivan's *HMS Pinafore*, at the chorus singing of 'Despite of all temptations, to belong to other nations, he remains an Englishman'.[3] 'God Save the Queen' began every concert, Queen

Previous page:
The artist C M F Goldie's impression of the First New Zealand Contingent's Defence of New Zealand Hill against the Boers on 15 January 1900 during French's advance on Pretoria. Captain Madocks is shown leading the charge with Lieutenant Jacky Hughes firing from the shoulder. *AUCKLAND WEEKLY NEWS, AIM*

Victoria, the 'Widow at Windsor', was venerated almost as a universal ruler, and Britannia truly 'ruled the waves'. For most New Zealanders it was unbelievable that two tiny African states could willingly choose to decline the benefits of membership of the 'greatest and most benevolent empire the world has ever known'. But the Boers did just that! The inhabitants of the republic of the Transvaal and of the Orange Free State were the descendants of the Dutch who settled the Cape as the first European colonists of Southern Africa. The Dutch had arrived in 1652, and established a thriving, self-contained community, before Britain won control of the Cape during the Napoleonic wars. Dutch Afrikaaners, unwilling to accept British domination, began their 'Great Trek' away from the Cape in 1836, moving with their religion, their republican government, their wagons, families and animals, some to create the Transvaal and some the Orange Free State.

The existence of these two republics in a British sphere of interest was for Britain an annoyance. Britain wanted the map of Africa splashed imperial red, from the Cape to Suez. An attempt was made to annex the Transvaal in the late 1870s, resisted militarily by the Boers in the first Anglo-Boer War of 1880–1: Britain's first 'white' against 'white' conflict since the Crimean War. A British force was thrashed by the mobile and straight-shooting Boers at Laingsneck and Majuba Hill. Reluctantly, Britain recognised the independence of the Afrikaaner republics at the London Convention of 1884, claimed it should superintend their foreign affairs, and simmered over an imperial defeat. The British Empire had been humiliated by a Boer army fewer in numbers than a British provincial town's population. 'Avenge Majuba' was a sentiment locked away in the British subconscious. When gold was discovered in the Transvaal in 1886 the republic's culturally myopic Calvinist farmers soon found their homeland overrun by prospectors and opportunists, mostly of Anglo-Saxon stock. Prosperity came to the Transvaal's monopolists. State revenue rose from $400,000 in 1886 to over $9,000,000 in 1899, and Johannesburg was transformed into a cosmopolitan city.

For the Afrikaaners it was a Midas touch of evil. The 'uitlanders' (foreigners) were 'godless', 'greedy', creating trouble by denouncing corruption in the Transvaal government, and demanders of voting rights. The 'uitlanders' wanted to take over the Transvaal, and in December 1895 Cecil Rhodes, Premier of Cape Colony, organised the 'Jameson Raid', an ill-organised attempt to do just that. It failed and the Boers began to rearm, with the most modern French and German weapons, recruiting foreign officers to command their artillery.

British business interests, the Foreign Office (annoyed at German government involvement in the republics), and the 'uitlanders', saw to it that throughout the Empire the press registered the cry for justice and franchise shouted by 'persecuted' Britons in the Transvaal. The *New Zealand Herald* declared that:

> *The Transvaal Boers are some of the lowest types of humanity I have ever encountered. They are unprogressive in every way, and strange as it may seem, the Zulus are infinitely to be preferred as a race…. The Boers live like pigs. Their homes, if homes they can be called, show it.*[4]

In New Zealand, as elsewhere in the Empire, the Boer was the victim of scurrilous denigration, portrayed as a foul-smelling, ignorant, backblocks farmer, surly and bullying in behaviour, and unfit to run a nation. Cartoons depicted horsed, bearded and aggressive Afrikaaners intimidating 'uitlander' women and children. Pamphlets portrayed the Boers as political recalcitrants, and Britain as beneficent and long-suffering.[5] The children's column in the *New Zealand Farmer*, run by 'Uncle Ned' added its denunciations.[6]

The Empire was psychologically conditioned for war, with propagandists ignoring the political reality, that the 'uitlanders' were actually demanding a franchise in the Transvaal that they were not entitled to in Britain, where it was not one man, one vote.

Even had gold not been discovered, and had the 'uitlanders' not arrived, Britain would most likely have sought a war of incorporation with the Boers. This was the age of the 'New Imperialism'. Between 1870 and 1900 the European nations expanded their colonial empires by nearly 150,000,000 people, by over ten million square miles. The battle for national pre-eminence in Europe was transferred to a global stage, with European states pushing to outflank each other by acquiring colonies and coaling stations. Britain, the owner of the world's greatest empire and navy, was very much involved. Harrison Wright's judgement is accurate:

> *A crescendo of tension and violence was reached at the end of the century with the massacre of twenty thousand Dervishes by Kitchener and his British troops at Obdurman.... The outbreak in 1899 of the three-year conflict between the British and the Boers in British Africa; and the Boxer Rebellion in China in 1900.[7]*

In antipodean New Zealand, with its population of less than 800,000, few knew or cared about a global perspective. From the 1870s, with the termination of the New Zealand Wars, the internal frontier was no longer militarily contested. New Zealand's eyes were now firmly on an external frontier, the Empire's frontier, and its leaders were anxious to show the colony's metal in the race for Empire.

'Killing Kruger with your mouth'

Richard John Seddon, since 1893 New Zealand's premier, robust, loud and Liberal party, was an ardent imperialist, annoyed that Britain had not secured Hawaii, and anxious to add Pacific dependencies to the British Empire. Fifteen days before hostilities commenced 'King Dick' Seddon responded to a War Office request for volunteers with a long speech to the New Zealand House of Representatives. Queensland and Canada had already offered volunteers and he had no wish for New Zealand to be left behind. Seddon offered an initial contingent of 200, all to be rough-riders, and good shots; preference to be given to those who would provide their own horses and gear. Emotion rather than logic permeated his oration to the House:

> *The flag that floats over us and protects us was expected to protect our kindred and countrymen who are in the Transvaal.... We are a portion of the dominant family of this world and we are of the English speaking race ... and wherever they are, no matter how far distant apart, there is a feeling of affection — there is that crimson tie, that bond of unity exists, which time does not affect, and as the years roll by it grows firmer, stronger.[8]*

The Leader of the Opposition, Captain W R Russell, seconded Seddon's motion to send troops, and his argument was repeated again and again by succeeding speakers: 'It is not for me, Sir, as an Englishman, to inquire deeply into the origin of the quarrel in the Transvaal'.[9] As the debate dragged on member sought to surpass member in expressions of loyalty and imperial

Wanganui Native Committee to the 'More Men' fund, who raised £80 and donated two horses towards equipping New Zealanders for South Africa. AUCKLAND WEEKLY NEWS, AIM

The Maori Coronation Contingent leading the South Island Battalion of the 10th Contingent to the Boer War, High Street, Christchurch, 1902. The troops are marching to the Christchurch railway station. WEEKLY PRESS, CANTERBURY MUSEUM

devotion. There were dissenters, but only a few. Robert McNab, soldier and historian, member of parliament for Mataura, was the most precise:

> *I have read the history of the Boer, and, if that question had to be decided in regard to justice or injustice, I say that the Boer beyond being a stubborn, and to our minds, a stupid people, are, in the right, and Britain is in the wrong.*[10]

Some criticism was veiled. Wi Pere, Member for Eastern Maori, pointed to England's sins of the past, and tellingly compared the poll tax imposed in New Zealand on Chinese immigrants to the Boer poll tax in the Transvaal.[11]

Pere's Maori brothers were not welcome at this war. Racism was alive and strong in the late 19th century. The War Office decreed that this was to be a white man's war. In New Zealand, despite Maori outrage and continued offers of recruits, the War Office stuck to its guns, even though Maori officers, NCOs, and other ranks, appeared on the New Zealand Volunteer rolls.[12] Had a Maori contingent reached South Africa it would have been surprised to see black Africans actually fighting on both sides; serving as porters, pioneers, railway gangers, and even as fighting soldiers. At the war's end Premier Seddon attempted to make amends to Maoridom by enrolling 31 Maori soldiers in the contingent to march at King Edward VII's coronation; and by promising (though not delivering) a Maori mounted rifle force of 5000 for imperial defence.[13]

Most of the actual dissenters to the war argued unpopular views: that Britain was being pushed into war by capitalist exploiters in South Africa, that this was not a war for the defence of New Zealand, that negotiation not war was needed in South Africa, and that it was an unjust war. Most did not press their objections to the vote. T E Taylor, prohibitionist, Seddon's fiercest political opponent, and member of parliament for a Christchurch seat, did, and assured his defeat at the 'khaki election' later in 1899.[14] J Hutcheson and J Scotland, who with Taylor deprecated the mood that had gripped New Zealand, were pelted with invective, and became the subject of ridiculing ballads. One of the least offensive proclaimed:

> *Shame:*
> *Scurrilous Scotland and treacherous Taylor.*
> *Go find other methods of venting your spleen.*
> *True men cheer brave warriors, soldiers and sailors.*
> *God guard all brave gallants who fight for the Queen.*[15]

Scotland, safely ensconced for life in the Legislative Council (New Zealand's Upper House) was the subject of the fiercest attacks. He had unwisely denounced those who volunteered for South Africa as 'loafers and larrikins who were only too glad to embrace the opportunity of getting a trip to South Africa at the public expense'.[16] Only a handful of parliamentarians finally opposed the sending of the contingent.

The first contingent's last act as it sailed from New Zealand was to give 'three hearty boos' for Taylor. It was one thing to embark for the Transvaal to fight for 'uitlander' liberty, it was quite another to allow liberty of dissent to opponents of the Empire's war at home. 'Jingoism', a term bequeathed to posterity by the arch-poet of Empire Rudyard Kipling, means bellicose imperialism. In 1899 jingoism had New Zealand by the throat. In Auckland a pantomime, of all things, became the focus of a patriotic demonstration, made all the more hysterical by the audience identifying volunteers for the first contingent amongst it. A contemporary newspaper report identifies the mood:

No sooner had the strains of 'God Save the Queen' died away than someone struck up 'Rule Britannia'. The audience joined in the chorus and also sang the well known song 'Sons of the Sea'. Mr Ernest Fitts afterwards came forward, in the uniform of the Heretaunga Mounted Rifles, to sing 'the songs of the Empire'. The Union Jack and the New Zealand flag were brought forward and entwined in the midst of enthusiastic cheering.[17]

Outside the safety of the legislature only a few New Zealanders had fortitude enough to challenge the jingoists. Father Patrick Cleary, the pro-Irish independence editor of the Roman Catholic journal, the *Tablet*, was one who did. He opined:

A correspondent who objects to the pacific tone which we had adopted declares that 'the manhood of New Zealand is for war'.... We would remind our bellicose friend that willingness to sit safely at home and send other people to hack and hew at each other, bore into each other's anatomy with bullets, and blow each other to smithereens with Lyddite and shells, is no necessary evidence of manhood.[18]

Trooper Callaway of the First New Zealand Contingent for the Transvaal.
AUCKLAND WEEKLY NEWS, AIM

Rutherford Waddell, the neo-socialist editor of the Presbyterian *Outlook*, also stood up to be counted, and prompted his readers to examine the 'Britain right or wrong' argument.[19] Black eyes, boycotted shops, and dismissal from government employment, marked the opposition of lesser figures. The *Waikato Argus* seemed to speak for a vast majority of New Zealanders when it proclaimed: 'There is only one sentiment throughout the Empire — we must win regardless of the cost in men or treasure'.[20]

Ten contingents of New Zealand troops departed for the war, and every departure was marked with patriotic celebration. The Wellington Opera House was packed for the first contingent's farewell prior to its embarkation on 21 October 1899. Province vied with province to give the lads the best send-off. Auckland provided the 2nd contingent (complete with a Hotchkiss gun attachment) with a boisterous send-off. The 3rd (Rough Riders) contingent, Canterbury's pride, and the Otago enlisted 4th (also Rough Riders) contingent, received equally flowery addresses and promises of public support, as did those contingents who followed.

'Will you kindly drop a shilling in my little tambourine'

Kipling was right! Those too old to fight, too young, debarred by their womanly sex, or secretly unwilling to go to war, were called upon to 'pay! pay!! pay!!!'. Farmers donated prize horses, merchants offered saddles and bridles to departing volunteers, communities offered money, women's circles knitted rugs and 'comforts', and churches held both prayer meetings and soirees. Far away, in Windsor Castle, the aged Queen Victoria knitted scarves, to be presented for acts of valour, one to each of her Empire's colonies engaged in the fight. Trooper H D Coutts received New Zealand's quota.[21]

Once the casualty lists appeared patriotic fund-raising for widows and their dependants became a matter of community conscience. Newspapers with as limited a reading public as the *Ohinemuri Gazette* published in full letters from boys at the front, stressing the need for community support.[22] Patriotic meetings, addressed by ubiquitous politicians, with processions, banners and bands, raised funds. Simon Johnson tells that in Auckland one procession of over 2000 citizens marched to the drill hall to hear speeches, to sing patriotic songs, and to listen to a recitation of Kipling's 'The Absent-minded Beggar', while collection mugs were passed from row to row.[23] In

Captain, officers and instructors of the Khaki Girls Brigade. These amazons were one of a number of women's volunteer corps that were formed to raise money for our boys in South Africa.
AUCKLAND WEEKLY NEWS, AIM

Christchurch, Women's Volunteer Corps, dressed in military uniforms, demanded donations in the streets, with a 'flying column' forcing cyclists to 'stand and deliver'.[24]

'Table Bay'

It was nearly one month's voyage from New Zealand to Cape Town's Table Bay, and the ten contingents were each and all kept busy aboard ship; with a 5.30 a.m. reveille, 'stables' at 6 a.m.; and drills, more 'stables' and fatigues, until 'lights out' at 10 p.m.[25] 'Smoke concerts' whiled away the evening hours. At Table Bay New Zealanders, most of whom had never before been abroad, stared in amazement at the line upon line of warships, transports, supply vessels and merchant ships in port. They had arrived in South Africa, and they were about to meet 'the enemy' — the Boers — moving north toward the front by rail in cattle trucks.

Their first lesson learnt in South Africa was that shiny brass buttons must be replaced with lustreless bone, that their proudly worn bronze 'NZMR' (New Zealand Mounted Rifles) and 'fernleaf' national identification mark must be removed, and that officers did not wear the uniform or badges of their rank. The explanation was simple — the Boers delighted in sharp-shooting at glittering targets, and at officers. Soon the New Zealand slouch hat was abandoned and replaced by a British topee, to prevent British riflemen confusing the New Zealand and Boer top-pieces.

Their second lesson was that war is ninety per cent boredom and only ten per cent action. This reality was deplored in a ditty by Trooper James Madill:

> *Grooming! grooming! grooming!!!*
> *Always ***** well grooming.*
> *From reveille to lights out*
> *It's grooming all day long.*
> *Trekking! trekking! trekking!*
> *Always ***** well trekking.*
> *From reveille to lights out*
> *It's trekking all day long.*
> *Biscuits! biscuits! biscuits!!!*

Three Waikato Volunteers of the First Contingent: Sergeant William Edward Mahood and Troopers William Fletcher Wallis and Thomas Joseph Holte Gaudin.
STOWERS COLLECTION

A Boer on horseback.
STOWERS COLLECTION, AIM

*Always ***** well biscuits*
From reveille to lights out.
It's biscuits all day long.[26]

Then came the most frightening lesson of all; that the Boer was an excellent soldier and that the Boer was initially winning the war. It did not take the New Zealand Mounted Rifles long to realise how misleading war propaganda was about their enemy. They discovered that the 87,000 Transvaal and Orange Free State citizen soldiers who faced the British Empire's might, were formidable, intelligent and enduring. Field Marshal the Viscount Montgomery's later assessment of Boer military aptitude is exact:

> *All were tough fighters, first class horsemen and with a natural sense of minor tactics. Although nearly all were mounted, they fought on foot. They were unexpectedly strong in artillery, and in this and other fields they were assisted by a number of European adventurers and experts. Their weakest feature was indiscipline: They disliked being organised and their officers could never count on all the men on their muster-roll being present to go into action.*[27]

Their artillery was German trained and with some German officers. Armed with 75 mm Creusot and Krupp field guns, their small regular force could hurl high explosive shells to a range of 8500 yards, and with their larger calibre 115 mm Creusot fire to a range of 11,000 yards.

Every Boer from the years of 16 to 60 was called up for the war, and 50,000 took to the field immediately the war began. Armed with the latest Mauser rifles, organised into commandos (companies), varying in size from 300 to over 1000, and dressed in ordinary farm garb (they possessed few uniforms), the Boers quickly showed themselves to be crack shots, resourceful and masters of informal warfare. Mounted on small fast ponies the Boers galloped to the battle front, dismounted to fight and specialised in surprise, ambush and concentrated fire from dug trenches and from behind rock walls. Their British opponents, unused to the veldt, nicknamed 'Rooinck' by the Boers (sunburned necks), were slow to realise the formidability of Boer tactics. General Kitchener, perhaps Britain's best commander in the theatre, early in the campaign foolishly remarked that:

> *The Boers are not like the Sudanese who stood up to a fair fight. They are always running away on their little ponies.... There are a good many foreigners among the Boers, but they are easily shot, as they do not slink away like the Boers themselves.*[28]

The war zone was mostly hilly, rocky and well suited to the mounting of ambushes by those who knew the terrain well — and the Boers made the most of their knowledge of likely ambush sites. In the New Zealand Defence Report from 1900, Parliament was apprised of the difficulties faced by its heroes in South Africa:

> *The strong kopjes [hills] are terrible affairs to tackle and the plains to cross them offer no cover at all.... [For the enemy] the rocky kopjes are just perfect cover, and it is only the guns bursting and the mounted men threatening their flank or rear that stirs them out, and then they just travel like deer to the next.*[29]

Merging into the landscape, and remaining hidden until a party of imperial or colonial troops were within a few hundred yards, the Boers then would unleash a fusillade of fire. As many spoke accentless English they easily acquired intelligence of imperial and colonial defence positions, sometimes by simply asking.

But the Boers were not supermen. In the first stage of the war they missed a glorious opportunity. Instead of a massed attack into Cape Colony, and through to Cape Town, their main force was divided and wasted on sieges of symbolic rather than military importance. Collective leadership and battlefield democracy led to compromise and marginally useful operations. Richard Stowers rightly assesses that this weakness continued down the line of command:

> *There was a tendency for Boer commandos to operate independently with little shared intelligence and few combined operations. The Boer morale, often suffering from sudden ebbings in discipline in ranks, left much to be desired. Taking leave without permission was considered normal behaviour. Even at the point of jumping a parapet to attack, half the Boer force would suddenly stay put — with no repercussions. Often a Boer would change units without permission, and if this didn't improve his position he would simply return to the old unit. Many even had servants and wives accompany them into combat zones.*[30]

Initially these Boer defects did not bring disaster. British military blunders were far more calamitous. E Kinnear brilliantly summarises early British military stupidity in one neat exchange between two British officers:

> *'It seems to me', said a well-known colonel of the guards, 'that our leaders find out the strongest position of the enemy, and then attack him in front'. 'It appears to me', put in his brother officer, 'that they attack him first and find out his position afterwards'.*[31]

The New Zealand and other colonial forces employed in the British imperial service contributed to the reversal of Boer success. Once Britain imported a reactive Commander-in-Chief, and learned how to copy and beat Boer tac-

Tons upon tons of oats for the horses. *Food for our horses was the biggest problem [and] there were ticks... we could scrape them off the tummies of our horses every morning by veritable handfuls.* Frank Perham. STOWERS COLLECTION, AIM

tics, then the superior discipline, strategic co-ordination and logistical capability of the Empire could triumph on the South African battlefields.

'Out on active service, wiping something off a slate'

New Zealanders fought in all three of the crucial stages of the South African war. Stage one began with the Boer sieges of Ladysmith, Kimberley and Mafeking, with three British imperial defeats in 'Black Week' (10–15 December 1899) at Stromberg, Magesfontein and Colenso, where three British generals tasted defeat.[32]

The first contingent arrived in November 1899, at a critical juncture in the war. Imperial forces and civilian townsfolk were besieged by the Boers in Ladysmith, Kimberley and Mafeking. Huge tracts of countryside were in Boer hands. Placed under the command of Major General J D P French, in his 1st Cavalry Division, together with the 6th Dragoon Guards, Scots Greys, Inniskilling Dragoons, some infantry, Rimington's Scouts, and a company of New South Wales lancers, the New Zealanders had inadvertently drawn the best of the British fighting generals as their commander.[33] French quickly observed the New Zealanders to be slack on saluting, below average in drill, but aggressive, eager and willing to be used. He used them at Jasfontein, where they took their first casualty, Trooper G R Bradford (formerly Regimental Sergeant-Major of the Ohinemuri Rifles), and then on 15 January at a critical incident near Colesberg.[34]

French had been sent to the northern Cape Colony in order to prevent further advances of Boer forces toward Cape Town. His plan was to continuously extend his front to overlap the Boer flanks, and by so doing force the enemy to over-extend, from which position he could push him back. Close to Colesberg, with its Boer garrison of about 10,000, French had taken the water supply base and forward outpost of Rensburg, which came under Boer fire from a hill three miles away. Later called 'New Zealand Hill', this prominence brought a company each from the Yorkshire regiment and the New Zealand Mounted Rifles into conflict with the enemy, with a New Zealand bayonet

Trooper Edward Wilmot Moore from Blenheim who was a member of the First NZ Mounted Rifles, Bloemfontein, April 1900. AIM

charge finally evicting the Boer. Trooper Alex Wilkie's 'literary memorial' to the event in nineteen verses has not won world fame for its poetry, but New Zealanders at the front and at home were captivated by its immediacy:

> *Have you ever heard the story,*
> *The British remember it still,*
> *The tale of Boer disaster,*
> *The Battle of New Zealand Hill...*
> *The order came in a twinkling,*
> *The hill must not be lost,*
> *New Zealand's men must take it,*
> *And hold it at any cost...*
> *The colonials charged the Dutchmen,*
> *They fought them hand to hand,*
> *They beat the Boer at every point,*
> *Those men from Maori land...*
> *Those men were the first colonials,*
> *To fight for the motherland,*
> *They gained the praise of General French —*
> *They made a brilliant stand.*
> *They proved to the mother country,*
> *What colonial men can do,*
> *Against an overwhelming force,*
> *New Zealand saw it through* [35]

The Boers were held and the second stage of the war followed with the arrival of Field Marshal Lord Roberts as Commander-in-Chief on 10 January 1900.[36] The Empire was now fighting back; and during the course of the year relieved Kimberley, forced General Cronje's surrender at Paardeberg, relieved Ladysmith, and then Mafeking, and in May 1900 entered Johannesburg and Pretoria.[37] Very soon in 1900, three and then four New Zealand contingents were in action — mounted riflemen, who, like the Boer, fought with rifles from the ground, mobile and effective in quick-moving clashes over the broad veldt. It was hot, dangerous and uncomfortable soldiering; a war of vast treks, as hard or harder on their mounts who were often without sufficient food, were short of water and were hard driven. Major M Craddock, commander of the second contingent, who arrived at Cape Town on 27 February 1900, joined the 1st Contingent on the march toward Pretoria. In a field entry he reported that between the date of the contingent's arrival and 28 August 1900 his troopers rode 2183 miles (3512 kilometres). Under 'Bob's' command (Field Marshal Lord Roberts) the fortunes of war had changed to favour the imperial forces, and daily distances between the front and the Boer capitals decreased. Although Trooper Frank Perham's 5th Contingent served in Rhodesia, and not in the Transvaal, his diary entry recorded a typical day's trek:

> *For the boys the routine of travel was to ride for a few hours, and then dismount and lead the horses for possibly an hour. To avoid the midday sun we would be on the trail at 3 a.m.; we'd halt at 7 a.m. for breakfast, then on again from 8 a.m. until 11 a.m., when we sheltered from the sun until 3 p.m. On again then until 7 p.m. ... when all hands would camp for the night.* [38]

When trekking time stood still, but once a fire-fight commenced time raced, and minutes encompassed a lifetime. Trooper G Harle Moore, of the 4th (Rough Riders) Contingent, in his description of his first action, records the confusion and surreal nature of the happening:

How Auckland received the news of the relief of Mafeking. The scene is Queen Street on Saturday night, 15 May 1900.
AUCKLAND WEEKLY NEWS, AIM

Gallopers darted about here and there delivering orders. The pom-pom of the fifteen-pounder came into action with a rumble and a clatter from somewhere in the rear, and took up a position in the front. Squadrons of mounted men moved out at a gallop, and occupied positions on either flank.... The bullets whistled overhead or passed close to us, and buried themselves with a nasty whirr-rp in the ground behind. At first one did not realise the danger; but when a horse, standing a few yards off, reared up and went down, all of a heap to rise no more, we quickly dismounted and sought the nearest shelter.[39]

On the road to the Boer capitals New Zealanders were at the fore of the relief of Kimberley on 16 February 1900, after its 124-day siege. The New Zealanders were 'put out' at the lack of enthusiasm on the part of the town toward their rescuers, and one trooper, tired of hearing about the harsh regime of the siege, commented that: 'the inhabitants we have seen so far look a great deal fatter and certainly cleaner and better dressed than we are'.[40] New Zealand units did not take part in the battle of Paardeberg Drift, on the Modder River, in the Orange Free State, whereafter the Boer General Cronje surrendered with 5000 troops on 27 February 1900. They were, instead, still with French, clearing the flanks for Roberts's advance upon Bloemfontein (the Orange Free State capital) up the Modder River. On 13 March 1900 the New Zealanders rode with Roberts's forces into Bloemfontein, but on 31 March 1900 had the first taste of a new style of warfare that was soon to dominate the theatre, guerilla warfare. General Christiaan de Wet surprised a column at Koornspruit, and in the defence of Sannah's Post the New Zealanders took casualties and 17 New Zealanders became Boer prisoners-of-war.[41] In August 1900 New Zealanders helped relieve Lt. Col. R S Baden-Powell (the later founder of the Boy Scouts) at Rustenburg, and in November took casualties in the battle of Khenoster Kop.[42]

New Zealand's only award of a Victoria Cross in the war occurred in an action on 28 January 1901, near Naauwpoort in the Transvaal, when Farrier Major W J Hardham, rescued the wounded Trooper McCrae, under heavy fire, mounting the wounded trooper on his own horse, and running alongside.[43]

On 5 June 1900 British imperial forces entered Pretoria, in September President Kruger fled to Europe, and when Field Marshal Roberts handed over his command to General Lord Kitchener on 29 November 1900 it looked as if it was all over, and that Roberts could enjoy his triumph in London.[44] His strategy seemed to have succeeded. He had held the Boers on the Natal front, engaged them on the western front, rolled up their centre in the advance from Cape Colony, and pushed their remnant into Portuguese East Africa.

Roberts's decision that there was only mopping-up to be done was premature. Following the taking of Pretoria the war entered its third stage, with the dispersed Boer field force resorting to guerilla warfare; raiding unexpectedly and effectively across a wide span, and forcing British imperial forces to tie up thousands of troops in lines of blockhouses, erecting barbed wire fences, using flying columns to pursue the elusive de Wet, B Viljoen, de la Rey and Smuts.[45] Given these unexpected and effective Boer raids Kitchener asked the New Zealand government to leave the 3rd, 4th and 5th Contingents in South Africa. Before the war was over, about 25,000 Australians, New Zealanders and Canadians, alongside the 60,000 colonial Africans, were gratefully accepted by the British government. According to Rudyard Kipling: 'All independent, queer and "odd, but most amazin' new"'.[46]

To crush the Boer guerillas, General Lord Kitchener initiated a new style response: of 'new model' drives, wherein mobile troops were used to sweep the enemy toward barbed wire and concreted machine gun emplacements. Like beaters in the Highlands of Scotland sweeping the deer towards the stalkers, Kitchener used his mobile forces to clear zone after zone of the veldt. To deny the Boer remnant food and supply, families were removed from their farms, their homesteads torched and their livestock slaughtered. Kitchener preferred to use colonial troops rather than British forces for these tasks. Trooper Frank Perham of the New Zealand 5th Contingent, was with the Kimberley Flying Column, and inadvertently reveals the dehumanising impact of these expeditions:

> *Coming to a farmhouse we delayed for a while to do some looting, but suddenly noticed that the Main Body of our Column and the guns were getting close to us, we hurried out to take up our positions again. Coming to a steep kopje, Phil dismounted and handing his horse to Bugler Chegwin to hold, he proceeded to climb to the top of the kopje. He had almost got*

there when he received a volley of rifle fire at almost point blank range. He stopped three bullets, a fatal one straight through the lungs, evidently a dum-dum or soft-nosed bullet as the hole where it left the body was large enough to put one's hand in.[47]

For de Wet and the 'bitter-enders' (as the continuing resistance was called) the war ended with their freedom of action blocked by barbed wire fences and lines of armed blockhouses, and with their stomachs shrunken for want of food as they moved from burnt-out ruin to burnt-out ruin. The end was bitter. At Langverwacht, on 24 February 1902, 24 New Zealanders died and 42 were wounded as they clashed with General de Wet's commandos.[48] Given the burnings, the lootings and the slaughtering of farm animals, it was hardly surprising that New Zealanders were shot by Boer 'bitter-enders' after the war had officially ended.

'And he's left a lot o' little things behind him'

Most New Zealand losses in South Africa were not from bullet wounds, but from disease. In the Anglo-Boer war the casualty rate from disease was double that of those killed on the battlefield. Enteric fever, nowadays called typhoid, was a constant threat in the Orange Free State and in the Transvaal. Malaria hit the 4th and 5th Contingents during their several weeks in Portuguese East Africa. Heat, flies, cold, wet clothes, together with an irregular and poorly balanced diet, increased the casualty rate. Infected water and poor sanitation contributed to enteric fever's 16,000 deaths amongst the British imperial force during the war (in contrast only 6000 died in battle!).[49]

Trooper Luke Perham, Third NZ Rough Riders, killed in action, 1900. AIM

For the sick and wounded the road to hospital care was a bumpy and dusty one. An expert eye witness paints a grim word picture of an end to one expedition:

> *The march back to the railway was even worse than the march out. The wagons were loaded with the sick and had to be dragged through the morasses so deep that bushes had to be cut and placed under the wheels to prevent them from sinking in. At Van Wyk's Vlei typhoid had broken out; ... It must have been a terrific journey for the five wagon-loads of sick. Only two had covers, so the rest huddled under tarpaulins. The wagons often bogged down and then all those who could stand were turned out to push.*[50]

Once the sick and wounded reached a field hospital what were their chances? Volunteer stretcher-bearers gently conveyed the wounded from ambulances unsuited to the stony veldt. It is just possible that New Zealand wounded were carried by Mohandas Gandhi, the father of Indian independence, a volunteer stretcher-bearer at the front. Inside the hospital tent, recovery and survival depended upon a mixture of factors: physical fitness, the placement of the wound, control of shock, the length of the waiting queue, and the aptitude of the surgeon. One New Zealand surgeon accompanied each of the smaller contingents, while sizeable contingents such as the 9th (1218 troopers) possessed two.[51]

The army surgeons of 1899–1902 knew about antisepsis, that putrefaction could be prevented by antiseptic solution such as carbolic acid, and ether and chloroform were employed as anaesthetics. But in a war all surgery is traumatic, performed in conditions that cannot be dictated or modified by the surgeon; and tired surgeons, under pressure, often picked up dropped instruments from the tent floor and adjusted spectacles and wiped their foreheads

The Ngapuhi Nursing sisters of Whangarei. AUCKLAND WEEKLY NEWS, AIM

with bare hands. Army surgeons of 1899–1902 worked bare-headed, bare-handed, ungowned, and their blood-soaked canvas aprons were hardly germ-free. The surgeon did what he could, as quickly as he could. Thomas Packenham describes a typical field hospital reception:

> *Everywhere lay the khaki helmets, crushed, blood-stained, and riddled with holes. Some of the men were delirious. They rolled off the stretchers and kicked about on the ground. One man, paralysed below the waist by a bullet in the spine, kept raising his head, staring with wonder at the limbs he could never move nor feel. The earth seemed to be covered with groaning men. In the evening it began to rain, and the men on the stretchers covered up with tarpaulins.... Outside the operation tent, men waited patiently for their turn. 'Keep yer chivey up, Joe', 'good luck to yer, old cock, you won't feel nothin'. Orderlies took the stretchers in through the open flap, as the endless work went on. Chloroform, examining, amputation. Legs rattled in the bucket, and dropped on the blood-stained grass.*[52]

Those likely to recover began a long journey, by road, train and then hospital ship, to England, nursed by volunteer women nurses, who after a fierce battle were finally permitted to serve in South Africa. The War Office had initially argued that soldiers preferred to be nursed by men, that South Africa was no place for women, and that women nurses flirted with their patients. There was no Florence Nightingale to put the generals in their place.

New Zealand nurses had quickly volunteered for the war and five from Christchurch and six from Dunedin soon arrived. Sister Teape, from Christchurch, the first to arrive in South Africa, was enraged by the army's failure to comprehend basic sanitation needs in Bloemfontein:

> *The place was a hotbed of fever, and the dreaded enteric raged everywhere; and no wonder, with... animals lying dead everywhere, water bad, buildings covered black with flies, and patients covered with vermin.*[53]

Nurse Nellie Redstone of Gisborne, who was one of the many New Zealand nurses to offer their services, and who had to pay their own fares to South Africa. NZ GRAPHIC

The New Zealand nurses who served in South Africa were mainly concerned with disease cases. Of the 232 New Zealand deaths in the war 139 were from disease. Of this 139, 57 per cent died of enteric fever, 25 per cent

Nurses in South Africa take afternoon tea. Nurse Emily Rowley from New Zealand is standing at the back left. Thirty-five New Zealand nurses served in the war, and their work set the seal on the value of military nursing. Initially, nurses were not allowed to tend patients — their duty was to supervise the medical orderlies. As the war dragged on this changed and where nurses were present standards of hygiene improved. These nurses wear mourning bands to mark the death of Queen Victoria. AIM

of pneumonia, and 6 per cent of dysentery.[54] The fouling and poisoning of water-holes was common practice by both protagonists during the war, and there was inadequate attention to sanitary drills. The bulk of New Zealand pneumonia deaths occurred on the returning troopship *Britannia*, when an outbreak of measles was accompanied by pulmonary complications. In the course of the war 2000 troops died of cholera and dysentery. The pseudonymous author of *The New Zealanders and the Boer War* chapters complaint after complaint by New Zealand nurses, attendants and doctors: of the poor facilities available for treatment, of red tape in the administration of British military hospitals, and of the length of time between a battle-front wounding and admission to proper care. In the same book there is undisputed praise for the care given to the sick and wounded by the New Zealand nursing sisters.

Both sides suffered on the veldt — from hunger, thirst, extremes of hot and cold, insufficient clothing and worn-out boots, as well as from killer diseases. It was worse for the Afrikaaner women, children and old folk; evicted from their homes and farms during Kitchener's 'model drives' — when homes were torched, crops destroyed and herds and flocks slaughtered, to prevent the supply of Boer commandos. In 'concentration camps' (their official British title) mostly tented, water supplies were often impure, sanitary arrangements unhygienic, clothing insufficient and food of poor quality. By May 1901 100,000 Boers, half of them children, were housed in 36 concentration camps. When the Boers counted their dead they found that only 12 per cent of their casualties had fallen in battle. A startling 65 per cent were children under 16 years who died in 'concentration camps'.[55] Twenty-thousand Boers died in camps that were insanitary, poorly run, insufficiently equipped with medical aids, and where hunger and malnutrition were common. Emily Hobhouse, the British social reformer, who visited some of these camps, came close to accusing the British of genocide in her newspaper reports. But it was not only whites who died in concentration camps. In a war not dissimilar to the American Civil War, where blacks fought on both sides, 13,000 black Africans, held in concentration camps by the British who refused to trust them, also died. Colonial troops largely resented their role in gathering civilians for concentration camp incarceration. One Australian trooper wrote:

I pitied the women and children who knelt before us and begged and prayed that their housing and food might not be destroyed, but it was an order and soon one of the most fertile valleys in the Transvaal was devastated.[56]

It is difficult to estimate how many New Zealand veterans of the Anglo-Boer war died of disease after their return. What is known is the New Zealand casualties statistic for the war. Of the ten New Zealand contingents, with a total death of 232 men, 59 were killed in action, 11 died of wounds and 25 were accidentally killed, while 133 died of disease.[57]

'When you've sung "God Save the Queen"'

New Zealand's heroes came home in dribs and drabs, as a contingent's time of service ended, or in parties of wounded, and in one case at the close of the Australian Commonwealth inauguration celebrations. The war had begun with Queen Victoria near the close of her record 64-year reign. It ended with her ageing son, Edward VII, the monarch of an empire 'upon which the sun never set', and during his reign the flames of imperialism would roar even higher. Colonial New Zealand welcomed the veterans back with prayers, parades, politicians' speeches and civic dinners; the colony basked in a euphoria of victory. Imperial pride was vindicated, the Anglo-Saxons had protected their own, and the sons and daughters of Empire had made old Mother England aware that they were growing up, and possessed muscle enough to be useful. New Zealand emerged from the war determined to increase her role as part of the Empire. In the years that followed school cadet units were raised and drilled and practised in marksmanship. The volunteer military system, unreliable and inefficient, was replaced by a conscript territorial army, on the Swiss model of every man a soldier. A battle cruiser, HMS *New Zealand* was offered to the Royal Navy, and paid for year after year by the New Zealand taxpayer. Calls for 'imperial federation', and for an 'imperial parliament', and for integration of New Zealand soldiers into the British Military, were loud and insistent.[58] Like a rowdy adolescent New Zealand wanted a say in the deciding of the imperial family's affairs.

Soldiers always expect to return to the land they have left behind, but they never do. It has always changed in their absence, and so have they. And after the lobster, the roast lamb or roast beef dinners, and after Major General Sir Hector MacDonald and Premier Seddon had laid their foundation stones 'to the memory of New Zealand's sons fallen in South Africa' what then? Those who returned received the colony's thanks, two campaign medals (Queen Victoria's and King Edward's, for the Queen died in 1901), and the challenge of finding jobs. As time went on the question of a national memorial was raised and Lord Ranfurly, New Zealand's governor, proposed that the national monument to New Zealand's fallen should be a home for needy veterans.[59] On 10 December 1909 the Ranfurly Veterans' Home was finally opened, on six hectares near Onehunga — a home for 32 single veterans and four couples. Those who returned were also determined to help each other, to support themselves through membership of the New Zealand Mounted Rifles Association, a body founded on SS *Orient*, on 22 January 1901, by troops bound for home.

The same plausible politician who sent them off to war welcomed them home. Seddon announced in September 1901 that returning soldiers might keep their rifles, providing they gave a written undertaking to keep them in order and promised to give them up if the authorities called upon them so to

Raised to fight for King and Empire.
COOPER ALBUM, AIM

do. Seddon had forgotten that the rifles were not his but belonged to the British War Office, and the British soon asked for them back. Those already returned to New Zealand said very strongly that 'a promise is a promise', and when military authorities attempted to relieve them they found their rifles strangely missing. When the 7th Contingent veterans on the transport *Manila* reached New Zealand, angry veterans aboard broke into the ship's armoury and seized their former weapons, and bandoleers, and took them home.

There was little chance of their return and Seddon and the army head-quarters would have done better to have left well alone. Many rifle butts had been artistically carved during the long nights on the veldt, and veterans had hunting plans for their much-loved .303s. One veteran insisted that as Seddon's Liberal Party argued for 'use-hold' land division (actually it was 'leasehold'), he had the right to the 'use-hold' of his rifle. 'Disgusted', in the *Otago Daily Times*, established his position with the utmost clarity:

> *Sir,*
> *I yesterday received a communication from the local defence office ordering me at once to return to the defence office my rifles and bandoleers brought from South Africa by me. Can you kindly inform me, sir, if this is an indication of the patriotism of the people of New Zealand?... We have had to live on a couple of biscuits a day, and have had no more than twenty hours' sleep for a whole week, lying out at night in the open, exposed to wind, rain, and heavy biting frosts.... P.S.... Sir, I've also got a couple Kaffir Assegais and a knob-kerrie. Perhaps they also would be of some service in arming the volunteer forces.*[60]

'Disgusted' and many of his disgusted comrades, won this battle. Army authorities soon found that the returned soldiers they visited were all 'inno-cent' men, with perfect alibis for the day the armoury was broken into. Few were able to give the slightest assistance in identifying or retrieving the miss-ing weapons. Despite the mysterious disappearance of these British Army weapons, in the decades that followed many a New Zealand deer fell to rifles and riflemen who had once ambushed a different quarry on the veldt — to British .303s, and also to the souvenirs brought home, Mausers and Martini Henrys, as spoils of battle.

What did those who fought in South Africa believe that they had achieved? For some it was sufficient to have engaged in an adventure that had taken them away from the insularity of antipodean isolation. Others believed the propaganda of militant imperialism, and assumed that they had defeated a dangerous challenge to the British Empire's mandate to rule in Southern Af-rica. Others were less sure, and remarked upon the likeness in build, horse-manship, marksmanship and farming interests of the Boer to the New Zealand farmer. Some believed that the Peace of Vereeniging, made between Boer and Britain on 31 May 1902, had settled it all. But at least one veteran realised that the Afrikaaner nation could not be absorbed into the British Empire by force. R H Bakewell, who served with the 9th Contingent, remarked in his diary:

> *The longer I am in contact with the returned troopers, and the men and officers of the 9th, the more clearly I see that the war will never be finished by them... We are only creating for ourselves another Ireland — does anyone suppose that anything can reconcile the Boers to British rule?*[61]

Back in New Zealand the war was recorded for posterity in another way, by the naming of streets and roads after South African war heroes and battles.

Trooper A Waata Kendall, Hokianga, who died in South Africa and who was one of the few Maori serving in the New Zealand Contingents. AUCKLAND WEEKLY NEWS, AIM

In several New Zealand towns and districts people still drive or walk along Kitchener Terrace, Mafeking Place or Pretoria Road — alas, too often, without knowing the origins of these place names.

In the village pub, over many a long beer, veterans chewed the fat over the war, and over their 'bosses'. 'Bob's' Roberts was venerated from afar; Kitchener was regarded as a tough, mean and successful professional, but French was respected and liked. French had treated them with respect and interest, and given them 'a fair go'. Trooper E Nopps won many a drink over his tale of General French and Captain Richard Hutton Davies:

> One day Captain Davies sent me as personal galloper to General French. Riding over the veldt he motioned me to ride beside him.... He was surprised to find that I, a Kiwi trooper, had been educated at Charterhouse.... Then he queried me about Davies and said that he was most surprised to find he was not a professional soldier. When I told him Davies was a highly competent surveyor and county engineer, the general said, 'ah, that accounts for it then. Nopps, I have employed your people on a number of important reconnaissance patrols. Well, Davies reports are models of accuracy and consistency and are always clearly illustrated with first class maps and sketches worthy of a military academy. As well, he is a first class squadron leader in the field — mark my words, Nopps, Davies will go a long way as a soldier'.[62]

French was right. Davies ended his career as Major General R H Davies, CB; after commanding the 20th Division at Ypres. In fact, the New Zealanders were lucky in their field officers. Major A W Robin concluded his military career as a major general and commander of New Zealand military forces. Captain W R N Madocks, the Charles Upham of the war (aggressive, unshakeable and personally committed to maximising enemy casualties), served as a brigadier general in the British Army in the First World War. Only one New Zealand contingent commander, Major T J Jowsey, of the 3rd Contingent, was disliked by his men. This difficult officer, with a chip on his shoulder over promotion, and all too testy over matters of seniority, was replaced by Davies — and not too soon his men affirmed.

Many of the junior British officers, who from time to time associated with the New Zealanders, received little respect. Their class consciousness annoyed egalitarian Kiwis, and their lack of soldierly skill was thought appalling. Corporal F Twisleton spoke for many when he wrote of:

> ... 'Nincompoops', men who if they had not possessed influence or money, would have been reckoned very inferior troopers had they joined the ranks. Can anyone imagine what the feelings of a sergeant or sergeant-major must be when he sees a sprat of a boy placed over him — a boy that ought to be at home with his mother.[63]

In Egypt, Gallipoli and France, some of the veterans who enlisted again for the First World War had their dislike of British officer arrogance reinforced.

'For a gentleman in khaki ordered south'

On Anzac Day in some New Zealand towns and villages the marching veterans still halt at the Boer War memorial, lay a wreath, and then march on. It is a distant war, a localised colonial war, dwarfed by the global contests that followed. But on the veldt, the ghosts of New Zealand's fallen still whisper in the wind the haunting question, 'Was this war worthy of our deaths — this war for Empire?'

The 'Rough Riders' of the 4th Contingent answer the question. On the slow railway journey from the front to Cape Town their train stopped often and they stretched their legs. At the little village of Norval's Point they came across a graveyard, and G Harle Moore tells of its impact on the returning veterans:

In this little plot we counted sixty-two plain wooden crosses, marking the last resting places of as many soldiers. Disease had been responsible for the deaths of no less than fifty-nine, mostly the dreaded enteric, one had been drowned, and another accidentally killed. The remaining cross bore the inscription, 'Shot on patrol', a simple phrase which conveys a good deal — but only to the initiated. Of the word 'patrol' the dictionary will offer a simple explanation; but the average layman has no idea of its meaning in warfare — especially in a war against an enemy like the Boer. It requires more than courage, more real pluck, to successfully carry out reconnoitring duties than to make a charge in company with a hundred of your fellows.... Two or three men walk their horses in a leisurely manner up to the kopjes to examine them for signs of the enemy. Finding none, the next cover is examined, and so on. The patrols are in the open, the Boers lurking behind boulders, hidden from sight. Probably the first notice the unlucky man has of the vicinity of the enemy is a volley fired at close range. Then it is a race for life. I have been with them scores of times, and have experienced the uncanny feeling that, in spite of every effort, creeps over you as you proceed closer and closer to some isolated kopje... From one kopje to another the patrol has to go — taking his life in his hands, doing work, which if necessary, is one of the most dangerous, arduous, and trying, in the service, and if you are shot there is no glory attached to your memory. A lonely grave in a strange land, a brief announcement in Regimental Orders — 'Number X, Trooper So-and-So, was shot on patrol today, and is struck off strength from this date'. Soon forgotten save by those who, thousands of miles away, will await in vain the return of a brother or son.[64]

The war that had begun with bugles, cheering and speeches, with a call to adventure and the great overseas experience, ended with scars on the veldt and the heart, and with the Last Post. In only thirteen years, in 1915, some of those who stopped at the Norval's Point graveyard would be at Gallipoli. Veterans twice, they could say with Chunuk Bair's Cyril Bassett: 'All my mates ever got were wooden crosses'.[65]

In the cemetery at Ladysmith. STOWERS COLLECTION

PART 3

The Great War of 1914-18

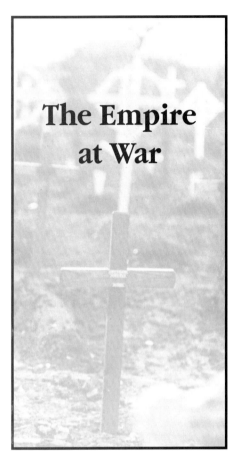

The Empire at War

The Boss said:... the whole of Europe's at war. The Duke and Duchess of Austria have been killed, and they're blaming the joker that done it on to Serbia, and they have declared war on Serbia. Russia declared war on Austria, Germany has declared war on Russia, and France and England are in a treaty with Russia and it looks as if they are both coming in at any time.

Charlie Clark, Wellington Infantry[1]

The assassination of the Archduke Franz Ferdinand, heir to the Austrian Hungarian Empire, and his wife at Sarajevo in Bosnia Herzegovina on 27 June 1914 was the spark that set Europe ablaze into what became the Great War of 1914–18. The causes are still subject to ongoing debate, but Imperial Germany's decision to invade France through neutral Belgium brought in a reluctant Britain who had originally guaranteed Belgium's neutrality. Britain's declaration of war on Germany ensured it would be a war that encompassed the world for her decision meant the British Empire was at war.

On 5 August 1914 when the Earl of Liverpool, Governor General of New Zealand, publicly announced that Great Britain had declared war on Germany, the people of New Zealand as part of the British Empire found themselves at war. We had no say in the matter nor did we want one. The British Empire was at war and as a loyal Dominion of that Empire that was good enough for us.

When New Zealanders went to war, they were ignorant of its causes and innocent of its meaning.

Ormond Burton, *The Silent Division*[2]

In every town in New Zealand cheering crowds took to the streets, and young men flocked to the recruiting halls keen to get away. To join the Expeditionary Force you had to join your local Territorial Unit. If you owned a horse you could try to get into the Mounted Rifles, if you did not then it was infantry or one of the other units such as artillery, engineers, signals and the service corps.

I was a surveyor down on the West Coast at Karamea. You couldn't work from the middle of June to August. The surveyor used to close up his camp and go into his office and complete his plans and bring them up to date which you can't do in a bush camp. I did it in my mother's place in Auckland. It was very obvious when it came to about the second of August 1914 that we were going to go to war. I worked for three days, day and night to put my stuff in order and then when war was declared I went down to try and join up but the infantry was already filled... but they said the Mounted Rifles wanted people. I walked along to the Mounted Rifles. 'Have you any vacancies for enlistment?' 'Yes', he said. 'Have you got a horse?' Just then a man said. 'By the way can I bring in both my horses?' 'No', I said, 'you are selling me one'. I went out to Devonport on the Ferry and picked up the horse. I rode it back out to Mt Eden. The next morning I was in camp at Potter's Paddock. Later on I swopped with a friend of mine who wanted to get into the Mounted Rifles. I wanted to get into infantry as I didn't think the Mounted Rifles would fight in Europe. Why did I join? I was an idealist.

12/1005 S Seddon, Auckland Infantry[3]

For King and Country?

New Zealanders went to war for every reason. The politicians, the press and the pulpit proclaimed that it was for King and Country, and indeed for some it was, but for many New Zealanders who had never been further than their own district or home town it was the chance to get away and see the world.

It was a mix of patriotism and adventure. I was always interested in battles, deeds that won the Empire. There was not the doubt and questioning that we have now. We were more simple-minded I think. We used to look at the map and see all the red areas [of the British Empire].

Dan Curham, Wellington Infantry Battalion[4]

I had been living with a stepmother and she didn't suit me so good so I thought it would be an opportunity to make a break — I'll go to war.

Henry Lewis, Otago Infantry Battalion[5]

'Well, I'm going to the war,' said Reg. So I says, 'Hold on, you can't go to the war. We've got a contract here to do and there's a lot to do in it yet!' So the Boss says to us, 'If England goes to war and if you want to go I'll cancel the contract and pay you day wages and take it off your bill at the store.'

Charlie Clark, Wellington Infantry Battalion[6]

I went down to Auckland and joined up. I suppose you could say I was looking for adventure. Today people would say we were brainwashed with patriotism. Britannia Rules the Waves on our side and Deutschland Uber Alles on the other. And now go out and kill each other.

Tony Fagan, Auckland Infantry Battalion[7]

I had a number of mates who were rugby men and that sort of thing and pals, I knew they'd all want to go. So in we got and the whole lot of us went together.

Joe Gasparich, Auckland Infantry Battalion[8]

I am in such a state of suppressed excitement that I can hardly write... The horror of such a war is thrust temporarily into the background by one's patriotism. As heat cures a burn and snow cures frostbite so the knowledge that Britain is at war for the moment cures the nausea of the whole thing.

George Tuck, Auckland Infantry Battalion[9]

Charlie Clark and a mate. CLARK FAMILY

Tony Fagan, an Auckland school teacher. FAGAN FAMILY

Dan Curham, a bank clerk of Wanganui. CURHAM FAMILY

Joe Gasparich (seated second left) with the other sergeants of the 15th North Auckland Company of the Auckland Infantry Battalion. GASPARICH FAMILY

The Rawene Boys go to war, August 1914. Third and fourth from the left in the front row are two brothers, Fred and Jim Price. Both migrated from Wales in 1912. Both served on Gallipoli and on the Western Front. Fred was wounded twice, and Jim was badly gassed in France and died as a result of this in the 1930s. HARRIS COLLECTION, AIM

Doing our bit for Empire

The infantry and mounted rifles units of the New Zealand Expeditionary Force (NZEF) were organised into provincial units based on the Territorial Regiments of Auckland, Wellington, Canterbury and Otago. Since the passing of the 1909 Defence Act part-time compulsory military training was an obligation for every young man once he reached his eighteenth birthday. This scheme had been organised by a British officer, Major General Sir Alexander Godley, and on the outbreak of war in 1914 this Territorial Force became the foundation of the NZEF which the people of New Zealand clamoured to send to show that they were loyal members of the British Empire. No one was sure where it was going to, only that it had to go.

There was no New Zealand badge and each infantry company or mounted rifle squadron wore the hat badges of their own local Territorial unit. For every one it was province first and until they got overseas being a New Zealander was not yet imagined. Each group reflected the character of the district that it drew its men from. In the Auckland Infantry the Third Auckland Company that was drawn from the city itself was known as the 'Wharfies Company', while the other companies reflected the bush and farming communities of North Auckland, Bay of Plenty and the Waikato.

Between 5 August 1914 and 12 November 1918, New Zealand, with a population of just over one million people, sent 99,263 soldiers, 539 sailors, 192 Royal Flying Corps and 550 nurses overseas to war. In addition, some 3370 New Zealanders are known to have left New Zealand and joined the British or Australian forces. New Zealand also sent 10,238 horses to war, but, because of quarantine regulations, only three returned.

The reinforcement soldier was not issued with a badge until he joined his unit at the front. Each reinforcement designed their own and bought them from the jewellers in the training camps at Featherston and Trentham. In late 1915 the New Zealand 'Onward' badge was produced and was popular as it gave the wearer immediate recognition as a New Zealand soldier. In the same way the lemon squeezer was originally only worn by the Wellington Infantry Battalion but by August 1916 it had become the distinctive hat of the NZEF except for the Mounted Rifles.

Sailing away on the great adventure

No one ever thought of not coming back.
Cecil Lovegrove, Wellington Infantry Battalion[10]

Few of the young men flocking to go to war ever thought what that word meant, or thought it might be they who would not come back. Like youth in every age they saw themselves as immortal. It was their mothers trying to hold back the tears who lived with a sense of impending disaster.

Monday [1914]

My dear Georgie
I tried to write last night to tell Dad, I could not face it alone. I had a good blub & feel better, of course I knew we could not hope to keep out of it, nor did I want to as I told the others if you were needed & you felt you ought to go; it will be very hard to part with any of you & I dare say it will mean the three, but I am ready to do my duty always as you are to do yours. Dad says they can't all go, I said I didn't see why not, you are here to take care of us & what right have you to keep [them] back if they wish to go. The Land won't be much use to us if you boys are not there to work it but please God you may not be wanted or if you are you will be spared to come back 'heroes' and take up your work again & we can do all the things we have planned together to make a lovely garden somewhere, with lovely beds of pansies. You had better tell Mr Skerman what you think of doing, it will make things easier for you; he will understand & you may want to give short notice. I have often thought about the song Men must work while women weep & wondered where it came from, now I know.

With much love from your ever loving Mother[11]

Here are young men of the Wellington Infantry Battalion wearing their distinctive lemon squeezers ready to go by train to Wellington. You can also see their issue caps attached to their epaulettes to stop them getting squashed. Note that one of them is carrying a drum for the company to keep step on the march.
AUCKLAND WEEKLY NEWS, AIM

William Douglas Knight (1892–1918). AIM

Ellen Knight was writing to her son George who has just told her of his intention to enlist. She and her husband Herbert lived in Dannevirke and had ten children, three daughters and seven sons. All three of her sons who were old enough went to war and never came back. The youngest, Herbert, was killed at Cape Helles at Gallipoli on 8 May 1915, George at Passchendaele on 12 October 1917, and Douglas on 1 September 1918 near Bancourt, France.

It was only at the final farewells on the wharfs as they boarded the transports that our young men started to realise what it meant to their families and the women they loved.

Then one fresh April morning as dawn was breaking through the mists, I went into Mother's room where she was waiting to greet me, and bade her goodbye. She gave me a brave farewell smile and her blessing, and I left her. We never met again.

E C McKay, Auckland Mounted Rifles[12]

Dear Mother
Have just time to scribble a line before lights out... Please post me my nugget outfit and a spare tin or two of nugget. There was some in the bottom of my tin box. Also post my heavy striped shirt and that pink singlet...

Edward Norman, Canterbury Infantry[13]

At 1 p.m. the ship cast off. What a din! What a scene! The blast of the ship's siren, the clanging of the ship's telegraph, the blowing of whistles, and the cheers of the troops and the crowd, all intermingled yet distinct. Truly a scene to stir any heart. Women were weeping and fainting, and the tense white faces of the men gazed upward in mute farewell. I must confess I felt a lump rise up in my throat, and as the ship slowly and majestically drew away from the wharf I felt that I should never return.

N M Ingram, Wellington Infantry Battalion[14]

With my mother I stood on the outskirts of the crowd near the entrance gates. She made a brave effort to be bright and happy, but when the fateful bugle sounded the call to every man to part and board the ship, the strain was a little too much and she almost fainted.

Eric Miller, NZ Engineers[15]

'Poppa goes to war.' The embarkation of troops from Wellington. AIM

One of the many transports that sailed from New Zealand with our boys. The local cinematographer is filming the departure from his stand on the horse and cart, and the film would be showing in the local picture theatres in the next day or so.
AUCKLAND WEEKLY NEWS, AIM

Plunging through the ocean

We have commenced our journey and are now plunging through the ocean, launched on the great adventure.

N M Ingram, Wellington Infantry[16]

New Zealand cargo and passenger ships were chartered by the Government to send our soldiers to war. Each was given the title: 'His Majesty's New Zealand Transport (HMNZT)' and a consecutive number of the sailing. This meant that a ship had a different transport number each time it was chartered. For example the *Maunganui* was in turn HMNZT Nos. 3, 17, 24, 30, 37, 49, 56, 68, 86 and 96. Conditions on board varied according to the type of ship. For the soldiers it could be the comparative luxury of a passenger ship with cooks' galleys built to cater for large numbers or it could be bunks in the hold of a cargo ship or horse boat made more unpleasant by poor food and the distinctive tang that horses gave to shipboard life.

For the soldiers and nurses on board ship keeping a diary to record their first overseas experience was obligatory. There are many diaries of the ship's voyage in libraries and museums throughout New Zealand. Sadly at the end of the voyage most of the diaries end as their writers are too busy learning the trade of soldiering to have time to keep up their diary as well as write letters home to the family, friends and girlfriend.

Seizing German Samoa

If your Ministers desire, and feel themselves able to seize [the] German wireless station at Samoa, we should feel that this was a great and urgent Imperial service...

Secretary of State for Colonies to Governor General of New Zealand, 6 August 1914.[17]

On 11 August 1914, five days after war was declared, the New Zealand Samoan Force totalling 1413 personnel was lined up on the Wellington wharf ready to sail. They were mainly Territorials from Wellington and Auckland and included six nurses amongst them. It demonstrated the efficient planning of Major General Sir Alexander Godley, the Commander of the New Zealand Defence

Forces, and his staff. The only delay was waiting for the wooden bunks to be fitted into the two Union Company steamships, *Monowai* and *Moeraki*, which sailed as HMNZT *1* and *2*, on 12 August 1914 with an escort of warships. The New Zealanders landed at Apia on 29 August 1914 without any resistance and German Samoa became the first German territory to be occupied during the First World War. It confirmed what many New Zealanders already believed — that this war, like the capture of Samoa, would be short and victorious. German administrators and merchants in Samoa were sent to New Zealand where they were interned on Motuihe Island in the Hauraki Gulf.

In Samoa the Advance Party of the NZEF soon found garrison life frustrating and the officers of the Force found it difficult to maintain the morale and discipline of these hastily trained citizen soldiers. In April 1915 the original force was withdrawn and replaced by a reduced garrison of 250 men who were over military age.

The first New Zealanders approach the landing at Apia on 29 August 1915.
ALBUM155, AIM

The Australian and New Zealand Army Corps (ANZAC)

In Egypt we joined with the 4th Australian Infantry Brigade and the 1st Australian Light Horse Brigade to form the New Zealand and Australian Division commanded by Major General Sir Alexander Godley. Together with the 1st Australian Division they became an Army Corps of two divisions commanded by Lieutenant General Sir William Birdwood and were called the Australian and New Zealand Army Corps (ANZAC). The New Zealanders camped separately from the Australians at Zeitoun, outside Cairo, while the Australians camped under the shadow of the pyramids at Mena.

Both countries provided staff for Birdwood's Corps Headquarters. Sergeant K M Little, a New Zealander working as a clerk at Birdwood's headquarters, made up an ink stamp with the Corps' initials on it to stamp all the incoming mail. Little is credited with the first use of the word ANZAC when he was heard to ask another clerk to 'throw me the ANZAC stamp'. ANZAC was adopted as the telegraphic address for the headquarters and it became the accepted abbreviation for the Australian and New Zealand Army Corps. In this way a new word was forged in the English language — Anzac.

The Anzacs in Egypt

Egypt, land of sun and sunset
Where our footsteps pause a while;
While the dirty unkempt Arabs
Barter fruit with native guile,
Half the world we've crossed to reach you,
Hearts were light and hopes were high.
Thinking that we came for fighting
But we're only 'Standing by'

Soldier's song, Egypt 1914[18]

SEEMS RUMMY ME GOING TO FIGHT A TURKEY

The New Zealanders arrived in Egypt in December 1914. They met and mixed with British and Australian soldiers while training and on leave in the streets of Cairo. We soon realised that while we had much in common with the other members of the British Empire, we were different in how we spoke, how we thought and how we did things. There was a growing self-recognition of being 'En Zeds' — New Zealanders.

Egypt also moulded New Zealanders from 'citizens in arms' into soldiers through camp life in tents at Zeitoun and hard training on the desert sands. Godley, the New Zealand commander, was a hard task-master who set very high standards and it seemed to the sweating, cursing New Zealanders that our best was never good enough for this unsmiling, aloof man whose highest praise was that we were 'almost as good' as a British Regular soldier.

Egypt was also a chance for a tram ride into Cairo and New Zealanders who had never been further than 20 kilometres from home were in turn horrified and fascinated by the teeming mass of people, and the poverty, smells, and strangeness of this new world. Everyone went to see the sights in the brothels of the Wazzir District, and after a few beers many stayed to sample. The venereal disease rate climbed accordingly among New Zealanders and Australians. Godley sent a number who caught the disease back to New Zealand as an example; but he also had prophylactic sets issued to his soldiers and set up treatment centres in the New Zealand lines for when they returned from leave.

The Anzacs looked down on the Egyptians and called them 'niggers' and 'wogs'. They were suspicious of the sellers in the markets who they thought were ripping them off and sometimes drunken Anzacs on leave ran riot. The first of these riots was on Good Friday in April 1915, but they happened a number of times during the war and usually involved both New Zealanders and Australians.

It was a real riot you know. They set the places on fire and the girls from the brothels were crawling along the ledges on the top of the buildings and fire engines would arrive and the boys would tip the fire engines over... It was quite a disgraceful day.

Tony Fagan, Auckland Infantry Battalion[19]

Leave in Cairo, February 1916. Two Gallipoli veterans at Luna Park roller-skating rink: Sergeant Rota Waipara (right) and Kahi Harawira (left). QEII ARMY MEMORIAL MUSEUM

Anzac
25 April 1915 – 20 December 1915

The First ANZAC Day: Anzac Cove, Sunday 25 April 1915

Where are the Lads of New Zealand to-night
Where are the 'nuts' we knew?
In Wellington, Auckland or Christchurch fair?
No, not there! No, not there!
They're taking a trip to the Dardanelles,
With their rifles and bayonets bright,
Facing danger gladly, where they're needed badly,
That's where they are to-night.

Popular song by R P Weston & P C Cole[1]

This I have no doubt will be the greatest day in our lives.

Richard Ward, Auckland Infantry Battalion[2]

At 4.30 a.m. on 25 April 1915 the First Australian Division of Lieutenant General Birdwood's ANZAC Force landed on an unnamed beach on the coast of Turkey. Due to a mistake by the Royal Navy it was the wrong beach, about three kilometres north of where they should have landed and the Australians were thrown into confusion by the unexpectedly rough country.

This was part of a combined landing by British, French and ANZAC troops under the command of General Sir Ian Hamilton. Its purpose was to seize the Gallipoli Peninsula which overlooked the Straits of the Dardanelles, the water-way leading from the Aegean Sea through to the Sea of Marmara and the Turkish capital of Constantinople (now Istanbul).

In early 1915 the Allies were desperately looking for a victory to break the stalemate of trench warfare that had bogged things down on the Western Front. The British Cabinet adopted Winston Churchill's scheme for a naval attack on the Dardanelles to break through into the Sea of Marmara and force the surrender of the Turkish government by threatening to destroy Constantinople by naval gunfire. The naval attack failed on 18 March 1915 and an Army was hastily cobbled together using everyone not yet committed to the Western Front. The Anzacs, who were becoming increasingly frustrated at being sidelined in Egypt, were included in this plan, and in early April they sailed for Lemnos Harbour on the Island of Mudros where they formed part of a large armada of ships gathered for the landing. No one anticipated when they left New Zealand that they would end up fighting the Turks, but we did not care, at last there was the chance for 'Bill Massey's Tourists' to do something.

Few of us, in fact none of us, ever thought we should get our baptism of fire on Turkish soil. How the world goes round and we with it.

Charles Saunders, NZ Engineers[3]

Auckland Infantry first New Zealanders to land

The first New Zealanders to land at 10 a.m. that morning were the men of the Auckland Infantry Battalion commanded by Lieutenant Colonel Arthur Plugge. They reinforced the Australians inland, but instead of a rapid advance the Anzacs were almost driven back into the sea by outnumbered Turkish soldiers fighting fiercely to defend their country. Australians and New Zealanders clung desperately to footholds on the second ridge inland which became the Anzac front line for the next nine months.

It was a matter of just a disorganised crowd of those fine brave fellows not knowing where to go, no-one in charge, no orders, no possibility of officers taking charge, because they were all scattered in the scrub. There was no planning... as we were not intended to land there in the first place among all those hills, ravines and precipices.

Tony Fagan, Auckland Infantry[4]

It was the men of the Auckland Infantry Battalion who were the first New Zealanders to reinforce the Australians and fight the Turks on the slopes of Baby 700, so called because it was 700 feet above sea level. Spencer Westmacott of the Sixteenth Waikato Company, who was wounded and would lose an arm, led the first group.

From the front, from the right, and now from the right rear the rifle fire was coming. The last got several of us, though we did not know it at the time, for a sniper lay there just on the edge of the plateau and picked us off as we showed up, one by one... Cowdray was the first to get it. He was talking to me one moment, the next his blood was pouring down his face from his forehead. He gave a surprised stare, then quietly laid his head on his rifle on the ground in front of him and was dead.

Spencer Westmacott, Auckland Infantry[5]

The 3rd Auckland Company on the beach at Anzac Cove waiting for orders, 25 April 1915. ALBUM 382, AIM

'Hanging on'. The Auckland Battalion in the trenches at Gallipoli, April 1915.
ALBUM 382, AIM

Chaos on the beach

Back on the beach the landing was turning into chaos as arriving boatloads of soldiers mixed with the growing numbers of wounded. Most New Zealanders who had religiously kept daily diary entries on the ship voyage and in Egypt had no time after they landed on Gallipoli. Some, like Major Percival Fenwick, a doctor who was tending wounded on the beach, left detailed accounts as well as photographs of conditions at Gallipoli.

> *There were numbers of wounded lying here close to the cliff waiting to be sent off to the ships. Every minute the number increased, and, as in addition fresh troops came ashore with mules and ammunition, the chaos became appalling... Violent bursts of shrapnel swept over us, and many wounded were hit a second time. Col. House was packing boats and lighters with these poor chaps as fast as possible, but the beach kept filling up again with appalling quickness. At one time more than 400 were lying on the stones waiting to be moved... A more hellish Sunday one could not conceive.*
>
> Percival Fenwick, NZ Medical Corps[6]

Most New Zealand dead have no known graves

Some 3100 New Zealanders from the New Zealand Infantry Brigade landed on Anzac Day and it is estimated that there were 600–700 New Zealand casualties. Almost all the New Zealand dead of the landing have no known graves. This became a feature of New Zealand's part in the Gallipoli Campaign. Our dead resulted from attacks against positions that the Turkish soldiers held or later regained. New Zealand bodies lay unburied around the heights of Baby 700 above Anzac Cove from the fighting in late April and early May 1915; around Twelve Tree Copse near Krithia at Helles from the unsuccessful attack on 8 May; on and below Chunuk Bair during the fighting from 6–12 August; and on Hill 60 in late August 1915. There are only 265 New Zealand graves on the Peninsula and many of these are of bodies found and buried after the war ended in 1918.

> *One of the two who lay farthest appeared to be a New Zealander, for the cover of a New Zealand entrenching tool lay beside the little patch of torn clothes and human remains. Part of the Narrows were clearly visible from this summit.*
>
> Charles E W Bean, Australian Official Historian, visiting Anzac Cove 1918[7]

Wounded waiting on the beach to be evacuated, 25 April 1915.
AUSTRALIAN WAR MEMORIAL

We were the amateurs and the Turks the professionals

When we and the Australians landed on Gallipoli on 25 April 1915 we were still amateurs with only a thin veneer of military skill. Today it is convenient to blame inept British generalship for the Gallipoli disaster. This is too easy. Hamilton's plan succeeded and he got his Army safely ashore, but once on the beach at Anzac Cove it was our inexperience and hasty changes of plan by the first Australian commanders to land that almost led to defeat and disaster that day. The Turks were heavily outnumbered, but a resourceful Lieutenant Colonel named Mustafa Kemal disobeyed orders and counter-attacked the Anzac bridgehead when it was still disorganised. His action was the difference between success and failure.

> *I don't order you to attack, I order you to die. In the time it takes us to die, other troops and commanders can come and take our places.*
> Mustafa Kemal, Turkish Commander opposing Anzac landing[8]

In the same way along the scattered Anzac line it was the initiative of individual soldiers and officers like Major Dawson, Second-in-Command of the Auckland Infantry Battalion, whose example prevented disaster on that first night.

> *About 15 yards from the crest we dug in like mad with our little entrenching tools — coffin trenches they call them... The Turks did not follow up immediately and this saved us — Dawson took charge from now on and held on like a hero.*
> Frank McKenzie, Auckland Infantry[9]

It would take days to sort out the Anzac casualties. Tired men were too busy digging in and defending the front line to think about the dead. For days after the landing men who had been separated from their battalions would suddenly come in long after they had been given up for dead.

> *Tuesday 27th April*
> *We gathered in all the Hauraki men we could find and mustered 99 out of our original 227.*
> Colvin Algie, Auckland Infantry[10]

Making good

> *It is officially announced that allied troops have been landed on both the Asiatic and European sides of the Dardanelles. The troops landed on the Gallipoli Peninsula have been engaged in hard fighting but are thoroughly making good their footing with the help of the fleet.*
> New Zealand Herald, 29 April 1915[11]

The first news that New Zealand received was of success. It was only later that the trickle of casualties grew into a constant flow of dead and wounded that filled the daily papers with faces of New Zealand's cost.

> *I am afraid it will be impossible to send accurate casualty lists for some time, as platoons, companies and battalions were so hopelessly mixed up, not only amongst themselves but also with the Australians, that it is impossible to tell whether many of the men missing are really killed or not, some keep dribbling in, even now.*
> Godley to Allen, NZ Minister of Defence[12]

Lieutenant Colonel Mustafa Kemal (later Kemal Ataturk, first President of the Republic of Turkey) commanded the Turkish reserves at Gallipoli on 25 April and disobeyed orders to counter-attack the Anzacs' landing. ALAN MOOREHEAD, *GALLIPOLI*

'The Landing'. AIM

'Anzac Bay' or 'Bloody Beach Bay'

An Order came out naming this bay Anzac Bay, after N.Z. and Aus[tralian]. Div[ision]. It does not matter what it is called. Perhaps it will some day be known as Bloody Beach Bay. God knows we have paid heavily for it.

Percival Fenwick, NZ Medical Corps[13]

Any illusion about the glories of war vanished for those New Zealanders on Gallipoli by nightfall on 25 April 1915. The New Zealanders ashore were full of praise for the Australian achievement that day, and while the rivalry that will always exist between our two countries soon resurfaced, a bond was forged that also continues.

The one thing about this skirmish is that it has bound the Australians and NZ's with loops of steel and friendships have been formed which will never be broken.

James Leys, Headquarters NZ & Australian Division[14]

Auckland soldiers who held the line with the Australians and who were originally thought to be among the missing. From left: Harry Erlam, Bill Jameson, Harold Lovell, and unknown. DAVY COLLECTION, 3RD AUCKLAND AND NORTHLAND BATTALION COLLECTION

Red Cross letter to Miss Elsie Morton regarding her brother. MORTON MS, ALEXANDER TURNBULL LIBRARY

Right and left, broadside onto the shore were the battleships steaming slowly and firing at the Turkish positions in crashing salvoes which went booming and echoing among the hills.

Spencer Westmacott, Auckland Infantry Battalion[15]

Nine months on Gallipoli

The beach that we hear so much about is a narrow strip of sand at the widest part. Not more than a chain. Rising from the edge of the beach are the little hills, about as steep as those rising from the Awatere at Tangihanga. When our men first landed the hills were covered with scrubby trees, not unlike holly, more prickly if anything. Most of this growth has been used up for firewood, and the hill face is riddled with dugouts. The beach is littered with every conceivable thing connected with modern warfare. There are three small jetties running out into the sea, these are used for unloading the barges. The stores being piled up on the beach, stacks and stacks of bully beef, biscuits, milk, jam, rifles, cannon ammunition, clothing, periscopes, and the Lord only knows what there is not there. That's Anzac for you.

J M Downey, NZ Artillery[16]

From 25 April until 20 December 1915 the ANZAC perimeter was a tiny foreign foothold on the Turkish coast. Until August the Anzacs clung to 400 acres — two ridges and the gullies between — and they clung by their fingernails to the inland ridge from Quinn's Post to the sea. It was called 'Anzac' after the people who held it. Our lack of success confirmed Hamilton's impression that we were still too inexperienced as soldiers and he concentrated on advancing from the south at Cape Helles with his British Regular soldiers. In many ways he was right. In those first days ashore the Turks took advantage of our lack of knowledge and discipline and threatened to push us back into the sea.

The New Zealand Infantry Brigade and an Australian Brigade were sent south to Cape Helles and used unsuccessfully to attack on 8 May 1915 and after many casualties were returned to Anzac.

Looking towards Anzac Cove from the sea. Men crowd the beach dwarfed by stacks of bully beef and biscuit boxes, while the slopes leading up Plugge's Plateau look like a New Zealand goldrush diggings. MORISON COLLECTION, QEII ARMY MEMORIAL MUSEUM

Fighting at Anzac

A man don't need a rifle, he hardly ever shoots,
He only needs a pair of shorts and a hefty pair of boots.
He needs a bloody shovel, to dig a bloody track,
And a bloody box of ammo to hump it, lump it, hump it,
To hump it on his back.

Anzac rhyme, Canterbury Infantry[17]

A New Zealander 'humping his bluey' at Anzac. WEBB ALBUM 338, AIM

This war was nothing like the Anzacs ever imagined. They quickly learnt that they were the amateur and 'Johnny' Turk the professional soldier. What was more he knew the ground and was grimly determined to defend his homeland from the invader. The cream of the Turkish Army took part in the Gallipoli Campaign, and were reinforced by thousands of volunteers, all determined to drive the invader back into the sea. By contrast the Anzacs had anticipated a rapid advance up the Peninsula and were not prepared or equipped for trench warfare. By cruel experience they soon learnt that the shovel, pick and entrenching tool were as important as the rifle and bayonet. Hatred of the Turk changed to grudging admiration for someone who was our equal as a soldier and who we found was human too.

Survival depended upon one's ingenuity. Anzac inventions included the periscope rifle and the jam tin bomb. Everything was scrounged or stolen to make up for shortages of timber, iron and building supplies. For many New Zealanders it was no different from the coal mines, gold diggings, gumfields or timber-felling at home. There was a job to do and you got stuck in and did it with whatever was available.

We soon found out that the Turks were first class shots who had the advantage of the high ground. Any moment of carelessness usually meant a bullet in the head. We had to beat them at their own game, and in each battalion the best shots became snipers.

> *You got that good, you could shoot the left eye out of a fly... If we could find loopholes, we'd shoot at the top of a loophole to bring the stuff down by tearing the sandbags, and loosening the earth and so enlarging the hole, and I am afraid that once or twice we split the end of our shot, so that when it hit it would branch out and make a mess.*
>
> Harvey Johns, Wellington Infantry[18]

Some like Jimmy Swan of the Wellington Battalion or Richard Walden of the Auckland Battalion became figures of legend at Anzac. Jimmy Swan would lie out in no-man's-land for days at a time using a Turkish Mauser rifle to disguise his presence.

> *I have been having a duel with [a] sniper this morning, he has been trying to stop me shooting at a machine gun but I stopped him first, I can see him kicking and struggling in the bushes 400 yards away. Poor Turk, if anyone comes through the bushes to help him, they won't value their lives. He will have to lay there until dark...*
>
> Jimmy Swan, Wellington Infantry[19]

In some places, such as Quinn's Post, the Anzac line was only five to ten metres from the Turkish trenches. It was impossible to put your head up and take an aimed shot with a rifle. To overcome this an Australian corporal devised the periscope rifle.

I'm handling a periscope rifle now... an invention of ingenious simplicity... Attached to the rifle-butt is a short framework in which two looking glasses are inserted, one glass at such a height that it is looking above the sandbags while your head, as you peer into the lower glass is a foot below the sandbags. The top glass reflects to the lower glass a view of the enemy trenches out over the top of the parapet. It is a cunning idea, simple and deadly...

Ion Idriess, 5th Light Horse, AIF (Australian Imperial Forces)[20]

The frames for the periscope rifles and the periscopes themselves had to be fashioned out of box wood and from mirrors stolen from the transport ships off shore, and were made by the soldiers in the trenches.

No New Zealanders or Australians had ever seen a hand grenade before landing at Gallipoli. Grenades were ideal for the trench warfare, and the Turks had plenty of them and were also skilled at using them.

The Turks had a good supply of bombs, mostly of the German 'cricket ball' type, but some of them, like our own, were home-made... [At Quinn's Post] To lie cowering in the darkness of that cramped evil smelling pit, and watch a big bomb sputtering among the corpses just against our loophole, while waiting for the burst, was an experience that no man could endure unmoved.

Cecil Malthus, Canterbury Infantry[21]

There were no supplies of British grenades available and like everything else at Anzac these had to be improvised, using whatever material was available. A bomb factory was set up on the beach to manufacture jam tin bombs, and each day scavenging parties were sent through the trenches collecting tin cans and shrapnel pieces.

Ours were made of tin with a small bag of ammonal as the charge in the centre of it — packed all round with .303 cartridges with the bullet snipped off flush with the brass — the bullets themselves inverted and packed in between the cartridges — then Turkish shrapnel, razor blades or anything at all put in to make up — the lid of the tin wired on with copper wire with the fuze projecting through it.

Charles Saunders, NZ Engineers[22]

Spotting and sniping with a periscope rifle. ALBUM 382, AIM

The jam tin bomb factory on the beach. Tins were scavenged from the trenches and then used to make bombs. These were often more dangerous for the thrower than for the Turk. AUSTRALIAN WAR MEMORIAL

Lieutenant Colonel William Malone of the Wellington Infantry Battalion. Fifty-six years old and a lawyer/farmer from Taranaki, he was the outstanding New Zealand battalion commander on Gallipoli. He died with his battalion on Chunuk Bair on 8 August 1915.
MALONE FAMILY COLLECTION

It was up to the ingenuity of the commanders to stop casualties among their men. One of the outstanding leaders among New Zealanders on Gallipoli was Lieutenant Colonel William Malone of the Wellington Battalion. He was a stickler for discipline and order, and each position that his Battalion took over was sorted out to his satisfaction.

First on Walker's Ridge, then at Courtney's Post and finally at Quinn's Post, Malone reorganised the defences by covering in the trenches with overhead protection, making covered shelters for the men to sleep under safe from artillery and grenades. At Quinn's Post Malone had a chicken wire fence erected to stop Turkish bombs and grenades rolling down onto the sleeping terraces below the crest.

> *I calculate that 100 rounds of rifle ammunition is fired every minute. That is 6,000 per hour, 144,000 per day. Add to this furious rifle firing at night, and not less than 200,000 rounds are spent daily by Turks. Shrapnel and shelling is incessant...*
>
> Percival Fenwick, NZ Medical Corps[23]

Initially untrained and frightened, soldiers fired at anything they saw or heard, real or imagined, and others fearing an attack would join in. Both sides did not have much in the way of artillery. For the Anzacs the small amount of land that they held meant that many of the few guns available could not be landed because there was no place to site them. Initially much of the artillery support came from the guns of the naval warships, but because of the closeness of the Turkish positions these could not be fired near to the Anzac front lines.

> *We have the Turks' guns sorted out to a tick here. In the morning one gun, we call it 'Christians Awake' comes over the beach on to a certain patch and as a rule the boys are very careful as regards cover until she starts and stops... Then we have 'Gentle Annie', 'Hell Fire Mack', 'Jack Johnston' and the 'Slug'. This one never fires until tea time or after.*
>
> Jimmy Swan, Wellington Infantry[24]

Few New Zealanders had seen an aircraft before Gallipoli but now they were a common sight with British seaplanes overhead from the seaplane carrier that was part of the British fleet as well as German Taube monoplanes. Both sides used aircraft to direct artillery fire and look for new trenches.

About twice a day our aeroplanes fly over the Turkish trenches giving the big guns marks to fire at, ranges etc [to] troops or guns, then they drop four bombs and as a rule somewhere among the Turks and depart. A German plane comes over now and again when ours are down but do not stop long...

Jimmy Swan, Wellington Infantry[25]

Life at Anzac

In places our trenches touch the Turks...One would never credit miles of enemy divided only by a narrow bank of earth: is it a wonder that men break down? The heat is intense; flies swarm the trenches in millions, the stench from the bodies of our men lying on trenches in front is choking and nearly unbearable. The world outside has great confidence in their men but I often wonder if they realise or try to realise what a hell the firing line is and know that every man desires and cannot help desiring immediate peace.

George Bollinger, Wellington Infantry[26]

Until August 1915 the Anzacs were besieged inside the ANZAC perimeter. They were overlooked by the high ground of Baby 700 above them, and hemmed in on the coast by Turkish artillery that fired at the barges bringing in supplies and reinforcements by sea. No one anticipated this stalemate and everything that was needed for trench warfare was in short supply. There was no iron, timber or barbed wire. Timber had to be salvaged from sunken barges at Anzac Cove. Unlike the Western Front there was no escape from the front line. Men could be killed by artillery and sniper fire almost anywhere

I saw a most amazing sight. A great mass of Turks coming over the hill... I had my gun trained on the very spot and all I had to do was press the trigger, and, of course, they fell all over the place. Dan Curham, Wellington Infantry. Firing a Maxim machine gun at Gallipoli. ALBUM 382, AIM

inside Anzac's 400 acres, where the garrison of almost 40,000 men used every available square centimetre of ground.

Men spent up to eight days in the front line, then eight days resting. 'Rest' at Anzac was hard work; carrying supplies up Shrapnel Valley and Monash Gully to the New Zealand positions at Quinn's and Courtney's Posts, or digging tracks and carrying water and ammunition up Walker's Ridge to the New Zealand positions on Russell's Top. It was not until the August offensive that fresh water wells were captured, and until then all the water had to be shipped in from the Greek Islands off the coast. Water came in kerosene tins and was often tainted from tins that had not been properly cleaned. Water was rationed to a quart (500 millilitres) a man per day which was not enough for men trapped in stinking pits two to three metres deep in the heat of a Turkish summer.

> *The heat was intense. So was our thirst and we got only half a bottle of water per man per day. We had any amount of biscuit and bully and once we got butter. Great was our delight when our first drink of tea came along the trench, passed from hand to hand in a kerosene tin. It was full of tea leaves, and by the time it reached our end of the trench it was muddy from the dusty walls — but it was nectar.*
>
> Ewen Pilling, Otago Infantry[27]

By early May the New Zealand battalions were less than half strength, but the battalions in the front line had to do their share of work as if they were still 1000 strong. In late May the New Zealand Mounted Rifles Brigade and the First Australian Light Horse Brigade left their horses behind in Egypt and reinforced Godley's New Zealand and Australian Division, but these two brigades together numbered less than an infantry brigade.

> *The heat of the sun, as the summer drew on, caused a plague of flies which bred and fed on the dead bodies, the latrines and the refuse of food, and which contaminated everything we ate. Dozens of flies were drowned in every dixie of tea we drank, and they would chase the food into our very mouths. The dust in the bottom of the trenches in which we slept, was alive with maggots...*
>
> Cecil Malthus, Canterbury Infantry[28]

The cookhouse of the 3rd Auckland Company at Anzac. ALBUM 382, AIM

86

There were no fresh vegetables available and soon every man had dysentery. Men who had been at the peak of physical fitness in early April wasted away. In the south at Helles there was more space and the sickness rates were not as high. British authorities were slow to increase medical supplies because they thought that the ill-disciplined colonial soldiers were wasting them. By August 1915 a fit man at Anzac was someone capable of standing up and holding a rifle. Doctors were ordered to stop evacuating sick men who in any other campaign would have been sent to hospital. Many died because of this.

> *I've seen men literally dying on the latrines, they couldn't get anyone to carry them to the latrines. They were buried on the latrines and were buried anywhere about.*
>
> Joe Gasparich, Auckland Infantry[29]

Life at Anzac was a struggle to survive. Good leadership was essential, and it was here that many inexperienced New Zealand officers failed. Men such as Godley, the New Zealand commander, Brigadier-General F E 'Earl' Johnston of the New Zealand Infantry Brigade, and Lieutenant Colonel Arthur Plugge of the Auckland Infantry Battalion showed their weaknesses and lost the trust of their men. Officers such as Brown, Hart and Young in the infantry and Meldrum and Mackesy in the Mounted Rifles showed their worth and would become the bedrock to New Zealand's reputation in the next three years of war. The outstanding New Zealand officer to survive Gallipoli was the commander of the New Zealand Mounted Rifles Brigade, Andrew Russell, a sheep farmer from Hawke's Bay. By the end of the campaign he commanded the New Zealand and Australian Division and would command the rearguard at Anzac for the last 48 hours.

A New Zealander at Anzac took each day as it came, the only thing that got you through was your mates; working together, sharing parcels from home, and letting you read their letters if your mail did not come through.

> *Of all the bastards of places this is the greatest bastard in the world. And a dead man's boot in the firing possy has been dripping grease on my overcoat and the coat will stink for ever.*
>
> Ion Idriess, 5th Light Horse, Auckland Infantry[30]

Letters from home kept men sane, but like everything else, writing paper was in short supply. Men wrote home on the indestructible Army biscuit, pieces of box wood, or any scrap of paper or cardboard they could find. 'Home' was now New Zealand and news from home was eagerly sought.

Major General Sir Alexander Godley who commanded the NZEF throughout the First World War. He was a highly capable administrator and worked hard for the good of the New Zealand Forces. This was rarely recognised by the men he commanded and he was hated by New Zealand soldiers who blamed him for the Gallipoli losses and his aloofness. SCHMIDT COLLECTION, ALEXANDER TURNBULL LIBRARY

Te Hokowhitu A Tu: The First Maori Contingent

> *Whatever you do remember you have the mana, the honour and the good name of the Maori people in your keeping this night... Do your duty to the last, and whatever comes never turn your backs on the enemy.*
>
> Chaplain Wainohu, First Maori Contingent[31]

The First Maori Contingent was named Te Hokowhitu A Tu, 'the seventy twice-told warriors of the war god', so named because 140 was the favoured size of the traditional war party or 'taua'. It landed 477 strong at Anzac Cove on 3 July 1915. They were attached to the New Zealand Mounted Rifles Brigade and occupied No 1 Outpost which soon became known as the Maori Pa.

The Regimental Badge of Te Hokowhitu A Tu.

They were first used as 'Pioneers' or labourers and they dug and enlarged the Great Sap that went from Walker's Ridge out to the outposts so that it was possible to move by day. They tunnelled under Quinn's and Courtney's Posts, and dragged water tanks to the top of Plugge's Plateau.

During the August offensive the Maori fought with the New Zealand Mounted Rifles as infantry. After heavy losses in August the Contingent was split up and its platoons allocated to the New Zealand infantry battalions which had been reduced from 1000 to 100–200 men.

Despite Maori bravery in the August fighting, four of their officers were sent back to New Zealand 'for unsatisfactory performance'. This and the splitting up of the unit angered both the men of the Contingent and the Maori people at home, and because of their protests three of the officers were eventually allowed to return. After Gallipoli the Maori Contingent formed part of the New Zealand Pioneer Battalion which on 1 September 1917 became the New Zealand (Maori) Pioneer Battalion.

Maori Contingent at No1 Outpost, which was called the Maori Pa, before the August offensive 1915.
E G WILLIAMS ALBUM 212, AIM

The battle for Chunuk Bair

A cold August morning in 1915
The mist was on the harbour, the constable had been
Oh Mother clutching her apron
Reported missing in action
They'd never come home to be heroes
Her boys from Rawene

Julie Collier, *Rawene Boys*[32]

In August 1915 the New Zealanders spearheaded the advance to seize the heights of Chunuk Bair on the Sari Bair Range that dominated the coast. This offensive involved the landing of a British Corps at Suvla Bay along the beach to the north of Anzac, as well as feint attacks at Helles to the south, and by the Australians at Lone Pine and at The Nek within the Anzac perimeter. The veterans at Anzac were exhausted, and their battalion commanders doubted their fitness to carry out the demanding roles they had been given.

Battalions that had landed a thousand strong and had received the 3rd and 4th reinforcements were now down to four or five hundred men... Most were thin and tired... They were shadows only of the men who had left Egypt so short a while before bursting with health and vigour...

Ormond Burton, NZ Medical Corps[33]

Like so much in the Gallipoli Campaign, a good idea for a breakout became too complex because Hamilton's planning staff did not appreciate the state of the men, and the difficulties of the country. One could understand this on 25 April, but by August 1915 there was no excuse for this blindness by the staff. Despite this the initial breakout went according to plan. But it was during the following days' fighting at The Nek and below Chunuk Bair that delays and indecision by both Australian and New Zealand commanders lost valuable opportunities and caused unnecessary casualties. Because of this the Auckland Battalion was decimated on Rhododendron Ridge on 7 August, losing 300 casualties in 20 minutes to no purpose.

We had a run of about 200 yds to the Turk trench and of course directly we appeared over the crest the machine guns opened on us and mowed us down...

Colvin Algie, Auckland Infantry[34]

In spite of this tragedy, before dawn on 8 August 1915 the Wellington Infantry Battalion under Lieutenant Colonel Malone seized the vital ground of Chunuk Bair, and for a moment the door was open to advance and seize the Straits of the Dardanelles. It was a New Zealand battle. All that day while two British battalions crumbled and ran on each side of them, the Wellingtons and the Auckland Mounteds held the hill.

The whole brunt of the heavy fighting was borne by our boys and it is so disappointing to find so little credit given them. They left their outpost line about 750 strong at 4.15 a.m. on the 8th and when relieved at midnight the same day they could barely muster the odd 50.

William Cunningham, Wellington Infantry[35]

It was an epic struggle against every man that the Turks could find because they too knew that Chunuk Bair was the key to victory or defeat on the Peninsula. Of all the days of battle in our history, if we as New Zealanders have a day and a dawn that is uniquely ours, it is 8 August 1915, the day we saw the Narrows from the hill.

It was just a mad whirl as far as I'm concerned. It was just a mad whirl but I can hear in the background... I heard it then and I can hear it at times today. 'Get the Bastard before he gets you.

Vic Nicolson, Wellington Infantry[36]

We held it for two days but inept decisions by New Zealand commanders meant that the one opportunity to break out was lost and on the night of 9/10 August 1915 we were relieved by British troops who were driven off the following morning on 10 August 1915. There was one further effort by the New Zealanders at Hill 60 in late August which failed and destroyed what was left of our fighting strength.

But the way men died on Chunuk shaped the deeds yet to be done by the generations still unborn... When the August fighting died down there was

It was up cliffs like this that the New Zealand Mounteds climbed on the night of 6/7 August to clear the way for the infantry to seize Chunuk Bair. E G WILLIAMS ALBUM 212, AIM

This is the scene at the Apex on the morning of 8 August 1915 showing soldiers of the 7th Gloucesters advancing after the Wellington Battalion towards Chunuk Bair. New Zealand machine guns can be seen on the crest at top left, while behind them in the dip are the staff of the New Zealand Infantry Brigade Head-quarters. These photographs are part of a series taken by W A Hampton of the Wellington Infantry whose pictures provide a record of the August offensive. A soldier in the same battalion remembered Hampton moving to one side as the Battalion was advancing under fire to take a photo and thought him crazy for doing so. W A HAMPTON COLLECTION, AIM

no longer any question but that New Zealanders had commenced to realise themselves a nation.

Ormond Burton, NZ Medical Corps[37]

'Nation' is a big word, but by August 1915 the New Zealanders on Gallipoli were fighting for themselves. War forced us to recognise that New Zealanders are uniquely New Zealanders, and that our goals and aspirations were not necessarily Empire goals. This was not seen immediately by the public at home, but became more and more obvious as this war dragged on and New Zealand's casualties continued to grow.

A nurse off Gallipoli

*4 weeks hard and terrible work... We anchor about half a mile from the firing line — guns going off all round us shaking the ship and startling the life out of me each time they begin — it's a dreadful place Gallipoli, dreadful and awful... the work is terrible — but we are needed badly....
To my dying day I will never forget this last six weeks.*

Charlotte Le Gallais, SS *Maheno* [38]

Charlotte Le Gallais AIM

In August 1915 the New Zealand Hospital Ship *Maheno* arrived off the Gallipoli beaches to assist in the evacuation of the wounded. On board were ten New Zealand nursing sisters, part of the hospital ship's staff, including Charlotte 'Lottie' Le Gallais who enlisted in July 1915 in the hope of seeing her beloved brother Leddra or 'Leddie' who was a member of the Auckland Infantry Battalion. Leddie was killed in July 1915 and the letters Lottie wrote to him were never received and were later returned to her in New Zealand. Lottie was one of the few New Zealand women to see Gallipoli, hear the sound of battle ashore, and pick up spent bullets from the *Maheno*'s deck as it steamed inshore to take on wounded. The impact of those weeks off Anzac stayed with her for the rest of her life.

John Duder was First Officer on the *Maheno* and he too shared in the shock of seeing the condition of the wounded.

We have 50 wounded onboard now the wounds are really shocking, two poor fellows aged 21 and 36 passed away half an hour after they came onboard, one was shot by shrapnel in the neck and the piece travelled down his body and lodged in his groin, the other poor fellow had his leg blown off at the knee and I never wish to see a sadder sight. He fought hard but we all knew he must die, our priest tried to comfort him and his last words were for his girl, he asked the priest to write to her and say that it was the thought of her and her example that had kept him straight and made him play the game, I have never heard such words from a dying man before and his very last word was his mother and the girl's name.

John Duder, SS *Maheno* [39]

The casualties of August overwhelmed the medical system. Here wounded are brought alongside a hospital ship. Many wounded lay on the beach for days and died while hospital ships waited offshore.
QEII ARMY MEMORIAL MUSEUM COLLECTION

Corporal Cyril Royston Bassett, Victoria Cross

All my mates ever got were wooden crosses.

Cyril Bassett, NZ Signals[40]

There was little official recognition of New Zealand's effort. Malone of the Wellington Battalion was blamed for the failure on Chunuk Bair, while the commanders and officers of British battalions that ran were decorated for bravery. Two New Zealanders received Victoria Crosses. One of these was Captain Alfred Shout who was mortally wounded fighting in the Australian force at Lone Pine. Cyril Bassett, a signals corporal from Auckland, was the only New Zealander in the NZEF to receive the Victoria Cross on Gallipoli. Bassett was awarded the Victoria Cross for his work on Chunuk Bair, laying and repairing telephone lines between the headquarters and the top of the hill. Bassett did not believe he deserved the award as he was only doing his job. He never spoke about it, and later on his own children only found out about their father's achievement from their school teacher.

Bassett VC. AIM

Failure at Gallipoli

After the failure of the August offensive the Gallipoli Campaign reached a stalemate. In December 1915 the Anzacs evacuated Gallipoli, followed by the British and French evacuation of Helles in January 1916. It left the bitter taste of defeat in everyone's mouths. There was no pride taken in the cleverness of the evacuation, only anger and sorrow at mates left behind in lonely Anzac graves and lying unburied on the slopes of Chunuk Bair.

New Zealand provided only a small fraction of the thousands of British, French, Australian and Indian forces that fought as part of the Allied forces in the Gallipoli campaign. Numerically our losses were minute when compared to the estimated 500,000 combined Allied and Turkish casualties. But in national terms our Gallipoli casualties were enormous and impacted on every town and community in New Zealand. Everyone knew someone who would not now be coming home.

The unknown dead on Chunuk Bair. This cemetery faces the Straits of the Dardanelles. The memorial lists 852 New Zealand dead who have no known graves. There are ten identified New Zealand graves, the youngest name that of Martin Andrew Perrson, aged 17, of the Wellington Battalion.
IMPERIAL WAR MUSEUM

New Zealand is paying every bit of her share for the Empire... I know our boys did well, but it is a big price to pay. God help their mothers when they see our casualty lists.

Percival Fenwick, NZ Medical Corps[41]

Today when you walk the old front line marked by cemeteries at each of the posts you become conscious that what you thought were broken sea shells underfoot are really broken bone shards.

No country went so far or paid so much to fight in this campaign. For most New Zealand survivors, Gallipoli was their war as sickness and wounds made them unfit for further active service.

8556 New Zealanders served on Gallipoli with the New Zealand Expeditionary Force. 2721 died.
4752 were wounded and this figure includes those wounded more than once.
Of the 2721 dead:
1669 have no known graves.
252 were buried at sea.
There are only 265 known New Zealand graves on the Gallipoli Peninsula, many of which were not found until after the war.

'In honour of the soldiers of the New Zealand Expeditionary Force 8th August 1915 From the Uttermost Ends of the Earth'. The New Zealand Ceremony at Chunuk Bair on 25 April 1990. DEFENCE OFFICIAL PHOTOGRAPH

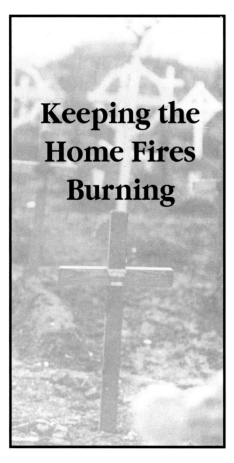

Keeping the Home Fires Burning

Fundraising and patriotism

Then suddenly the First World War was upon us... At first, it all seemed rather remote, and we were inclined to think more in terms of the South African war. We all felt quite pleasantly excited, and we went around assuring ourselves and everyone else that it wasn't likely to last longer than three weeks, and at the very outside, we gave it three months.
As it became apparent that it was not going to be over as rapidly as we had anticipated, we all became terribly patriotic.... We attended innumerable patriotic concerts where somewhat elderly women sang:

> *We don't want to lose you,*
> *But we think you ought to go*
> *For your King and your country,*
> *Both need you so!*
> *We shall want you and miss you,*
> *But with all our might and main,*
> *We will cheer you, thank you, kiss you,*
> *When you come home again!*

Laura Hardy, Onehunga[1]

The outbreak of war in August 1914 was greeted with cheering and parades throughout New Zealand. Men swamped the local recruiting halls, and anxious mothers and proud fathers suppressed their fears and quietly consented as under-aged sons joined the provincial battalions of the New Zealand Expeditionary Force.

War was seen as a job for the men. The women's role was to accept their loved one's enlistment, cheer them on their way, write them letters, look after the home and cheer them back again. The loss of a loved one was portrayed as part of the sacrifice in the cause of King and Empire. There was no formal public role for women in New Zealand other than to be a good mother and wait, so women devoted themselves to voluntary patriotic and fundraising efforts in countless war related causes. Hundreds of patriotic societies were formed all raising money for every cause imaginable. These multiplied to the point where they had to be regulated under the War Funds Act of 1915, and a Federation of New Zealand War Relief Societies established. A New Zealand Red Cross Society was established which channelled the work of thousands of women volunteers in providing parcels, gifts and money to run the YMCA canteens in the training camps in New Zealand, England, Egypt, France and Belgium. The efforts of the YMCA, YWCA and Salvation Army were also important and by 1918 goods and money totalling £6,481,002 had been raised by patriotic societies in New Zealand.[2]

Knitting for our boys

First aid classes swelled... and knitting guilds sprang up like mushrooms. We took our socks and balaclavas to church and knitted like mad all through the sermon. Two plain, two purl became hopelessly mixed up with the text, and if we did rather lose the thread of the Canon's discourse, we at least got our heel turned.

Laura Hardy, Onehunga[3]

Britannia leads the way along Queen Street in Auckland on Saturday 14 November 1914 as part of 'Belgium Week' in one of the many processions and days to raise funds for Belgian widows and orphans and other deserving wartime causes. *AUCKLAND WEEKLY NEWS*, AIM

Nothing was too good for our boys overseas. Everyone started knitting, and families and communities combined to send Christmas parcels and letters. In one month in January 1917 the New Zealand Expeditionary Forces Post Office in London received 680,000 letters and parcels for delivery to soldiers in England and France, as well as redirecting 32,000 items for those transferred or hospitalised.[4]

Christmas gifts for soldiers outside Wellington Town Hall with the women who supervised the packing on behalf of the Red Cross Society. *AUCKLAND WEEKLY NEWS*, AIM

Women's work

Girls permeated into every sort of work, and took over jobs which we had always looked upon as the man's prerogative. They even worked in the banks! We tolerated it, as we were sure that the moment the war was over, they would all be sent packing, but to say we were horrified was putting it mildly.

Laura Hardy, Onehunga[5]

Women replaced men in many industries and businesses. This was not as dramatic as in the armament and explosives industries of Europe, but was no less important. In clerical work and typing they took over jobs that men had been doing. Less obvious was their work in family businesses and farms. As the men went to war they filled in, often in an unpaid capacity, behind the counter, and in the milking shed, with the children also helping out.

Living standards changed very much during the war years. Jack became as good as his master, and Jill, at least in the matter of clothes, often a little better than her mistress. It was the beginning of a new era of silk stockings and fur coats for everyone who could afford them, and as wages had soared tremendously there were few people who need go without.

Clothes became very dashing, and skirts were worn a full five or six inches from the ground. It took quite a long time to get used to seeing the female ankle so fully displayed, and we thought it was really not quite nice.

Laura Hardy, Onehunga[6]

For many in New Zealand the war brought prosperity and opportunities. Race days were popular and if it were not for the casualty lists it was sometimes hard to believe that New Zealand was at war.

We had a meatless day once a week, more for the look of the thing than because of any acute shortage. It was really not hardship as we quite enjoyed the change of food, and thinking out new vegetarian dishes was most interesting. There was no rationing, and we had as many clothes, and as much butter and sugar as we wanted.

Laura Hardy, Onehunga[7]

To fill the place of men going to the front, women were trained as telegraph operators. AUCKLAND WEEKLY NEWS, AIM

'We think you ought to go'

Middle aged and strong minded ladies employed their spare time in presenting white feathers to undeserving men, many of whom had already been to the war, and had returned permanently disabled. These misguided females were well and truly snubbed, and this unpleasant phase did not last long.

Laura Hardy, Onehunga[8]

Initially New Zealand successfully maintained our numbers overseas with volunteers encouraged to join by recruiting booths in city streets. By 1916 the casualty rates on Gallipoli and the formation of a New Zealand Division in France required 2000 men to sail from New Zealand each month. Camps were set up at Trentham and Featherston, each capable of housing 6500–7500 men in huts and tents. A man could volunteer but after passing his medical he was then sent home to await his call-up notice to come into camp. This was done by monthly reinforcement drafts marching into camp for 15 weeks' training before going overseas.

By 1916 the provinces with smaller populations could not meet their quotas of reinforcements and conscription was brought in under the 1916 Military Service Act which came into effect on 1 August 1916. It was a clever piece of legislation. Voluntary enlistment continued for each reinforcement draft, but if there was a shortage in the monthly requirement that could not be filled with volunteers then a ballot would be held to make up the numbers.

'The first gamble in human life'

'The first gamble in human life' was held on 16 November 1916 by the Government Statistician and his staff. After the draw there was morning tea for the young ladies who it is quite possible will draw their sweetheart's cards...

Truth, 18 November 1916[9]

The first ballot under the Act to make up a shortfall in volunteers in 23rd Reinforcements was held on 16 November 1916.[10] Conscription ensured

The 18th Reinforcement on the march from Featherston to Trentham. Women volunteers give refreshments at the top.
AUCKLAND WEEKLY NEWS, AIM

The officials drawing the marbles for the first ballot under the 1916 Military Service Act. AUCKLAND WEEKLY NEWS, AIM

'equality of sacrifice' and was generally accepted by the New Zealand public. It enabled New Zealand to ensure that its forces overseas were kept at full strength with trained reinforcements. This was a major factor in maintaining the calibre and reputation of the New Zealand forces on the Western Front and in Sinai and Palestine. The Act divided the eligible male population into two divisions. The First Division consisted of all single men, including those with dependants; the Second Division were married men and were placed in priority according to the number of dependants — those with the least number were called up first. The first ballots for married men took place in October 1917, and they marched into camp in January 1918. By the end of the war married men with two children were being called into camp.

The Fourteen

When I was only semen in a gland
Or less than that, my father hung
From a torture post at Mud Farm
Because he would not kill. The guards
Fried sausages, and as the snow came darkly
I feared a death by cold in the cold groin
And plotted revolution.His black and swollen thumbs
Explained the brotherhood of man

James K Baxter, *Pig Island Letters* [11]

Conscription was opposed by the New Zealand Labour Party and by individuals on both religious and philosophical grounds. Every man balloted had the right of appeal and Military Service Boards made up of prominent civilians were established to hear appeals. However the Government took a hard line against 'shirkers' as they called them. Individuals who refused to come into camp when balloted were arrested and in some cases those who refused training were forcibly sent overseas to join the New Zealand forces in England and France.[12]

On 14 July 1917 fourteen objectors were shipped off on the *Waitemata*. They included Archibald Baxter who wrote of his experience in *We Will Not Cease*, a restrained and factual account of the treatment he and the rest of the

Fourteen received at the hands of the New Zealand Military authorities in England and France. They were sent as an example to other conscientious objectors. Once in England and France if they did not conform they were broken.

> *He said I must know, myself, that I would be beaten eventually; I must know that I would be broken.*
> *'And if I am broken, what good should I be to the authorities or anyone else?'*
> *That doesn't concern us. It's your submission we want, Baxter, not your services.*
>
> Archibald Baxter, *We Will Not Cease*[13]

Public concern over reports of brutality to the Fourteen made our Government stop sending objectors overseas without training. Conscientious objectors were sent to prison camps in New Zealand and by late 1918 there were 208 objectors in prison.[14]

Conscription of the Waikato

> *These people are mine. My voice is their voice... I will not agree to my children going to shed blood. Though your words be strong, you will not move me to help you. The young men who have been balloted will not go... You can fight your own fight until the end.*
>
> Te Puea Herangi, from *Te Puea* by Michael King[15]

Initially conscription only applied to Europeans but in June 1917 conscription was also applied to the Waikato-Maniapoto tribes. This was because of their unwillingness to provide their share of reinforcements to the Pioneer Battalion. The Waikato were not prepared to fight until the injustices they suffered from the land confiscations carried out by the Crown after the invasion of the Waikato in 1863 were corrected. In the end the conscription of the Waikato was enforced not because of a lack of numbers of Maori volunteering for service with the Pioneer Battalion, but because other tribes resented the Waikato not doing their share. They put pressure on the government to make Waikato conform. Conscription was enforced and numbers sent to camp at Narrow Neck in Auckland, but the war ended before any were sent to the front.

A recruiting appeal to the Waikato Maori from the Hon. James Allen, Minister of Defence. *AUCKLAND WEEKLY NEWS*, AIM

Aliens amongst us

*We heard terrible tales of the cruelty and barbarity of the Germans, and
of their wanton destruction of everything in their path. We saw moving
pictures of the actual fighting on the battlefields and then we saw movies
of the results of the use by the enemy of dum-dum and soft nose bullets.*
Laura Hardy, Onehunga[16]

The patriotic fervour that marked our reaction to war also had an ugly side to
it. Spy mania swept the country, and suspicious lights and behaviour were
reported. Those with German backgrounds bore the brunt of our mistrust.
Anti-German hysteria was fuelled by the reports of German atrocities in
Belgium, the execution of Nurse Edith Cavell, and the sinking of the *Lusitania*.
We wanted to believe it was true. Aliens of military age were interned on
Motuihe Island in the Hauraki Gulf and on Soames Island in Wellington Harbour.

To have a German-sounding name was enough, even if the family had
been in New Zealand for many years. There were outbreaks of violence. A
butcher's shop in Gisborne belonging to Frederick Wohnsieder was ransacked
on New Year's Eve 1914, and further incidents were reported in Wanganui
and New Plymouth in 1915. In 1916 Lady Stout and Madame Ida Boeufre
founded the Women's Anti-German League; its aim being 'to root out the Hun
Hog'.[17] The League protested 'against the employment of Germans, sons of
Germans, and naturalised Germans in our army or in any position of trust
where they can obtain information detrimental to our country's interest'.[18]

Soldiers who had fought with distinction for New Zealand on Gallipoli
were not immune, and were accused of enlisting in order to shoot good New
Zealanders in the back. This intensified in 1916 when Private William Nimot,
the New Zealand-born son of a naturalised German family from Carterton
serving with the New Zealand Division in France, deserted to the Germans. It
was the only case of desertion to occur in the New Zealand forces in the First
World War. In France anyone with a German-sounding name was sent back
to England. An act was passed removing school teachers with German parents from their positions in schools. Ironically many of these dismissed teachers were then conscripted for overseas service.

Vowing to fight on until Germany's total
surrender. Cathedral Square,
Christchurch. *AUCKLAND WEEKLY NEWS*, AIM

The casualties mount

As we scanned the lists it almost seemed a positive relief to see the name of a relation [or] a friend in the wounded column. 'Now he's safe for a while, anyway,' we thought.

Laura Hardy, Onehunga[19]

The casualty lists carved scars across New Zealand's heart. The war that was to be over by Christmas 1914 seemed as if it would never end. The reports of victories on Gallipoli and in France and Belgium began to ring hollow as list after list of casualties was published. No one was untouched, and despite the crowds gathering on each anniversary of the start of the war and vowing to fight until Germany's total surrender, there was growing war weariness. By late 1917 there was a 'growing feeling in New Zealand that the willing horse is being worked to death.'[20]

The entry of the United States into the war on 21 April 1917 led to a debate in Parliament that our nation's efforts should shift to food production and that there should be no increase in our commitment of the New Zealand forces at the front, other than maintaining what we had there already.

New Zealand had led the way with our introduction of conscription. Canada had followed belatedly, but the Australian public had refused in two referenda to bring in conscription. An Empire's cause now seemed to be less important than the long-term impact of our casualties on New Zealand. As it turned out James Allen, our Minister of Defence, achieved an outward display of support for Britain while managing to limit requests to use New Zealand reinforcements outside of the New Zealand Division in France and the New Zealand Mounted Rifle Brigade in Sinai and Palestine. However, putting New Zealand interests first was a feature of our political dealings with Great Britain in 1917 and 1918, and evidence of a emerging sense of identity and national self-interest.

The return of casualties on the *Willochra*, July 1915. *AUCKLAND WEEKLY NEWS*, AIM

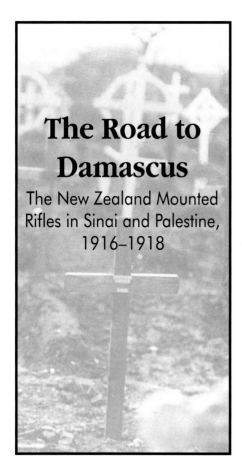

The Road to Damascus

The New Zealand Mounted Rifles in Sinai and Palestine, 1916–1918

Who could have dreamed when the Regiment left Auckland that men of it, before they returned, would stand... on Christendom's holy place. Who could have imagined that the paved streets of Bethlehem would resound with the march of New Zealand horsemen as they moved forward to the conquest of Jericho?

C G Nicol, *The Story of Two Campaigns*[1]

After the evacuation from Gallipoli the New Zealanders returned to Egypt, and when the New Zealand Division went to France in April 1916 the New Zealand Mounted Rifles Brigade, with brigades of the Australian Light Horse, formed the Australian and New Zealand, or ANZAC, Mounted Division. Two-thirds Australians and one-third New Zealanders, this body of horsemen became a key part of the mobile fighting force of the British army protecting the Suez Canal against Turks in the Sinai desert. It was as mounted riflemen that New Zealanders had won a reputation as fighting soldiers in the Anglo-Boer War; we were to confirm that in the Sinai deserts and high country of Palestine. Unlike British cavalry, who still carried the sword and lance as weapons, our mounted rifles fought with rifle and bayonet, and machine gun.

Mounted troops always fought as infantry when the pressure was on. The work of the horse was to get his rider as near the scene of action as possible, in quick time.

Ted McKay, Auckland Mounteds[2]

The New Zealand Mounted Rifles Brigade remained with the ANZAC Mounted Division for the rest of the war, retracing the routes of the Crusaders in Sinai and Palestine — routes that had been followed by Alexander the Great of Macedon, Saladin and the Crusaders, Napoleon of France, and now mounted soldiers of two distant lands.

... we were just about a forgotten unit on a forgotten front.

Ted McKay, Auckland Mounted Rifles[3]

Today the Sinai Campaign conjures up visions of Lawrence of Arabia leading bands of camel-mounted Arabs. New Zealand's role has been largely forgotten, yet in three years of warfare New Zealanders fought alongside Australians as part of one of the largest bodies of mounted horsemen in the history of warfare.

The New Zealand Mounted Rifles Brigade

The New Zealand Mounted Rifles Brigade consisted of a brigade headquarters and three regiments of Mounted Rifles: Canterbury, Auckland and Wellington, with the 1st NZ Machine Gun Squadron, a NZ Mounted Field Ambulance, a NZ Mounted Signal Troop and a NZ Mobile Veterinary Section. The strength of the Brigade was approximately 1850 men and 2200 horses. It was a small, tight-knit family of horsemen, and these close bonds were emphasized by the

On the road to Damascus. The 'En Zeds' on trek. QEII ARMY MUSEUM

provincial background of each of the mounted regiments. Each numbered 523 men and 616 horses drawn from the Territorial regiments in New Zealand.

> *So the Auckland Regiment consisted of the 3rd, 4th, and 11th Squadrons coming from their parent regiments, 3rd [Auckland] Mounted Rifles, 4th [Waikato] Mounted Rifles, 11th [North Auckland] Mounted Rifles. The Wellington Regiment was composed of the 2nd, 6th, and 9th Squadrons coming from Queen Alexandra's 2nd [Wellington West Coast] Mounted Rifles, 6th [Manawatu] Mounted Rifles, and the 9th [Wellington East Coast] Mounted Rifles. And the Canterbury Regiment consisted of the 1st, 8th and 10th Squadrons, from their parent regiments the 1st Mounted Rifles [Canterbury Yeomanry Cavalry], the 8th [South Canterbury] Mounted Rifle, and the 10th [Nelson]Mounted Rifles.*
>
> C Guy Powles, *The New Zealanders in Sinai and Palestine*[4]

'Fiery Ted' Chaytor and his commanding officers

Each squadron reflected the character of the district from where its horsemen came. Each also reflected the character of its leader and it was here that the New Zealanders were fortunate in having men who had served in the Anglo-Boer War and who had been further tested on Gallipoli. The Brigade commander was Brigadier General E W C Chaytor. 'Fiery Ted' was a professional soldier of the New Zealand Staff Corps. He had earned a reputation during the Anglo-Boer War in South Africa where he commanded the 3rd New Zealand Contingent before being severely wounded. Chaytor was again badly wounded on Gallipoli, but recovered to be appointed commander of the New Zealand Mounted Rifles Brigade. His wounds made horse-riding difficult and did nothing for his temper, which accounted for his nickname.

Chaytor's commanding officers were also men of character and skill. 'Old' John Findlay, a farmer from South Canterbury who had seen service in South Africa, commanded the Canterbury Mounted Rifles.

Charles Mackesy, an accountant and land agent from Whangarei, commanded the Auckland Mounted Rifles. A noted horseman and rifle shot, 'Ger-

The New Zealand commander Brigadier General E W C Chaytor was perhaps the first general in modern warfare to conduct an aerial reconnaissance when he flew over the advancing Turkish forces.
ALEXANDER TURNBULL LIBRARY

Colonel 'German Joe' Mackesy.
ALEXANDER TURNBULL LIBRARY

Brigadier General 'Fix Bayonets Bill'
Meldrum. ALEXANDER TURNBULL LIBRARY

man Joe' was already a legendary figure in the Mounted Rifles. The number of Mackesys in the regiment led to the 11th North Auckland Mounted Rifles (NAMR) Squadron being known as 'Nearly All Mackesy's Relations'.[5] Mackesy lost a son on Gallipoli and he was fiercely protective of the welfare of his men. When the Auckland Mounteds reached the Palestine border 'the old colonel halted his men, rode on alone past a boundary pillar, took off his hat, and thanked God that he had at last been permitted to enter the Holy Land.'[6]

William Meldrum, a lawyer farmer from Hunterville, commanded the Wellington Mounted Rifles. Known by his men as 'Fix Bayonets Bill', Meldrum was the obvious successor to command the New Zealand Mounted Rifles Brigade when Chaytor was appointed commander of the ANZAC Mounted Division in 1917.

New Zealanders with the Imperial Camel Corps (ICC)

The Arabs say that at creation when the beasts of the earth were formed, there were left over a lot of remnants out of which was made a camel, and the parts are not hard to identify. The head of a sheep was placed on the neck of a giraffe, which was attached to the body of a cow, and the neck bent itself in shame at being put to such use. The tail of an ass was appended, and the whole was set on the legs of a horse, which ended in the pads of a dog, on each was stuck the claw of an ostrich, and the monstrosity, evidently being considered a failure was banished to live in the desert.

John Robertson, *With the Cameliers in Palestine*[7]

Other New Zealand units were raised and attached to British and Australian formations: the 15th and 16th Companies were raised and formed part of the 4th Battalion of the Imperial Camel Corps Brigade.

The Camel Corps was later disbanded in Palestine and the New Zealand members re-formed as the 2nd NZ Machine Gun Squadron which was attached to the 5th Australian Light Horse Brigade. Indeed these were some of the few New Zealanders to complete the road to Damascus. The NZ Engineer Field Troop was part of the 1st [ANZAC] Field Squadron of the ANZAC Mounted Division and No 4 Company NZ Army Service Corps was part of the ANZAC Mounted Divisional Train. A NZ Rarotongan Company was raised as a Labour Corps and served with the British 21 Army Corps.

A New Zealand Wireless Troop served in Mesopotamia and Persia in 1916–17. In 1918 a group of veteran New Zealand officers and non-commissioned officers from France became part of 'Dunsterforce' under Major General Dunsterville. In this forgotten war small parties of New Zealanders led groups of Armenian irregulars in Armenia and Persia against the Turks. A handful of New Zealanders were also sent as instructors with the North Russian Expeditionary Force and were still fighting alongside the White Russians against the Bolsheviks in 1919.

We have been carrying on as usual, sending up 'iron rations' for transference to 'Abdul' per medium of our artillery. I can say that so far we have not let the guns run out — or anywhere near it — and our Brigadier General Royal Artillery reckons one Rarotongan equal to three white gunners when it comes to handling heavy shell.

A Bush, Rarotongan Company[8]

Egypt

Our brother New Zealanders in France were a mighty army: we were a very little army. They faced a weight of metal unknown to us because they were much more bunched: they were static in filthy trenches, while we had the advantage of mobility. Even if it meant staring at a sand hill the exact double of one we stared at yesterday, at least it was a change. So far as weather conditions went, there was not much to choose. They shivered and froze in the numbing cold of a European winter; we sweltered and drooped in enervating, soul-scorching heat. But they had one advantage we lacked. When wounds and sickness or a lucky break took them to the Old Country, they moved among their own kith and kin, and enjoyed a fellowship that we longed for and could not find. Our leave periods were spent among alien people: no bond of language, custom, religion or history linked us to those who were our reluctant hosts. They met and were welcomed into the homes of gracious British women: we met only foreign prostitutes, their home a brothel.

Ted McKay, Auckland Mounted Rifles[9]

Aotea Home, Moascar. ALEXANDER TURNBULL LIBRARY

Egypt was the home base with the training depot at Moascar, near to which was the Aotea Home. This was established by Lady Godley at the beginning of the Gallipoli Campaign. It served as a rest home for New Zealanders for the remainder of the war.

To my Darling Mother,
This is a great place and a great credit to those in charge & the people of NZ who so generously subscribe to it. If they only know how much the boys appreciate Aotea. I am convinced they will not regret the money and gifts that they give...[10]

Caring for the sick and wounded

The first contingent of 50 New Zealand nurses arrived in Egypt on 18 June 1915. They dressed in the grey and scarlet coats of the British Army nurses with a silver badge of fernleaf and a red cross to represent New Zealand. During the Sinai Campaign a railway line was built as the British force advanced, and hospital trains returned the wounded to Egypt.

We are right in the thick of things now, wounded and sick coming in faster than we can take them... As every few patients go out a fresh batch is put in and another surgical ward downstairs has had to be used for gastro-enteritis and dysentery cases. The men say it is just like heaven to be here and one feels that one cannot do enough for them... some are absolute wrecks. The men who left here just a week ago are coming back now wounded.

Sister C Anderson, New Zealand Army Hospital Cairo, August 1915[11]

In the desert the wounded were carried on the backs of camels.

These consisted of two canvas stretchers balanced horizontally, one on each side of a specially constructed saddle. In these the wounded men could either sit or lie at full length, and were shaded from the sun by a small canvas hood. The jolting motion of the camel frequently was most trying to the badly wounded men, but it was sometimes a case of this kind of carriage or death.

John Robertson, *With the Cameliers in Palestine*[12]

Sister Condick and her hospital train at El Arish. WILLIAMS ALBUM 213, AIM

'Mates'

... we loved our horses with a feeling that went deeply into our beings. They were more than mounts to shift us from spot to spot — they were cobbers.

Ted McKay, Auckland Mounteds[13]

On operations it was the bond between man and horse that determined the success of the New Zealand Mounted Rifles Brigade. Desert conditions weeded out the weak. A New Zealand trooper in the Mounteds was at constant war with the harsh climate and sands of the Sinai desert or the rugged hills and disease of the Jordan Valley. The horse always came first.

On the order to dismount being given, built-up ropes would quickly be taken off the horses' necks and up into one long line. Then while the horseholders in each section looked after the horses, the remainder would set to work with pick, shovel, and bayonet to stretch and anchor down the horse lines. This done, the horses would be tied on the line, off-saddled, perhaps given an opportunity to roll, if the ground was soft, groomed, and then fed. The patient animals always knew the order 'feed up' which was greeted with a chorus of hungry whinnyings and much pawing of the ground.

Then, and not till then, the men would set about making themselves as comfortable as circumstances allowed. Bivvies would spring up all over the area like magic, often supported, if sticks were scarce, on two bayoneted rifles, the bayonet being driven into the ground, while the butt of the rifle carried the canvas or blanket. As dusk fell, hundreds of tiny fires would flicker brightly in the gathering gloom, as shadowy figures moved about in preparation of the indispensible billy of tea to wash down 'hard tack' and 'bully'.

A Briscoe Moore, *The Mounted Riflemen in Sinai and Palestine*[14]

Making camp in the Palestine Hills. WILLIAMS
ALBUM 216, AIM

Indeed the horse was the true hero of the Sinai and Palestine Campaign. During the war New Zealand sent 10,117 horses to war, 5908 as remounts for the New Zealand Mounted Rifles Brigade. The Australians of the Light Horse brigades swore that their New South Wales 'whalers' were the best horses in the desert. We New Zealanders, too, had no doubts.

> *They say the men of the N.Z. Army are second to none, we may truly say that horses are of a very similar nature because it is absolutely marvellous how they have stood up to the work. They have actually been without water for 48 hours carrying its own feed with feed for the man and all equipment and ammunition and travelled about 50 or 60 miles on drift sands and hills. I think we can say that the N.Z. horses are the hardest animals of this kind after this trial of endurance in such a hot climate. At Romani battle one could hardly bear one's hand on their back owing to the heat caused by the hot sun.*
>
> J Masterman, Wellington Mounteds[15]

In the New Zealand Mounted Rifles 1402 horses were casualties in 1917–18, 370 being killed in action. Perhaps the hardest task that faced the New Zealanders was the disposal of the horses in Egypt on demobilisation. Those that were not passed to other mounted units were shot by their riders rather than pass into civilian Egyptian or Arab hands.

> *I am quite sure they would like to get back to their native land [New Zealand] where they could have a good feed of green grass and a scamper round the paddock...*
>
> J Masterman, Wellington Mounteds[16]

Photographs of a desert war

There was little time for diary keeping in the desert, and today it is difficult to find the details or collection of letters for Sinai and Palestine comparable to those of the New Zealanders' experiences on Gallipoli and on the Western Front. The record of who they were and what they achieved has to be found in what remains. An important source is the roll book of the Auckland Mounted Rifle Regiment which is the record of the men who came from the Auckland Province. It was written at the time in neat copperplate handwriting in the canvas-bound ledger book which was carried in a metal trunk on one of the pack horses in the regiment's headquarters throughout the campaign. It shows the wear and tear of three years of warfare and contains all the names and information of those who served with the regiment in Egypt, Gallipoli, Sinai and Palestine. Occupation, next-of-kin, their time with the regiment, the courses they attended, where they fought, when they went sick or wounded to hospital, and when and where they died. Similar records exist for the Canterbury and Wellington Mounted Rifles.[17]

One of the most important sources that survive are the collections of photographs of the campaign. Perhaps because it was so difficult to keep a diary, everyone seemed to have a camera and there are more action photos of New Zealanders in combat from Sinai and Palestine than for the Western Front where personal cameras were forbidden and censorship rules strictly enforced.

While many photo collections have no individual identification, some outstanding collections such as the five captioned albums of Lieutenant Gordon

Weary after battle. Hebron Road, November 1917, after the taking of Beersheba. WILLIAMS ALBUM 210, AIM

Williams who served in the 9th (Wellington East Coast) Squadron of the Wellington Mounted Rifles have survived and allow us to glimpse some of the realities of this mounted warfare.

Gordon Williams's troop

Williams commanded a troop of horsemen which was the equivalent of a platoon but much weaker in numbers, each troop being about 18–20 strong on operations when one took out those who were sick in hospital, on leave, and on courses. Each troop consisted of four sections of four men.

> *The section of four men being the smallest working unit of a mounted regiment, one man generally attending to the commissariat, and did the cooking and tea-making in mess-tins and billies, while the other three looked after the four or more horses... Newcomers in reinforcement drafts reaching the Brigade for the first time quickly had selfishness knocked out of them, and under the rough chaff and good-humoured patience of their experienced comrades, quickly learnt the necessity of co-operation in all things, and the valuable lesson of always helping others beside themselves.*
>
> A Briscoe Moore, *The New Zealanders in Sinai and Palestine*[18]

Gordon Williams's photographs chart the trekking and fighting of the New Zealanders as they took part in every major operation east of the Suez Canal from April 1916 until the Armistice in 1918. They record the difficult breaking in of the brigade with the desert patrols into the Sinai in defence of the Suez Canal in early 1916.

> *By mid-May, the heat raged across the sand; the sharp outlines of the dunes seen in the early morning light would melt into shifting, simmering mirages as the sun climbed higher or be blotted out in the dust of the khamsin, which frequently blew for three days and sometimes longer. Man and horse were tested to the limit when temperatures rose above 120° Fahrenheit in tents under the palms... Sometimes men were so parched when they reached camp that they would fling themselves from their horses and drink the brackish water from the same troughs.*
>
> A J Hill, *Chauvel of the Light Horse*[19]

A section of four mounted riflemen in Gordon Williams's troop: Corporal Knapp the section commander, Denys, W Creswell and H F Wilson. WILLIAMS ALBUM 213, AIM

'Johnny Turk'

The Turks' advance on the Suez Canal was stopped and he was then gradually pushed into the Sinai desert towards the Palestine frontier in a series of battles in which we played a major part. The Turkish attempt to seize the Suez Canal was defeated by hard fighting at Romani in August 1916. It confirmed the Anzac soldier's admiration for the fighting qualities of the Turkish soldier. It was a war where principles were maintained by both sides.

> On the 25th [July 1916] there came a polite note dropped from a German aeroplane warning our ambulances that their red cross flags were not sufficiently visible from the air, a matter to which the ambulances gave serious attention.
>
> A J Hill, *Chauvel of the Light Horse*[20]

Turkish machine gunners. AIM

Turkish Standard Bearer with escorts. AIM

I don't think for a moment that the Turk either hated or despised us. Those pregnant months on the ridges and gullies of the [Gallipoli] Peninsula had given each force a wholesome respect for the other...

Ted McKay, Auckland Mounteds [21]

The Bedouin and the massacre at Surafend

We collected all the Bedouin on the desert hostile or otherwise and sent them to a compound near Cairo. They were filthy creatures. They never washed and just lived in the sand with palm shelters. They live on dates watermelons and corn and whatever they can exchange for the dates they collected.

J Masterman, Wellington Mounteds [22]

The Bedouin of the deserts were mistrusted by Anzac and Turk alike who both looked on them as the scavengers of the desert and likely to kill any wounded man or straggler of either side who fell into their hands.

This distrust of the Arabs came to a climax after the armistice when the New Zealand Mounted Rifles Brigade camped at Richon. Nearby was the Arab village of Surafend. One night a New Zealand soldier was killed trying to stop a thief found looting his tent. The thief's tracks led towards Surafend. The next night the New Zealand Mounteds surrounded the village, herded out the women and children, then attacked and beat to death all the men they could find, killing 20–30 and then setting the village ablaze.

Surafend was a blot on the reputation of the New Zealand Mounteds. They acted out of a tribal loyalty in revenge for what happened to one of their own, and their officers looked the other way when it happened. Because of this General Allenby, the Commander-in-Chief in the Middle East, did not include New Zealanders in his final list for honours and awards at the end of the war.

Sergeant Stellin with some of his dusky friends. WILLIAMS ALBUM 213, AIM

I was proud of you as brave soldiers, but now I am ashamed of you as cold blooded murderers.

General Allenby to the NZ Mounted Rifle Brigade after the massacre at Surafend [23]

Desert stunts

... the shuffling of horses' feet... the clink of stirrups and bits... Some men fall asleep in their saddles and are carried on in uneasy oblivion by their understanding mounts — others remain awake in a world of moving shadows and distorted images.

A Briscoe Moore [24]

An operation in the Sinai was one of night marches in long columns of horsemen enveloped in clouds of dust. Tired men on equally tired horses. It called for energy, resource and endurance from all ranks as regiments would cover 40 miles of heavy sand in 30 hours. The Battle of Magdhaba in December 1916 saw extreme demands made on men and horses; great distances were covered with long periods without water, and it showed the growing professionalism of the Division with the Mounteds and Light Horse capturing Turkish infantry positions with rifle and bayonet.

It's a hell of a life. We need a spell and so do the mokes... If I ever get out of this don't talk desert to me. The only shelter from the sun is what we can rig up with our blanket. All manner of insects attack us at night, and at dawn they are relieved by an army corps of vicious flies... I suppose we are dinkum crusaders, but we don't look it or feel it. In the next war I'm going to be a rum buyer in Jamaica.

unknown New Zealand trooper quoted in C G Nicol, *The Story of Two Campaigns* [25]

Segeant Eion Robertson on trek between Mustagidda and Arnussi. He was killed at Rafa. WILLIAMS ALBUM 211, AIM

The advance of the Rafa redoubts showing No 2 Troop, 9th Squadron Wellington Mounted Rifles making the last advance before the final charge. Sgt Robertson took this photograph just before he was shot and killed. One man is falling and three of those who were killed in the charge are shown in this picture. WILLIAMS ALBUM 211, AIM

In January 1917 the Anzacs crossed into Palestine and success at Rafa was followed by the frustration of the first battle for Gaza when, after a day's hard fighting, the Australians and New Zealanders who had fought their way into the outskirts of the town were ordered to retire, and withdrew in a 'confused night of intense darkness, the Khamsin blowing; the troops disheartened by lack of success; horses and men exhausted.' [26]

Operations stagnated in front of Gaza throughout the hot summer. The Turks established an entrenched line over 32 kilometres long to Beersheba and limited the Anzac Mounteds to a war of outposts, trench digging, reconnaissance and patrolling or 'stunts' as they were known.

Robby's [Sergeant Eion Robertson] grave. WILLIAMS ALBUM 213, AIM

Auckland v. Wellington at El Arish with crowd in background — score 0–0.

Bully beef, biscuits and a bottle of water

Like Gallipoli this war was fought on a diet of bully beef and biscuits.

> *Bully beef needs no introduction but the Army biscuit was the creation of a genius. It was about four inches square by one half inch thick, and perforated here and there, presumably to give breathing space to the weevils that boarded and lodged in so many of them. It was so hard that the strongest teeth gave up the unequal struggle...When speaking of war atrocities don't fail to include the army biscuit ration.*
>
> Ted McKay, Auckland Mounteds[27]

Water dictated where many of the battles were fought as both armies depended on water to survive, and the oases in the desert that had wells were fiercely contested as the Turks knew that without water the British army could not advance.

> *... the usual allowance was one bottle per man per day; not over generous in such a climate... But even in the midst of our own water worries we could spare a thought for the plight of the poor horses. Until we reached Palestine at the beginning of '17, they never knew the taste of one drop of fresh water. The water in the all-too-few wells that served their needs, had a saline taste abhorrent to man and beast.... But at least we had the means of voicing our grievances and could parade sick, or complain to the right quarter, but our splendid, overwrought horses just broke their great hearts and spirits in silence. What grand gallant animals they were!*
>
> Ted McKay, Auckland Mounteds[28]

Two Up and Crown and Anchor

> *The tastes of Australians and New Zealanders ran more to 'Two up' and 'Crown and Anchor' but these games were not allowed to be carried out within the lines, so in dusk the 'schools' assembled out in the sandy wastes where the faint light of their few candles could not be seen from the camp. Especially after a pay day, the 'schools' would boom at night, when various schemes were adopted by rival 'ringmasters' to attract custom. Some would have free biscuits and lemonade distributed amongst their patrons at intervals during the evening; others would have a free issue of cigarettes and chewing gum, while their exhortations to the motley crew who were in various states of dress and undress, and composed of men from the four corners of the earth urged their patrons to stake their piastres on their*

fancy in a manner that would have turned an American sideshowman green with envy — 'Shower it in thick and heavy,' they urged, 'You pick 'em and I'll pay 'em,' 'I'll hide 'em and you find 'em,' 'Throw it in my lucky lads, they come here in wheelbarrows and go away in motorcars.' 'Speculate and accumulate,' 'Pour it in, lads. We are the Good Samaritans you read about.' 'Here's where you get the oscar for your next trip to Cairo.[29]

John Robertson, *With the Cameliers in Palestine*

Men were rested with spells on the seashore where swimming in the salt water healed desert sores on both horses and men. It was time for rugby, concerts and sing-alongs, catching up with letters from home and gambling.

Thoughts of home

*Jaded and gay, the ladies sing: and the chap in brown
Tilts his grey hat; jaunty and lean and pale,
He rattles the keys — some actor bloke from town —
God send you home; and then A long, long trail;
I hear you calling me; and Dixieland...
Sing slowly — now the chorus — one by one
We hear them, drink them; till the concert's done.*

Siegfried Sassoon, Kantara, April 1918[30]

Army concerts naturally varied in detail, but there was one sort of common denominator to them all. Everybody nibbled peanuts, and the crackling rustle of peanut shells was as much a part of the show as the National Anthem... We wanted the stuff we used to hear with Mum and Dad and the girl friend and in the main we got it. It goes without saying that smutty yarns went the rounds and lasted their little day, but the fellows who ran these shows for us knew what we wanted and ministered to our unspoken desires to have the old songs we heard at home.

Ted McKay, Auckland Mounteds[31]

Letters and meeting newly arrived mates from the home town was the only contact with home. Writing was often difficult on operations and usually caught up with during rest spells.

Writing to a soldier becomes a one-way affair if he wills it so. The temptation to use the field service postcard, with its terse, standardised assurances was almost resistless when duty and obligation demanded letter writing, but inclination leaned towards sleep, or gambling or yarning.

Ted McKay, Auckland Mounted Rifles[32]

Yet even when they did not write themselves, receiving the mail was one of the few constant delights.

I felt I had been cheated a trifle one sweltering day when a Patriotic gift parcel reached me. It held a heavy muffler, a warm balaclava and a couple of pairs of thick socks, eminently suited for wear in the frozen mud of Flanders, but not quite what the well dressed warrior wore in desert country.

Ted McKay, Auckland Mounted Rifles[33]

The summer of 1917 climaxed in the Battle for Beersheba, with the Mounteds taking Tel el Saba, the key to the Turkish position. This was followed by the fighting north of Beersheba on the coastal plain in the advance towards Philistia. At Ayun Kara on 14 November 1917 the New Zealand Mounted Rifles had 44 killed and 81 wounded.

Fruit market, Ludd. WILLIAMS ALBUM 213, AIM

When it is remembered that a mounted rifle regiment dismounts for action only a little over two hundred men and that the Regiment was far from full strength, the eighty nine casualties suffered by Auckland give some indication of the fierceness of the engagement. There were probably not more than... one hundred and forty men in the line.[34]

Hard fighting in Palestine

November 1917 was a month of hard fighting north of Jaffa, and the Brigade was again exhausted when it was rested in early 1918 among the vineyards and orchards of the Jewish settlements of Richon le Zion.

Richon is the first Jewish colony in Palestine, and is some seven miles south of Jaffa. It has special associations for the New Zealanders as the severe action of Ayun Kara was fought near there on November 14th, 1917... On entering the colony the morning after the fight the people gave us a great reception, and wine, fruit, brown bread, etc, were showered on us in great profusion — a very welcome change after some six weeks on hard tack.

Harry Frost, Auckland Mounteds[35]

The New Zealanders were much surprised when they met the Jewish settlers and one of the women asked in English for the whereabouts of a New Zealander in the Auckland Mounteds. 'I would like to find him for he is my son.' They met shortly after.

In February 1918 the New Zealanders entered Jerusalem.

It was a fitting day for our introduction to the Holy City, a day of calm and peace and sunshine: war and all its blood and sorrow seemed remote

Lonely graves on the Jericho road. ALEXANDER TURNBULL LIBRARY

and impossible at that moment. We halted and gazed, moved on slowly and gazed again, each one in his own way thinking that this was a unique and unforgettable moment in his life, a memory that would fade only with life itself.

Perhaps it was best summed up by one of the drivers named Joe, a tough lad with a free-flowing gift of invective, entirely lacking in any outward sign of religious enthusiasms, and about as imaginative as a boiled egg. Joe strolled over and said, apropos of the surroundings, 'Makes you think a bit don't it Mac?' I agreed that it did.

Ted McKay, Auckland Mounteds[36]

Victorious and exhausted

The war finished for the New Zealanders eight months' campaigning in the Jordan Valley with two raids into the mountains of Moab towards Amman. While the New Zealand Mounted Rifles remained in the Jordan Valley, the 2nd New Zealand Machine Gun Squadron, who were attached to the Australian Light Horse, got along the road to Damascus where their war ended. Victory over the Turks also saw the victory of disease over the now exhausted brigade.

In the first 12 days of October the ambulance admitted over 700 cases of malaria, most of it malignant. The New Zealand Brigade lost at least a third of its strength.

A D Carbery, *NZ Medical Services in the Great War*[37]

The New Zealand Mounted Rifle Brigade have become the forgotten men in New Zealand's history. Yet by what ever measure one chooses, it was one of the finest groups that New Zealand has ever raised. In three years of warfare casualties totalled 1786 including 640 killed in action, died of wounds and from sickness.

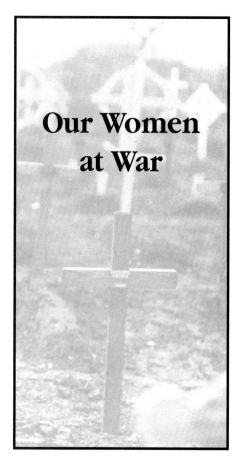

Our Women at War

The first volunteers

Although six New Zealand nurses went to Samoa with the Samoan Expedition-ary Force in August 1914, New Zealand women had to fight hard to get overseas as the government was initially reluctant to send nurses with the New Zealand Forces. Many New Zealand nurses took the initiative and joined the Australian and British nursing services. Ella Cooke was one of these. Ella was born in Auckland in 1885, the youngest and a twin in a family of eight living in Grafton Road. Ella trained as a nurse at Auckland Hospital and worked as a Native Health Nurse in the Waikato before going to England with her twin sister in July 1914. They arrived after war had been declared and Ella volunteered to nurse in France 'to fill the gap in some hospitals caused by nurses going on active service.'[2] She left for France in November 1914 to serve with the French Flag Nursing Corps. Ella worked at a base hospital at Bernay near Rouen for six months and treated French wounded, many of whom arrived at the hospital straight from the trenches.

> *Many had been in the trenches for weeks, and several explained to me that they had not had their boots off for 4 months. You can imagine the state most of them are in. Many have swollen feet and frozen up to the ankles; most I am afraid will lose both feet, and many the legs up to the knees.*
>
> Ella Cooke[3]

At a time when New Zealand was still regarding the war as a great adven-ture that would be over by Christmas 1914, Ella was one of the few New Zealanders who had seen its realities.

> *I am sure most people do not realise what this war means unless they could see these poor suffering men. I am also nursing numbers of Germans, and they are really most respectful to me, and very helpful in every way they can. Although as a nation they hate the English, they always ask the Frenchmen to send along the 'Nurse Anglais' to them.*
>
> Ella Cooke[4]

Ella's patients included French Moroccans who 'simply hate the Germans'. One day there was an 'awful smell' from the room of one of them, 'and a German's head was found under his bed!'

On New Year's Day 1915 her German patients thanked:

> *me for all my trouble with them, and that after the war my name shall be known far and wide in Germany... They too were longing for peace, and they wished me long life, good luck, prosperity and the best of good wishes for the year 1915... I was quite taken aback and thanked them as best as I could for their good wishes, and said that my greatest wish was that peace should reign. After which they gave 3 cheers for 'Nurse Anglais'.*
>
> Ella Cooke[5]

After six months Ella returned to England, intending to return to New Zealand, but was persuaded to join the Queen Alexandra's Imperial Nursing Service Reserve. After training at Aldershot she was posted to No 17 General Hospital at Alexandria in Egypt in September 1915.

> *My Army uniform and clothes are early Victorian and... I think I'll present them to the Auckland Museum when I arrive home. My outdoor dress is of grey, bodice well-boned. We wear little capes always with uniforms faced with red.... You never in your life saw a more old fashioned turn out.*
>
> Ella Cooke[6]

Neither Ella nor her uniform came home. She nursed in Egypt for two years and was killed crossing a railway line behind the hospital.

New Zealand nurses for the front

> *There were so few uniforms, recalled Miss Emily Hodges of Fendalton, that on embarkation, her group was presented with two bolts of material and two sewing machines and were instructed to make their own. The sisters were so sea-sick that it was some time before that was achieved.*
>
> Elisabeth Ogilvie, *Nursing in the First World War*[7]

Ella Cooke. AIM

The demand for trained nurses eventually overcame the reservations of the New Zealand Government. The first contingent of 50 New Zealand nurses, under Matron Hester McLean, sailed for London in April 1915 and they were posted to hospitals in Cairo. By the end of the war 550 nurses had served with the NZEF and approximately 100 others served with other forces or with the British and French Red Cross.

> *The New Zealand sisters served in every theatre during the war — with distinction. They gained a reputation for adaptability and resourcefulness.*
> *They nursed in Alexandria and Cairo, treating wounded men from Gallipoli on the sandy banks of the Nile. They were in hospital ships in the Mediterranean and crossed the Channel in the horrific days of the great 'pushes'. They brought refugees from Siberia and were in hospital trains in Palestine. They nursed wounded men in the searing heat of the Persian Gulf.*
>
> Elisabeth Ogilvie, *Nursing in the First World War*[8]

On our hospital ships

> *The ship is beautiful. 'The New Zealand Hospital Ship' it is and has been subscribed to by all the people of New Zealand and she is a great white huge monster — three great red crosses on either side and green stripes — she just looks like what she is — an errand of mercy for all you men — and very proud I am to be one of the staff.*
>
> Charlotte Le Gallais[9]

Nurses were also selected for the two New Zealand Hospital Ships, *Maheno* and *Marama*. The *Maheno* sailed on its first voyage in July 1915. The *Maheno* also carried the second contingent of New Zealand nurses who disembarked at Port Said to work in the New Zealand hospitals in Egypt. A party of them sailed for Salonika with No 1 NZ Stationary Hospital on the transport SS *Marquette* which was torpedoed almost in sight of Salonika at 9 a.m. on 23 October 1915.

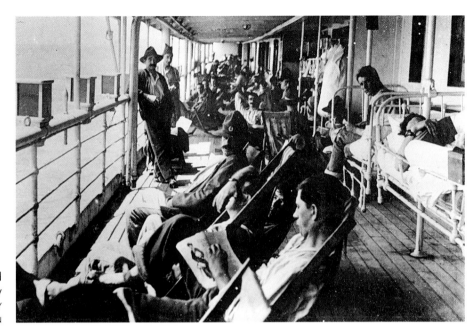

Coming home, New Zealand wounded and convalescents on board the New Zealand Hospital ship *Maheno*. QEII ARMY MEMORIAL MUSEUM COLLECTION

[The Marquette] went down in 7 minutes... Ten were lost, 4 at present are here and very ill — the Matron has never spoken since — she went grey in one night... poor Rogers and Hilyard... both went down; Rogers and another nurse unidentified washed ashore and both buried at Saloniki; Isdell had her arm broken — Fox they say her back was broken, another nurse both legs; Rattray had two nurses keeping her up for hours, they were holding on to spars and with hands crossed these girls kept Rattray up until she became mental and died of exhaustion... Hilyard sang 'Tipperary' and 'Are We Downhearted' until she died.

Charlotte Le Gallais[10]

New Zealanders nursing in France

They learned to sleep to the sound of the guns and the bombs falling nearby For a time the work at Hazebrouck was very strenuous: 350 cases were admitted during one day and three operating theatres were going day and night. During the winter the sisters suffered severely from trench feet. It was impossible to put on boots or shoes. Many times the sister [who] attended a man with trench feet who was admitted as a patient, could if she had chosen, show a condition worse than her patient.

Miss Hester MacLean, 'New Zealand Army Nurses'[11]

No 1 New Zealand Stationary Hospital at Wisques. ALEXANDER TURNBULL LIBRARY

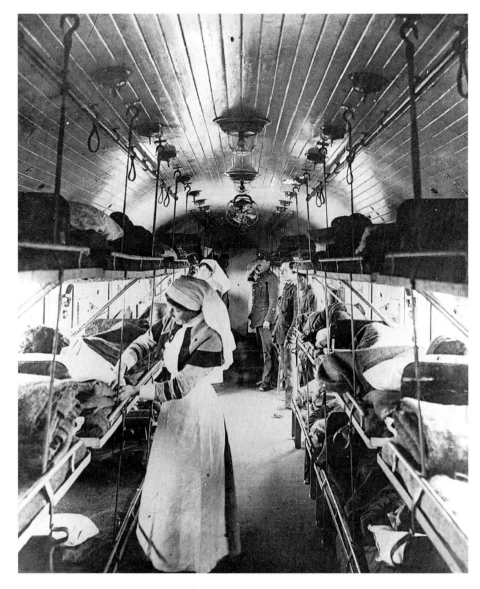

A hospital train in France. First stage of a wounded soldier's trip to 'Blighty'. BRITISH OFFICIAL PHOTOGRAPH, QEII ARMY MEMORIAL MUSEUM

New Zealand nurses worked at the New Zealand Stationary Hospital in France and also with the British and French forces. The New Zealand Stationary Hospital was established at Amiens in France in July 1916 and included 35 NZANS (New Zealand Army Nursing Service) sisters. Six of our nurses were also sent to work as part of special surgical teams in the more forward Casualty Clearing Stations. In May 1917 the hospital moved to Hazebrouck where it functioned as a Casualty Clearing Station taking the overflow from other stations closer to the front line, and specialised in head wounds. Heavy shelling by a long range gun in August saw the hospital evacuated to Wisques near St Omer where it expanded to accommodate 1000 beds.

Nancy Robertson

Nancy Robertson completed her nursing certificate at Auckland Hospital and was accepted in the Queen Alexandra's Imperial Nursing Service Reserve of the British Army in November 1916. She sailed from New Zealand in October 1917 and on arrival in England was posted to 5 Casualty Clearing Station in France where she served for the remainder of the war. Her fiancé and later husband, Arthur Page, served as Quartermaster Sergeant in the NZEF and returned to New Zealand before her.

Ellen Brown. AIM

Ellen Brown

All men being brought in were given oxygen until their blue cheeks assumed a natural colour. Thereafter they were moved to wards upstairs where careful nursing and plenty of whisky effected a cure! She used 'Octopuses' — oxygen bottles in the centre while men wore attached masks on the beds radiating from the centre, like tentacles.

Elisabeth Ogilvie, *Nursing in the First World War*[12]

Ellen Brown volunteered in 1914 to nurse overseas and joined the Australian Army Nursing Service in Egypt, where she nursed Australians and New Zealanders wounded from the Gallipoli Campaign. She served in France and on hospital ships returning wounded to Australia. In France during the influenza epidemic of 1918 Brown showed her nursing skills in not losing any of her patients to the epidemic. By 1918 she was Matron-in-Chief of the Australian Nursing Service. She returned to New Zealand as Matron at Queen Mary Hospital, Hanmer Springs, before her marriage to Donald Manson, manager of St Helen's station.

Ellen Brown (seated left) with some of her helpers in Egypt. AIM

Nursing in New Zealand hospitals in the United Kingdom

The New Zealand War Contingent Association established a hospital at Walton-on-Thames in England to cater for New Zealand wounded from Gallipoli. After our Division moved to France in 1916, this became No 2 New Zealand General Hospital. No 1 New Zealand General Hospital came from Egypt and took over Lady Hardinge's hutted hospital built for Indian soldiers at Brockenhurst in the New Forest. Known as 'Tin Town', it consisted of two wings each of ten wards as well as the Balmer Lawn Hotel and the Forest Park Hotel which were both used as hospitals. Oatlands Park was later established for New Zealand limbless patients or 'limbies'. No 3 New Zealand General Hospital was established at Codford and also established was the New Zealand Convalescent Hospital at Hornchurch. By 1918 New Zealand hospitals in the United Kingdom could accommodate 6495 patients. From 1 May 1916 to the demobilisation after the war there were 70,000 New Zealand admissions to hospitals in the United Kingdom; over 25,000 to Walton-on-Thames, and over 20,000 to Brockenhurst.[13] This large number of hospitals meant that there were always shortages in nursing staff. This got worse when male medical orderlies were sent to France in 1917 and replaced by Volunteer Aid Division nurses, or VADs. It was hard, demanding work for the both the nursing sisters and volunteers.

Volunteers for our boys

Some linger for a friendly chat,
Some call me 'Mother' — Think of that!
And often at the magic word,
My vision grows a little blurred
The crowd in khaki disappears,

I see them through a mist of years:
I see them in a thousand prams —
A thousand mothers' little lambs...

CALT *YMCA*[14]

Many New Zealand women who were not professional nurses paid their own fare to England. Together with New Zealand women living with their families in Great Britain, they bought their own uniforms, and worked unpaid as volunteers in the clubs, YMCA camp canteens and as VADs in the New Zealand military hospitals and convalescent homes in England and France. None of these women ever qualified for medals because they were never officially in the services. As so often with women's work it was essential, exhausting, but unpaid, and, apart from the thanks of the men themselves, unrecognised.

Gladys Luxford was one of these. Her father, Padre Luxford, was a New Zealand military chaplain who had been wounded and lost a leg on Gallipoli. After recovering from his wounds, Padre Luxford was appointed as Chaplain to No 2 New Zealand General Hospital at Walton-on-Thames. His wife joined him from New Zealand and Gladys was also allowed as VADs were badly needed.

Volunteers and convalescing New Zealand soldiers in the Kia Ora Club, Brockenhurst.
QUALIS ALBUM, QEII ARMY MEMORIAL MUSEUM

Ward interior. New Zealand General
Hospital No 2, Walton-on-Thames.
ALEXANDER TURNBULL LIBRARY

I now became a very small cog in the big military machine that was functioning to win World War One. I was sent into the big nurses mess room, to see how I got on, & eventually worked my way up to the senior waitress. This meant waiting on the matron's table, & no other waitress could start till this table was served... Matron was sympathetic with me and asked me if I would like to work in the wards, which delighted me. This was against my parent's wish, but Matron overruled this, & said she had always wanted me in the wards... I was lucky to be in [Ward] 5, with Sister Nutsey as charge sister... The first morning two deaths, second morning three deaths, & the patients blamed me; the old superstition regarding parsons and their kin, was held in those days, so wasn't I thankful that the third morning no deaths.

The staffing of [the] ward consisted of three sisters and five VADs. There were 36 beds in ward, eighteen each side and a side room. At one stage the Empire was represented by two NZ sisters and one Canadian, the VADs, one English, one Scottish, one South African, one Australian, and one New Zealander... It was a happy ward with work, laughter, sympathy and kindness intermingling...

I will never forget the Matron announcing at dinner time the last shot has been fired. There was absolute silence; & the thought no more soldiers killed, & the return to NZ soon.

Gladys Luxford, VAD No 2 NZ General Hospital Walton-on-Thames[15]

Margaret Swarbrick was one of the many
British VADs working at No 1 New Zealand
General Hospital at Brockenhurst. AIM

122

Ettie Rout and members of her Volunteer Sisterhood worked tirelessly in Egypt, England and France. Women also staffed the YMCA Lowry Hut Canteen at the New Zealand Reinforcement Depot at Etaples. The photo shows volunteer staff at the NZ YMCA Lowry Hut at the New Zealand Training Depot, Etaples, France. Left to right: Miss Eaton (Wales), Miss Carr (Napier) and Miss Russell (Auckland). The lines of exhaustion are etched on the women's faces from long hours in the canteen serving tea and cakes and talking to soldiers to whom these New Zealand women represented perhaps the last link before joining the Division and going into the trenches. OFFICIAL PHOTOGRAPH, H SERIES, AIM

Bringing home the girl of my dreams

By early 1919 there were 250 applications to marry each week from New Zealanders waiting to return to New Zealand; it was estimated that shipping for 2000 wives and families would be needed. For many young men wartime conditions and a brief eight days' leave in Great Britain led to romance and marriage, and the frustration of waiting for a boat to take them back to New Zealand after the Armistice. Many of the men had been wounded and had no occuption to return to in New Zealand. Their wives and families faced a difficult future in a strange land very different from the one they knew.

New Zealand sergeants, their wives and families going to their new home in New Zealand on the *Remuera*. G S RICHARDSON ALBUM, AIM

'On the Fringe of Hell'

The New Zealanders on the Western Front 1916–1918

We're here
Because
We're here
Because
We're here
Because we're here

To the tune of *Auld Lang Syne*[1]

'Under the sign of the Silver Fern': The New Zealand Division

Our New Zealand Division fought on the Western Front in France and Belgium from 1916 to 1918. It took part in the battles of the Somme in 1916, at Messines in June 1917, and before Passchendaele in October 1917. It spent Christmas 1917 in the Ypres Salient, then hurried to the Somme again where it played an important part in stopping a German breakthrough towards the city of Amiens during the German offensive, in March 1918. It then spearheaded the British offensive which ended for New Zealanders at the fortress town of Le Quesnoy in November 1918. We ended the war with the reputation of being one of the outstanding fighting divisions of the British armies on the Western Front.

'Mademoiselle from Armentières'

> *One thing you never have to worry about your wardrobe, because you have everything on your back. Where I put my tin lid now is my home... Having boska weather... Some queer places about here Soph, these froggies must be great Church people, every little village you go into they have a fine big Church, but can't they put the nips in. Went in to buy you some lace, but Christ I did get a shock. I told them I did not want to buy the village, a man would want a 100 pounds to buy anything here, eggs cooked eightpence each. I think you had better come over and start an egg and chip shop.*

Bert Gill, Canterbury Infantry[2]

When it arrived in France in May 1916 the 20,000-strong New Zealand Division had only been in existence for three months and was a mixture of untried reinforcements fresh from New Zealand and battle-weary Gallipoli veterans. Gallipoli for all its difficulties had not prepared the New Zealanders for conditions on the Western Front. Here we were a small part of what was to become five British armies totalling over 50 divisions. Each army was made up of two or three army corps, each of three or four divisions. We and the five Australian divisions belonged to I and II ANZAC Corps, but in France divisions were moved wherever they were needed, and in battle when a division was exhausted with too many casualties, it was replaced by a fresh one. Because of this the New Zealand Division fought on the Somme in 1916, and again on the Somme in 1918, as part of a British corps. By 1918 the Australians had formed an Australian Corps with their divisions, and the ANZAC Corps no longer existed.

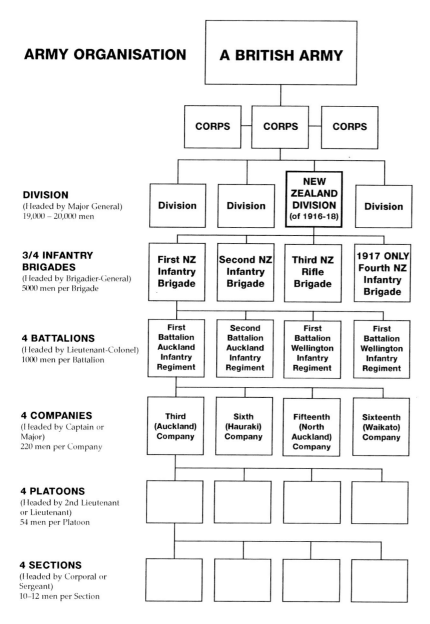

ARMY ORGANISATION

A BRITISH ARMY

CORPS | CORPS | CORPS

NEW ZEALAND DIVISION (of 1916-18)

DIVISION
(Headed by Major General)
19,000 – 20,000 men

Division | Division | **NEW ZEALAND DIVISION (of 1916-18)** | Division

3/4 INFANTRY BRIGADES
(Headed by Brigadier-General)
5000 men per Brigade

First NZ Infantry Brigade | Second NZ Infantry Brigade | Third NZ Rifle Brigade | 1917 ONLY Fourth NZ Infantry Brigade

4 BATTALIONS
(Headed by Lieutenant-Colonel)
1000 men per Battalion

First Battalion Auckland Infantry Regiment | Second Battalion Auckland Infantry Regiment | First Battalion Wellington Infantry Regiment | First Battalion Wellington Infantry Regiment

4 COMPANIES
(Headed by Captain or Major)
220 men per Company

Third (Auckland) Company | Sixth (Hauraki) Company | Fifteenth (North Auckland) Company | Sixteenth (Waikato) Company

4 PLATOONS
(Headed by 2nd Lieutenant or Lieutenant)
54 men per Platoon

4 SECTIONS
(Headed by Corporal or Sergeant)
10–12 men per Section

Organisation of the New Zealand Division within a British Corps.

New Zealanders in the trenches at Armentières. You can see from the tidiness of the sandbag wall that this is likely to be a showpiece trench in the support lines some distance behind the front line.
IMPERIAL WAR MUSEUM

Empty graves waiting to be filled at Armentières. J HILLIARD FAMILY COLLECTION, NATIONAL ARCHIVES

Life in France for the New Zealanders started in the trenches at Armentières in northern France. This was regarded as a nursery where 'new boys' were gently blooded into the realities of trench warfare. It was anything but gentle between May and August 1916. This was a period of intense activity to coincide with British preparations for the Battle of the Somme which began on 1 July 1916. Just as on Gallipoli, we mostly inexperienced New Zealanders had to learn the intricacies of trench warfare the hard way, under the critical gaze of the British high command. It almost destroyed us, and the cemeteries dotted round Armentières have enough fern leaves carved on stone to show how difficult this was.

'Ariki Toa': Andrew Russell, New Zealand's fighting chief

Despite our inexperience, we made good because of the calibre of the man in charge, Major General Sir Andrew Russell, a sheep farmer from Hawke's Bay who although a Territorial soldier was totally professional in what he demanded of his men and of his staff. By trial and error he forged us into a honed and efficient fighting machine. But unlike many other generals of that era, he never forgot that the strength of the Division was flesh and blood. He was given the title 'Ariki Toa' (the fighting chief sent forward to lead) by the Maori people on his return to New Zealand in 1919.

Major General Sir Andrew Russell. OFFICIAL PHOTOGRAPH, H SERIES, ALBUM 418, AIM

The first priority is the care and welfare of the men, the rest [is] nowhere.
Major General Sir Andrew Russell, NZ Division[3]

The Diggers

The New Zealand soldier was known as a 'digger' or 'fernleaf'. The soldier term 'digger' did not come from the goldfields as is often believed but from the exploits of the New Zealand Pioneer Battalion on the Somme in 1916 where they earned the reputation of being the 'digging battalion' and were referred to as 'Diggers'. By the end of 1916 this was the common term to describe any New Zealand soldier, and was then adopted by Australian soldiers in 1917 who were also part of the two ANZAC Corps. The term 'fernleaf' came from the distinctive New Zealand identifying or tactical sign of a silver fern set within a black circle.

The New Zealand Division 'All Black' rugby team also wore the silver fern on their black jerseys. On the Western Front the New Zealanders did not see themselves as 'Anzacs' but as 'En Zeds'. The New Zealand Division was a national army in miniature, fiercely proud of its identity, and as determined as Russell, its commander, to be the best. In August 1916 we ensured our distinctive appearance with the adoption of the 'lemon squeezer' as the head dress of the NZEF.

Totally professional despite our amateur status

Although regarded as amateur citizen soldiers, the New Zealand digger was generally better trained than his British or Australian counterpart, and this advantage increased as the war went on. This was due to the organisation of the recruiting and reinforcement system in New Zealand. No matter when soldiers volunteered they had to wait until they were called up by groups or reinforcements into the training camps at Trentham and Featherston.

After training they were sent overseas for more advanced training in New Zealand camps in England, and again for further training at the New Zealand training depot at Etaples in France, before finally being sent to the Division. This process could take up to ten months, and the introduction of conscription in 1916 ensured that New Zealand was one of the few countries that kept its division up to strength with trained men. This and the calibre of our leadership were the foundation of our outstanding reputation. It built on what have become recognised as characteristic traits of New Zealanders; a strong sense of individual initiative, an unassuming ability to get on with different nationalities, a willingness to conform, and an almost dour determination to win. We fought in the same way as we played rugby, by ensuring the percentages were in our favour with trained soldiers, and careful planning and preparation.

New Zealanders in training before the battle of Messines. OFFICIAL PHOTOGRAPH, H SERIES, ALBUM 418, AIM

A bloody stalemate

Pity for the tired men,
Up the line and down again —
Tramping where their comrades fell.
Flotsam on the fringe of hell.

M E Hankins, Chronicles of the NZEF[4]

By 1916 the Western Front was a bloody stalemate. A line of trenches stretched from the English Channel to the Swiss Frontier. It was a form of siege warfare with soldiers of all armies living in trenches separated by no-man's-land in between. To get out of the trenches and advance was to risk death from machine-gun fire. Men burrowed through the ground and protected themselves in dug-outs and bunkers with connecting trenches that were often covered with roofs made of sandbags and earth heaped over sheets of corrugated iron resting on wooden supports. Barbed wire entanglements often hundreds of metres thick protected the front lines. In these entanglements were outposts occupying shell holes manned by groups of men to give early warning of any attack, report enemy patrols, or to snipe and kill any unwary soldier who showed himself in the opposing front line.

Left billets about 3 & went to second line trenches, & waited there till dark. Trenches only half finished, rottenly drained, & very muddy. This mid-summer too. Our front line only 5 outposts out in No Man's Land... Our post in old slightly damaged German shell-proof hut. Only allowed to talk in whispers, & make no noise, especially at night. Two sentries on at night, & one at day time. All must remain awake all night, but sleep all day except when on sentry.

G C Latimer Clark, Auckland Infantry[5]

The front line was often a series of strong points connected by trenches. Men scraped little coffin shelters in the trench walls where they tried to sleep. There were underground dugouts for the company headquarters with bunks for the officers and signallers, but most British soldiers in the front line lived in the trenches, finding shelter where they could during their stint in the line. Each division was responsible for part of the front and each of its brigades might hold a sector, rostering its four battalions through in rotation, eight days in either the front or support lines, and then eight days in billets in reserve where they provided working parties and carried out training.

Behind the front line was the support line which also had a network of trenches and here dugouts and shelters were more common. This was connected to the front line by communication trenches which were used to take up supplies and reinforcements and bring out casualties. In low-lying areas the trenches were built up above ground with sandbag walls. The trench was built to a standard pattern which zigzagged its way across the countryside. In quiet areas trench systems became very sophisticated with drainage systems and neat sandbag walls held up by wooden supports.

Behind the lines were rest areas and billets where men were housed or 'billeted' in French and Belgian villages, often in barns and factories. Rest involved physical fitness training, sports days and rugby competitions. Each battalion had its own band, and a concert party was formed and concerts and films were given nightly in the Divisional theatre. Beer was sold in the canteens and soldiers could go to the local estaminets for egg and chips, beer and wine.

Life in the trenches

> *Day by day we dig new trenches,*
> *Bury war-created stenches,*
> *Build up castles in the mud, and drain the floor,*
> *Night by night the big guns thunder,*
> *Trench and castle rend asunder;*
> *And at dawn we start to dig and build once more.*
>
> K L Trent, *New Zealand at the Front*[6]

In the trenches men worked by night and tried to sleep by day. Patrols, wiring, repairing and replacing sandbags, laying wooden duckboards, carrying up supplies and ammunition were all done at night. Before dawn soldiers would 'stand-to' and the men would line the trench a metre apart peering into no-man's-land in case there was a surprise attack. When daylight came men 'stood down' and tried to sleep. This was difficult in daylight as they would be disturbed by others moving along the trench. Men were lucky to get three or four hours' broken sleep a day and were always dead-tired.

A British soldier on sentry duty in the front line looking through a periscope. You can see that he has made himself as comfortable as possible. He is sitting on his overcoat, and has his cigarettes and matches and a watch to tell him how long he has on duty before someone else takes over. Empty ammunition boxes were inserted into the trench walls and these held ammunition, hand grenades and trench stores. QEII ARMY MEMORIAL MUSEUM

A zone of death

Our platoon got shelled like hell — shrapnel simply rained. Jim Walker and I were completely buried. I was dug out alive. Jim, my pal dead. Going unconscious underground was an awful experience — suffocating was awful. Will never forget... — quite mad when got out.

Owen Le Gallais, Auckland Infantry[7]

Each side tried to prevent the other from improving their trench systems, which had to be done at night. Flares were sent up and snipers fired at any movement. Machine guns fired at random by day and night along the barbed wire barriers. Artillery fired at artillery, and guided by reconnaissance aeroplanes shells were fired at the trenches and barbed wire to break them down, and at the communication trenches and roads leading to the front line to prevent supplies coming forward.

This zone of combat was a zone of death where a man could be shot by a bullet, blown to pieces by an artillery shell or mortar bomb, choke to death from gas, freeze to death in winter, drown in the mud in the spring thaw, or go mad with the constant fear that was everyone's companion.

If anybody says that the day of the horse transport is over, then let them come and see what the old geegee is doing in this war. As far as the eye could reach teams were hauling gear to the big dumps... and to the batteries and their ravenous guns.

W K Wilson, NZ Rifle Brigade[8]

The soldiers hated the suffering that war inflicted on animals, particularly on the 3000 or so horses and mules that were part of the New Zealand Division. Only the rats that fed off the dead were loathed and killed. Stray dogs were adopted, named, fed, and trotted along with the men as they trudged through France and Belgium for three years of war.

Bert Gill, a New Zealand 'Digger'

Had a lovely dream the other night. I dreamt I was back, [home in NZ] if it was only true, and I was talking to Nancy, what fun I was having with her, just how she would be now too. I can picture her to a T. I woke up and suddenly discovered I was laying in France with a dam lump of dirt sticking in my back, and a couple of dam shirt rats [lice] giving me hell... I could of cried.

Bert Gill, Canterbury Infantry[9]

Henry Herbert Gill, or Bert as he was known, was a typical New Zealand digger. Bert was a married man, balloted under the Military Service Act. It was only after he was balloted that he found that his wife Sophie was pregnant with their first child. After training in New Zealand and England, Bert went to France as a member of the Canterbury Regiment in 1917. In the routine of the trenches Bert often lost track of the days, but on every seventh day he wrote home to his wife Sophie and his daughter Nancy:

It is one big joke this Soph and the sooner the dam joke is finished the better because I am fed up... They have got us back to the old bullshit/drill again, saluting by numbers, forming fours and all that dam rot...

Bert Gill, Canterbury Infantry[10]

Typical barbed-wire entanglements — no-man's land. QEII ARMY MEMORIAL MUSEUM

Bert Gill did not want to be in France. He was a reluctant conscript and like most older married men he found the routine of soldiering irksome and longed for home. Like many in his situation he made the best of it, recording war's realities in his letters home. His letters and many like them can be found in the Auckland Museum Library collection and in similar institutions throughout New Zealand.

I have been into the firing line, the front one at that. It is a peculiar sensation the first time going in puts the fear of God in your heart... a man lives like a rat, burrows a nest out for himself with a shovel, and there he gets for the night. Don't do anything but watch out, each man has his turn, gets what sleep he can.

Bert Gill, Canterbury Infantry[11]

Out of the front line it was a time to rest and retrain and write home. His letters record the training, his impressions of France, his home town friends and acquaintances whom he meets, and when in the trenches, the discomfort and the universal fears that were shared by citizen soldiers on both sides.

Big stuff at times puts the wind up a man, can hear the big shells coming, some one will say, here the bugger comes, and then we duck into our hole like a rabbit.... The baths are allright we get here, hand all your dirty clothes in one window, and go to another window and get clean ones. No washing only our face which is not very often.

Bert Gill, Canterbury Infantry[12]

It was the simple things that made the war endurable; letters from home, hot food, a good bath and the company of your mates.

Excuse the writing Soph because I am writing this on my gas mask, and diggers keep getting in the light, some playing cards, some swearing, some singing, never heard such a din in all your life.

Bert Gill, Canterbury Infantry[13]

Up to Div baths today for bath & change of clothes... Received gift parcel tonight from the Marlborough Patriotic Society Blenheim, NZ containing tobacco, chewing gum, writing paper & envelopes, sheep tongues, sardines, extract of meat & a handkerchief. Ben Smart, Headquarters 2 NZ Infantry Brigade.[14] OFFICIAL PHOTOGRAPH, H SERIES, ALBUM 418 AIM

The Division tried to give each man a bath at least every ten days and set up bath units for each brigade of 5000 men. Soldiers entered the bath unit and undressed, handing in their clothes and valuables before moving into the showers. After a hot shower, clean underwear, shorts and socks were issued and their uniforms and valuables returned. While they were in the showers the seams of their jackets and trousers were ironed by French women employed as laundresses and seamstresses by the Division. This was to kill the lice that laid eggs in the seams, particularly the armpits and crotch where the soldier's body heat helped them hatch. However, the clothing changes were only a temporary respite and within hours men would be scratching themselves again. Supporting the baths was the divisional laundry which disinfected, washed and mended all the dirty underclothes, socks and towels.

A cross-section of New Zealand transported to France

The baths and laundry were all part of the large and complex organisation that was the New Zealand Division. As well as the infantry and artillery brigades, engineers and Pioneer Battalion, it included workshops, supply and transport units, a concert party and film show or 'Perriots' as they were known and the YMCA, which provided free or 'buckshee' coffee, cocoa and biscuits, as well as writing paper at specially organised canteens. There were other New Zealand units outside of the Division including an artillery brigade, a cyclist company, a squadron of mounted rifles, a tunnelling company, a field bakery, and a light railway-operating company that ran ammunition and supply trains on specially laid light rails forward to the supply dumps behind the lines. In 1918 New Zealand began to form a Tank Battalion and men were sent to England to train but the war ended before they received their tanks. At any one time the NZEF in France and Belgium numbered over 21,000 with as many again in training or convalescing in the camps and hospitals in England.

Mud and misery

Life in the trenches was a misery. Men lived in their clothes for weeks at a time, only taking their boots off to change socks, which in winter was a daily requirement to overcome 'trench foot' when untended feet went rotten in the damp and wet.

Working party going up to the front line.
OFFICIAL PHOTOGRAPH, H SERIES, ALBUM 418, AIM

Cookhouse in the support trenches.
OFFICIAL PHOTOGRAPH, H SERIES, ALBUM 418, AIM

…it don't take much to make the trenches slippery. You would of laughed the other night. I was coming back from work dark as it could be, and slippery as one thing, meets a cove and here am going off a treat and the other cove just the same, walked for about a hundred yards and he said, 'Hell is that you, Bert, I thought I knew your voice' and it was Dick Adam, damned if I knew him it was so dark.

Bert Gill, Canterbury Infantry[15]

There were no sleeping bags, only a single blanket and a soldier's great-coat which he wrapped around himself to sleep. Food came from the company and battalion cookhouses set up in the support trenches and delivered to the front line in specially insulated containers to keep it warm. It was 'sandbag duff' and bully beef in every variety as stews, rissoles or in the tin, with bread and tea, while soldiers wrote of what they imagined was on the table back home in New Zealand:

roast beef and rhubarb and cream for tea while in the trenches, everything comes to us in sand bags, the duffs are made in them, the fluff and string that a man eats, he will be passing a few sand bags or else a few feet of rope one of these days.

Bert Gill, Canterbury Infantry[16]

Living for the mail from home

I got seven letters from NZ. 3 from Mother, 2 from Lyell, 1 from Bill Morris and one from Aunt Jean, but yours have not arrived yet. Funny I got the last lot a week before the usual mail, but may get them any day. I hope they have not come a gutser, am looking forward for them. I always go for your letters first, then Mothers, and then the others.

Bert Gill, Canterbury Infantry[17]

It was the mail and parcels that made a difference, and which reminded men that there was another life away from the war. Bert never got home to see his Soph and Nancy. He was badly wounded with gunshot wounds to the chest, right forearm, legs and thigh during the New Zealand advance on 26 August 1918 and died in a military hospital in France on 2 October 1918, a month before the armistice ended the war.

Bert Gill was one of 12,483 New Zealanders to die in France. Of these, 4722 have no known graves. In some cases these were destroyed by artillery fire and could not be traced. In other cases the dead were among the thousands of bodies that littered the battlefields of the Somme and Passchendaele.

A terrible lot of poppies grow about here in the corn, they look lovely mixed up with the wheat and oats, some delicate colours to, I think they must plant them.

Bert Gill, Canterbury Infantry[18]

Burying an Otago soldier. OFFICIAL PHOTOGRAPH, H SERIES, ALBUM 418, AIM

Heroes of New Zealand

Bert Gill did not see himself as a hero, he was simply doing his job. It was the same for those who were singled out for honours and awards for bravery. Honours and awards were allocated by quota, and no matter how many were recommended, only a certain percentage were approved. Ten New Zealanders received the Victoria Cross on the Western Front, but all were soldiers. Although New Zealand officers were recommended, none of these got past Russell the New Zealand commander who believed officers should not get the award no matter how outstanding the act of bravery as they were only doing their job. The New Zealanders who were awarded the Victoria Cross can be seen as a random cross-section of typical New Zealand soldiers.

Travis's work was invaluable, so capable was he of gently surprising some Germans having their morning cup of tea and leading them gently back

into our lines.... It is not going too far... to say that no individual soldier contributed to our success more than Travis, V.C.

Major General Sir Andrew Russell, Commander NZ Division[19]

Perhaps the most outstanding soldier in the New Zealand Division in France was Dick Travis, a sergeant in the Otago Regiment. He and his gang roamed no-man's-land taking prisoners and bringing back valuable information for the New Zealand commander. Travis was killed by artillery fire in July 1918.

'The Big Pushes'

The German positions that had been stormed one by one were marked by lines of concrete blockhouses — ferro-concrete five feet thick.... They had withstood storms of fire and had enabled the Germans to hold their line with relatively small garrisons of machine gunners.

Ormond Burton, *The Silent Division*[20]

In 1914 the German armies had seized most of Belgium and the important industrial and rail centres of northern France. Once it was obvious that Paris could not be taken quickly they were content to dig in and hold on to what they had won, while they concentrated on defeating the Russians on the Eastern Front. The Germans developed effective defensive tactics that included concrete bunkers and pillboxes manned by machine-gunners protected by barbed wire that dotted the plains of northern France and Belgium in a chequerboard pattern. These can still be found when you visit the New Zealand battlefields at Messines and Polygon Wood. For three years the French and British armies endeavoured to break through the German defences and drive them back to the German frontier on the Rhine. Each breakthrough attempt was a massive undertaking involving the stockpiling of thousands of tons of ammunition, and the movement and supply of hundreds of thousands of men.

Traffic passes unheedingly. At another place about 100 yards from the road, the Germans have got onto a battery and two gun pits are blown up, some drivers get a bit nervy and chase their teams along, mostly they take it all in a days work. About 400 yards in front of the battery which is receiving German attention, two large 'two up' schools are in full swing. The men don't appear to hear the shelling, all their care about is — can the man with 'Kip' head the pennies or not. When a shell catches a few of them, the stretcher bearers and the ambulance men pounce on them and cart them off. The mighty machine never stops. Men take it all as a matter of course, and when they have been sometime on this job they become fatalists and it is just as well it is so.

Francis Twisleton, New Zealand Pioneers[21]

These 'pushes' were dreaded by the veterans, and for each one the high command looked for ways to break through the stalemate. This saw the introduction of technological innovations, such as chemical and gas warfare, the growing size and accuracy of artillery, the use of wireless, the development of aerial warfare, and the introduction of the armoured tank.

Did I ever tell you about these tanks, they do some good work. Great looking affairs and they can go anywhere, stop at nothing, go straight through a

Sergeant Dick Travis VC, DCM, MM, Otago Regiment — New Zealand's 'Upham of the Western Front'. ALEXANDER TURNBULL LIBRARY

Communion for New Zealand soldiers before the battle of Messines, June 1917. OFFICIAL PHOTOGRAPH, H SERIES, ALBUM 418, AIM

fence, don't look for a gate, up hills over roads, any damn where at all. Can't explain the thing exactly, but will tell you all about it when I get back.

Bert Gill, Canterbury Infantry[22]

Technology ahead of tactics

In each case the wish to use something new was not always matched by the tactics employed by the Army commanders on the ground. Until 1918 they used the bodies of their men to bash through barbed wire and German machine guns, and failed.

Now from two directions, half-right, half-left, came the hissing of many bullets, the herring-bone weave of machine gun cross-fire... I glanced right and left and saw the Platoon, thirty of them, crumple and fall, only two going on... A few yards farther on I was nearly knocked down by a tremendous blow in the upper right arm and spun sideways... Pain came the next moment.

Alexander Aitken, *Gallipoli to the Somme*[23]

*If you want to find the old battalion,
I know where they are, I know where they are,
If you want to find the old battalion,
I know where they are,
They're hanging on the old barbed wire.
I've seen 'em, I've seen 'em,
Hanging on the old barbed wire*

John Brophy and Eric Partridge, *The Long Trail*[24]

Gas and grenades

We had been served out with cloth helmets saturated in some foul chemical designed to absorb chlorine while the unfortunate wearer choked to death from natural causes. In France we had received the box respirator which

Gas mask inspection for a New Zealand battalion in the support line. OFFICIAL PHOTOGRAPH, H SERIES, ALBUM 418, AIM

in danger areas were carried on the chest ready for instant use. These covered the face with a rubber mask. A clip on the nose meant that all breathing had to be through the mouthpiece which connected with a tin of chemicals. Drawing a breath was a laborious business which pretty well immobilised you at the time...

Ormond Burton, Auckland Infantry[25]

Grenades were ideal weapons for trench warfare and while certain men were selected as 'bombers', everyone was trained to throw them. There were also rifle grenades, fired from a rifle by a special cartridge. The British Mills Bomb was patterned like a pineapple so that it blew into chunks when it exploded. It was ignited by pulling the pin out, which released the lever, and then you had five seconds before it went off. The German grenades were known as Stick Bombs because of their wooden handles. A string had to be pulled before the grenade was thrown.

The guns

I was one of the gun crew, and I actually fired 43 rounds. This is the first time I've let Fritz have a few, and while I was sitting on the trail handle pulling the lanyard I wondered what damage they were doing.

Bert Stokes, NZ Field Artillery[26]

Artillery was seen as the key to achieving a breakthrough by destroying the German trenches and carving gaps through the wire. The soldiers in the trenches hated the artillery. A shell could land without warning, killing and maiming while leaving others beside them untouched.

One shell landed in the trench near us and gave one of the healthiest and strongest of men shell-shock.... he was half-dazed and jumping at every sound of shell or gun. I told him he would have to go back. He said he wouldn't. That the boys would call him cold-footed. I insisted and after a moments silence he broke down and wept. A nice thing shell-shock, when

A New Zealand 18-pounder in action.
OFFICIAL PHOTOGRAPH, H SERIES, ALBUM 418, AIM

it makes a half-witted snivelling kid of a hard-headed man. And 'tis a knowledge of these things and of seeing good men flinch from duty when their nerve is gone — that, hangs like a waiting beast on its opportunity, that darkens the soul of a man.

George Tuck, Auckland Infantry[27]

On the Somme and at Passchendaele weeks and weeks of artillery fire reduced the landscape to a desert of overlapping shellholes. As winter approached these filled with rain, drowning wounded men who had sheltered in them to escape the gunfire and reducing those who survived to helpless misery.

I have seen human bodies used as temporary railway sleepers and as fascines for moving guns over. I have seen bodies and parts of bodies scattered all over the place lying and decomposing. I have seen roads along the sides of which men — horses and wagons have been lying in broken tangled masses. I have seen men killed by shells, fall in the mud of the road and the traffic go on just the same. Nothing is safe.... Men are smashed and patched if possible and sent back to be smashed again... and so it goes on... But enough of this its 'Just the War'.

Charles S Alexander, Auckland Infantry[28]

We New Zealanders were successful in all but one of the big pushes in France and Belgium, but both successes and failure cost New Zealand dearly in lives and maimed men. Success on the Somme in 1916 cost 7408 New Zealand casualties in 21 days, Messines 3700 in eight; Passchendaele was both success and failure, success on 4 October and failure on 12 October when in four hours of fighting New Zealanders suffered 2700 casualties in the worst day of war in our history.

They had poured out their blood like water. The bodies of 40 officers and 600 men lay in swathes about the wire and along the Gravenstafel road.

Hugh Stewart, *The New Zealand Division*[29]

A 'Blighty one'

Men prayed for a 'Blighty one', which was a wound bad enough to get them out of the trenches and invalided back to Great Britain or New Zealand. Getting the wounded off the battlefield was the job of the stretcher bearers.

We've worked till we got past caring
In the stinking poisoned mud,
And we've gone on stretcher-bearing
With our stretcher soaked in blood.

R B Lambert, *Chronicles of the NZEF*[30]

The doctor and his assistants work at top speed. A dab of iodine on a torn scalp, a pad of lint, a bandage tightly twisted round, and the casualty ticketed up... Next... a smashed hip and a broken leg... His trousers are ripped up, the wounds covered, a rough splint tied from armpit to ankle to steady the limb as the lurching stretcher is carried over the torn ground... So the procession goes on without end.

Ormond Burton, *The Silent Division*[31]

... we had six men to a stretcher and then began the hardest toil I have ever done in my life. Stout leather straps are fastened round one's neck and go down each side to the handles of the stretcher where the loops fit over. Two men walk on each side to stop the sway of the stretcher and help

Stretcher parties, including one of German prisoners, bring in wounded as artillery bursts behind them. QEII ARMY MEMORIAL MUSEUM

138

Doctor bandaging a New Zealand soldier in the front line. OFFICIAL PHOTOGRAPH, H SERIES, ALBUM 418, AIM

lift over trenches, shell holes and any obstruction at all. Positions are changed from time to time and in the dark we stumbled along through thick mud as it had rained during the day. Often we were shouted at by men manning batteries that we were heading straight into the mouth of cannon. The noise all the time of the guns was terrific and at times we had to wait and put the poor wounded man down to rest or let the guns fire. Finally at 7.30 a.m. we got back to a point where the horse transport or wagon could relieve us of our patient... The carry must have been five miles and in the dark it seemed like twenty and I have every sympathy for our patient who not only had his wound to distress him but had to suffer the additional torture of a swaying stretcher handled by men of unequal height stumbling along without being able to see where to put their feet.

Colin Gordon, NZ Medical Corps[32]

'Blighty'

I want to stroll down Bond Street,
Lord, what memories it brings!
I want to see shop windows
Full of flimsy useless things
I long for Piccadilly
And its crowd of lovely girls
With their neat silk-stockinged ankles
And their captivating curls.

C R Baker, *New Zealand at the Front*[33]

Apart from being wounded, the only other escape from the trenches was an eight-day leave pass which came round about once a year, if you were lucky, and if there was not a 'big push' on at the time. It was a chance to visit relations in Great Britain or see the sights of London or Paris. British soldiers on leave had their homes and families to go back to. While many New Zealanders had relations in England to visit, many did not, and the sights and temptations of London led to New Zealand soldiers having one of the highest rates of sexually transmitted diseases of all the forces of the British Empire. This continued until, at the tireless urging of Ettie Rout, the New Zealand authorities began the free issue of prophylactics to our soldiers.

The NZ Club in Russell Square is a fine institution. All NZers gather here and it is their general headquarters while on leave. I took the boys to a fancy boozer or two that I know of.... One bar was half full of mere girls, all of them drinking and using the choicest of soldier's language.... A soldier especially a New Zealander or an Australian have no need to walk about on his own and if you happen to have a few whiskies in and... you hook on to one of these birds you never know where or how the affair is to end...

W K Wilson, New Zealand Rifle Brigade[34]

Paris offered the same temptations.

Arrived Paris 1AM... Taken to YM at barracks, and given feed, & then a lecture on women, & then driven in lorry to flash hotel. Slept till 9, then rose & departed in full pack to Hotel Modern. ([NZ] Club) Got room with 2 beds, all to myself. Fair French damsel seized me & escorted me to the underground station, paid my fare as I had no coppers, & then shook my hand & said goodbye. So they are not <u>all</u> bad. This Hotel Modern is some show. Saw a lady guide re ride in Bois de Boulogne. (20 fr[anc]s) Left at 1PM, had half an hour in the underground, then over 2 hour ride in the Bois de Boulogne, & got back about 5.15. Went to the Folies Belgiere in the evening and got back 11.30.

G C Latimer Clark, Auckland Infantry[35]

New Zealand soldiers convalescing in England. UK SERIES 1368, AIM

Latimer Clark was killed on 30 September 1918.

The End

1918 was the year of New Zealand successes, when its leadership and training gave it the numbers and staying power that other British and Empire divisions lacked. Russell demanded success at minimum cost in New Zealand lives and achieved it with a series of victories. We earned the reputation of being the 'Silent Division', one who got on and did what had to be done without any fanfare or nonsense.

> *I do believe the New Zealand soldier is about the best in the World. I think I have told you before that he is not a great one for singing and laughing, in fact he is rather dour. But on the whole he is intelligent, and if he is told what he has to do, and understands the reasons for it, he is very good. And I must say they are responsive in a quiet subtle way, and they do appreciate it if their offcers look after them and try to lead them properly.*
> Reg Richards, NZ Rifles[36]

Personal cameras were prohibited in France and unlike Gallipoli and Sinai and Palestine this was strictly enforced. All photos were taken by the Official New Zealand photographer and film cameraman, Henry or 'Movie' Sanders, who was a newsreel cameraman with Pathé Frères and was specially enlisted to take film and photographs of New Zealand's efforts on the Western Front. Thomas Scales of Pathé Frères was also enlisted to take similar films and photographs of New Zealanders in England.

> *We now have a divisional photographer appointed to us. He is a regular cockney 'tout', not even a New Zealander and has never been to New Zealand... The pictures will of course be appreciated in N.Z. and you will probably see many more now of our own troops than formerly in the papers... He has a cinema apparatus too and poor old 'movie' as we call him was up close to the line soon after our last big fight to take photographs and got caught... in a barrage. He had his wits nearly scared away and instead of taking pictures he sat in a shell hole all day.*
> G Cory-Wright, NZ Divisional Headquarters[37]

Official artists, George Butler, Alfred Pearce and Nugent Welch, were also appointed to paint and record scenes from New Zealand battlefields for a

King George V presents medals to New Zealanders on Salisbury Plain while a film cameraman captures the moment for history. BRITISH OFFICIAL PHOTOGRAPH, QEII ARMY MEMORIAL MUSEUM

Arthur J Lloyd, 'Soldiers of the New Zealand Division advancing', October-November 1918, Oil. AIM

proposed national war memorial museum. There were also many artists in uniform, both amateur and professional; such as the Auckland artist Arthur Lloyd who was in the NZ Machine Gun Battalion and sketched life in the trenches.

His painting is of the final stages of the successful New Zealand advance towards Le Quesnoy in 1918. It shows the stark realities of war. The diggers who are part of a machine gun team advance behind the leading battalions who have just captured the burning village in the distance. Prisoners are coming back under guard, and the men keep trudging forward, ignoring the signs of recent battle around them. Lloyd shows that war kills both sides, German and New Zealander, and we can see from the twisted bodies of the dead that death in battle is horrible and far from glorious. The dead mule also shows what artillery does to flesh when it ricochets off the cobbled roads. War inevitably destroys both the body and the spirit, and these victories in France had a cost which New Zealand paid in full.

Lloyd and other artists like him, such as John Weeks and W A G Penlington, often let their sketches record their war in place of the more conventional diary. Weeks was a member of No 3 Field Ambulance and painted an ink and watercolour drawing of each location occupied by the Ambulance during the war, using the blank side of casualty report forms for his paper.

It was after the surrender of the old fortress town of Le Quesnoy that we heard that on the eleventh hour of the eleventh day of the eleventh month of 1918, the Great War had ended in an armistice.

In this hour for the first time since facing the enemy my mind allows itself to really believe that I shall see you all again.

George Tuck, Auckland Infantry[38]

So on a cloudless day of sunshine we steamed past the yellow cliffs of Coromandel, into the Hauraki Gulf, past Tiri lighthouse, through the Rangitoto channel where yachts and launches picked us up, round North Head and so up the Waitemata through the circling boats to the wharf while all the sirens sounded and the bells rang. Immense multitudes thronged every pier, and street, and eminence that gave some view of the 'Hororata' as she swung so slowly to her berth at the Railway Wharf.

Ormond Burton, Auckland Infantry[39]

Rolling home,
Rolling home,
Rolling home,
Rolling home,
By the light of the silvery moo-oo-oon!
Happy is the day
When you draw your buckshee pay
And you're rolling, rolling, rolling, rolling home.

John Brophy and Eric Partridge, *The Long Trail*[40]

We garrisoned the Rhine at Cologne for Christmas 1918 and then it was time to go home to New Zealand. OFFICIAL PHOTOGRAPH, H SERIES, ALBUM 418, AIM

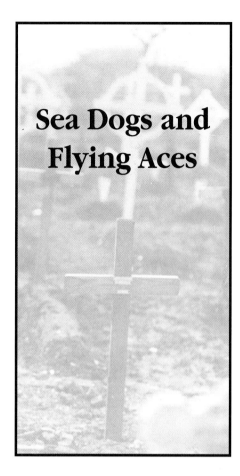

Sea Dogs and Flying Aces

HMS *Philomel*: 'our first ship'

In August 1914 at the start of the First World War New Zealand had already reluctantly decided to follow Australia's example and establish her own division of the Royal Navy with New Zealand-manned ships.[1] A Naval Advisor, Captain Hall-Thompson, had been appointed, and on 15 July the obsolete P-Class light cruiser HMS *Philomel* was commissioned as New Zealand's first naval unit with a Royal Navy crew and a number of New Zealand boy-seamen enlisted for training. On 15 August 1914 *Philomel* sailed with two other P-class cruisers, *Psyche* and *Pyramus*, both of which also had a number of New Zealand crew on board, as escort to the two transports *Moeraki* and *Monowai* carrying the Samoan Force of the NZEF which landed and seized German Samoa on 30 August. HMS *Philomel* then assisted in escorting the New Zealand Main Body of the Expeditionary Force from Wellington to Albany in Western Australia on 16 October 1914.

Initially this convoy of ten transports carrying 8574 men and 3818 horses was to sail from New Zealand in late September.[2] However our government was not prepared to risk the lives of our men while cruisers of the German Pacific Squadron were at large in the Pacific and our battle cruiser HMS *New Zealand* was on the other side of the world with the Grand Fleet in the North Sea. The ships remained in port until more and better armed escorts arrived, including the Japanese cruiser *Ibuki*. At Albany the *Philomel* left the convoy and together with the *Pyramus* started to patrol the Indian Ocean in search of the German cruiser *Emden*. Fortunately for both ships the *Emden* was sunk by HMAS *Sydney* off the Cocos Islands on 9 November 1914. Had they found her first the *Emden* could have sunk them both before they came in range with their guns.

After this the *Philomel* was tasked with patrolling the Red Sea and disrupting Turkish coastal traffic by boarding and sinking coastal dhows. Throughout 1915 and 1916 the ship operated in the Mediterranean and the Persian Gulf. In February 1916, Able-Seaman Knowles, RNR, was the first New Zealander belonging to a New Zealand ship to be killed on active service when a

HMS *Philomel* COOKE ALBUM, AIM

landing party from *Philomel* was fired on by Turkish soldiers near Alexandretta, and three crew were killed and three wounded. The *Philomel* returned to New Zealand in March 1917 and was paid off to finish her career as a training depot and floating accommodation alongside the Devonport Naval Base.[3]

HMS *New Zealand*: 'a lucky ship'

New Zealand's principal contribution to the Royal Navy was the provision of the battle cruiser HMS *New Zealand.* Although it had few New Zealanders on board during the First World War, its exploits were the focus of New Zealand public attention.

On 22 March 1909 the New Zealand Prime Minister Sir Joseph Ward shocked both New Zealand and the British Empire by offering to buy 'one first-class battleship and if necessary two' as a gift to the Royal Navy. This was in response to the threat by the German Imperial Navy to build a fleet of battleships to rival the strength of the Royal Navy. Somewhat bemused by the New Zealand offer the British Government accepted and the keel for HMS *New Zealand* was laid on 20 June 1910. She was launched by Lady Ward on 1 July 1911, and commissioned under the command of Captain Lionel Halsey on 19 November 1912.[4]

The battle cruiser concept was the brainchild of Admiral of the Fleet Jacky Fisher. These were very large, very fast, heavily gunned but lightly armoured ships designed to hunt down and defeat fast commerce raiders, as well as scout the enemy's battle fleet. Armour was sacrificed for speed, and to gain four precious knots, four inches of armour were taken off the ship's armoured belt around its side. This lack of protection did not matter if the battle cruisers were employed in the role they were designed for and used their speed to keep out of the range of battleships and their heavy guns. However because of their size they were included in with the battle fleets.

Between 1906 and 1914 Britain built ten battle cruisers and Germany six. HMS *New Zealand* was a battle cruiser of the Indefatigable class which included the *Indefatigable* and *Australia*. This was the second class of battle cruisers built for the Royal Navy, and the last with 12-inch guns. Both *New Zealand* and *Australia* had slightly heavier armour than the *Indefatigable* but all three ships had inadequate deck-armour protection. This was common to all British battle cruisers. They looked big enough to be battleships but as the Battle of Jutland in 1916 would show they were fatally flawed. That is unless fate had given the battle cruiser special protection as was the case with HMS *New Zealand*.

In January 1913 HMS *New Zealand* sailed to New Zealand to show us the ship we had given the British Empire. She arrived at Wellington on 12 April 1913 and received a tumultuous welcome everywhere she went. She toured both islands, visiting or anchoring off almost every port, and in ten weeks HMS *New Zealand* was visited by nearly half a million people. Those who could not visit saw her image in the illustrated weeklies or on screen at the local picture theatres. During the visit the ship was given a Maori piu piu and a greenstone tiki to be worn by the ship's captain whenever the *New Zealand* was in action. A Maori chief in Rotorua foretold that the ship would be in action three times and be hit but would survive with few casualties.

During the First World War our HMS *New Zealand* was one of the very few of the British capital ships to take part in all three naval battles in the North Sea with no casualties. Her sister ships were not so lucky. The *Indefati-*

HMS *New Zealand* at Nelson on 8 June 1913. F N JONES COLLECTION, ALEXANDER TURNBULL LIBRARY

Sub-Lieutenant Alex Boyle of Christchurch in 1908. RNZN MUSEUM COLLECTION

gable blew up with the loss of almost its entire crew at Jutland and HMAS *Australia* never saw action. The *Australia*, or *'Kangaroo'* as she was known, was in the Pacific during the first battles and then in early 1916 she collided with *New Zealand* while changing course on a foggy night and was damaged seriously enough for her to miss the Battle of Jutland.

Lieutenant Alex Boyle from Christchurch was one of three New Zealand officers serving on *New Zealand*. Boyle was the only New Zealander to remain with the ship throughout the war and was in charge of the twin 12-inch guns of X Turret at the stern of the ship.

Boyle kept a diary which tells us of life on HMS *New Zealand* during the war. On Monday 3 August 1914 the *New Zealand* was with the Grand Fleet in Scapa Flow. What followed was typical of the *New Zealand's* patrols for most of her war in the North Sea.

> *Vice Admiral Sir David Beatty came on board and addressed the men on the Quarter Deck. He made a very impressive speech saying how he trusted all the men to do their jobs and it was 'one thousand pounds to a gooseberry war was coming...' That evening New Zealand sailed. At 3 am 'heard by wireless War was declared on Germany. The first remark made by many 'We have got a medal anyhow'.... Spent next day searching North part of N[orth] Sea for hostile ships, saw nothing.*[5]

On 28 August 1914 HMS *New Zealand* joined Beatty's First Battle Cruiser Squadron off Heligoland Bight in a scheme to draw out German warships into a trap. The plan worked. *New Zealand* was the last ship in Beatty's battle cruiser line firing on German light cruisers and destroyers.

> *We opened fire with A turret at the flashes but couldn't see the hull of the ship. As she drew aft all turrets commenced [firing] mine in the stern last and then all I could see was the mast heads and occasionally the bow and stern. The rest of her was envelloped [sic] in black smoke from bursting shells. She was only 4000 yards off. We fired for 20 minutes getting off 82 common shells at her, until her guns were silenced.*[6]

Boyle's X Turret at the stern 'only fired 14 as the smoke from the other guns made it impossible to see half the time...'. The target was the German light cruiser *Koln*, which continued firing though heavily out-gunned.

> *Not one of her shots hit us. They nearly all went over. I could see her after gun firing till the end. When the smoke cleared you could see all her funnels down and masts gone and she was burning amidships... Anyhow it took 5 battle cruisers some 20 minutes to finish her off. I suppose the whole squadron fired about 350 rounds of common shell from 13.5" and 12" guns. The noise was terrific... It was a very inglorious victory considering our superiority and I think the Germans very, very gallant fellows.*[7]

On 24 January 1915 *New Zealand* was again one of Beatty's battle cruisers when they intercepted the German battle cruiser squadron off Dogger Bank. The *Blucher* which was the rear-most ship in the German line was heavily hit, and became the target of the British battle cruisers.

> *We all then attacked the 'Blucher' and fired off and on at her till 11.50 at ranges decreasing to 5600 when she blew up and sank. It took an awful lot of shot to kill her. For the last half hour shells from our 4 ships were continually hitting her and she was generally on fire. It was really a very pretty sight but pretty nasty for them. At the end we could see all their men*

The *Blucher* heels over and sinks during the Battle of Dogger Bank. IMPERIAL WAR MUSEUM COLLECTION

fallen in on the Q[uarter] D[eck]. Destroyers were sent to pick up survivors they got to her just before she blew up... Personally I don't feel at all satisfied with the day. Our shooting was not over good, we ought to have done more damage...[8]

Poor shooting such as this came to haunt the British battle cruisers at the next engagement which was the major naval battle of the First World War between the British Grand Fleet and the German High Seas Fleet off Jutland on 31 May 1916.

[Boyle] was having tea when suddenly somebody came in and said 'some ass of a light cruiser reports two enemy destroyers in sight and the smoke of a fleet behind them'. Everybody said 'what awful rot' and went on eating. Five minutes later, off went the bugle for action stations. We all flew. I to my cabin to get life saving waistcoat and glasses and eventually to my turret, the faithful one in the stern [X Turret] which I have had ever since it was built... suddenly the order came 'German Battle Cruiser in sight' Load! I looked through my slit in the armour and behold, there they were — five of them — a very long way off.

The sort of feeling one gets when going to the dentist to have a tooth out comes over you. Let's go and get it over. Nobody can truthfully say they enjoy these things. I know I don't...[9]

After about an hour's delay the range gradually decreased and at about 5 o'clock the British and German battle cruisers opened fire on each other at a range of ten miles.

It then came on thick around the Huns and we could hardly see them, while we were in clear weather and silhouetted against a clear sky. This was our undoing as they could see their fall of shot and correct it, and we had great difficulty in seeing ours. They shot well. At about 5.15 there was a roar and a blaze astern. I looked and saw the poor 'Indefatigable' go sky high. She must have been hit in a magazine. It was a dreadful sight. When the smoke had cleared away there wasn't a sign of anything at all with the exception of one raft with two men hanging on to it. They were saved later. I had hardly finished looking at this, when the 'Queen Mary' did the same thing. Her foremast part went off, and her stern came past us sticking right up in the air with the screw going round. When she got abreast of us the stern went up with an appalling explosion. Bits flew everywhere, some came aboard us. How anybody was saved from either ship I simply can't think.[10]

HMS *Indefatigable* explodes after being hit by shellfire at Jutland. *It was a dreadful sight. When the smoke had cleared away there wasn't a sign of anything at all with the exception of one raft with two men hanging on to it.*[11] IMPERIAL WAR MUSEUM COLLECTION

This struck me as a good start for an action which seemed to be going to last hours. I began to wonder when our turn to go balooning [sic] was coming. I didn't have to think long, as suddenly there was a terrific explosion alongside us and the whole place became filled with dense yellow smoke. I shipped smoke pads goggles and everything we are supplied with and slipped down into the turret expecting every moment the magazine would go up. Nothing happened. My gun stopped firing of course, and everybody started coughing. There was absolutely no panic and as soon as the smoke cleared, we found everything worked properly and went on firing. Not a soul was hurt. After a few rounds however, the turret wouldn't train and consequently we had to stop firing. I retired into the smoky bowels of the turret and found everybody very cheerful but a little shaken. I then started off on a tour of inspection of the rollers on which the turret revolves... perspiring freely, partly from fright and partly from exertion we found a shell had hit the armour that protects this roller path and a large bit had been knocked in on the roller. We moved this and some splinters that had got between the rollers and tried to train on the enemy who by this time were on our other beam. So all this time we had been sitting with our backs to the Huns. Not at all nice. Alas she would not move so I decided to be really brave and proceed outside the turret and see if there was anything stopping her outside. There was nothing so a further inspection of the rollers was necessary... I found bits of shell in the rollers, removed them and to our joy the turret went round and we were soon hard at it again... I've never seen anything like it — not only were we fighting the Hun Battle Cruisers but what seemed to be most of the High Seas Fleet as well. There were literally miles of ships and the sea round us boiling with falling shells. It seemed utterly impossible that a ship this size should live in such an inferno. She did and without being hit once again. It was when the High Seas Fleet first came in that the 'Invincible', 'Inflexible', and 'Indomitable' joined us and within three minutes of arriving the poor 'Invincible' went up with a roar. I didn't see her, thank goodness...

At about 7.10 [pm] the Grand Fleet appeared and relieved us a bit. We still went on having small actions with the Hun B[attle] C[ruisers] whenever possible and it was during these actions that I really did see some damage done...[12]

The action went on into the night... staring into the darkness expecting every minute to be attacked by their Destroyers... The other ships in the fleet were hit many more times than we were, but no serious damage done. Our sailors say the Maori's face we have painted on our central top saved the ship. If we painted it out now, I believe they all would mutiny. We are not going to try. The 'Kangaroo' [HMAS Australia] was not there. When the enemy fires at you, you can see the dull red flash of their guns, and then a cluster of dots getting bigger and bigger as they tear towards you. One knows it's no good ducking or getting behind anything, so the only thing to do is to sit still and hope they won't hit you. Get somebody to throw heavy stones at you while you sit still in a chair, and see how you feel.

It's a nice little game, this War. I shan't be sorry when it is all over.[13]

Jutland was *New Zealand's* last engagement. There was only the monotony of patrolling the North Sea for the rest of the war. She took part, however, in the surrender of the German High Seas Fleet. In 1919 HMS *New Zealand* returned to New Zealand with Admiral of the Fleet Viscount Jellicoe, who would later become our Governor General. On her return to England she went into reserve and, though little more than ten years old, was dismantled and scrapped at Rosyth after the Washington Naval Treaty of 1922 between the United States, Britain and Japan drastically reduced the number of battleships and battle cruisers in the Royal Navy.

HMS *New Zealand* in the foreground being scrapped in 1923 at Rosyth, Scotland. NATIONAL ARCHIVES OF NEW ZEALAND

Pelorus Jack of HMS New Zealand

A bulldog named Pelorus Jack was given to the ship by a New Zealand resident in England and became the ship's mascot. The original Pelorus Jack met an unhappy end, being burnt to death after falling down the forward funnel, and was 'Discharged Dead' from the Navy on 24 April 1916. His successor, as Jack had requested in his will, was also a 'bull pup of honest parentage, clean habits, and moral tendencies'.[14] He too was named Pelorus Jack. It was Jack's wish that 'no Dachshund or other dog of Teutonic extraction' be permitted on board HMS New Zealand except only by way of rations for his successor. Pelorus Jack the Second was on the ship in the Battle of Jutland and was gun-shy ever after, 'bolting for his life every time a gun is fired.'[15]

HMS New Zealand was a battle cruiser of the Indefatigable class. She was built by the Fairfield Shipbuilding and Engineering Company at Govan on the Clyde. She measured 590 feet in length, 80 feet in breadth, and displaced 19,000 tons. Turbine engines of 44,000 horsepower driving four propellers gave her a maximum speed of 26 knots. The turbines were powered by 31 coal-burning boilers, and were later converted to burn oil-fuel. New Zealand carried 3170 tons coal, plus 840 tons of oil. Coal consumption per day was 192 tons at 14 knots, the economical cruising speed, and 790 tons at full power. This gave a radius of action of 3360 nautical miles at 23.5 knots and 6690 nautical miles at 10 knots. She carried a crew of 806 in 1913; this increased to 853 by 1919 and 1070 by 1921. Her armament consisted of eight 12-inch guns in twin turrets, sixteen 4-inch guns and two submerged torpedo tubes. She carried sixteen twin 24-inch searchlights. HMS New Zealand cost £1,684,990 plus a further £98,200 for her guns. New Zealand paid for her gift battle cruiser by raising a loan at three and a half per cent over 18 years repaying approximately £140,000 a year until 1927, four years after the ship was scrapped.

Lieutenant Alex Boyle (left of sign) and the crew of X Turret of HMS New Zealand after the Battle of Jutland. Pelorus Jack (the Second) can be seen above the sign in the centre of the picture.
RNZN MUSEUM COLLECTION

New Zealand's other 'Sea Dogs'

I am very sorry to say this business gets on one's nerves. Can you imagine three weeks and over at sea, waiting and watching; we never have our clothes off until we return to Base; we never know the pleasure of a real sleep, only snatches of it; it is, I assure you, enough to kill an iron man, let alone a human being.

Lieutenant Commander William Sanders, VC, DSO, RNR[16]

Lieutenant Commander William Edward Sanders, VC, DSO, RNR. AIM

New Zealand provided many seamen both to merchant ships and to the Royal Navy. Many of these were members of the Royal Naval Reserve. One was the Auckland sailor William Edward Sanders who had earned his master's ticket on the coastal ships working New Zealand waters. When war broke out he journeyed to England, and joined the Royal Naval Reserve as a sub-lieutenant in April 1916.[17]

Sanders served on the Q-ships. These were the so-called mystery ships which looked like inoffensive sailing vessels but were heavily armed with hidden guns. Their task was to defeat the German submarines attacking the convoys and merchant shipping supplying Britain. They sailed alone and seemingly helpless to lure German submarines to the surface where they could use the submarine's deck gun rather than waste a torpedo.

Sanders commanded the topsail schooner *Prize*. In April 1917 it was attacked by the German submarine U.93, which surfaced and opened fire, hitting the Q-ship a number of times and setting it on fire. A specially rehearsed 'panic' crew appeared to abandon ship and U.93 closed to within 70 metres to finish it off. Sanders, still on board with his gun crews, ran up the White Ensign and opened fire. They hit the submarine's gun and destroyed the conning tower, throwing its captain and a number of the crew into the sea where they were taken prisoner. It was thought the submarine had sunk, but the badly damaged U.93 managed to limp back to port.

After this battle Sanders was promoted to Lieutenant Commander and awarded the Victoria Cross. Two months later he was again in action and was awarded the Distinguished Service Order (DSO). On 14 August 1917 the *Prize* was torpedoed and sunk by the German submarine U.48 with the loss of Sanders and his crew. The *Prize* was one of 16 Q-ships lost to submarine attack in 1917. German submarine commanders no longer risked surfacing and sank lone merchant ships without warning.[18] In 1921 the Sanders Memorial Cup was presented for New Zealand inter-provincial yachting in memory of this outstanding New Zealand seaman and naval commander.

Sanders's actions were matched by other New Zealanders in the Royal Naval Reserve. Wybrants Olphert, Ernest Low and Frank Worsley are some whose services were recognised. Wybrants Olphert was an English-born master mariner with the New Zealand Shipping Company. As a lieutenant commander with the Royal Naval Reserve he commanded the Q-Ship *Salvia* and received the Distinguished Service Order and Bar (i.e., was awarded it twice) for actions against German submarines. The *Salvia* was also torpedoed in 1917 and Olphert taken prisoner.[19]

Ernest Low was born in Nelson and was serving as a marine engineer on the inter-island steamer SS *Wahine* when it was called up for war service and the crew enlisted as naval reservists. The *Wahine* had an adventurous war serving as a despatch vessel at Gallipoli, and then as a mine layer in the North Sea from 1916 to 1918 laying a total of 11,378 mines off German ports. Low was also awarded a Distinguished Service Order. He returned to New Zealand with the *Wahine* in 1920, and remained with the ship for 21 years.[20]

Frank Worsley was a master mariner from Akaroa. He captained the *Endurance* in Ernest Shackleton's South Polar Expedition from 1913–16. When the *Endurance* was trapped in the ice and crushed, Worsley navigated Shackleton's open boat 1300 kilometres to South Georgia and made the winter crossing of the island on foot to bring help for his crew. As a lieutenant commander in the Royal Naval Reserve he captained two Q-ships and was awarded the Distinguished Service Order for actions against German submarines. He was awarded a Bar to the Distinguished Service Order for his work behind Soviet lines as a member of the North Russian Expeditionary Force to Archangel in Russia in 1919.[21]

You find New Zealanders everywhere. It was a New Zealander, Lieutenant Commander George Dennistoun of the Royal Navy who sank the German gunboat *Hermann von Wissmann* on Lake Nyasa in 1915 which became the basis for C S Forester's tale of *The African Queen* and the film starring Humphrey Bogart and Katherine Hepburn.[22] These are just some of those known, to which must be added the unrecorded service of hundreds of New Zealand seamen who crewed merchant ships, and served as reservists throughout the war.

German raiders in New Zealand waters

Here was a ship, to all outward appearances just an ordinary large modern steamer on her way from Wellington to Sydney, and with just the usual crew to be seen at their duties on deck. Yet this ship was in reality a heavily armed cruiser; a pirate months at sea and existing on the fuel and provisions she commandeered from captured ships.

Roy Alexander, *The Cruise of the Raider 'Wolf'* [23]

In the First World War there was no threat of invasion to New Zealand. It was also too far for German U-boats or submarines to travel. The threat was from German surface raiders, both warships, such as the cruiser *Emden* that was sunk by the Australian cruiser HMAS *Sydney* in November 1914, and armed merchant ships acting as raiders that attacked shipping around the New Zealand coasts or on the sea routes to Europe with mines, guns and torpedoes. The most successful raider in New Zealand waters was the converted cargo ship *Wolf (II)* which sailed from Germany under the command of Captain Karl-August Nerger on 30 November 1916. The *Wolf* carried seven 150-mm guns, four torpedo tubes, 465 mines, and an armed seaplane nicknamed *Wolfchen*. Its task was to lay mines off the major ports in South Africa and India, and then attack British merchant shipping. The voyage would take 15 months during which she steamed 102,400 kilometres, sinking 13 steamships with her mines, and capturing or sinking another seven steamships and seven sailing ships; totalling 114,279 tons.[24]

During this epic voyage the *Wolf* laid mines around New Zealand in June 1917, and the flight by its seaplane *Wolfchen* was the first flight of an armed warplane in the New Zealand area. Three ships were sunk by mines laid by the *Wolf* in New Zealand waters, including the passenger steamer *Wimmera* which was mined and sunk in the passage between North Cape and the Three Kings in July 1918, one year after the mines were laid.[25] By this time it was known that mines were in the area, and instructions were issued for ships to avoid the passage. Captain Kells of the *Wimmera* ignored the warnings and was one of 26 passengers and crew who went down with the ship.

But to issue mine warnings in the Tasman Sea in those days was akin to warning surfers at Bondi to beware of crocodiles, or to caution hikers outside Auckland to watch out for man-eating tigers.

Roy Alexander, *The Cruise of the Raider 'Wolf'*[26]

Count Felix von Luckner, 'The Sea Devil'

Before I gave an order to sink any of the many ships we accounted for, I took care to see that even the ship's cat was safe.

Count Felix von Luckner[27]

A daring but humane fighter, von Luckner commanded the *Seeadler*, which because of its captain has become the most well known and romantic of the German raiders in the Pacific. Formerly the *Pass of Balmaha*, she was a three-masted full-rigged American sailing vessel which had been seized by the Germans as a war prize for carrying a contraband cargo of cotton.[28]

She sailed from Germany in December 1916 armed with two 105-mm guns and disguised as a neutral Norwegian sailing ship. In 13 months' raiding the *Seeadler* captured and sank three steamships and 13 sailing ships, totalling 30,099 tons. Its luck ended when the ship called at the uninhabited island of Mopeha in the Cook Islands for water. On 2 August 1917 a heavy sea drove the ship ashore and wrecked it. Von Luckner set out three weeks later with a crew of five in one of the two ship's boats that survived in an endeavour to capture an island schooner and then return and rescue his crew. Their presence was reported in the Fiji Islands and von Luckner and his well-armed crew surrendered to Police Officer Hills and the crew of the island trader *Amra*, all of whom were unarmed as the Governor of Fiji had refused Hills permission to carry firearms.[29]

Von Luckner and his crew were taken to New Zealand and imprisoned. Von Luckner and Lieutenant Kirscheiss, who had accompanied him in the boat to Fiji, were held with German internees from German Samoa on Motuihe Island in the Hauraki Gulf. Here von Luckner engineered the escape of Kirscheiss, some German naval cadets and himself by manufacturing swords, knives, a working sextant and a dummy machine gun. They also painted an imperial German ensign onto a bedsheet belonging to one of the cadets. Stealing the prison commander's motor launch they then captured the coastal scow *Moa*. The armed cable ship *Iris* was alerted and gave chase and caught up with the *Moa* off the Kermadec Islands. After a warning shot was fired across the *Moa*'s bow, von Luckner surrendered. He was imprisoned at Ripapa Island in Lyttelton Harbour and was again planning to escape when the war ended.

Flying aces: The first New Zealanders to fly in combat

Every man that took to the air in that first great air war must have been endowed with unusual courage: when every facet of air fighting had to be discovered for the first time; and the very machines in which they flew were so accident prone that merely being airborne was almost as dangerous as being under fire. Whatever their nationality, whether they were fighter pilots, who attracted the widest publicity, or aerial gunners who received none, courage was their hallmark.

Richard Bickers, *The First Great Air War*[30]

A Caudron Mark III E2 aircraft. AIM

Flight Lieutenant William Wallace Burn of the New Zealand Staff Corps, our first professional military pilot. He was killed in action, Mesopotamia, 30 July 1915.
AUCKLAND WEEKLY NEWS, AIM

In 1914 New Zealand had one trained military pilot, Lieutenant Wallace Burn of the New Zealand Staff Corps, and a single military aircraft, the Bleriot monoplane *Britannia*. Both were sent to war.[31]

In 1915 as New Zealand's 'only qualified aviator belonging to the Defence Forces of the Dominion', Burn was loaned to the Indian Government after New Zealand and Australia received a request for pilots for Mesopotamia where the Indian Army was fighting the Turks. Burn was the New Zealand contribution to the Australian 'Half Flight' of four pilots, 40 mechanics, mules and an aircraft workshop. At Basra in Mesopotamia they joined with two pilots including New Zealand-born Major Hugh L Reilly of the Indian Army to become the Mesopotamia Flight of the Royal Flying Corps under Reilly's command.[32]

The Mesopotamia Campaign of 1915 started in administrative chaos and logistic muddle and ended with the disaster of Kut where Major General Townshend's force surrendered to the Turks. In this confusion the Mesopotamia Flight just had to make do and improvise. The aircraft were a mix of ancient under-powered French-designed Maurice Farman 'Shorthorns' and 'Longhorns' (so-called because of the shape of their undercarriage), or 'Rumpties' as they were known, and Caudron aircraft. Each carried a pilot and an observer as crew.

> *Practically nothing was known about flying in tropical climes [and there was] little experience to show the effect of heat and sun and dust on engines and fabrics. Temperatures often exceeding 40 C, navigation was difficult over a largely featureless terrain and beginning in June, a strong, dust-laden NE wind called the Shamal 'blew all day for several weeks.' The flying speed of the Farmans on a calm day did not exceed eighty kilometres an hour and when the Shamal blew 'they simply moved backwards in the face of it'.*
>
> Nick Lee-Frampton, *Anzac Pilots over Mesopotamia — 1915*[33]

The Flight first went into action on 31 May 1915 and provided invaluable air reconnaissance for Townshend's advance. Turkish positions were plotted on maps, and urgent messages dropped to the troops on the ground in tins with streamers attached. (Radio-equipped aircraft were not introduced until September 1915.) The aircraft were also used for directing artillery fire by dropping 'smoke balls' on the target. Bombing was equally primitive. The first one kilogram bombs were dropped by hand by the observer over the side of the aircraft. When the 20 pound (9 kilogram) aeroplane bombs arrived, the bomb-racks supplied with them would not fit, and the bombs were dropped through an improvised hole cut in the cockpit floor.

On 30 July 1915 two Caudron aircraft were returning to Basra. Reilly piloted one and the Australian Lieutenant G P Merz the other, with Burn as his observer. Both aircraft were forced to land with engine failure. Reilly was fortunate to land near a village where the Arabs were friendly. Merz and Burn were not so lucky. They force-landed near a camp of Arabs who attacked and after a running battle killed them. Merz and Burn were the first professional military pilots of the Australian and New Zealand forces to die in war. Ironically because he was attached to the Royal Flying Corps in Mesopotamia, Burn's name never appeared in the New Zealand Roll of Honour. His brother Trooper R B Burn of the Canterbury Mounted Rifles was killed at Gallipoli during the night advance on 6/7 August 1915, seven days after his brother's death.[34]

Learning to fly the New Zealand way

In those early flying boats instructor and pupil would sit side by side. There was no intercom and communication was by signs and a lot of yelling. Air speed indicators were not carried. A taut piece of string from which a fluttering tape indicated drift acted as an artificial horizon for straight and level flying. A good or bad turn in the air was judged by the weight-on-the-seat-of-the-pants method.

David Mulgan, *The Kiwi's First Wings*[35]

In 1915 the two brothers and pioneer New Zealand aviators, Leo and Vivian Walsh, with financial support from R A Dexter established the New Zealand Flying School 'with one home-built flying boat and one self-taught instructor'.[36] The seaplane was the first one to be designed and built in the Southern Hemisphere and the instructor was George Bolt. The school's first home was in a shed built of car cases at Orakei, and from 1916 in similarly constructed hangers on the foreshore around the old stone Melanesian mission building at Kohimarama.

The first three pupils; Geoffery Callender, Keith Caldwell and Bertram Dawson started in October 1915. The fee was £100 and if successful they would graduate with the Royal Aero Club certificate. Graduates would be accepted as second lieutenants in the Royal Flying Corps and on arrival in England three-quarters of the course costs would be repaid.[37] On 28 Novem

A Walsh brothers' seaplane on the Waitemata. *AUCKLAND WEEKLY NEWS*, AIM

155

The New Zealander who destroyed a Zeppelin; Flight Lieutenant A Brandon of Wellington leaving Buckingham Palace after being invested with a DSO by His Majesty the King. *AUCKLAND WEEKLY NEWS*, AIM

ber 1915 Callender became the first New Zealand-trained pilot to fly solo, and both Caldwell and Callender graduated on 22 December 1915. In 1916 a class of 12 students enrolled, and by January 1918 the class size had increased to 25. Students provided their own tents to live in and paid board of £1 a week. Originally it took five to six months to train a pilot, but as the number of aircraft at the school increased this was reduced to three months. Fifteen pilots graduated in 1916, and by the end of the war 110 pilots had graduated from the school. This included the first Maori pilot, Charles Barton, who was commissioned into the Royal Air Force in February 1919.[38]

A film taken by Charles Newham in 1918 shows the daily routine at the New Zealand Flying School.[39] It was run on military lines and pupils 'learned how to build as well as how to fly machines' as the school was also an aircraft factory where the seaplanes were rebuilt and maintained.

A second school, the Flying Training School, was set up at Sockburn in Christchurch in 1918.[40] New Zealand was unique in that its pilot training was run by private enterprise, with both schools dealing direct with the British Government. Together both schools graduated 224 pilots with Royal Aero Club certificates, of which 203 were commissioned. Only 68 of these, most New Zealand Flying School graduates, arrived in time to see action.

New Zealanders in the Royal Flying Corps

Almost 1000 New Zealanders served in either the Royal Flying Corps, Royal Naval Air Service, or Royal Air Force after it was formed by combining these two services on 1 April 1918. At least 70 died and some 17 became prisoners of war. The first New Zealand pilot to capture the public's imagination was Second Lieutenant Alfred de Bathe Brandon who was the first New Zealand airman to be awarded the Distinguished Service Order in October 1916. During the Zeppelin airship raids on London, Brandon destroyed Zeppelin LZ 15 on 31 March 1916, and later severely damaged Zeppelin LZ 33 which was also hit by ground fire and crashed on 23 August 1916. The New Zealand Division had just arrived in France and Brandon's exploits inspired many to apply for transfer to the Royal Flying Corps.[41]

New Zealand flying aces

The Walsh brothers' first two graduate pilots, Caldwell and Callender, both won distinction in Europe. Callender rose to the rank of Captain in the Royal Flying Corps and was awarded an Air Force Cross and the Silver Star of Italy. Keith Caldwell or 'Grid' as he was known joined the Royal Flying Corps in April 1916 and was sent to France in July. He served in 8, 60 and 74 Squadrons, commanding the last in France from April 1918 until the end of the war. 'Grid' Caldwell was awarded the Distinguished Flying Cross and Bar, together with the Belgian Croix de Guerre. Altogether he was credited with 25 German aircraft and while he was regarded as an 'excellent pilot it was considered that had his marksmanship been better, he would probably have become one of the greatest aces of the war.'[42] He was the most successful New Zealand fighter pilot of the First World War.

Graduates included Captain Ronald Bannerman who joined the Royal Flying Corps in March 1917 and flew Sopwith Dolphins with 79 Squadron during the British offensive from August to November 1918. Bannerman shot down 17 German aircraft and was awarded the Distinguished Flying Cross and Bar.[43] He and pilots such as H F Drewitt, A W and F S Gordon, W W Cook, and R Russell proved the value of the Walsh bothers' flying school.

Many New Zealanders applied to become pilots while serving in the trenches in France. One of these was Keith Park, who was born in Thames and on leaving school worked as a purser with the Union Steamship Company. Park served with the New Zealand Field Artillery on Gallipoli, was commissioned and then transferred to the British Regular Army as an artillery officer in 29 British Division. He was wounded on the Somme in 1916 and classed as 'unfit to ride a horse'. This allowed Park to become a fighter pilot on the Western Front.

> It may seem strange that I was considered unfit to ride a horse but fit to fly an aeroplane. But tradition was still strong in those days of horse-drawn artillery — and an officer and gentleman was expected to ride into battle on a charger.
>
> Major Keith Park, 48 (Fighter) Squadron, Royal Flying Corps[44]

Park was posted to 48 Squadron flying Bristol Fighters in July 1917 and flew with it for the rest of the war. He was appointed to command the squadron in April 1918. Park shot down a total of 20 German aircraft and was also shot down twice. He was awarded the Military Cross and Bar and the French Croix de Guerre. He remained in the Royal Air Force after the war and rose to the rank of Air Chief Marshal.[45]

> He was covered with blood all over, although his only wounds were a grazed forehead and a damaged finger; but this was something in the nature of a miracle, because his machine had been shot about in the most amazing manner. In fact I cannot imagine how it held altogether; bullets had ripped it in scores and clusters until there was hardly an untouched portion anywhere. He had accounted for two Huns, but from his own appearance and that of his machine, one might have imagined him fighting the whole German Air Force single-handed.
>
> Vincent Orange, Coningham[46]

Another to earn similar fame was the Australian-born, New Zealand-raised Arthur 'Mary' Coningham who served with the NZEF in Samoa and Egypt. After being discharged unfit for active service, Coningham sailed for England and enlisted in the Royal Flying Corps in 1916. In France he flew de Havilland DH2 and DH5 fighter aircraft with 32 and 92 Squadrons, shooting down 14 aircraft, and being wounded twice. He commanded 92 Squadron in France from July 1918, flying the outstanding SE 5A fighters. Coningham always led from the front and was awarded the Distinguished Service Order, Military Cross and Distinguished Flying Cross. Coningham remained in the Royal Air Force after the First World War, reaching the rank of Air Marshal.[47]

It was men like Park and Coningham and the many other New Zealanders who remained in the Royal Air Force that established the foundation of New Zealand's reputation for pilots that would be again evident in the Second World War.

Remember

'They had poured out their blood like water'

No country sent its soldiers as far as New Zealand did to fight in this most unnecessary of wars. Few countries suffered as many losses. By 1928 the final tally of New Zealand casualties numbered 18,166 deaths and 41,317 wounded, a total of 59,483 out of 100,444 soldiers and nurses who went overseas.[1] An enormous price for a country that in 1914 had an estimated population of 1,089,825, of whom 243,376 were of military age.

The lingering impact of these immense losses is still a feature of the New Zealand landscape, where cenotaphs on lonely hills on country roads carry more names than can be justified by today's farmhouses. It is the same in every town. Each has a memorial to its 'boys' who went to war and never came back.

We have to remember that each of these names was a telegram delivering anguish and uncertainty to a New Zealand family. *'Living, wounded, dead, or missing. Face the words — one must be true'*. In many cases for families; it was the not knowing and the waiting that added to the agony. Each death was a rock thrown into the pool that is small town New Zealand, and the ripples spread. No one was untouched. Each week the centre pages of the illustrated papers displayed the faces of the dead and wounded. At the same time young men who had turned 20 were still being farewelled from the local hall, presented with an inscribed watch and a soldier's bible, each promising to do his bit for King and Country, and going off to war.

Almost a generation of the best men were wiped out, and throughout my life I have been conscious of this deprivation. In all walks of life many of those who would have been the leaders were missing. The ineptitudes of the decades between the two wars, both in Europe and in New Zealand, may in large measure be due to this. Not only these men, but those who would have been their children are missing, and we have had to do our best without them.

Douglas Robb, *A Medical Odyssey*[2]

Coming home

Most wounded men simply wanted to put the war behind them and pick up from where they had left off. Many young men had never established themselves in a trade or career. At 18 they had pushed their age up a year or two with the connivance of a sympathetic Staff Sergeant at the local Territorial drill hall, and had gone off to war. Soldiering and the comradeship of the trenches was the only profession they knew. Looking back from the distance of New Zealand these young veterans were glad to be out of it. They had hated the senseless regulation of army life, the food, the dirt, lice, flies and disease. The ever-present smell of quicklime on the latrines and the dead, the distinctive stink of which also lingered. They also felt guilty that they had survived and good mates had died. There had been no sense to the killing. It was better put behind them, resettlement on the land or in a small business offered that chance, but war and its effects refused to go away.

Our heroes still lie in France. NZ OFFICIAL PHOTOGRAPH, H SERIES, AIM

THEIR·NAME·LIVETH·FOR·EVERMORE

The names of New Zealand dead in an English churchyard. ALEXANDER TURNBULL LIBRARY

Well you would go for an interview [for a job], everything was satisfactory until they saw your discharge certificate and that you were no longer fit for active service, and they would say, 'Oh well, we will let you know', and they didn't let us know.

Henry Lewis, Otago Infantry[3]

For the veterans the 1920s became years of struggle, years of being in and out of sanitariums and hospitals and leaving the wife to cope. They sought escape with their wartime comrades. This was the paradox that war had left with them. For all its insanity and horror the Great War provided men and women with a sense of comradeship and belonging which many of them could never find again when they came back to New Zealand. Many clung to unit associations and as time passed grew to treasure the memories of those years which were kindled at every annual reunion.

Alec, Max, Bill, and Josephine who was 'knee high to nothing' all went off to war. The family lived at Maungakaramea in Northland. Josephine went nursing and was at the New Zealand hospital at Walton-on-Thames in England. Dad (Alec) ended up in there too. Josephine was called 'Spitfire Kate'. She didn't marry until she was 75 and learned to drive after she was married. Too independent and a real nursing sister. Dad had been gassed in one lung in France and always slept sitting up for the rest of his life. He was tough and hardy and lived to 89, and his brothers did as well. They never talked about the war — only at commemoration times and then it came out. All had been kauri bushmen before they joined up. They went away with their mates, and that comradeship lasted all their lives.

Betty Stewart (née Adams)[4]

It was not just the dead that we lost. We sent the fittest we had. They sailed full of the immortality of youth. They saw death in war in all its sense-lessness and were pushed to breaking point. They came back still young in years but conscious of their own mortality. They had pushed themselves to the brink and could never push themselves that far again. The government

'The Casualty List'. AUCKLAND WEEKLY NEWS, AIM

looked at re-establishing soldiers on the land and the Discharged Soldiers Settlement Act was passed. Crown land was allocated and private land purchased and divided up into blocks and balloted to soldiers. It was one of many such initiatives.

> *Conditions for the soldiers' first year were primitive, even for fit young men; but not many of these fifty-five were fit. One or two were badly wounded and had perhaps been granted farms because they had young sons to help. Some had lung damage from mustard gas. Many had gunshot wounds. Others had health seriously impaired by trench diseases. All had suffered emotionally and mentally, a few seriously so.*
>
> Sidney M Perry, *Soldiers of the Mangateparu*[5]

They were a crippled generation. Tony Fagan who had fought on Gallipoli and in France went to see his former commanding officer, Arthur Plugge, who had commanded the Auckland Battalion at Gallipoli. Headmaster of Dilworth School, Plugge was one of New Zealand's Gallipoli heroes. Fagan found him share-milking at Taupiri and living in a lean-to alongside the milking shed.

> *Those that war destroys aren't those who are killed or wounded. The real casualties are those who come back, and who have to go on as if nothing has happened.*
>
> Tony Fagan, Auckland Infantry[6]

Anzac Day: joy and sadness

> *Men of our islands and our blood returning*
> *Broken or whole, can still be reticent;*
> *They do not wear that face we are discerning*
> *As in a mirror momentarily lent.*
>
> *A glitter that might be pride, an ashy glow,*
> *That could be pity, if the shapes would show.*
>
> Allen Curnow, *Attitudes for a New Zealand Poet II*

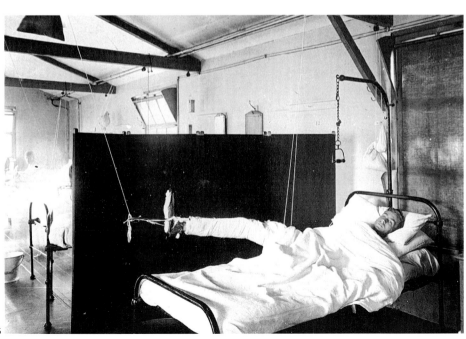

Alive, but....NZ OFFICIAL PHOTOGRAPH, UK SERIES

160

It started spontaneously in 1916 when large crowds gathered throughout New Zealand to mark the first anniversary of Anzac Day. Anzac Day was also remembered among the men of the New Zealand Division in France and among the Mounted Rifles in Egypt. In the New Zealand convalescent camps and hospitals in England members paraded and were inspected by Sir William Birdwood who commanded the Anzac Corps at the landing, and a ceremony was held in Westminster Cathedral with Australians and New Zealanders parading down Pall Mall.

At the front and in the camps Anzac Day was a day for sports, entertainment and a few beers. It was for remembering mates who had gone and enjoying the fellowship of those that remained. It was different in New Zealand. Here Anzac Day was a day of mourning for the dead. Except for 1917 it has always been held on 25 April each year and has become the day we remember all New Zealanders who fought and died in war. It has not got the heroic and national overtones that accompany the day in Australia where the focus is on the parade of those who fought as much as remembering those that died. Now as the number of veterans of the two world wars dwindles it has become a day of discovery for us, where generations who have never experienced war look at the names and ask who were they and why did they go?

The first shiploads of wounded arrived back on the *Willochra* in July 1915. These were the first of 41,315 wounded who arrived back during the war in 95 ships. Those fit enough were picked up from the wharf or station and driven through the town as heroes. It was a role they wore with diffidence. It was impossible to talk about what war was like, and the family that came to greet them did not know what questions to ask.

> *When I came back from the war I landed in Auckland. An uncle of mine came down to meet me from the boat. He took me to his home in Devonport and left me with a couple of aunts of mine. One of the aunts touched the single pip of the Second Lieutenant's rank on my sleeve and said: 'What did you get that for?' I didn't get time to answer. The other aunt said. 'Kate, you're not to ask questions. You're not supposed to ask questions.*
>
> *I went home to a father, mother and four sisters and no one ever asked me what it was like. For seventy years no one ever asked me what is was like.*
>
> Cecil Burgess, Wellington Infantry[7]

Fred Rogers of the Otago Battalion returns to ANZAC for the seventy-fifth anniversary in 1990. DEFENCE PUBLIC RELATIONS

Returned servicemen, attended to by Boy Scouts, outside Parliament Buildings, Wellington. ALEXANDER TURNBULL LIBRARY

Of the 18,166 New Zealand
dead of the First World War:
12,483 died in
France and Belgium
2721 died during the
Gallipoli Campaign
381 died in
Sinai and Palestine

Many of our dead lie in
unknown graves:
4227 in France and Belgium
1684 at Gallipoli
61 in Sinai and Palestine

Opposite: (top) General Godley inspects New Zealand's wounded veterans before their return home. ALEXANDER TURNBULL LIBRARY; *(bottom left)* The machine gun detachments of the German defence were manned by their best soldiers, who were prepared to fight to the last to stop the British attack. AIM; *(middle)* Mr William Massey, the New Zealand Prime Minister, and Sir Joseph Ward receive a haka from the Pioneers. ALEXANDER TURNBULL LIBRARY; *(bottom right)* New Zealand soldiers cheering victory and the promise of returning home. IMPERIAL WAR MUSEUM

This page: (top) Piko nei te matenga — When our heads are bowed with woe. The burial of Lieutenant Colonel G A King, Ypres 14 October 1917; *(middle)* The Division was sated with death and more meant little; *(bottom left)* Men of the 9th Hawke's Bay Company of the Wellington Regiment receive their tot of rum; *(bottom right)* The price of victory. ALL QEII ARMY MEMORIAL MUSEUM

PART 4

The Second World War
1939-1945

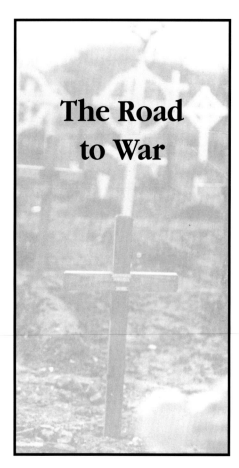

The Road to War

In simplest terms the question who or what caused the Second World War can be answered in two words: Adolf Hitler.

Eric Hobsbawm, *Age of Extremes*[1]

To make Adolf Hitler, Chancellor and Führer of Germany, solely responsible for the number of wars that merged to become the Second World War of 1939–1945 is too simple an answer, but it is a good place to start. Of all the wars that New Zealand has been involved in, the Second World War was most clearly a 'just' war where the evils represented by the Fascist powers were real and had to be opposed.

Hitler's ambitions brought war to Europe in 1939, but the conflict was hastened by the aggressive ambition of Mussolini in Italy, Stalin in the Soviet Union, and the military-dominated government of Imperial Japan in Asia. Each was prepared to fight to achieve its national aims. By contrast the human and economic costs of the First World War had exhausted the democracies of Europe and America.

The Rising Sun

China's abundant natural resources are an indispensable element in both our economic development and our defence.

Japanese Defence Plan of 1923[2]

In the First World War Japan had been one of the Allied powers and had gained control of the Caroline, Marshall and Mariana Islands, former German colonies in the Pacific. The growing power of Nationalist China and the Soviet Union and the impact of the economic depression in the 1920s alarmed Japan. The Japanese Imperial Army ignored weak Japanese civilian governments and set out to expand Japan's economic power by military action in Asia.

Manchuria was invaded in 1931 and a puppet state, Manchukuo, established. In 1933 Japan withdrew from the League of Nations. China came under growing Japanese military pressure and in 1937 open war broke out. The city of Nanking fell to the Japanese Army and the massacre, rape and looting which followed revealed to the West the nature of the horror and atrocities that became characteristic of Japanese military expansion in the eight years of war that lay ahead.

War!

Both with gratitude for the past, and with confidence in the future, we range ourselves without fear beside Britain. Where she goes, we go. Where she stands, we stand.

Prime Minister Michael Savage in a radio broadcast to New Zealand, 5 September 1939[3]

On 1 September 1939 Germany invaded Poland. In New Zealand Michael Savage's Labour Government proclaimed a state of Emergency to prepare us for war. On 3 September at 9.30 p.m. New Zealand Standard Time we declared war on Germany, together with the United Kingdom, France, India, Australia

Previous page:
Kittyhawks being maintained at Emirau Island in the Bismarck Archipelago.
NZ HERALD

and Canada. Our weak and ill-equipped Territorial Forces were mobilized and the coastal defences manned. The two cruisers of the New Zealand Division of the Royal Navy went to sea. HMS *Achilles* sailed for America and the HMS *Leander* took our few regular infantry soldiers to guard the important cable station at Fanning Island in the Pacific.

On the outbreak of war Savage was already a very sick man and would die on 27 March 1940. From the outbreak of war his Deputy Peter Fraser carried the burden as acting Prime Minister; it was a role he would fulfill throughout the war. Despite Savage's statement of willingness to follow Britain, it was a willingness tempered by the knowledge of 60,000 New Zealand casualties in the First World War and reinforced by the determination to ensure that New Zealand's national interests were never forgotten. No advice that Britain offered would ever again be accepted unquestioned. Fraser refused to let the First Echelon of the Second New Zealand Expeditionary Force sail 'unless more adequate naval protection was provided.'[4] Fraser asked for a battleship, and because of this the battleship HMS *Ramillies* escorted the New Zealand convoy to war. Despite having gone to prison for sedition in the First World War, and having voiced his opposition to conscription as recently as April 1939, Fraser, like Churchill in Britain, was New Zealand's man for the crisis.

Off to war

Leaving home finally was a dreadful experience. Dad was okay but Mum and the girls were very upset. Mum had a brother in the 1914–1918 war, and although he returned, she did not expect me to be so lucky. She was distraught and very fearful for my safety. The mail-coach driver tooted the horn. 'Get on the bloody bus and go, lad,' said Dad. 'Mum will recover.'
Shorty Lovegrove, NZ Divisional Cavalry[5]

In 1939 New Zealand was far less prepared for war than we had been in 1914. Our Territorial Forces had been run down to almost nothing during the Depression of the 1930s and we lacked modern arms and equipment. We

Milestones to war

1919	Treaty of Versailles
1931	Japan invades Manchuria
1933	Hitler appointed Chancellor of Germany
1935	Italy invades Ethiopia
1936	Germany re-occupies the Rhineland
1936–37	Spanish Civil War
1938	11 March Germany annexes Austria
	29 September the Munich Crisis, when British Prime Minister Neville Chamberlain announces 'Peace in our time'
1939	14 March Germany occupies Czechoslovakia
	7 April Italy invades Albania
	23 August Hitler and Stalin sign a non-aggression pact
	1 September Germany invades Poland
	3 September France, United Kingdom, Australia, India and New Zealand declare war on Germany
	6 September South Africa declares war on Germany
	10 September Canada is now at war with Germany
	17 September USSR invades Poland
	27 September Warsaw, the capital of Poland, falls

Volunteers lined up in the Rutland Street Drill Hall to register with their chosen units. AUCKLAND WEEKLY NEWS, AIM

The Second Echelon march down Queen Street before departing our shores, April 1940. *THE WEEKLY NEWS*, QEII ARMY MEMORIAL MUSEUM

went to war expecting old men who had been good soldiers 20 years before, and who had done little military training since, to lead the next generation of young men. We were wrong, and had to learn by our mistakes in Greece, Crete and North Africa, at the cost of many New Zealand lives, until we finally forged an effective New Zealand Division by the end of 1941.

On 6 September 1939 Cabinet authorised the mobilisation of a Special Force of 6600 volunteers between the ages of 21 and 35 for active service within and beyond New Zealand.[6] By 5 October enlistments totalled 14,983. Our government now offered Britain a complete infantry division to be raised in three echelons each of 6600 to serve in the Middle East.[7]

Freyberg, VC

Major General Bernard C Freyberg, VC, DSO who had retired from the British Army in 1937, offered his services to the New Zealand government and was selected to command what would become the Second New Zealand Expeditionary Force (2NZEF). It was much more than a Division, it was our nation's army, manned by New Zealand citizens; the focal point of public interest and the visible evidence of our war effort. The New Zealand government gave Freyberg the powers to match, and he could appeal over the heads of his superior military commanders direct to the New Zealand government if he thought his New Zealanders were being wrongly employed or faced serious casualties for no good purpose.

The First Echelon entered camps at Papakura, Hopuhopu, Ngaruawahia, Trentham and Burnham on 3 October 1939. Recruiting also began for 28 (Maori) Battalion. The First Echelon sailed for Egypt on 5 January 1940. It was followed by the Second Echelon, including 28 (Maori) Battalion, on 2 May 1940. Because of the fall of France, they were diverted to the United Kingdom to assist it against the threatened German invasion. The Third Echelon sailed on 27 August 1940.

It took eighteen months before the New Zealand Division was ready for operations. It assembled at the bleakest period in Britain's history, with Europe overrun and its bases in Egypt threatened by Italy. Our division was seen by the British High Command as a source of urgently needed manpower. When Italy entered the war, Freyberg had to strike the balance between vital training and supporting operations by O'Connor's Western Desert Force in Libya. He provided signallers and transport, and reluctantly allowed personnel from Divisional Cavalry and 27 (Machine Gun) Battalion to be temporarily detached to the Long Range Patrol, later better known as the Long Range Desert Group (LRDG). They were to remain temporarily detached until 1943. Freyberg's New Zealand Division was not complete in Egypt until joined by the Second Echelon from the United Kingdom on 3 March 1941. Three days later on 6 March 1941 the first of the Division embarked for Greece.

Egypt

Thursday, 25th April 1940. Anzac Day. Have read and reread of the Anzacs but never thought that one day I would be one myself. Let's hope I and everyone else measures up to their standard.

Clarence Moss, 27 (Machine Gun) Battalion[8]

Sailing for war. WICKHAM COLLECTION, AIM

Egypt became the training base of the New Zealand Division as it gradually assembled throughout 1940 and lemon squeezer hats were once again seen in Cairo's streets. The Second New Zealand Division, 18,000 strong,[9] consisted of three infantry brigades; 4, 5 and 6 Infantry Brigades, each with its regiment of 25-pounder field guns. (So-called because of the weight of the shell that it fired). Each infantry brigade had a battery of anti-tank two-pounders, which were later replaced by six-pounders, whose members were mainly New Zealanders who had enlisted in England, a battery of Bofors anti-aircraft guns, engineers, a machine gun company firing Vickers machine guns from 27 (Machine Gun) Battalion, signals, transport, ordnance and everything else needed to make each brigade of over 6000 men, vehicles and equipment work effectively.

Unlike the First World War, where the battalions were named after their province, they were now only numbered: 18, 21 and 24 were from Auckland; 19, 22 and 25 from Wellington; and 20, 23 and 26 from the South Island. As the diagram below shows, each brigade had one battalion from each district with 28 (Maori) Battalion being usually attached to the 5th Brigade.[10]

Soldiers of 28 (Maori) Battalion on leave in London. JORDAN COLLECTION, AIM

2ND NEW ZEALAND EXPEDITIONARY FORCE
2NZEF
(Maadi Camp, Egypt)

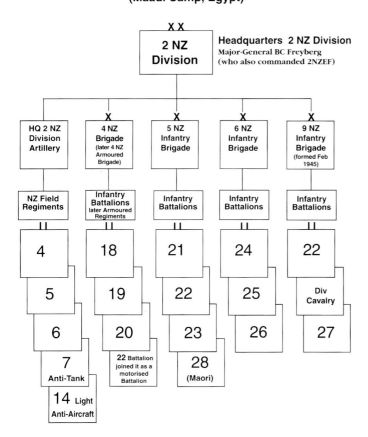

Organisation of the Second New Zealand Division. This diagram does not show signals, cavalry, engineers, transport and supply organisations. AIM

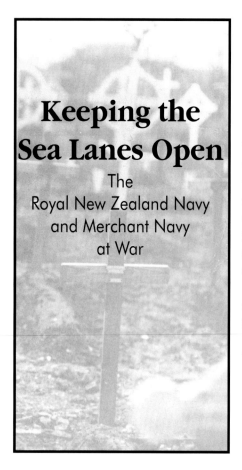

Keeping the Sea Lanes Open

The Royal New Zealand Navy and Merchant Navy at War

Our Cruisers: HMNZS *Achilles*, *Leander* and *Gambia*

We started the war as the New Zealand Division of the Royal Navy[1] with the two modern 6-inch gun cruisers of the Leander class, HMS *Achilles* and *Leander*, the minesweeping trawler *Wakakura* and our first ship, *Philomel*, which was now a hulk tied against the Navy Wharf at Devonport in Auckland. A number of small ships were hastily commandeered and used for port inspections or fitted as minesweepers. Four-inch guns were fitted to protect our merchant ships, and the Union Steam Ship Liner *Monowai* was requisitioned and fitted out as an armed merchant cruiser.

The *Leander* first took a garrison to Fanning Island, and *Achilles*, commanded by Captain W E Parry, took up war station patrolling the South Atlantic off South America searching for German transport ships and surface raiders.

'Make way for the Digger flag!': Achilles *at the River Plate*

> *The gun crews worked liked galley slaves, loving it all, with no time to think of anything but the job. The whole of the Turret from top to bottom thought that the action lasted about twenty minutes. The rammer numbers were very tired towards the end, but they did not appear to notice that till it was all over... Men lost all count of time.*
>
> Turret Officer, HMS *Achilles*[2]

In company with the cruisers *Exeter* and *Ajax*, *Achilles* fought the first naval action of the war against the German pocket battleship *Admiral Graf Spee* on 13 December 1939.

> *When the alarm rattlers sounded in the* Achilles, *a signalman with a flag under his arm ran aft shouting: 'Make way for the Digger flag!', and proceeded to hoist a New Zealand ensign to the mainmast head to the accompaniment of loud cheers from the 4-inch gun crews. For the first time a New Zealand cruiser was about to engage the enemy.*
>
> S D Waters, Royal New Zealand Navy[3]

The *Admiral Graf Spee*, commanded by Captain Hans Langsdorf, was an armoured cruiser armed with six 28-cm (11-inch) guns which had been specially designed to circumvent the provisions of the Washington Naval Treaty by giving Germany cruiser-size ships with much heavier fire-power than normal for ships of this tonnage. The *Admiral Graf Spee* had sunk nine merchant ships in the Indian Ocean before sailing to intercept a convoy in the River Plate area. There it ran into the three cruisers of Force G, commanded by Commodore Harwood, that had been searching for it. In the 80-minute battle that followed *Exeter* was badly damaged and forced to withdraw. *Ajax* and *Achilles* were also damaged and withdrew out of range but continued to shadow the *Admiral Graf Spee*, which had received enough damage to make it unseaworthy for the dash back to Germany. The *Admiral Graf Spee* sailed into Montevideo in neutral Uruguay where Langsdorf was told he would have to sail within 72 hours or face internment. On 17 December Langsdorf sank his ship outside the harbour and committed suicide. This was hailed as a

The forward guns of *Achilles* while their crews take a spell after the action. RNZN MUSEUM

major victory, and *Achilles* and her crew returned to New Zealand to a heroes' welcome on 23 February 1940. British casualties numbered 72 killed and 47 wounded, of which four of the killed and nine of the wounded were from *Achilles*.[4]

Leander *sinks* Ramb I

Leander was tasked with convoy protection duties in the Red Sea. This was followed by convoy escort duties in the Indian Ocean and on 27 February 1941 *Leander* sighted a merchant ship that refused to answer signals. It proved to be the Italian raider *Ramb I*.

> *When ordered to stop she hoisted the Italian ensign and opened fire at 3000 yards. A few shell splinters hit the* Leander, *who fired five salvos in one minute. It was then seen that the Italians were abandoning ship and that their flag had been struck. Their ship had been hit many times, and through a large hole in her side it could be seen that she was burning.*
>
> S D Waters, *Leander*[5]

The Italian raider *Ramb I* on fire after being hit by *Leander*. RNZN MUSEUM

Almost a New Zealand cruiser

In 1941 our government agreed to man and maintain a third Leander class cruiser, HMS *Neptune*, which, since now we had the Royal New Zealand Navy, would become HMNZS *Neptune*. It never happened. En route to New Zealand, and with a fifth of its crew New Zealand sailors, *Neptune* was retained in the Mediterranean for escort and shore bombardment duties. At 1 a.m., 19 December 1941, *Neptune* ran into a minefield and hit three mines in rapid succession. Attempts to reach the ship saw an accompanying destroyer also hit a mine. Captain O Conor, commanding *Neptune*, refused further assistance and being close to an enemy coast with daylight approaching the other ships had to withdraw. By then the *Neptune* hit a fourth mine and sank in heavy seas. Sixteen seamen, including the captain, survived the night on a raft but when picked up by an Italian warship six days later only one seaman remained alive. More than 750 men died, 150 of them New Zealanders. It remains our worst naval disaster.[6]

> *I clearly cannot help. God be with you.*
>
> Signal on the news of the sinking of HMS *Neptune*[7]

At war with Japan

Both cruisers and the *Monowai* were involved in escort work in the months following Japan's surprise attack on Pearl Harbor, and it was the *Monowai* that was first involved with the Japanese navy when it unsuccessfully fired on a Japanese submarine on the surface off Fiji in January 1942. *Leander* was the first New Zealand ship to take an active part in the Guadalcanal campaign (escorting transports carrying United States Marines) from September to November 1942; the critical phase of the battle for control of Guadalcanal and the sea routes around it. *Achilles* relieved *Leander* in December 1942 and continued the vital convoy escort role as part of the American Task Force. On 4 August the Task Force was attacked by Japanese aircraft off Guadalcanal.

> *I remember the action stations being sounded and my action station was in the high power switchboard and I'd no sooner got there and the telephone rang and they said 'X' Turret was out of action so we took all the power off from 'X' Turret, and the ship gave quite a lurch when she was hit.... it wasn't until after we'd fallen out from action stations that we saw the damage that had been done. There were about 11 killed instantly and two died later on.... We heard afterwards it was rather lucky it hadn't hit a few yards back because it may have gone through the after magazine which would have been the finish of us. I take my hat off to some of the seamen boys. They were only young lads and they cleaned up what was left of the blokes with a shovel and bucket and never turned a hair. It was a pretty frightful mess.*
>
> Heath Simcox, RNZN, HMNZS *Achilles*[8]

After temporary repairs, *Achilles* returned to Auckland and then went to Britain for a major refit. It would be two years before it returned to New Zealand. In April 1943 the *Monowai* was also released from navy service for use as a fast troop transport in European waters. In the United Kingdom, *Monowai* was converted to an assault ship or Landing Ship Infantry (LSI) as they were known, and fitted with 20 assault boats capable of landing 800 troops at a time. *Monowai* took part in the D Day Landings on Normandy, landing British and Canadian soldiers on Gold Beach. In total *Monowai* carried 73,000 Allied soldiers to France in the coming months, and was then employed in the Mediterranean and Indian Ocean.

Leander *torpedoed off Kolombangara*

> *The supply fans roared to the demand for higher air pressure as the engine throttles were eased open for full speed. Stop! Full astern! Full ahead!... Our boilers pulsated and roared. Furnace flames spat out with every salvo. Dull thuds around us. Bombs? No, enemy shells exploding in the sea, more likely. Loud speakers told us that our force had run into a Japanese cruiser and destroyer squadron. The ship quivered as the salvoes thundered. A crash — sudden darkness — the ship lurching and heeling over — an almost incredible silence.... With communication lines dead and in semi-darkness we did our best to give steam. Slow ahead! All day we flogged those boilers. Nightfall saw us safe in harbour, battered, torn, but not beaten.*
> Stoker, RNZN, No 3 Boiler Room, HMNZS *Leander*[9]

After Kolombangara, cement was mixed for temporary repairs to *Leander* at Tulagi Harbour, Florida Island. RNZN MUSEUM

HMNZS *Leander* rejoined the American fleet in the Pacific in March 1943, and after convoy work joined an American Task Force in the Solomons. On the night of 13 July 1943 she was part of an American Task Force off Kolombangara which intercepted Japanese ships of the 'Tokyo Express' running reinforcements to the island of New Georgia. Both sides opened fire and discharged torpedoes. The Japanese light cruiser *Jintsu* was sunk, but in the confusion of the night action the *Leander* was hit by a Japanese torpedo. It blew a huge hole amidships in her port side, exploding in the No 1 Boiler Room, killing everyone there and flooding five compartments. Seven members of the 4-inch gun above the explosion were also blown overboard and killed, a total of 27 dead. The ship was out of action and in danger of sinking. Its survival was a tribute to the leadership of *Leander*'s captain, Commander S W Roskill, and his training of the crew.

Damage to the side of *Leander* in dock at Auckland. RNZN MUSEUM

HMNZS **Gambia** *and* Achilles *join the British Pacific Fleet*

HMNZS *Gambia*, a light cruiser of the Fiji class, was lent to New Zealand to replace the *Leander*. It and the recommissioned *Achilles* served with the British Pacific Fleet in operations off Okinawa and in the Sea of Japan. Both were involved in defending the fleet against Japanese air attacks, including Kamikaze (Divine Wind) suicide attacks. The *Gambia* was struck in one of these attacks while the 'Cease hostilities against Japan' signal was flying, announcing the end of the war.[10]

Our small ships

The loss of the *Niagara* off the Hen and Chicken Islands to German-laid mines in June 1940 prompted our government to expand our small fleet of minesweepers. Thirteen minesweeper trawlers were built in New Zealand during the war to meet the threat of first German- and then Japanese-laid mines off our harbours. During these sweeping operations the trawler HMS *Puriri* hit and was sunk by a mine in the Hauraki Gulf on 14 May 1941 with the loss of five of her crew. Three anti-submarine minesweeping corvettes, HMNZS *Kiwi*, *Moa* and *Tui*, were built in Scotland for the Royal New Zealand Navy, and arrived in 1942. Four Scottish Isle-class trawlers, each of 560 tons,

HMNZS *Gambia* bombarding Kamaishi in Japan, August 1945. RNZN MUSEUM

173

were also purchased, and 12 Fairmile anti-submarine motor launches were built in Auckland between 1942 and 1943.

On the outbreak of war with Japan the converted coaster HMNZS *Gale* was sent to Fiji and became the first of our many small ships to serve in the Pacific. In late 1942 the four ships of 25 Minesweeping Flotilla, *Matai*, *Kiwi*, *Moa* and *Tui*, began anti-submarine and escort duties in the Guadalcanal-Tulagi area and our flotilla would remain there for the next two and a half years.

Kiwi *and* Moa *sink Submarine I-1 off Guadalcanal*

> *He gave the order to ram. At the same time he thought he'd better let the engine room know what was going on. So he shouted down the voice pipe, 'Stand by to ram.' When the voice came back from the engine room, 'What the hell do you do when you ram?' He replied, 'I don't know, I've never done it before.'*
>
> David Graham describing the actions of Lieutenant Commander Gordon Bridson, RNZNVR, commanding HMNZS *Kiwi*[11]

On the night 29–30 January 1943 the *Kiwi* and *Moa* were patrolling off the north-west coast of Guadalcanal when the asdic watch on the *Kiwi* made contact with a submerged vessel some 2800 metres away. The *Kiwi* immediately began a depth-charge attack, while the *Moa* maintained watch with its asdic sonar detector. After three depth-charge runs the submarine was forced to surface and both ships attacked at full speed, illuminating the submarine with star-shells and firing high explosive from their 4-inch guns and 20-mm Oerlikon cannon.[12]

The submarine opened fire with its heavier 5-inch gun, while *Kiwi* rammed and holed it near the conning tower. Landing barges were seen lashed to the submarine's deck and fully equipped soldiers were seen to jump overboard. *Kiwi* rammed it twice again with illumination from both its own searchlight and that of *Moa*. The *Moa* took over the action as *Kiwi*'s bow was damaged in the ramming and her 4-inch gun too hot to use. The submarine endeavoured

The explosion of a depth charge dropped by a destroyer in the Hauraki Gulf.
RNZN MUSEUM

HMNZS *Kiwi*, 1946. RNZN OFFICIAL PHOTOGRAPH

The remains of the Japanese I-1 submarine sunk by *Moa* and *Kiwi* off Guadalcanal. RNZN MUSEUM

to escape but ran aground on a submerged reef and was destroyed. It was the I-1 Submarine, three times the size, twice the length, and faster than the New Zealand corvettes and as heavily armed as both. Its destruction by our small ships was a major achievement.

The following night *Moa* and *Tui* were on patrol and engaged four Japanese barges off Guadalcanal, sinking two, with the *Moa's* 4-inch gun crew being wounded when Japanese fire ignited the cordite charge at the gun. In April 1943 *Moa* was sunk in an air attack in Tulagi Harbour. The little ships were kept busy on patrol and escort duties. In 1944 they were joined by the New Zealand-based Fairmile motor launches that operated as the 80 and 81 Motor Launch Flotilla on anti-submarine patrol and escort duties in the Solomons.

Unsung heroes: Battle of the Atlantic

I was an apprentice deck officer as a 16-year-old with the British Tanker Company... The convoy itself comprised about 50 per cent tankers. There were three British Tanker Company ships; British Security, British Freedom, and British Splendour, which I was on. We were in one of the central columns of a 32-ship convoy. I was on watch on the port wing of the bridge in the morning about 11 o'clock when there was an explosion which didn't seem to sound very loud, but the ship absolutely heaved out of the water. I couldn't see anything. I ran to the stern of the bridge around the superstructure and there was what was left of the leading ship in the left

About 7000 New Zealand officers and ratings served with the Royal Navy during the Second World War. Our naval strength peaked at 10,635 in September 1944, of whom 4901 were serving in the Royal Navy. We served everywhere on every type of craft from battleship to midget submarine, and in every water from the Arctic to the Sea of Japan.

175

On the signal bridge of a cruiser escorting convoys to Russia. QEII ARMY MEMORIAL MUSEUM

column of the convoy. It was obviously carrying a lot of munitions, because in the time I got to the end of the bridge it was virtually gone. There was no deck left and it was carrying Hudson Bomber fuselages on deck and I could see this aircraft body come down. We thought we were under air attack. The next minute the ship following it, which was carrying aviation fuel, turned hard a starboard to avoid the wreckage, and it was hit by a torpedo, and I had a grandstand view of that as it was coming straight towards us. It was hit and the flames shot up as big as the ship and it was very much like the atomic bomb. And I believe we had a torpedo go across our stern by about 15 to 20 feet, or something like that. I feel that the submarine had stopped engines and waited for the convoy to come up to it, and fired fore and aft tubes for best effect, and it certainly achieved that. Anyway those two ships went. We were ordered to disperse as our escort was an armed merchant cruiser and couldn't do anything in that situation, so we dispersed to all points of the compass. For the next two days we heard distant explosions without any idea what was going on. Then destroyers came out from Iceland and started to round us up, and got us into a convoy and then a Norwegian tanker was sunk, and each night there was explosions.

Frank Pugsley, Merchant Navy[13]

His mother said he went away a schoolboy and came back an old man.
Olwen Pugsley[14]

New Zealand's merchant navy has become the forgotten service of the Second World War. Our sailors served with many shipping lines, including those that serviced New Zealand ports such as the Union Steamship Company, Shaw Savill and the New Zealand Shipping Company. On the outbreak of war the government took control of all shipping services. In 1940 German raiders sank a number of New Zealand ships, including the *Niagara*, which struck a mine laid by the German raider *Orion*, taking with it eight tons of gold and half of New Zealand's entire stock of small arms ammunition which was en route to the United Kingdom to make up for their shortages after the fall of

France and the evacuation of the British Expeditionary Force from Dunkirk. Fortunately there were no casualties.

On 26 August 1940 the *Turakina*, en route to Australia, was attacked by *Orion*. The *Turakina's* master, Captain James Laird, elected to fight rather than surrender. He managed to send a distress signal giving latitude and longitude and stating that he was being shelled by an enemy ship. After being reduced to a blazing hulk the *Turakina* was sunk with two torpedoes. Thirty-five were killed, including the captain, 73 were taken aboard the *Orion* and landed in Bordeaux eight months later and interned in Germany. On 27 November 1940 *Orion* and her fellow raider *Komet* sank the passenger liner *Rangitane* with the loss of 16 lives.

The war saw the steady attrition of merchant ships. Seamen in ships on the New Zealand Register in 1940 numbered 2990. One hundred and ten merchant seamen are known to have been killed and 123 interned during the war.[15]

Flying with the Fleet Air Arm

More than 1000 New Zealanders joined the Fleet Air Arm of the Royal Navy, 738 of whom were commissioned. We numbered 10 per cent of the officers of the Fleet Air Arm, and our percentage in the British Pacific Fleet was much higher. Many New Zealanders opted for the Fleet Air Arm when it became obvious that the pilot surplus from 1944 onwards left little prospect of flying with the RAF. As service with the Fleet Air Arm was considered close to suicidal, there were not so many volunteers and so New Zealanders filled the gaps. We could be found on every aircraft carrier in every theatre of war from the Battle of the Atlantic to the final attacks on the Japanese mainland.

A deck-landing on HMS *Illustrious*. RNZN MUSEUM

Pilots being briefed for an attack on the battleship *Tirpitz* in April 1944. AIM

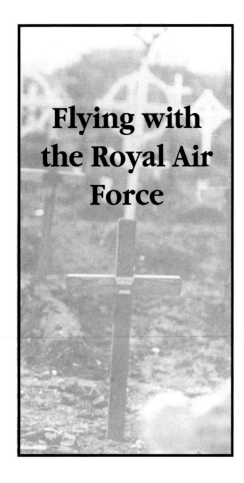

Flying with the Royal Air Force

Empire Air Training Scheme

We were all young and full of fun and they worked the guts out of us.
Bill Simpson, RNZAF, 109 Squadron RAF[1]

The Royal New Zealand Air Force (RNZAF) was established in 1937. On the outbreak of war we saw our role as being the provider of trained aircrew to serve with the Royal Air Force (RAF). A New Zealand quota was agreed under the Empire Air Training Scheme which would see New Zealand train 880 pilots a year, and in addition send partly trained personnel — 520 pilots, 546 observers and 936 air gunners — to Canada, where they would complete their training before being posted to the RAF.[2] When this was agreed there was little perceived threat to New Zealand itself, and it was felt that this could be met by coastal surveillance and reconnaissance against surface raiders. So all that we kept in New Zealand were instructional and maintenance staff, plus the three bomber-reconnaissance squadrons which formed our home defence. Everything was aimed at getting manpower to Britain and by the beginning of 1941 we had exceeded our quota targets, providing 1480 fully trained and 850 partly trained pilots per year.[3]

> *There were about 20–30 NZ's here & our 35 so we are quite a few, there are also Aussies and Canucks. We are in long dorms in 2 high bunks about 50 to a dorm. The conditions and food are not a patch on Taieri.... I'll probably be able to send home some silk stockings later. I'm feeling great & look forward to starting flying when our course starts.*
> Jack Sherwood, RNZAF[4]

Despite the growth of RNZAF squadrons in the Pacific, on the entry of Japan into the war the major contribution of our Air Force was the provision

New Zealanders trained under the Empire Air Training Scheme arrive in Britain, September 1940. JORDAN COLLECTION, AIM

of trained aircrews to the RAF. We were part of a Commonwealth contribution that allowed Britain to expand its first-line combat squadron strength from 332 squadrons in September 1942 to 635 squadrons by the end of 1944. Indeed, until the invasion of Italy, it was the only tangible British offensive in Europe. We were almost too efficient and by 1944 the supply of pilots and aircrew outstripped Britain's ability to provide aircraft. Hundreds of New Zealanders were diverted to the Fleet Air Arm or returned to man our squadrons in the Pacific.

> *The training scheme has been the kernel of our air power. Without it we would have been nowhere with everything in the shop window and no reserves on the shelves.*
>
> Sir Arthur Harris, Bomber Command, RAF[5]

New Zealand Squadrons of the RAF

In the late 1930s, as events in Europe pointed towards war, New Zealand took steps to bolster its tiny air force by ordering 30 of the latest twin-engine Wellington bombers. The first six, along with their New Zealand crews, were just about to fly to New Zealand from England when war was declared. These and the remaining bombers were allowed to stay with the RAF, and became the basis of the famous No 75 New Zealand Squadron RAF. It was the first of seven designated New Zealand squadrons to serve with the RAF.

These 'New Zealand' squadrons were not completely manned by New Zealanders. It was RAF policy to deliberately dilute nationalities throughout the RAF and not place any emphasis on the designated national squadrons. As a result New Zealanders flew in every area of operations in every theatre of war from the maritime patrols against U-boats over the Atlantic to flying Blenheim bombers over Burma in support of the XIVth Army.

There were already New Zealanders in the RAF when war was declared, including many who had served in the First World War and who were now of senior rank. One such New Zealander was Keith Park who commanded No 11 Group and played a key role in the Battle of Britain in 1940. He commanded the RAF on Malta during its siege in 1942, then the RAF in the Middle East and finally was Allied Air Commander-in-Chief in South East Asia with the rank of Air Chief Marshal. Arthur Coningham, another flying ace from the First World War, began the Second World War as a group captain in Bomber Command, commanded the Western Desert Air Force, then the 1 Tactical Air Force in Italy, and finally the 2 Tactical Air Force for the invasion of Europe and the advance on Berlin. Our pilots played a leading role in the first years of the war.

> *I got into a position to fire on the first enemy fighter and saw it go down, leaving a trail of thick, black smoke. It was then my intention to go after the second Messerschmitt; but he got a third shot into me and my engine stopped… I was well over Germany. I could only glide back to France. The second Messerschmitt might get me, but I did have a go at him. He passed underneath me and I let fly at him, but it was no use without an engine.*
>
> *He beat it, and I steered for France. Then the motor caught fire and smoke poured backward. I thought I was done for. I tried side-slipping in the approved style, but it made no difference. I was prepared to jump, but found that the straps of my parachute harness had slipped. So I had to stay there.*

New Zealand Squadrons with the RAF

- No 485 was a fighter squadron flying Spitfires.
- No 486 was first a fighter then a fighter bomber squadron flying Hurricanes, Typhoons, then Tempests.
- No 487 was a bomber squadron flying Venturas and then Mosquitos. It carried out the famous Amiens Prison raid which allowed imprisoned French resistance members to escape. Squadron Leader L H Trent won the Victoria Cross with this Squadron over Amsterdam on 3 May 1943.
- No 488 was a fighter squadron flying Beaufighters and Mosquitos.
- No 489 was a torpedo-bomber squadron with Coastal Command flying in turn Beauforts, Hampdens and then Beaufighters. In 1945 it formed an Anzac Strike Wing with an Australian and British squadron.
- No 490 was a flying boat squadron with Coastal Command flying Catalina and Sunderland flying boats.

'Cobber' Kain, the first British flying ace of the war. JORDAN COLLECTION, AIM

Flight Lieutenant D J Scott, DFC and Bar,
Hurricane and Typhoon pilot.

The fire went out for a while and then started again. The fumes were so
bad that I turned on my oxygen to breathe. I managed to glide far enough
to land on an aerodrome a few miles behind the Maginot Line. The fire
had stopped again. I climbed out and fell flat on my face.

'Cobber' Kain, RAF[6]

This was the stuff of newspaper legend. During the so-called 'Phoney
War', before the fall of France, 21-year-old New Zealand Flying Officer E J
'Cobber' Kain, flying Hurricanes, became the first British air ace of the war,
with 14 aircraft to his credit, before being killed in an aircraft crash in June
1940. It was the month that France fell, and while there were flying aces to
replace him, the war suddenly lost its glamour and became a grim battle for
survival.

Four New Zealanders commanded fighter squadrons during the Battle of
Britain and 95 fought as fighter pilots. It was the Hurricane and Spitfire pilots
such as Des Scott, Al Deere, Johnny Checketts and others who captured the
public attention. We were also strongly represented in both Bomber and Coastal
Commands, but they got little limelight. It was with Coastal Command that
Flying Officer Lloyd Allen Trigg was awarded a posthumous VC in attacking a
U-boat on 11 August 1943 after his aircraft had been set on fire. None of the
crew survived.

Flying with 75 (New Zealand) Squadron, RNZAF

There were the two battleships directly below us. How we weren't blown
out of the sky I do not know. What with the 'FLAK' bursts and the crew
yelling their heads off all inter-communication was lost. I dropped the
bombs but did not see where they landed. We arrived back to base with a
badly riddled aeroplane and a very subdued air crew.

J D Fletcher, RNZAF, 75 (NZ) Squadron RAF[7]

J D Fletcher was a Flight Sergeant and Observer with the RNZAF who trained
in Canada under the Empire Air Training Scheme and was posted to 75 (NZ)
Squadron at Feltwell Airfield in England in November 1941. The Squadron

A Spitfire being prepared for flight. AIM.

began operations with the Vickers Wellington bombers. It was in a Wellington bombing raid by 75 Squadron on 7 July 1941 that Sergeant-Pilot James Ward RNZAF climbed out onto the wing of his aircraft to extinguish an engine fire and became the first New Zealander to be awarded the VC in the Second World War. Ward was killed on a bombing mission over Germany on 15 September 1941, five weeks after the award. In May and June 1942 the Squadron took part in the first of the 1000-bomber raids. It was re-equipped with Stirling four-engine bombers in late 1942 and took part in the Battle of the Ruhr and in 'gardening', or minelaying, operations in 1943 and early 1944 with heavy losses. It was re-equipped with Lancaster Bombers in early 1944 and was tasked on bombing missions over Germany. By the war's end the Squadron had completed 8150 sorties, dropped 21,630 tonnes of bombs and laid 2344 mines.

New Zealand Officer May at the controls of his Lancaster bomber. RNZAF MUSEUM, WELLINGTON

> *Was shot down while bombing ESSEN on 25th March 1942, and spent the rest of the war in the 'Bag' in Stalag VIII B. Lamsddorf, Uber Silecia... We had a full load of incendiaries on board and were supposed to get there first and light up the target... 'WE ARE ON FIRE.' We had been hit right in the incendiaries. I tried the 'FIRE EXTINGUISHER' but the fire had too much of a hold.*
>
> *When I heard that announcement I knew that I wouldn't be going back to base that night. My first thought was for my MUM, how she would take it. My eldest two brothers had been in the 1st World War, poor Mum deserved something better than this.... One of the chutes was on fire so the W/op [Wireless Operator] & 2nd Pilot went out on the same chute. Unfortunately when the chute opened the 2nd Pilot was thrown off....[8]*
>
> *I remember putting my feet out of the escape hatch and the slip-stream whipping me out before I had a chance to change my mind. Counted 5 to make sure I was clear of the burning plane before I pulled the rip-cord... Some Jerry soldiers got a long ladder and helped me down. They then had to protect me from the civvies who wanted to 'do me in'.*
>
> J D Fletcher, RNZAF, 75 (NZ) Squadron RAF[9]

A bombed London street after German night raids. LAUSEN COLLECTION, AIM

A Wellington Bomber of 75 (NZ) Squadron bombs up for a raid. AIM

Lloyd Noble's war

Lloyd Noble's war is typical of that of many New Zealanders who joined the RNZAF and flew with Bomber Command in the RAF during the war. A bomber raid was a highly complex planning exercise, similar in intelligence assessment and planning to a major attack on land. Target decisions would be made at Headquarters Bomber Command by mid-morning and within 10 to 12 hours some 800 four-engine bombers, both Halifaxes and Lancasters, would be on target with an additional 200 Mosquitos in essential supporting and target-marking roles.

While Lloyd Noble talks about his being an 'easy tour', his account helps us to grasp the nature of the risk our airmen took. It is difficult to imagine

Wellington crews, including that of Sergeant Pilot Henry 'Filo' Cotton, DFM, RNZAF (fifth from left, front row). He was 22 years old when he was killed in an aircraft crash in Palestine in 1942. There is a lamp of everlasting flame dedicated to his memory in St Aidan's Church, Remuera. AIM

what it must have been like in the early years of the bomber offensive. Perhaps that can only be fully understood by looking at the casualty lists.

An 'easy' tour?

My crew was a Commonwealth one: pilot and aircraft captain from South Africa, bomb aimer from New Zealand, wireless operator from Australia, mid-upper gunner from England and rear gunner from Wales. At the conversion unit we were joined by a flight engineer. He was Canadian.... we went in August to 1666 Heavy Conversion Unit at RCAF [Royal Canadian Air Force], Wombleton, Yorks, and there met up with the aircraft we were destined to fly in 'Operations Against the Enemy' or 'ops' — the Handley Page Halifax. These were clapped out old Mark II's and V's with Merlin engines and a great number of ops to their credit. Flying could be dicey and casualties were not unknown as we were to find out.

In early September 1944 we reported to 102 Squadron, RAF Pocklington, East Yorks, and immediately commenced familiarisation on the Halifax Mark III. It had more powerful Bristol Hercules XVI engines and was a superior aircraft. On 17 September together with another new crew, also skippered by a South African, we were dispatched over the North Sea to drop time-expired bombs. The other crew disappeared. So before I had flown a proper operational sortie and experienced a welcome from angry Germans 14 men had been killed. This would have been quite normal for many crews. A few days later in response to acute fuel shortages affecting the British army at Arnhem, our squadrons in 4 Group were loaded with 750 gallons of petrol in 165 jerrycans per load which we delivered to Brussels. We flew low to avoid radar detection and in daylight. Thankfully our fighters had subdued the enemy because I hate to think what might have happened if a Folke Wolfe 190 had found us. We did five of these.

Then on 6 October 1944 we made our first operational sortie to Scholven-Buer synthetic oil plant just north of the Ruhr. On the way to the target two Halifaxes from neighbouring Free French squadrons collided and we flew through the debris. There were no parachutes to come out of the aircraft. Our 102 Squadron lost no aircraft but 16 of the 23 aircraft on

Lloyd Noble's Stirling crew. From left: Flight Sergeant Wates RCAF, Flight Engineer; Flight Sergeant Walker RAAF, Wireless Operator; Flight Officer Noble RNZAF, Navigator; Captain Watson SAAF, Pilot; Flight Officer Murrell RNZAF, Bomb Aimer; Sergeant Lewis RAF, Rear Gunner; Sergeant Williams RAF, Mid/Upper Gunner. NOBLE COLLECTIOM, AIM

183

A Manchester bomber in flight. JORDAN
COLLECTION, AIM

The morning after an RAF bombing raid
on the Krupp Works, Essen, in Germany.
AIM

the raid suffered varying degrees of flak damage. Our ground staff counted 77 holes in our aircraft. A navigator well through his tour told me I should be unfortunate to have a tougher op than that. I also recall that on entering the mess a Squadron Leader with First World War ribbons took me by the arm, led me to the bar and said 'give this young officer a pint.' The WAAF barmaid later told me I was ghostly white. I had not long turned 20.

Lloyd Noble, RNZAF, Navigator Bomber Command[10]

Noble noted that despite the damage to aircraft, October 1944 was the first month in the war that 102 Squadron had lost no aircraft and had no crewmen killed. It did not happen again until April 1945.

The price we paid

We had four years away from home growing up from callow youths to seasoned old men seeing death in all its guises.

Bill Simpson, RNZAF, 109 Squadron, RAF[11]

Bombing up a Mosquito fighter bomber. *The Mosquito was beautiful to fly. It was a small cockpit and you were jammed in. It was fast, it would reach a high altitude. It carried the same bomb load as a Flying Fortress with a crew of two compared with a Fortress's crew of 10.*[14] Bill Simpson, 109 Squadron RAF. LOWSON COLLECTION, AIM

Our casualty figures reflect the part we played. In October 1944 New Zealanders attached to the RAF peaked at 6127 out of a total of 10,950 New Zealanders who are known to have served with the RAF during the war. Of these, 3285 were killed, at least 138 seriously wounded, and 568 became prisoners of war.[12] That 30 per cent of all New Zealanders who were attached or served in the RAF were killed beggars the imagination. While not diminishing our air effort in the Pacific, our 338 dead, 58 seriously wounded and four prisoners in this theatre pale in comparison to the costly battle of attrition we fought over Europe. Our contribution has been clouded by post-war debates on the morality and effectiveness of the British mass-bombing offensive. However, what cannot be questioned is the bravery and professionalism of the crews who flew on operations over occupied Europe knowing that the odds of completing the 30 sorties that made up an operational tour were always against them. Certainly the countries of occupied Europe recognised our contribution.

Norway will never forget that men of Australia and New Zealand, in spite of the grave danger to their own countries, went on fighting for our sake on battlefields here.

Admiral H Riiser-Larsen, representing the Norwegian Air Force, 1944[13]

Burying the dead of 75 (NZ) Squadron.
AIM

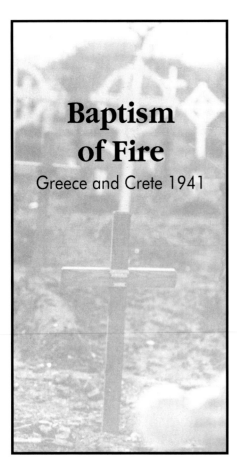

Baptism of Fire
Greece and Crete 1941

The Anzacs in Greece

We did what we went there for and saw some fighting. Our show comprised a dawn attack by the Germans while we were on the Yugo-Slavian front. The odds were greatly in their favour and they had the element of surprise on their side but we beat them easy and what was left after a couple of hours pretty hot fighting surrendered under the white flag. That was the only scrap we had and as you will know we withdrew from Greece without actually meeting up with his troops again. Certainly saw plenty of his airforce however... the dive-bombers and fighters gave us a deuce of a time. Very sorry to leave the country... the people took it very well, and could still wave us a cheery good-bye as we passed through the villages with their homes... bombed in ruins. But war is a dirty business at any time.

Vincent Salmon, 19 Battalion[1]

In March 1941 the New Zealanders, together with 6 Australian Division and 1 British Armoured Brigade, found themselves in Greece as part of 'W' Force to assist the Greek armies defend Greece against the anticipated German invasion. This was the first time that Freyberg's New Zealand Division had been committed to operations. All of Europe except Greece had fallen. In hindsight this was a hopeless military undertaking that should never have been contemplated. Both the Australian and New Zealand governments were reluctant to see their forces committed to an enterprise with the potential to be another ill-fated Gallipoli Campaign. On 6 April 1941 Hitler launched a full-scale invasion of Yugoslavia and Greece using ten Wehrmacht divisions.

The New Zealand Division defends Servia and Olympus Passes

There you are, sonny, you have only got to live till 6 o'clock tonight to be a ------ Anzac.

General Blamey to Captain R Morrison, 25 Battalion, on passing him the message about the formation of the Anzac Corps, 12 April 1941[2]

The invading German forces broke through the weak Greek Army and outflanked the 'W' Force positions. The 6 Australian Division and the New Zealand Division became the Anzac Corps under the Australian General Blamey and were committed to a series of withdrawals from potentially strong positions that always had too few forces to defend them.

At Servia and Olympus Passes the brigades of the New Zealand Division had dug in and with artillery support slowed down the German advance, but they were by-passed on both flanks, including the New Zealand position on the east coast at Platamon, and both brigades had to pull out by night, march back to their transport and withdraw while under constant German air attack.

As in all withdrawals someone has to fight the rear action while the other troops get out. It fell to the lot of our artillery to do the job. About 8.30 p.m. just as it was getting dark and our forces had been safely on the road to the evacuation point we withdrew. As we came out the shells were bursting round us — mortars I think they must have been — and we could see the

186

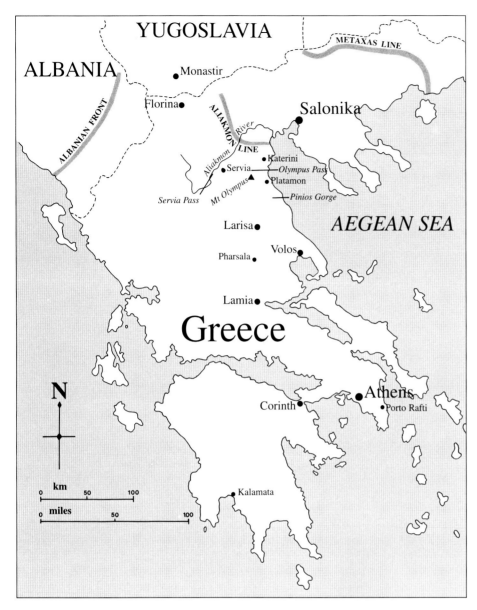

Burnt-out ammunition truck in Greece.
HAWKINS COLLECTION, AIM

Disaster in Greece, 1941. AIM

German tanks, blazing wrecks on the road a few hundred yards below us where our shells had caught them trying to break through.

Buster Snelling, 6 Field Regiment, NZ Artillery[5]

Evacuation

Friday, 25th April, 1941. Anzac Day. Mostly N.Z. and Aussies fighting this rearguard action. Today is a critical day and if the Germans come fast there is a chance we may be encircled and trapped.... Have had a talk to myself and am ready for whatever happens. After all this is what I have spent eighteen months training for. It is obvious that the show is drawing to a close — just a matter of the individual result — death, prison or escape.

Clarence Moss, 27 (Machine Gun) Battalion[4]

By late April the collapse of the Greek armies led to the decision to evacuate 'W' Force. This started on 24–25 April 1941 using ships of the Royal Navy and continued until 1 May 1941. Thousands were left behind, many making their own arrangements to get away from ports on the Greek coast.

Roadside scene in Greece during the retreat of the New Zealand Division to the evacuation ports. QEII ARMY MEMORIAL MUSEUM

I was too tired to be worried by anything when Pat told us that the ship had sailed without us. I merely sank to the ground and fell asleep 'all standing'. But with the dawn came a move and we scattered for cover to hole up for the day.... Instead of being well on the way back to Egypt, we were still in Greece, sans truck, sans grub, sans equipment, sans almost everything except hope.

E Saunders, 6 Field Regiment, NZ Artillery[5]

Nursing in Greece

Twin sisters Marini and Muriel Jackson trained at Auckland Hospital to become registered nurses in 1928. During the Second World War they both joined the New Zealand Army Nursing Service (NZANS). Marini's overseas service began with three months at Pinewood Hospital in England, treating soldiers sent home to recuperate. She was then posted to the Middle East as a Theatre Sister at a front-line tent hospital. On 1 March she awaited another transfer, but fortunately, the nursing sisters were left behind to follow three weeks later. Fortunately, because on 25 March only hours before leaving for Greece, Marini briefly met her sister, just arrived from New Zealand.

March 25 1941: Met Boo [12.15 a.m.]. Simply marvellous — talked until 3 a.m. Visited Monica Mackay. Drank bottle whisky, then to bed. Up 6 a.m. finished packing. Caught train 9 a.m. at Cairo Station for Alexandria. Boo came to station to say goodbye. Greece.

Diary, M E Jackson[6]

Packed on every available ship, and exhausted after days of withdrawal, troops sleep wherever there was room to lie down. QEII ARMY MEMORIAL MUSEUM

Marini Jackson spent a month in Greece, where casualties poured in and the nurses often worked 24-hour days in atrocious conditions. Towards the end of April the troops and medical staff were forced to retreat

April 24: Left Kiffissia 4 p.m. for port of disembarkation. Unable to travel by train so travelled all night in trucks... Road mod. dangerous. Very long

convoy with blazing lights. Hold ups en route. Lucky to get through.
April 25: Stopped en route for breakfast, then went on. Truck capsized
with 19 of us. Also air attacks & land bombed. Most uncomfortable. Spent
most of day 12 miles from port in cemetery until dark when we went in an
ambulance to port. Went aboard destroyer. Great feeling of security after
a very trying journey. On board at midnight.[7]

The cost

The Greek Campaign was a disaster for the British Commonwealth Forces.
Some 62,612 Commonwealth personnel served in Greece: casualties numbered
903 killed, 1250 wounded, and 13,958 taken prisoner. Of these 16,720 New
Zealanders served in Greece: 291 were killed, 599 wounded, and 1614 taken
prisoner. This included Sergeant Jack Hinton of 20 Battalion who was awarded
the VC for his action at Kalamata on 28–29 April when this small port crammed
with reinforcements awaiting evacuation was attacked and overrun by Germans.
Hinton took part in a spontaneous counter-attack during which he was
wounded and taken prisoner.

Defending Crete 1941

Tuesday 20 May 1941
at 7am. the air raid started. Anything up to a hundred planes over and
fighters and bombers swooping and diving and machine gunning. It was
a great sight... Then the big heavy troop carriers came over and as they
passed overhead out tumbled paratroopers. An amazing sight. We opened
up with everything we had and I don't believe more than 30% of them
were alive when they landed. Quite a war for a while. Then over came
another crowd and once more we hammered them. They reckon about
ten thousand troops were landed. I think the big majority of them dead...
We're doing pretty good.

Clarence Moss, 27 (Machine Gun) Battalion[8]

Lacking vehicles, weapons, radios and equipment, 4 and 5 Brigades of the
New Zealand Division were landed on Crete with what each man could carry.
They were 7000 of the 35,000-strong mixed garrison of British, Australian,
New Zealand and Greek forces. The island's geography made its defence
difficult, but it was decided that Crete must be held because of its potential as
an air base for a future bombing offensive in the Balkans against such targets
as the Ploesti oilfields in Romania.

Little had been done to prepare the defences of the island which were
now made the responsibility of the New Zealand commander Major General
Bernard Freyberg. He formed a headquarters from a handful of his divisional
staff, and Brigadier Puttick assumed command of the New Zealand Division

Marini (top) and Muriel Jackson. Muriel
served in Cairo and then in Italy, only 12
miles from the front. In March 1944 her
diary recorded: 'At Prezenzaro. Maj. Gen.
Kippenberger admitted... Amp R & L legs.
Very ill.' AIM

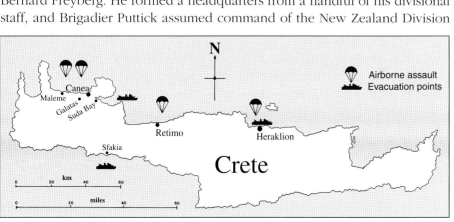

Crete, May 1941, showing the locations of
the airborne assault and the evacuation
points. AIM

189

which formed an ad hoc 10 Brigade from divisional troops and Greek forces in addition to the existing 4 and 5 Brigades. Freyberg's plan for the defence of Crete has been criticised but, within the limits of his resources, it was sound. He positioned 5 Brigade, the strongest brigade he had, to defend the Maleme sector. Its brigade commander, Brigadier James Hargest, knew that the airfield had to be held at all costs and briefed his battalion commanders accordingly. Every soldier defending Crete knew that the paratroopers would come after the bombing and strafing by the Luftwaffe.[9]

> *Well the attack came early one morning after the dive-bombers and fighters had a pretty continuous go to silence any ground opposition. Then came the huge silvery gliders carrying troops and dozens of planes literally dropping parachutes in their hundreds, both troops and stores. Some of them landed barely 150 yards from us. This with the planes circling barely more than 200 ft up above our heads. You can imagine the roar of the engines intermingled with the crackle of machine guns and rifles as the battle started.*
>
> Vincent Salmon, 19 Battalion[10]

Maleme lost, Crete lost — New Zealand's mistake

When the Germans came on 20 May 1941 they were killed: at both Retimo and Heraklion the German landings were annihilated. They were also facing defeat at Maleme, and a German withdrawal was discussed. However Lieutenant Colonel Leslie Wilton Andrews VC, commanding 22 Battalion, lost his nerve and withdrew his battalion from Point 107, the vital heights above the airfield at Maleme, on the first night of the invasion. His men had held it all through the day and when night fell his companies were still in location. Leaving his forward companies behind, Andrews withdrew back on the other battalions of the Brigade.

> *About 4 p.m. the Hun started to land troop carriers both on the drome [Maleme] and along the beach. We gave them hell. Getting pretty hot around our positions and we are being sniped at pretty badly. However it was a great surprise when we were told we are getting out. 'Bring the gun locks and spare parts but leave the guns.' Couldn't understand it at all...*
>
> Clarence Moss, 27 (Machine Gun) Battalion[11]

They came right on schedule and as they dropped we killed them. QEII ARMY MEMORIAL MUSEUM

Maleme covered with German gliders after the fall of Point 107. QEII ARMY MEMORIAL MUSEUM

The planned immediate counter-attack at Maleme by the other battalions in 5 Brigade was abandoned on Andrews's advice and for most of the night Point 107 remained deserted until occupied by German paratroopers the next morning. The allowed badly needed German reinforcements to be flown in the next day. Andrews's actions sealed the fate of Crete.

A counter-attack on Maleme was not launched by Brigadier Puttick until the early morning of 22 May 1941. Both 20 and 28 (Maori) Battalions pressed forward to the outskirts of the airfield, but were unable to continue by day because of German air superiority, and they had to withdraw. It was during this counter-attack that Second Lieutenant Charles Upham displayed the courage and leadership that would earn him the first of his two VCs. Sergeant Alfred Clive Hulme displayed the same qualities on the day of the landing and at Galatas, and was also awarded a VC. A crack shot, he stalked and killed German snipers until he was wounded on 28 May 1941.

Sergeant Alfred Clive Hulme, VC. QEII ARMY MEMORIAL MUSEUM

Evacuation

After the failure to recapture Maleme no matter how bravely the New Zealanders, Australians and Cretans fought at Galatas and on the long trek over the mountains to Sphakia, defeat was inevitable.

> *Pretty strenuous time marching 50 miles on foot within three days until we reached the beach from which we were evacuated. The Hun followed us up not, I think, that he relished it as he must have suffered pretty severely but often as not we would have a scrap on our hands in the daytime and then march again at night. The Maoris deserve a lot of praise. Our unit was beside them one morning when they went in on a bayonet charge — a Maori haka first and then Maori war cries as they charged. Did they love it. The Germans didn't. They broke and ran for nearly a mile until the Maoris decided to call it a day.*
>
> Vincent Salmon, 19 Battalion[12]

The Royal Navy lacking air cover suffered severely in evacuating the Crete garrison, losing three cruisers and six destroyers, and seventeen other ships damaged. Our Prime Minister, Peter Fraser, was in Egypt and it was at his insistence that the naval evacuation from Sphakia continue for one more night until 30 May.

German paratroopers fighting for Crete.
QEII ARMY MEMORIAL MUSEUM

Capture and escape

Another 10 days of dodging Jerrys, climbing mountains and going hungry, with our boots all worn out. We were captured by a patrol while we were bathing our feet in a stream and were sent to a large prison camp on the coast near Galatas.

Ray Riddell, 27 (Machine Gun) Battalion[14]

Ray Riddell was a despatch rider and was stationed at Suda Bay protecting the anti-submarine boom at the harbour mouth. After being sunk, he got ashore, managed to dodge the Germans and headed for the evacuation beach at Sphakia. But he arrived too late and was taken prisoner. Soon, however, he and others escaped and made their way to the coast.

We crawled through the wires, up over the road and then dived down into the vines; we seemed to make a hell of a row crossing the road but neither shot nor yell followed us. We kept to the olive trees and away from houses, often passing German Paratroopers, still hanging with their 'chutes caught in the branches — all had been shot and by this time had started to smell.

We assembled on the beach (75 of us), and there she was. A black shape [of a British submarine] creeping closer and closer. A Naval Officer paddled

D Hawkins in a 'little grass hut' on Crete.
HAWKINS COLLECTION, AIM

The counter-attack by 20 and 28 (Maori) Battalions towards Maleme. It was too late and when daylight came there was no progress because of German air superiority. QEII ARMY MEMORIAL MUSEUM

a canoe ashore with a thick rope tied to it. The non-swimmers went out along the rope, each with a swimmer beside him to see that he didn't get into difficulties. It was the biggest, prettiest and most comfortable ship that I had seen for many a long day. We were in Alexandria before I could get the grin off my face.... After 14 days' leave I was back in the desert in action again. It was August 27th when we left Crete and on November 27th; exactly three months later, I was taken prisoner by Rommel at Sidi Aziz with about 800 others and marched into the 'Pen' at Bardia where I had to cool my heels for seven weeks before the South Africans released us.

Ray Riddell, 27 (Machine Gun) Battalion[15]

Many New Zealanders escaped by boat or submarine or were hidden in the hills until captured or killed by the German and Italian garrisons.

The cost

Crete cost New Zealand 671 dead, 967 wounded and 2180 captured (including 488 wounded), a total of 3818 out of the 7702 New Zealanders on the island. Crete was also the graveyard of a number of New Zealand reputations and doubts were raised about Freyberg's performance. While Freyberg took the blame for the loss of Crete, he was badly served by his New Zealand subordinate commanders who did not carry out his orders.

The Crete Campaign scarred the hearts of the New Zealanders who fought there because we knew that we were better than the Germans who attacked us. We could not understand why this battle was lost. We also gained an enduring image of the courage and hospitality of the Cretan people who risked their lives to help nearly 300 New Zealanders escape to Egypt after the island was captured.

We were fed by the people of Mescla for about 15 days sometimes getting 3 or even 4 meals a day and sometimes going for 2 days without anything, depending on the conditions and the food situation. The villagers knew that if caught feeding or helping us in any way, that they would be shot and their homes burned, but it didn't seem to worry them. How they hated the Germans.... We saw a patrol kill two Cretans in the village of Larchi — an old man and a young simple boy — because they complained when the Jerries stole their potato crop. Before dawn one morning, the Jerries surrounded the village below ours and shot 28 Cretans, 6 British and 2 New Zealanders caught... because someone had fired a shot at the patrol the previous day.

Ray Riddell, 27 (Machine Gun) Battalion[16]

To the population and the military forces on Crete

It has been brought to the notice of the German Supreme Command that German soldiers who fell into the hands of the enemy on the island of Crete have been illtreated and even mutilated in a most infamous and inhuman manner.

As a punishment and reprisal therefore is announced as follows:

1) Whosoever commits such crimes against International laws on German prisoners of war will be punished in the manner of his own cruel action, no matter be he or she a man or a woman.

2) Localities near which such crimes have been perpetrated will be burned down. The population will be held responsible.

3) Beyond these measures further and sharper reprisals will be held in store.

The German Supreme Command

To the population and military forces on Crete. AIM

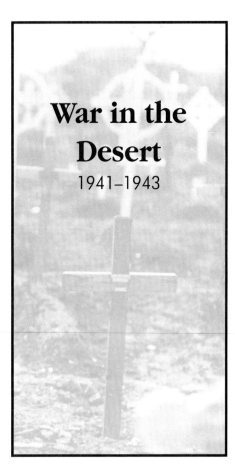

War in the Desert
1941–1943

Afterwards, a long time afterwards, I met the New Zealanders again, in the desert below Ruweisat ridge, the summer of 1942. It was like coming home. They carried New Zealand with them across the sands of Libya. This was the division that had saved the campaign of 1941 at Sidi Rezegh. The next year when Rommel came into Egypt, the same division drove down from Syria and up along the coast road against the tide of a retreating army to meet him, and waited for him near Mersa Matruh. They held there for three days. By the evening of the third day, the whole of the Afrika Corps had lapped round them and closing in. Ordered to come out, the New Zealanders attacked by night led out their transport through the gaps they cleared, boarded it, and drove back to Alamein. Through all the days of a hot and panic stricken July they fought Rommel to a standstill in a series of attacks along Ruweisat ridge. They helped to save Egypt, and led the break-through at Alamein to turn the war.

John Mulgan, *Report on Experience*[1]

After the evacuation of Crete, Freyberg had to rebuild his Division. He also had to re-establish the New Zealand Prime Minister Peter Fraser's trust in his ability to look after New Zealand's small national army. This had been badly shaken in Greece and Crete. As we regrouped and trained Hitler invaded the Soviet Union. His armies, after initial outstanding success, were fought to a standstill and gradually driven back in five years of bloody savagery that had no parallel in any other theatre of war, except perhaps the Pacific.

Fighting Rommel

Always treated the Germans with respect but tolerated the Ities. They were a poor comical crowd.... Two things I learnt. The enemy is a human being just like one's self, and that things never turn out as bad as they seem at the time.

Clarence Moss, 27 (Machine Gun) Battalion[2]

Moving out on night training in the desert.
QEII ARMY MEMORIAL MUSEUM

194

During the North African Campaign General Irwin Rommel out-thought every British commander except Montgomery. After the failure of two British attacks — Operations 'Brevity' and 'Battleaxe' — Winston Churchill replaced General Sir Archibald Wavell with Lieutenant General Sir Claude Auckinleck as Commander-in-Chief Middle East.

There was a vast gulf between the professional approach of Rommel's Afrika Corps and that of the British Army in North Africa. German tactics were built on the initiative of the junior commanders and on the close co-operation between infantry, armour and anti-tank guns. By contrast there was no co-operation between British tanks and infantry, and British commanders in North Africa from the Army commander down were generally men of mediocre talent, lacking in initiative and vision. Talented Commonwealth commanders, such as the Australian generals Blamey and Morshead, were never considered to be suitable for higher command appointments at corps or army level — a British regular officer was always the first choice.

Learning the hard way

The whole Division here… An amazing sight. Thousands of vehicles moving over the desert like an army of ants… dwarfed by the hugeness of the desert… The method of night travel is simple. No lights and no smoking but scattered through the columns are vehicles with red lights at the back. One watches these vehicles and keeps position. In addition the route is marked at intervals with dim green lights which show only one way.

Clarence Moss, 27 (Machine Gun) Battalion[3]

In November 1941 Freyberg's New Zealand Division, 20,000 strong and with 2800 vehicles, played a major part in 'Operation Crusader' which was mounted by the newly formed Eighth Army to destroy Rommel's Afrika Corps and relieve the garrison in Tobruk.

Into action: a German 88-mm anti-tank gun crew reload while their previous target burns in the distance. McGUIRK COLLECTION, AIM

In the first four days of fighting most of the British tanks were destroyed. Without tank support we New Zealanders opened the way to Tobruk and bore the brunt of Rommel's counter-attack in days of confused desert fighting at Sidi Rezegh and Belhamed. The New Zealand infantry was asked to achieve what British armour could not, and did so at heavy cost. This was some of the hardest fighting that the Division was involved in during the war. Operation Crusader was finally won after Rommel's supplies were exhausted and he was forced to withdraw from El Agheila.

> *The Germans poured in a terrific hail of machine gun fire and shells. Saw a 25 pounder near us get a direct hit. Saw the whole gun team just seem to reel back from the gun. Three killed... Trucks were burning, all the guns had been silenced and still the hail of lead continued. All one could do was keep one's head down. Had the gun ready for action. At this stage I was chain smoking. Thought each smoke would be my last so thought I might as well enjoy them. Really didn't feel frightened — life just seemed grim... Then the tanks came through. No use opening up on them. Too late even to smash the gun. I fully expected the Huns would just wipe us out. A tank comes near and a German tommy gunner motioned us up. We get up with our hands up.*
>
> Clarence Moss, 27 (Machine Gun) Battalion[4]

> *Once you have smelt rotting human flesh, you never forget.*
>
> Laurie Lennard, 27 (Machine Gun) Battalion[5]

Operation Crusader cost New Zealand 982 dead, 1699 wounded and 1939 taken prisoner. There were a further 124 killed when 80 New Zealand wounded were lost in a ship evacuating wounded from Tobruk, and 44 prisoners were drowned when the ship taking them to captivity in Europe was sunk. And while bloody fighting raged in the desert, the New Zealanders were concerned about Japan's entry into the war and the threat this presented to New Zealand.

> *One of us would go over every evening at 6 p.m. to hear the news from the B.B.C. While there heard that the Japs had come into the war.*
>
> Lawrie Birks, 14 Light Anti-Aircraft Regiment[6]

The North Africa Campaign, 1941–1943.

AIM

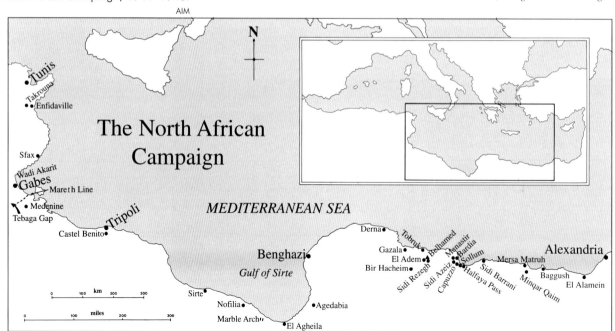

Keeping in touch. A signaller at work in the radio truck. QEII ARMY MEMORIAL MUSEUM

Back into action at Minqar Qaim

> *The bombers are not so bad, but the strafing is frightening. I try to be philosophic. Get scared just the same. Some of the chaps jittery. Dug in and just finished lunch and a bit of a discussion when, 'Whee' a shell whistled over. To ground like a flash. It's absolutely amazing how instinctively one hits the ground. Into our pit and over whistled another to land a couple of hundred yards away and in direct line with the pit. If he comes down a couple of hundred it's going to be warm round here.*
>
> Clarence Moss, 27 (Machine Gun) Battalion[7]

In June 1942 Rommel once more advanced and although ULTRA intelligence had given the British warning of his plans he defeated the Eighth Army at Gazala, captured Tobruk, and advanced on Egypt. Freyberg's New Zealanders, now named the Second New Zealand Division, were rushed back into battle. Freyberg refused to occupy Mersa Matruh, where he believed he could be surrounded and by-passed, and instead occupied a position south of this at Minqar Qaim on a low desert ridge covering the coastal road. Though we were prepared to make a stand, the rest of the Eighth Army continued to retreat and on 27 June Freyberg was wounded and the Division, commanded by Brigadier L M 'Whisky Bill' Inglis, was surrounded and cut-off. New Zealand artillery held off the Germans and that night, led by 4 Brigade and 28 (Maori) Battalion, we cut our way through the German forces. It was at Minqar Qaim that Captain Charles Upham VC continued to show his leadership and bravery.

> *With the 20th rushed Charles Upham. Those who saw him at the start noticed the huge load of grenades he carried, some said in a sandbag, but certainly in a stuffed haversack slung around his shoulders... They watched him with his bag of grenades, tossing them at every target he saw, regardless of the risk of wounding himself from the explosion of his own bombs. It was throw... throw ...rush in — another truck — throw — rush.*
>
> Kenneth Sandford, *Mark of the Lion*[8]

New Zealand infantry link up with British armour and open the corridor with the Tobruk garrison on 27 November 1941. Corporal Roy Thomas and Private Ted Walker are the leading two New Zealanders. QEII ARMY MEMORIAL MUSEUM

We joined the other divisions of the Eighth Army on a defensive line at El Alamein where the Qattara Depression limited Rommel's ability to bypass the British defences.

The lack of co-operation between British armour and infantry continued in the battles of Ruweisat Ridge and El Mreir. Each time our infantry attacked and captured the objective in a night attack, the promised daylight support of British armour never happened. We watched in helpless frustration as German counter-attacks overran our positions, taking hundreds of New Zealanders prisoner, including the wounded Upham, whose leadership in this fighting would be rewarded with a Bar to his Victoria Cross.

It was at Ruweisat that Sergeant Keith Elliot won his VC, by fighting his platoon out from where it was trapped by German tanks, knocking out machine gun and anti-tank positions, and being wounded four times in the process. The strength of the Division was reduced from 20,000 to 13,000 in a month of bitter and fruitless battle. The soldiers did everything asked of them, it was the generals that let them down.[9]

By the time the battles of the Alamein line were over, in June and July 1942, the Commonwealth soldiers of the Eighth Army had lost faith in their commanders, hated British armour and held Rommel in high regard. Our distrust of British armour led us to form our own armoured brigade out of 4 Brigade. After it was decimated in the defeats of June 1942, it was withdrawn from battle and changed from infantry to armour.

Desert warfare

Lieutenant Colonel Howard Kippenberger, DSO (left), and Captain Charles Upham VC. 'Kip' would command 2 New Zealand Division at Monte Cassino in Italy and would lose both legs after standing on a mine. Upham would be wounded and taken prisoner at Belhamed in July 1942 after displaying the fearless leadership that would see him become the only combat soldier in history to win a double VC. QEII ARMY MEMORIAL MUSEUM

The war in the desert had an effect, one way or another, on each and every one of us who served there. It was a unique experience. The desert had a mystical quality — very few who were there did not come under its thrall. It was so different in its sounds, sights and smells...

The sounds of the desert war: heavy shells landing, crump... crump, crump... crump, sounding so innocent but creating havoc among the

New Zealand graves at Point 175 after the November battles at Sidi Rezegh. AIM

poor devils at the receiving end: the rustle of high-flown shells: the distinctive rattle of a German Spandau and our Bren guns answering: the whip-crack of the famous German 88-mm anti-tank gun: the movement of tanks and transport over the next ridge (friend or foe?): the quiet talk of men at night: the rattle of equipment and the odd cuss-word: the drone of unseen bombers passing.

The smells: the odour of your mate's socks after days of wearing… the good smell of stew and rice for your evening meal: the brackish smell of water from your water-bottle: the cloying smell of unburied dead.

C W Hollies, 21 Battalion[10]

Leave in Cairo

During the desert campaign there were periods of training in Egypt with night leave in Cairo. There entertainment included the Kiwi Concert Party, swimming, days at the races, rugby and cheap beer in the New Zealand Soldiers' Club.

These cabarets are more or less blood baths! Saw a fight. Drunken N.Z. started it. Got a glass smashed in his face. The other chap — a Greek by the look of him — drew a knife. The mob took to him and half killed him. I watched but kept out. They could have murdered each other for all I cared. The N.Z. was chiefly to blame…

Clarence Moss, 27 (Machine Gun) Battalion[11]

As in the First World War our government was reluctant to employ women with our forces overseas, apart from nursing sisters in the hospitals and later the VADs. However, in August 1941, Meryll Neely became the first woman officer appointed in New Zealand and was selected to lead a group of 30 women to serve in the New Zealand Forces Club, Cairo. The Tuis, as they were known, became the first of the Women's Auxiliary Army Corps (WAAC), which included the Tuis working in the clubs, first in Cairo, and later in Bari and Rome. The VADs assisted the nursing staff in the hospitals, first in Egypt and later in Italy, and eventually numbered some 200. The first 20 WAACs

Terry Vaughan of the Kiwi Concert Party leads them in a song. QEII ARMY MEMORIAL MUSEUM

199

Meryll Neely, the first woman officer appointed in New Zealand, achieved the rank of Senior Commander. When hostilities ended in Europe she was released to work for the United Nations Refugee and Rehabilitation Agency's headquarters in Albania. AIM

trained as shorthand typists and reached Egypt in April 1944. By the end of the war they numbered some 200 in Egypt and Italy. The men had mixed feelings about them being there, especially as they seemed to be monopolised by the officers in their time off.[12]

> *Had a talk to a very nice N.Z. girl in the club. Very nice girls but competition too fierce for them to take any interest in 'Pongos'. Too many officers about. As far as the average 'Pongo' goes its B.... silly bringing these girls over here. Plenty of Greek girls etc. could have been engaged over here. Good luck to the girls — they think they are aiding the war effort and having a thrilling adventure at the same time.*
>
> Clarence Moss, 27 (Machine Gun) Battalion[13]

More than a Division

The Second New Zealand Expeditionary Force was bigger than just 2 New Zealand Division. It contained the administrative headquarters which included pay, postal, welfare, the training depots, reinforcement units, hospitals, and everything else to enable this New Zealand army to function. New Zealanders provided members to the Long Range Desert Group (LRDG) and the Railway Operating Group. In addition a forestry company was raised from skilled workers in New Zealand and sent to the United Kingdom.

The LRDG was formed in July 1940 to carry out vehicle patrols deep behind the Italian front line on the Libyan border with Egypt. The border defences on the coastal roads were by-passed by operating south in the Great Sand Sea. Despite Freyberg's reluctance, New Zealanders of the Divisional Cavalry provided the men for R and T Patrols, as they were called. Each patrol initially numbered two officers, 28 men and 11 vehicles, and operated far behind the front lines observing and reporting traffic moving to the front and occasionally carrying out raids to gather intelligence and prisoners.

Sergeant Keith Elliot waits pensively at attention before receiving the Victoria Cross from Montgomery. AIM

Battle of El Alamein

...here we were in the line, not much like the unbroken lines of trenches of the last war, just guns in uneven lines, or groups each in its pit, vehicles of all sorts all over the place in all directions, tanks large and small, Bren-carriers, tank-carrying vehicles and their trailers, armoured cars, gun-tractors of various sorts, 3-tonners, utility cars, staff-cars, jeeps and motor-cycles.

Lawrie Birks, 14 Light Anti-Aircraft Regiment[14]

By now it was Auckinleck who had lost Churchill's confidence and he was replaced by General Sir Harold Alexander. Then Lieutenant General Bernard Montgomery became Eighth Army commander after its intended successor was killed when his aircraft was shot down. Montgomery took over a tired, dispirited force that had lost faith in itself, and lacked the procedures and training to beat their opponents. He instilled it with the will to win.

We had heard strange stories of this man. One of which we wholly approved, was the first thing he did on taking command was to clean out the General Staff Officers from their comfortable Cairo offices and apartments (including mistresses in many cases) and move them out into the desert under canvas.

C W Hollies, 21 Battalion[15]

ULTRA intelligence allowed Montgomery to defeat Rommel at Alam Halfa in late August, early September 1942. Freyberg's division played an important role in this battle and became Montgomery's spearhead at the Battle of El Alamein which began on 23 October 1942.

By 10 o'clock the din was terrific, every field gun, near and far, firing at the rate of at least two rounds per minute... The scene was lit by the flashes, while between the crash of explosions could be heard the whine of shells as they passed over our heads... [At the guns] some of the men were bleeding from the nose and ears before the finish, from the concussion...

Lawrie Birks, 14 Light Anti-Aircraft Regiment[16]

Lieutenant General Bernard Montgomery, Commander Eighth Army standing in front of a General Grant tank. The Battle of El Alamein was a classic set-piece battle of attrition that suited his style and became his personal triumph. AIM

A Vickers Machine Gun post of 27 (Machine Gun) Battalion at El Alamein. AIM

El Alamein was the turn of the tide. After this battle the distinctive black diamond signs of 2 New Zealand Division marked the 3200-kilometre route that we drove through Egypt, Libya and Tunisia until the end of the North African Campaign. We fought, in turn, the battles at Sollum and Halfaya Pass on the Libyan border; the New Zealand left hooks at El Agheila and Nofilia; then the defensive battle at Medinine; and the third left hook at Tebaga Gap, during which Lieutenant Ngarimu won a posthumous VC during 28 (Maori) Battalion's attack on Point 209. We were professional and battle-hardened, but the strains of war were showing. Freyberg was conscious of this. On many occasions he did not press home the advantage he had, perhaps because he feared too many New Zealand casualties against an enemy he knew was in retreat.

It finished with the battle at Enfidaville below the heights of Takrouna before the final surrender of the German and Italian forces in Tunisia to General Freyberg on 13 May 1943. The German 90 Light Division asked if they could surrender to us because we had fought against them throughout the campaign.

Middle East or the Pacific?

Read one of John [A] Lee's election pamphlets. Two points appeal. Firstly he maintains the Div. should go home and fight in the Pacific. I think in general the Div. heartly agrees. This Div. has done enough. N.Z. should maintain one Div. only — in the Pacific. One Div. is all N.Z. can maintain. Lee advocates close co-operation with the Americans. Bugger the Yanks! Let's fight with the Australians. Second point is that our wages should be increased with war bonds. Quite agree. The men and boys in N.Z. get high wages, the girls are apparently having a wonderful time...

Clarence Moss, 27 (Machine Gun) Battalion[17]

We New Zealanders lost 2755 dead, 5036 wounded and 3622 taken prisoner in the North African Campaign between November 1941 and May 1943. At the

Soldiers of the German 90 Light Division surrender to the New Zealand Division.
HAWKINS COLLECTION, AIM

end we were short of men and exhausted. During 1942 the demands of the Pacific meant that few reinforcements reached 2 New Zealand Division and after the Battle of El Alamein, Peter Fraser asked that the Division be returned to New Zealand for service in the Pacific. He was, however, persuaded by Churchill and President Roosevelt that this would disrupt essential shipping. Fraser agreed to leave the Division in North Africa until the end of the Tunisian Campaign.

The question of where we would serve was discussed by the New Zealand government in May 1943, and it was agreed that it would remain in the Middle East. The uncertainty over its future ruled the Division out of contention for the Sicily landings, and provision was made for the 6000 members of the original echelons to have furlough leave to New Zealand.

It was an unsettled period, made worse by disquieting stories from home.

Italian soldiers surrender to the New Zealanders at Enfidaville, 1943. ALBUM 105, AIM

The reinforcement are a mixture of veterans and lads fresh from N.Z. Chaps eager to get first hand news of N.Z. Mostly pertaining to Yanks. Apparently the Yanks are not popular with our chaps. Heard some rather incredible tales — based I suspect on jealousy especially concerning N.Z. girls… the reinforcements bring tales that upset the boys… one of our chaps had a letter from his wife. A Yank visits her and he's the 'Most cultured man she's ever met'! The chap is worried. It's not the best. Time the Yanks were out of N.Z. This Div. could go home and do those jobs in N.Z. N.Z. not big enough. Yanks not to blame it's the way of soldiers the world over.

Clarence Moss, 27 (Machine Gun) Battalion[18]

On a roll. The Second New Zealand Division moving up Halfaya Pass. HAWKINS COLLECTION, AIM

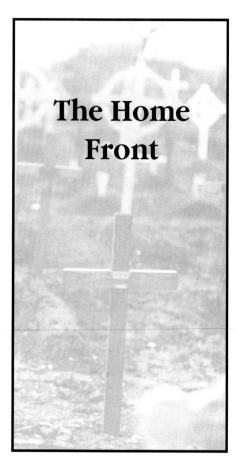

The Home Front

War on our doorstep

... this little island is no longer in the safety zone, but right in the danger zone — and we have found it difficult to convince people that the enemy is right at our back door.

Hon. R Semple, Minister of National Service at launching of Auckland's Home Guard[1]

On the outbreak of war, the government called for volunteers and took power to govern by regulation, but after the initial excitement New Zealand settled down to work as usual. To many, the war seemed far away and people trusted in the protection offered by the British base in Singapore. Our main effort was seen as sending forces to Europe and maintaining a supply of agricultural produce to Great Britain. But in late 1940 German raiders engaged with New Zealand shipping in the Pacific. Finally, in December 1941 the bombing of Pearl Harbour brought the war indisputably to our very doorstep. The illusion of British protection finally disappeared with the fall of Singapore early in 1942. Darwin was bombed soon after and New Zealand hurriedly reviewed its home defence.

'Preparation without panic'

Steps were taken to increase the numbers of home defenders; 4600 men of the Territorials and National Military Reserve were immediately posted as fortress troops or given coast guard duties and some 21,000 Territorials were 'mobilised for the duration'; a further ballot would call up another 27,000 Territorials, and more volunteers were called for the National Military Reserve. A major programme of construction got under way and all around the country camps were built to provide troop accommodation.

Barbed wire was coiled along our North Shore beaches, and searchlights and guns installed. A net from North Head stretched across the harbour

Captain Dixon at Gun Battery, Auckland Harbour. AIM

Coastal Defence Searchlight Crew,
Auckland. ALEXANDER TURNBULL LIBRARY

*entrance to trap submarines. At some stage,… public air raid shelters were
built, notably a large one under Albert Park. The Home Guard and ARP
became active. But where were the men to defend us? Mostly in North
Africa or in German prisoner-of-war camps.*

from Lauris Edmond (ed.), *Women in Wartime*[2]

The number of coastal batteries around the country was increased and
additional artillery installed. Two 4-inch guns from the front of the Auckland
Museum were installed at Fort Takapuna, Narrow Neck, Auckland. Fort Cautley,
at North Head, was extended and on Waiheke Island an enormous underground complex was built with three large gun emplacements connected by
tunnels. Coast watch stations were set up at strategic points and our main
harbours had defence booms extending from one side to the other. Home
Guard troops and Territorials erected wire entanglements along the beaches,
and training in signals, coast watching and aircraft spotting was stepped up.

God Defend New Zealand: The Home Guard

From the start there was concern at the government's initial lack of action in
providing for New Zealand's home defence, and there was considerable
pressure to set up a citizen's army to defend our rural coastline. Volunteer
Home Guard units sprang up around the country based on the self-reliant
British Home Guard system.

In August 1940, the Home Guard gained recognition by the War Cabinet
as a semi-military organisation which would provide pickets, patrols and sentries and co-operate with the Army if the need arose. Early the following year
Government appealed to borrow weapons for the Home Guard; in April all
privately owned rifles were impressed and finally, later that year, consign-
ments of rifles were received. The impressed weapons, which included many
Anglo-Boer War and First World War rifles, were marked with a white stripe
before issue as a reminder that they were to be returned to their owners.
Membership reached 100,000 in May 1941 and soon after the Home Guard
was transferred to Army control.

Children in front of barbed wire
entanglements on Takapuna Beach. AIM

Wellington Home Guard parading, 1941.
NZ HERALD, AIM

By late 1943 the immediate threat of Japan had receded and the Home Guard was put into reserve. They had operated for nearly three years and a total of 123,242 men served. Their presence was reassuring and important for public morale and provided an opportunity for many to make a contribution to the war effort.

At home

My grandparents lived with us. I remember the world map on the wall above the settee; Grandpa referred to it daily as he listened to the war news. He had pins that he moved from place to place as armies advanced or retreated.

from Lauris Edmond (ed.) *Women in Wartime*[3]

Keeping up with the news was a constant pre-occupation for those at home; the radio, the daily and weekly newspapers and the newsreels at the cinema all provided a means of keeping track of loved ones. *The Weekly News*, as in the First World War, regularly published lists of casualties and those believed missing in action. The local papers were censored, but you didn't know what was being withheld. The BBC brought news from the front into most homes; letters arrived, sometimes censored, and then there was what you heard from the neighbour.

I remember going into people's houses where sons and brothers had been killed and it's an aspect of the war that's been forgotten largely, the gloom that's cast through the house, the special kind of grief. Because there's no body, nothing to concentrate the grief on, it was a lost grief. It was an appalling experience.

Kevin Ireland[4]

While those at home continued to go about their daily lives, always present were thoughts of those who were absent — and the fear of seeing their names in the growing casualty lists.

Girl Guides making camouflage nets. The Girl Guides Association of New Zealand knotted 5000 camouflage nets. They also gathered rosehips and raised funds for an air ambulance.[5] WAR HISTORY COLLECTION, ALEXANDER TURNBULL LIBRARY

Kids...

The war was an important part of children's lives. Some never knew their fathers, or grew up with no father at home. Many were too young to understand what was happening, but all received a mixture of impressions: from their parents; from the playground; from radio serials and weekend films; from their own involvement in the war effort; seeing young men leaving, and learning that some wouldn't return.

Many books, games and toys had a wartime theme. Children listened to Peter the Pilot on radio ZB on Tuesdays and Thursdays, and by eating Diamond O-tis porridge every morning could collect cards of war heroes and battleships to paste into their annual album.

Older children were involved in the war effort: collecting pennies for copper-trails; gathering scrap metal, seaweed, ergot, rosehips and foxgloves; and collecting books to send to servicemen. Others helped make camouflage nets and 'hussifs' (sewing kits) and joined mothers and older sisters in knitting circles. Boys with bicycles were enlisted as messengers for the Emergency Precautions Scheme. School children took part in air-raid drills and some homes had air-raid shelters in the backyard.

Auckland Air Raid Test. The Chief Warden, Mayor Sir John Allum, at the emergency control centre under George Court & Sons building. NZ HERALD, AIM

'Doing your bit' — the war effort

The Emergency Precautions Scheme

> *... so far we have been fortunate in not having had an enemy attack us, we know not the day nor the hour it may come. We have thousands of men training as Territorials and Home Guardsmen, to be ready to defend our shores, our homes and our lives. So may I ask... that we, another section of the civilian population asked to do our share, be not found wanting, willing and efficient to do those things expected of us in the cause of freedom.*
>
> J Park, Mayor of Onehunga, 10 August 1941[6]

The August 1940 Emergency Reserve Corps Regulations linked the Emergency Precautions Scheme (EPS), the Women's War Service Auxiliary (WWSA) and the Home Guard under the National Services Department. Emergency Precautions Schemes became compulsory for all local authorities and a major recruitment drive began. Within six months 80,000 people were enlisted. Each municipality was to have its own scheme, led by the local Mayor as Chief Warden, and towns were divided and mapped into blocks and sections with a network of local committees led by wardens or sub-wardens. The local schemes were responsible for air-raid shelters, anti-gas precautions, lighting controls, evacuation procedures, auxiliary fire brigade, emergency communications, demolition work, water supply and the protection of vital points. They also provided guidance for and policed public observance of Emergency Regulations. A central communications control system was set up and messages were to be carried by car or motorbike, on bikes or on foot. Boy Scouts and young women were enlisted as runners. A works section was responsible for rescue and demolition, clearing streets, and repairs to gas, electricity and water supplies. Separate Emergency Fire Services were set up and trained to deal with incendiary bombs and small fires. Fire wardens and fire patrols used their own cars, wore armbands, and had wooden shovels, rakes, bucket pumps, hoses, dry sand, choppers and lanterns.

As the possibility of an air attack became more likely, additional precautions were taken; slit trenches and air-raid shelters were built, fire-watchers were posted to night duty, key buildings like the Fire Station were sandbagged, and a series of full-scale air-raid drills were held in all the main centres. Citizens received pamphlets and notices about what to do in an air raid, and

NZ Red Cross Transport Driver. NZ HERALD, AIM

were warned to have buckets of sand and drums of water available in case of fire.

Lighting restrictions were introduced in March 1941; the aim was reduced lighting, especially in coastal areas. Street lighting was eliminated or fitted with blackout shields, cars had to have headlights adjusted and in private homes there were various means to prevent light escaping. In Auckland and other centres the EPS arranged several trial blackouts of the whole city in late 1941.[7]

> *… at school we were constantly reminded that an invasion could be imminent because we were given a piece of tape, a cork and a piece of wood to keep with us all the time. The piece of wood and the cork had holes bored in them so that the tape could go through and we were to hang this around our neck and on the piece of wood we were to write our name and address… We were told to put the cork between our teeth if shelling or bombardment started and scarper into the hills…*
>
> David Burdan, Gollan's Valley, Eastbourne[8]

Screening suburban windows. *NZ HERALD*, AIM

Rationing and 'making do'

We have no eggs. We don't know when we are getting any. We don't care.
Notice in a Wellington shop, November 1942[9]

Petrol rationing, introduced in September 1939, led people to experiment with alternative fuels. Some gave up and reverted to horse and gig, and bicycles became popular, although rubber shortages made it difficult to replace tyres. Petrol rationing was in place until 1946 and was re-imposed in 1948–49. Special rations were available to those involved in EPS work. From 1942 a wide range of foodstuffs and clothing was rationed as New Zealand concentrated on producing food, uniforms and equipment for our own forces to Britain and later for the Americans. Many items remained rationed until the late 1940s as we embarked on the post-war Food for Britain campaign. For example, the 8oz butter ration imposed in late 1943, was further reduced to 6oz a week in June 1945 and was not increased until October 1949.

Manpowering

As more industries were declared 'essential' for wartime production another form of conscription was introduced. All men and many women had to register with the Manpowering authority, and people began to be directed into essential industries. Many women joined the workforce at this time, and at harvest time university students and the armed forces helped out. In the summer of 1943–44 full-time students were manpowered during their vacation which was extended over March. At Pukekohe, near Auckland, the Americans also lent a hand. As the threat from Japan receded many men in the Territorials were placed on reserve and redirected into essential industries.

A small boy clutches his ARP pouch and identity tag during the air-raid alarm. In 1942 the wearing of ID tags was widespread and many forms were used from stitched labels and wooden tags to expensive discs. In Auckland the Mayor arranged for cheap silver-plated copper discs to be made available at one shilling each. In five months more than 20,000 had been sold.[10] *NZ HERALD*, AIM

Fundraising and patriotic activities

As productive as the paid workforce were, many voluntary workers devoted thousands of hours to patriotic activities — fundraising, knitting and preparing food parcels for the men overseas. Their work was co-ordinated by the National Patriotic Fund Board. Under its auspices, a number of organisations such as the YMCA, the Navy League, the Lady Galway Patriotic Guild and the Joint

Meat rationing begins: a diner in a city restaurant looks on as a waitress clips the coupon for his meat course. Except for fresh pork, meat was not rationed until May 1944, but rationing remained in force until 1948. NZ HERALD, AIM

Council of St John and the NZ Red Cross were appointed as agents to carry out fundraising activities.

Patriotic welfare work included the supply of 'comforts' and recreational huts for the overseas forces and the relief of distress caused by enemy action in Britain and allied countries. Provincial Patriotic Councils were also responsible for the entertainment of men in armed forces camps and on leave in their districts, for the knitting of woollen comforts, for patriotic gift parcels and, through the St John and Red Cross Joint Council, for the distribution of parcels to prisoners of war. Fundraising took many forms including privately-held fundraising evenings, street appeals, sweet stalls and cake stalls, concerts, penny trails, art exhibitions, garden parties, concerts and Queen Carnivals.

National Patriotic Fund Board 'Comforts' being packed in Wellington, 1940. Four parcels, or 'comforts', a year were sent to each serviceman, containing a cake, biscuits, sweets, tinned fruit, tinned coffee and milk, meats, cigarettes, soap, razor blades, foot powder, fruit salts, hankies, writing paper, playing cards, small books, and so on. As well the Red Cross sent a parcel a week to each of New Zealand's 8469 prisoners of war. The Patriotic Fund Board publication, Comforts for the Armed Forces, gave advice on what to put in a parcel, and provided recipes for some of the contents. ALEXANDER TURNBULL LIBRARY

Women at work 'for the duration'

My girl cousin from the South Island was in the Land Army. She plucked dead sheep and buried them and handled bales of hay. She wore a uniform and was described as a Land Girl. I longed to be useful and applied to the Labour Department for work in essential industry. I was put to work in the mail room of the Auckland Post Office where women were replacing the young men who had gone to war. I had a bedsitter in Grafton Road and worked staggered hours.

from Lauris Edmond (ed.), *Women in Wartime*[11]

Women tram employees, Wellington, 1944. In 1942 the Auckland Transport Board took on their first women conductors who soon became New Zealand's first female workers to achieve equal pay. In Wellington some women were employed as gangers, but there was such an outcry that this work was prohibited by government. In 1944 the recruitment of women for tram work ceased in most areas. ALEXANDER TURNBULL LIBRARY

The Second World War opened up new areas of employment for women. Many entered the workforce voluntarily, others were manpowered into essential industries. In 1939 there had been 180,000 women in the workforce; by 1943 this had risen to 228,000 plus another 8000 in the armed forces. However, as the range of employment available to women increased their willingness to take on tedious and unpleasant work decreased.

On the whole, when the men came home women moved out of jobs that were believed to be the preserve of men. They either returned to traditional female occupations or to domestic life. But some industries, the Public Service, the Post Office and the banks, for example, retained a higher proportion of women workers than they had previously employed. In the Public Service the number of women in the workforce rose from 5 per cent in 1939 to 25 per cent in 1946. Overall pay rates rose, from 47 per cent of men's pay in the mid-thirties to 60 per cent in 1945. During the war women herd-testers and Auckland tram conductors were the first women to be employed on equal pay, and in 1943 the public service launched its first effective equal pay offensive.[12] Women's expectations also rose.

Between 1941 and 1942 three women's service units were formed: the Women's Auxiliary Air Force (WAAF), the Women's Royal New Zealand Naval Service (WRNZNS) and the Women's Auxiliary Army Corps (WAAC). Women could also join the Women's Land Service which was established in 1940. The first three services were retained as peacetime forces when the war ended.

New Zealand soldiers, US soldiers and land girls working side by side on a 900-acre government farm at Patumahoe take time out for tea. SGT ALLEN, US ARMY SIGNAL CORPS, *NZ HERALD*, AIM

Outsiders

After a time barbed wire starts to play on your mind and you continually think about it, and dream about it — in fact I still dream about it and it's thirty years ago.

A New Zealand guard remembers Featherston Camp[13]

By 1943 there were mobilisation and training camps spread throughout New Zealand. The first group to enter camp were volunteers. But there was a strong feeling that everyone should do their bit and conscription was introduced. In 1944 the issue of equality of service came to a head and these camps became a seat of rebellion.

There were other camps too, for 'outsiders': for refugees here at our invitation; for 'enemy aliens' whose freedom was believed to prejudice New Zealand's security; for defaulters, who had refused military service; and for prisoners of war, taken in action in the Pacific. And the war revealed that we were not very tolerant of outsiders. Around the country a number of groups demanded strong action against 'communists, disloyal elements and enemy aliens'.

The furlough men

'Every man once, before volunteers are called upon twice.'[14] This was the slogan of a group of Hamilton furlough men. Part of the first furlough draft of 6000 came home in 1943, and they resolved not to return to the front for a second tour of duty until everyone had done their share. When orders came in January 1944 to prepare to embark for the Middle East, married men with children, men aged over 41 years and Maori were exempt from further service and others were medically down-graded; and only 1637 men were still eligible. The majority of these were unwilling to return to the front.

In Hamilton a meeting of more than a hundred men resolved to disobey orders to return to camp. They met the south-bound train carrying men back to camp with banners and leaflets and by the time the trains arrived at the camps they were virtually empty. The rebellion spread and was taken to the public with parades and protests. The government attempted to contain the mood of rebellion by imposing censorship on matters that were 'destructive

Ormond Burton leading a Christian Pacifist Society poster parade in Wellington, 1940. One of New Zealand's most outspoken pacificists, Rev O E Burton was a World War I hero. In the Second World War he spent two years and eight months in prison and was dismissed from his position as an ordained Methodist minister. *NZ HERALD, AIM*

Hautu Camp. AIM

of civilian morale on our own country or disruptive of unity of our forces at home or abroad.'[15]

Ultimately, those who refused to return to the front were arrested and charged with desertion. Court-martials took place and the men were found guilty and given a 90-day sentence, suspended subject to appeal. The first appeal quashed the findings of the court martial as the men had not actually deserted. However, the Government decided to dismiss the 552 men of the first and second furlough drafts who still refused active service. This decision was reversed immediately after the war when the dismissals were cancelled and privileges restored.

'... a disgrace worse than death'

> *For us Japanese, to become a prisoner-of-war was a disgrace worse than death, and a serious crime deserving no less than death.... to become the prisoner-of-war of an enemy country meant the end of one's life as a fighting man and... the end of one's life as a human being.*
>
> Michiharu Shinya[16]

Michiharu Shinya, captured by Americans at Guadalcanal, was one of 687 Japanese held as a prisoner of war at Featherston Camp. The camp, on the site of the First World War military camp, was built in 1942 at the request of US Army authorities to accommodate Japanese taken prisoner in the Pacific.

On 25 February 1943, 240 of the Japanese prisoners at Featherston Camp refused to parade for work. Two Japanese officers requested and were refused a conference with the Camp Commandant. When the prisoners still refused to parade a warning shot was fired, which narrowly missed one of the officers, but may have killed the man behind him, and the Japanese rose to their feet (ready to charge or escape?). A second shot was fired, the prisoners threw stones, and the guards fired 70 rounds of Thompson sub-machine gun ammunition and 150 rounds of .303 rifle ammunition. In 15 to 30 seconds 31 of the Japanese were dead, 17 fatally wounded and 74 injured. Six New Zealanders received gunshot wounds, one of whom died and ten New Zealanders were wounded by stones.[17]

Dissidents

> *At the age of thirty-three I became a law-breaker. Until then I'd been a most respectable, law-abiding citizen, churchman, lay-preacher...*
>
> A C Barrington[18]

> *If we don't win this war we shall be faced with extermination. There is no place in this community for a conscientious objector, except possibly in a mental hospital.*
>
> H D Acland, Canterbury University Council[19]

Pacifists and conscientious objectors received almost unanimous public disapproval. Most, like A C Barrington, were respectable law-abiding citizens, and shared his abhorrence of war and violence. By refusing to serve when conscripted, many found themselves detained 'for the duration'. Of 7000 men who appealed against conscription, 800, mainly conscientious objectors, had their appeals dismissed outright and were sentenced to detention camps. The rate of appeals dismissed in New Zealand was far higher than in Britain or Australia as was the severity of the sentences handed out.

When I arrived there was a terrible atmosphere in camp. To me it looked like a concentration camp... barbed wire fences, searchlights, drills. The spirit of most of those blokes there, was broken.

Ian Hamilton[20]

Behind barbed wire, Hautu Camp. Hautu, near Turangi, was the most severe of the camps and included a punishment block and solitary confinement cells for persistent rule-breakers. AIM

There were five main detention camps.[21] They were intended to be less comfortable than army life and less punitive than prison. In effect conditions were spartan and the rules were harsh. There were punishment blocks and solitary confinement for those who broke the rules, persistent rule-breakers were sent to prison; mail was censored and no criticism of camp conditions was tolerated. Visits were allowed only from immediate family members and these were infrequent because of the difficulty of getting to the camps. Generally the men were resourceful and overcame monotony and boredom by organising debates, lectures, hobby classes and drama performances.

Some 300 men were released in June 1945 but 260 were still confined in March 1946. After release the men remained subject to the loss of certain civil liberties; they were banned from employment in the public service; they were not able to vote until the 1951 elections and the teaching profession kept its doors closed to defaulters until the early 1960s.

Many conscientious objectors were associated with religious groups or peace organisations such as the Christian Pacifist Society and the Peace Pledge Union. Some were exempted from active service on the basis of their deeply held convictions, but because of their outspoken promotion of peace were arrested and imprisoned for disturbing the peace and other subversive activities. The 1940 Public Safety Emergency Regulations gave police the power to prohibit meetings and processions, to arrest speakers and distributors of leaf-

G Riethmaier, the wireless operator on board *Seeteufel*, 1938. G RIETHMAIER COLLECTION

lets, and to search private premises without warrants.[22] As well as themselves being penalised, the wives and families of pacifists also suffered.

> *Waikato are not going to the war. If any of the young men want to they can. Those that do not wish to go will be able to assist... with kai.*
>
> Te Puea Herangi[23]

In 1942 the Security Intelligence Bureau subjected the leadership of the King Movement to an investigation. Te Puea was well-known for her pacifist stance, deriving from King Tawhiao's declaration of peace in the 1880s. She was also accused of having German sympathies; her German-derived name and the hospitality she had shown in 1938 to Count von Luckner made her a suspect. But her pacifism did not interfere with the conscientious decisions of others and Te Puea actively supported the war in non-combative ways. And, as she told Prime Minister Peter Fraser: 'Look, Peter, it's perfectly simple. I'm not anti-Pakeha; I'm not pro-German; I'm pro-Maori.'[24]

Enemy aliens

> *We didn't know why they were taken. We were told later they were enemy aliens but they were not members of the Fascist Party, they were naturalised New Zealanders.*
>
> Maria Lamacchia[25]

When war broke out approximately 3400 people resident in New Zealand were classified as enemy aliens. Of these, about 180 were interned on Somes Island in the middle of Wellington Harbour. They were a mixture of nationalities — Germans, Austrians, Italians, Japanese, a few German Samoans and Tongans, and a handful of others. Some were brought to New Zealand from other Pacific Islands, a few were recent arrivals in New Zealand, but others, like the 38 Italians, mainly from Island Bay, had lived in New Zealand for some time and were leaving wives and children to fend for themselves. These were men whose support of Italian nationalism, expressed through membership of the Fascist Party or the Wellington Garibaldi Club, had made them suspect.

> *I came home from work and there were 2 detectives. Of course, I was loaded up with Christmas presents, because it was just before Christmas; they said, 'We have a pleasant surprise...'*
>
> Gregor Riethmaier[26]

Sentry on Somes Island, Wellington. G RIETHMAIER COLLECTION

Gregor Riethmaier came to New Zealand in 1938 on the *Seeteufel* as a crew member for von Luckner. He decided to stay and when war broke out was working in Auckland at the Dominion Breweries. Two days before Christmas, 1939, Gregor Riethmaier was arrested as an enemy alien. He and six other Germans were taken to Papakura Military Camp for the night, and then by train to Wellington and Somes Island where they spent the next five and a half years. At first Gregor helped the island's caretaker with milking; for two and a half years he was camp carpenter and supervised the camp workshop; then, during his last year, he managed the canteen. While in camp he studied towards a Bachelor of Commerce degree through the Army Education and Welfare Service and gave book-keeping lessons to other internees.

For a single man life as an internee was not bad. The worst thing was not knowing when you would get out. When he was finally released in October 1945 Gregor was surprised to learn that he could remain in New Zealand.

*... then war started. Though people were nice and friendly to start with,
suddenly some of them dropped us... we were 'enemy aliens'. We were not
'Jewish refugees' anymore...*

Margot Phillips[27]

In the two years preceding the war New Zealand had received approximately 1000 refugees from Central Europe, most of them Jewish refugees from Hitler's Europe. These people, as German nationals, were classified as 'enemy aliens' and treated with suspicion. A few, because of their communist sympathies, were interned on Somes island and initially shared quarters with German Nazis. For the refugees it was ironic now to be classified as enemies, and they argued for a separate classification as 'refugee aliens' which would more accurately reflect their status.

Initially the refugees were seen as a security risk, and not given a role to play in New Zealand's war effort, but this, in turn, brought accusations of refugees not playing their part yet profiting at the expense of our men fighting at the front-line. The RSA, *Truth* and the British Medical Association argued that the government should control the commercial activity of aliens and that when the war ended they should return to Europe. In general, these attitudes changed after the war.

'The Invited'

*We had a final welcome on the platform of Pahiatua Station. Then the
New Zealand soldiers helped us onto some trucks and took us to our new
home... A place of our own in a distant land.*

Krstyna Skwarko[28]

Another group of refugees arrived in Wellington in November 1944. 700 Polish children, mainly orphans, with accompanying adults, were given a home at Pahiatua. Initially envisaged as a temporary stop-over, the camp became a 'Little Poland'. Later, when the possibility of returning to Poland became more remote, steps were taken to integrate the children into a New Zealand way of life — they were here for keeps.

Love and laughter

Entertainment

*Auckland became a drab town. Only very young or older men were still
around. Clothing was rationed, and women no longer cared about their
appearance. Houses went unpainted. At one time electricity was rationed
and on the North Shore we sat in the dark or with candles for an hour
each night. The atmosphere of dreariness and the undercurrent of
loneliness were pervasive.*

from Lauris Edmond (ed.), *Women in Wartime*[29]

In country districts the war effort created an unprecedented level of activity, but in the cities the absence of so many men seemed to have the opposite effect. In fact, there were the usual range of things to do; movies, hotels, dance-halls, and more besides, as Queen Carnivals and fundraising events were staged in the towns. There were also visiting artists, and in 1943 the Kiwi Concert Party took leave of the front-line troops to make a lightning tour of New Zealand raising funds for the Patriotic Fund Board.

Gracie Fields singing to servicemen at the Auckland Military Hospital. She received an enthusiastic welcome and seats for her two public concerts were sold out. THE WEEKLY NEWS, AIM

215

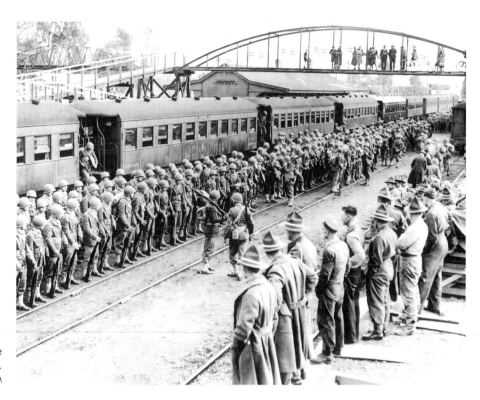

US Forces arriving at Papakura in late 1942 watched by their Kiwi counterparts.
NZ HERALD, AIM

In June 1942 the first American troops arrived in Auckland. Suddenly, drab Auckland was full of pretty, well-dressed young women. Hair was styled and make-up came out of drawers. The Americans wore well-cut uniforms and were well paid. When they took a girl out, they gave her flowers, and they were free with presents of stockings, cartons of Camel and Chesterfield cigarettes, chocolates — all wartime luxuries to us. They were entertained by patriotic societies and invited to private homes. The New Zealand girls fell for them, and New Zealand men were jealous.

from Lauris Edmond (ed.), *Women in Wartime*[30]

American forces began arriving in New Zealand in June 1942 when a convoy of seven ships arrived at Princess Wharf with troops of 145 Regiment and US Army 37 Division. New Zealand took on a new role, providing bases to marshal and train troops, to treat the sick and wounded, and facilities for rest and recreation. Camps set up in and around Wellington were able to accommodate 21,000 men and in the Auckland region there was accommodation for another 29,500 men. A number of publications, New Zealand and American, provided the American troops with an introduction to life in New Zealand.

The American camps had their own recreational halls, and special service clubs were set up, which provided American home comforts — hamburgers, doughnuts, Coca Cola and coffee. Some New Zealand women volunteered to work for the American Red Cross as 'Grey Ladies', providing welfare services and hospitality for Americans recuperating in hospitals and rest homes like the Kia Ora Rest Home in Parnell. 'Rest and Recreation' took Americans to other parts of the country; warm welcomes and hospitality were given at Turangawaewae and at Whakarewarewa. Americans were also welcomed into New Zealand homes and treated to cups of tea, home-made scones and lamingtons, roast lamb, mint sauce and baked potatoes. The generosity of New Zealand mums in providing hospitality during times of food rationing was matched only by the generosity of the Americans themselves.

New Zealand women appreciated the attention they received from the Americans: gifts of flowers, chocolates, cigarettes and nylons. But there was another side to fraternisation which caused local concern. The number of sly grog outlets rose dramatically, and New Zealand's first policewomen were appointed to help police cabarets and private clubs. The number of brothels also increased, as did the number of illegitimate births and the incidence of venereal disease. Special Public Health Nurses were appointed to check up on women who had been named as contacts by American servicemen.

The Americans were less popular among New Zealand men and when our troops arrived home on leave, they were quickly put onto trains and dispersed, for fear of 'trouble'. And they did not like what they found — New Zealand had changed while they were away, and they found 'their' women monopolised by the Americans who were different, exciting, and had more money to spend. Several disturbances involving New Zealanders and Americans occurred, the most well-known being the 'Battle of Manners Street' in Wellington.

New Zealand wives of US servicemen with their children aboard the *Permanente* at Auckland. NZ HERALD, AIM

> *Thank God we had some time in New Zealand. We loved the place even if we were pounded around... Oh yes, there were fights in the streets of Wellington. We understood what it was all about. The New Zealanders resented our favouritism with their women. Our men were done over in the Wellington lavatories, but I think we gave as good as we got.*
>
> Bill, US Marine[31]

> *One cold day, en route to Victoria Park, our final place before departure, we marched down to Stanley Bay. New Zealanders were lining the streets, silent, cheering and waving, yet some with tears in their eyes. It was a very emotional departure...*
>
> Oden S Smith, (950th AAA AW-BN) US Army[32]

By the time the last US troops left in October 1944 over 100,000 had visited New Zealand. Although the camps were dismantled, the facilities which remained were put to use. The Western Springs Camp provided transit housing for Auckland's desperate housing situation. For many New Zealanders this had been their first real contact with foreigners and a foreign country. Up until now our main overseas contact and travel destination was Great Britain, and many of us still saw ourselves as British. While some said there had been too many and they stayed too long,[33] many New Zealanders had enjoyed this contact; the Americans gave us a taste for a different lifestyle.

For some New Zealanders the contact was an enduring one; nearly 1400 New Zealand women married US servicemen. Some followed their husbands to the States and settled there, others later brought their American husbands back to New Zealand.

At the same time New Zealand became 'home' for war brides from elsewhere; from Canada, where the RNZAF had done their training, from Britain, from Greece and Crete, and from Germany. From late 1945 a number of ships arrived in New Zealand bringing nervous young women to rejoin husbands and meet their new families in a strange country.

The Pacific War

War comes to New Zealand, 1941–1945

In the beginning

In April 1939 the Pacific Defence Conference attended by representatives from the United States, Great Britain and Australia was held in Wellington to examine the Japanese threat to the Pacific. Its recommendations included the need for New Zealand to ensure the protection of those islands that could serve as potential bases for the Japanese in the South Pacific. On the outbreak of war, HMS *Leander* sailed with a small Regular garrison for Fanning Island to protect the cable station there.

Defending Fiji

> We marched off the Rangitira *in khaki shorts and shirts, and in 1914 puttees, carrying fixed bayonets, and showing the N.Z. flag; and when we had marched the three miles into Samabula Camp through the rain, we became just as wet under our rubber waterproof capes (through perspiration) as outside.*
>
> L J Read, 30 Battalion[1]

In November 1940, 8 New Zealand Infantry Brigade consisting of 29 and 30 Battalions was sent as garrison to Fiji. Eventually a third battalion for the Brigade was raised from reinforcements and by combining smaller units. Our 'Coconut Bombers' in Fiji, as they called themselves, were bottom in priority for equipment, transport and weapons, and became a training pool for reinforcements for 2NZEF in the Middle East. They were commanded by Freyberg's rejects; those officers and non-commissioned officers he had thought too old for wartime command. They now showed their worth in the tropics with untried men. It seemed that everything was happening everywhere else but in the South Pacific, although visiting Japanese provided the occasional scare. Then, one day, it was no longer playing.

> *Increasingly as time went on, we had alarms and spent many nights manning our mosquito infested trenches. On one such occasion (it*

HMS *Leander* at Devonport before leaving for Fanning Island with the first Regular soldiers to leave New Zealand as a body for overseas service. AIM

Signals Platoon 29 Battalion, Fiji. L J READ, AIM

happened to be December 7) one of the civilians called out from his house that he had just heard on the wireless that the Japs had bombed Pearl Harbour. We told him not to be silly, but when we got back to camp we found that it was true enough. We were still woefully short of arms but soon proper web equipment, Bren guns and mortars began to arrive. This wasn't the only thing to arrive, because, very shortly, another brigade joined us from New Zealand. We ceased to be the B-Force and became the Third Division 2 NZEF. In my unit I got a further 400 men and instead of being the Reserve Battalion we now became the 34th.

Lieutenant Colonel F W Voelcker, DSO, MC, 34 Battalion[2]

Sons of the 'Rising Sun'

The war in the Pacific began with the Japanese surprise attack on the Pacific Fleet at the United States Naval Base, Pearl Harbor, Honolulu, on 7 December 1941. This attack brought the previously neutral United States into the war. New Zealand, the United Kingdom and the Commonwealth declared war against Japan, and it became a world war when Germany and Italy declared war on the United States on 11 December 1942.

> *From New Year's Day we've had some exercise of attacking the enemy's area, but I couldn't concentrate... I must keep it in my mind that everybody takes part in building the New World. We knew our group was going to Taiwan. We drank sake for good luck in battle... Tonight (16/1/1942) I went to the city and had a good time there. It was the last day...*
> Translation of a Japanese soldier's diary taken from a body on Bloody Ridge, Guadalcanal, 1942[3]

This unknown Japanese soldier is one of the many who would die in the Battle for Guadalcanal in August 1942, the high-water mark of the Japanese advance into the Pacific. May 1942 found the Japanese with victories beyond their wildest expectations; Thailand, the Philippines, Malaya, Singapore, Borneo, the Dutch East Indies, Burma and large tracts of China were under Japanese control. The seizure of Papua New Guinea and an advance onto Samoa and Fiji would isolate Australia and New Zealand. Who knew what opportunities might result from further victories?

This string of successes was finally stopped by the United States' victories in the Coral Sea and at Midway in May and June 1942.

Sons of New Zealand

Things are going from bad to worse and then to bloody awful...
Peter Kinder, RNZAF[4]

Peter Kinder was one of a number of New Zealand pilots defending Singapore. His diary is a record of British unpreparedness and inaction.

It is becoming increasingly difficult to answer questions by the public as to where our planes are, because if we tell them the truth they would panic. One plane serviceable in the whole of Singapore yesterday!
Peter Kinder, RNZAF[5]

The New Zealanders included the men of No 1 Aerodrome Construction Company who built airfields in Malaya only to see them used by the Japanese, and the pilots of No 488 New Zealand Squadron flying the obsolete Brewster Buffalo fighter which was totally out-classed by the Japanese Zero. As January progressed, the out-dated Buffalo fighters were shot out of the sky, and the few Hurricanes hastily assembled were not enough to match the Japanese. Most of the time was spent 'on bended knees avoiding bombs'.[6]

On 1 February the British forces retired over the causeway and Singapore was besieged. On 12 February Kinder's squadron was evacuated by ship. Kinder was on one of the last boats to leave Singapore before its fall.

After the fall of Singapore New Zealand now accepted that its fate depended on the military resources of the United States. Though Churchill wanted our forces to remain in the Middle East, they stayed because Roosevelt also agreed that this was where they were best employed.[7]

It was in the islands of the South Pacific that New Zealand initially committed its remaining meagre resources. Fiji was reinforced by 14 Infantry Brigade, made up of three battalions, to form 3 New Zealand Division of the Second New Zealand Expeditionary Force in the Pacific, or 2NZEF(IP). This was achieved by diverting the Eighth Reinforcements for Freyberg's division in the Middle East, and marked the start of our military juggling act, as the government tried to balance the need for sustaining our war effort in the Middle East and Europe with the growing threat from Japan.

A Brewster Buffalo fighter at Singapore.
RNZAF COLLECTION

Fijian units were enlisted for the defence of Fiji and New Zealand officers and non-commissioned officers were seconded to them as cadre. A similar force was enlisted in Tonga under New Zealand command and in Samoa one New Zealand Warrant Officer commanded a Samoan force of 150 men. In mid 1942, 3 New Zealand Division was replaced by American forces. The Division returned to New Zealand and went into camps in South Auckland and the Waikato.

Coast-watchers of the Pacific

Japs coming. Regards to all.
New Zealand Coast-watcher, Southern Gilbert Islands, August 1942[8]

A coast-watching system was started in the South Pacific in September 1939. It was a primitive system, relying on sightings by islanders or traders that were often taken by canoe or mail to an island which had radio communication, so a report could take weeks to arrive. The initial concern was with armed German merchant raiders, such as the *Orion*, who were active in the Pacific in the first two years of the war. The growing threat of war with Japan, however, led to the establishment of a large South Pacific coast-watching network with improved communications under New Zealand Navy control. Military personnel were drawn from New Zealanders already in Fiji and the radio operators were civilian Post and Telegraph employees. They were needed to operate the 58 stations in the Pacific.[9] Each of the civilian operators would be accompanied by two soldiers who were volunteers from the men too old for service in the Middle East. In addition, observers and local radio operators were enlisted from the islanders. For most it was a lonely, monotonous existence with little happening from week to week until the tide of Japanese expansion lapped against the Gilbert and Ellice Islands, overrunning the coast-watching stations and capturing 17 New Zealand personnel. These men were initially imprisoned on Tarawa and then executed after the first American bombing raid on the island on 15 October 1942. Seven of these were civilian radio operators and were later given posthumous military rank. Their fate also led to the remaining civilian coast-watchers being enrolled into the New Zealand Army in December 1942.[10]

The coast-watchers provided invaluable information about Japanese movements against Fiji and Samoa. New Zealanders were also active as coast-watchers in the Solomons, which was under Australian control. A New Zealander, Nelson Dyett, also ran the radio station on Pitcairn Island.

Taking a break in a roadside stream, Fiji.
AIM

> *My job was to set up the radio station and act as a coast-watcher to report on any enemy shipping, especially Q-ships which had operated in the area in the First World War. On Pitcairn I had to rig up a power supply from the four-cylinder petrol motor to my house and I put up an antenna between two coconut trees. That worked very successfully. I was also asked to set up a meteorological office and send daily weather reports. For four years I kept in daily contact with ZLW in Wellington on Tinakori Hill and with Suva... There were about 150 people on the island and about twelve ships a year, down from about thirty a year before the war.*
>
> *We followed the course of the war through the BBC and from Radio America. Otherwise we just kept on doing the job and reporting to New Zealand... I didn't get any recognition for my work except for a mention in the war history, but I did survive.*
>
> Nelson Dyett, Radio Operator, Pitcairn Island[11]

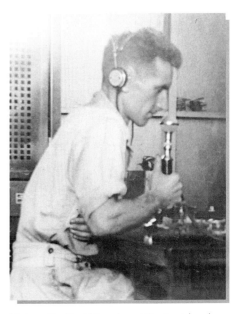

Nelson Dyett at his set on Pitcairn Island.
DYETT COLLECTION, AIM

Captain Edward Cakabau of the Third Battalion Fiji Infantry Regiment briefs his men before a patrol on Bougainville. AIM

Pacific commandos

I very soon realised that this kind of fighting was nothing like that for which we had trained; nor was it found in the books. For a start you had to fight in thick jungle. The huge trees created an artificial twilight even on a sunny day and, with visibility restricted by this darkness and the undergrowth to, at the most, ten yards, operations resembled night fighting... The jungle blanketed sound and amazing situations would develop suddenly with machine guns firing at ten or fifteen yards' range. There was practically no aimed shooting because there was very little to aim at. The hand grenade, Bren and Tommy guns were ideal but the rifle and bayonet comparatively useless... A sort of glorified 'blind-man's bluff' for rather high stakes.

Lieutenant Colonel F W Voelcker, DSO, MC, 3 Battalion Fiji Infantry Regiment[12]

The Fiji Military Forces eventually sent 12,000 soldiers to fight in the Pacific from a population of 120,000. Two New Zealand trained and officered commandos, each 200 strong, fought with the American forces on Guadalcanal and New Georgia. The commandos included an attached element from Tonga. They earned an impressive reputation for patrolling and jungle fighting at heavy cost in killed and wounded. In April 1943 the First Battalion Fijian Infantry Regiment went to the Solomons, to earn a reputation as fighting soldiers on Bougainville. In March 1944 the Third Battalion joined the First Battalion on Bougainville, where it fought as part of the American XIV Corps. A Tongan platoon fought as an integral part of this Battalion. Some 325 New Zealanders were attached to the Fiji Military Forces during the war.[13]

Island-hopping

The Third New Zealand Division trained in the Hunua Ranges, just south of Auckland, under its new commander Major General Barrowclough. He had returned from the Middle East, where he commanded 6 New Zealand Brigade with distinction at Sidi Rezegh. Barrowclough found that the government's

222

Bougainville islanders armed for a patrol.
AIM

intention to raise a second full-strength division to serve with the Americans in the Pacific could not be realised. We simply did not have enough men. In January 1943 the Division moved to New Caledonia for training and by June it had 8 and 14 Brigades and a cadre representing 15 Brigade. This latter group was disbanded and the Division served for the rest of its existence with only two brigades. It was smaller than its equivalent American division, and this placed limitations on how it could be used. Reinforcements were limited and our Pacific division was never destined to play more than a small but valuable supporting role.

The battle for naval, air and ground control of Guadalcanal saw the United States evolve the 'island-hopping' strategy built on air and amphibious re-sources that isolated Japanese garrisons and left them to 'wither on the vine'. It involved seizing an island with the amphibious forces of the United States Marines and securing a perimeter within which engineer construction units, or Seabees, would build an air base for planes to strike at the next strategic island target. Once air superiority and naval control had been gained on the seas around the next target, an amphibious landing would be mounted to gain sufficient space to build an airfield, and so it went on.[14] The island had no value for its own sake, only for how it could serve as an airfield or port, and often it was not necessary to seize the entire island, only enough to secure the airfield.

In August 1943 3 New Zealand Division sailed for Guadalcanal. The evi-dence of the fierce battles between the Marines and Japanese was every-where evident, and as we settled into our sector, Japanese bombers overhead reminded us that we were finally in a war zone.

Vella Lavella

'I don't like this jungle', Roy would say. 'I like to be where you can hear the trams going by.'

Oliver Gillespie, *Pacific Kiwis*[15]

14 Brigade going ashore at Guadalcanal.
AIM

35 NZ Anti-Tank Battery at Maravari, Vella Lavella. AIM

Bill Pearson was an armourer sergeant with 29 Battalion. Auckland born, and a letterpress machinist before the war, he was one of the first casualties on the beach at Falamai on Mono Island when he was killed by mortar fire on 27 October 1943.[17] His tent mate and best friend Ted Stephenson was killed on the same day. *In a beautiful wee spot overlooking a quiet bay in the Pacific he rests, waiting the day when His Lord will come for him...*[18] AIM

In late September 1943 Barrowclough's Division was given its first operational role. Our 14 Brigade was tasked to land on the island of Vella Lavella, where a beachhead for an airfield had already been seized by an American combat team, and clear the island of Japanese. It was the start of a difficult operation which saw the three battalions of the brigade carry out weeks of hard patrolling. They encircled the island by 'barge-hopping' from bay to bay, all the while conscious of sudden raids by Japanese dive-bombers which gave urgency to each beach landing. The estimated 1000-strong Japanese garrison lost some 200–300 killed before the rest were successfully evacuated. We lost 32 killed and 31 wounded. The dead lie in the cemetery at Maravari, alongside the Americans who were killed in this campaign.

While 14 Brigade was tackling Vella Lavella, 8 Brigade landed on Mono and Sterling Islands in the Treasury Islands group to the north as a prelude to the major landing by the United States Marines at Empress Augusta Bay on the west coast of Bougainville.

Mono Island

The initial landings on Mono were purely a New Zealand affair.[16] Mono Island is the main island of the Treasury group and is situated south of the then Japanese-held island of Bougainville. It was an ideal radar site to cover the Bougainville landings and also provided a good harbour that could be used as a staging area for ships during the invasion. For the first time Barrowclough's New Zealanders were given a real task that had some operational significance.

Only one area was assessed as suitable for the landing of the heavy earth-moving equipment needed for airfield construction, and this was Falamai. It was here that the main New Zealand assault went in on 27 October 1943, by elements of 8 Brigade, while overhead aerial support included aircraft from Nos 15 and 18 Squadrons RNZAF.

In appalling conditions of rain, mud, heat and dense forest, the coastal zone was consolidated. A small force, known as Loganforce after its commander and based on a company from 34 Battalion, advanced into the area held by the Japanese and set up a radar station which started operations on 31 October 1943, just in time for the Bougainville invasion the following day.

Training for jungle warfare in the Pacific in the Hunua Ranges, south of Auckland. AIM

Japanese resistance ceased by 12 November with 233 dead and eight captured. The Mono landings were a model in planning and co-operation between New Zealand and American units. It showed the Americans that we were professional and knew our stuff. However, the progress of the campaign meant that we would have only one more opportunity to demonstrate it.

Nissan (Green) Island

> *From conception to completion I consider that the Green Island operation was a remarkably fine operation.*
>
> Admiral W F 'Bull' Halsey[19]

The first two operations by the New Zealanders in the Solomons Campaign had been brigade-level operations. The Nissan or Green Island landings was the only one at divisional level. The Green Islands group consisted of a small circular coral atoll made up of three islands, the largest one was Nissan Island, with two small islands, Barahun and Sirot. It was wanted as an airfield and motor torpedo boat base for the attack on Rabaul. The New Zealand operation was a superb piece of co-ordination and planning involving ships and resources that had to be gathered together from where they were spread throughout hundreds of kilometres of the Pacific. Barrowclough left nothing to chance and, given the nearness of Rabaul, was happy to use his divisional sledge hammer to crack quite a small nut.

A battalion-size reconnaissance was mounted by 30 Battalion on Nissan Island on 30 January 1944 to establish suitable landing sites and likely airfield locations. This was followed by the landing of Barrowclough's headquarters and 14 Brigade on 15 February. Apart from air attacks mounted from Rabaul, the landing was largely unopposed. By nightfall on the first day the landing craft of all shapes and sizes had unloaded.

There were two actions against the small Japanese garrison in the days following the landing. The first was on 17 February on Sirot Island, while it was being cleared by B Company, 30 Battalion. It was difficult fighting in thick jungle at ranges between five to ten metres. On 20 February equally

Tanks at Tanaheran. A Valentine tank going in after pockets of Japanese resistance. QEII ARMY MEMORIAL MUSEUM

difficult fighting occurred on Nissan Island, when a large part of the Japanese garrison was discovered dug in near the village of Tanaheran. They were finally beaten by a combination of tank and infantry fire. It was the only time New Zealand tanks were engaged in the Pacific campaign.

> *All told 52 dead Japs were counted in the area and on the beach below, in addition to which were eight killed by the section of 16 platoon. Souvenir hunters promptly seized rifles, hilt-encrusted swords three feet long worn by the officers, and rising sun flags taken from the insides of helmets and from the khaki clad bodies where they were worn under the uniform next to the skin.*

Oliver Gillespie, *Pacific Kiwis* [20]

A fortunate shortage of men

Trophies of war. AIM

The seizure of the Green Islands group was the virtual end of the Solomons Campaign. Rabaul was reduced and impotent. The South Pacific campaign was over; a two-pronged strategy had carried the United States forces under General Douglas MacArthur towards the Philippines, while the United States Naval forces under Admiral Nimitz advanced from island chain to island chain through the central Pacific towards Japan. There would have been no role for New Zealand ground forces in this. We would have been sidelined on the same costly and needless mopping-up operations which became the fate of the far more powerful Australian forces. We were spared this because we had run out of manpower and, wisely, our government, acting on American advice, decided that we were better employed in Italy. In March 1944 Barrowclough's Division was withdrawn to New Caledonia and gradually reduced to a cadre as reinforcements were sent to Italy or returned to essential industries in New Zealand. Finally on 19 October 1944 it was disbanded. It was the RNZAF and Royal New Zealand Navy (RNZN) that would continue New Zealand's fighting efforts in the Pacific.

A patrol sets out across a tidal creek on Vella Lavella. AIM

I was in the Islands for about four years. I came back once when I had malaria. I didn't see a Japanese soldier all the time I was there. I heard plenty of shooting though, and I was wounded one time when the man behind me fired his Bren gun and shot coral splinters into the back of my leg. We didn't really know what was going on. We were more concerned with our own business really. I was ready to go to the Middle East but they told me to go home instead. I was too old.

Leon Missen, 3 New Zealand Division[21]

Enjoying the sea and sun near South Point, Nissan Island. AIM

Interrogating Japanese prisoners on the beach at Mono Island. QEII ARMY MEMORIAL MUSEUM

227

Kiwis over the Pacific: the Royal New Zealand Air Force in the Pacific

When Japanese invasion of New Zealand seemed imminent in the early part of 1942, a desperate scheme was developed under which even Tiger Moths were to be armed with 25-lb anti-personnel bombs and used against the invasion forces.

Charles Darby, *RNZAF: The First Decade 1937–1946*[22]

Twelve Lockheed Hudson bomber-reconnaissance aircraft out of the 36 New Zealand possessed were sent to Fiji in December 1941 and February 1942.[23] These were the most modern aircraft we had, and they were committed to the Pacific to meet the Japanese threat. The remaining aircraft in New Zealand were either obsolete or training aircraft and included 221 Tiger Moths, Avro 626, Hind, Vincent and Vildebeest reconnaissance aircraft, and a single Walrus seaplane. They were no match against Japanese aircraft but each was allotted a wartime role.

Indeed Japan's entry into the war forced the RNZAF to convert from an organisation designed to provide trained air crew for the RAF to a truly independent air force with its focus on the Pacific. Initially there were not the aircraft available for New Zealand to do this, but it was eventually agreed that the RNZAF would expand to a force of 20 squadrons by April 1943.[24]

Operations from Henderson Field

The task of the reconnaissance crews was perhaps as arduous as any in the campaign. In the first two or three months camp facilities were still primitive and crews on early morning patrols had to take off without breakfast. Eventually tea and a piece of toast were provided, but it was not until the squadron established its own cookhouse facilities that it was possible to ensure that crews had a meal before going on operations. They flew for long periods without seeing anything but had to be constantly alert, not only for possible targets but for hostile fighters. When they found enemy shipping it was usually too strongly defended for them to attack,

Robert Prentice (second from left) in front of 'T' for Taieri. Prentice got his pilot's licence in 1937 and was an instructor at the Auckland Aero Club. He became a flying instructor in the RNZAF before doing a number of tours flying Kittyhawks in the Islands. PRENTICE COLLECTION, AIM

PV1 Venturas at Henderson Field on Guadalcanal in 1943. *NZ HERALD*, AIM

and the most offensive action they could take was to radio back to base giving the position of the ships and call up striking forces of American bombers to deal with them.

Squadron Leader J M S Ross, RNZAF [25]

No 9 Squadron, flying Lockheed Hudsons, was deployed to New Caledonia in July 1942 until March 1943 conducting maritime and anti-submarine patrols. No 3 Bomber-Reconnaissance Squadron, also flying Lockheed Hudsons, was deployed first to Espiritu Santo and then to Henderson Field on Guadalcanal on 24 November 1942 to conduct reconnaissance and bombing patrols on the sea approaches. The battle for Guadalcanal was essentially a battle for the airfield at Henderson Field, and this was the target for Japanese air and ground attacks. When the New Zealanders arrived we found it was a period of intense air activity with Japanese aircraft over every other night and Japanese fighters contesting the air space over the island. On 2 April 1943 a Hudson piloted by Flight Lieutenant Maxwell McCormick destroyed a Japanese float-plane — the first enemy aircraft shot down by our air force. [26]

RAF Venturas bombing up at Emirau Island for a mission against Rabaul, 1945. AIM

Fighters over the Solomons

An RNZAF PV1 over a lagoon at Green Island. CLARKE COLLECTION, AIM

As far as was possible at the time, each RNZAF aircraft had its own air and groundcrew and, since we all came from the same part of New Zealand, we named ours 'Wairarapa Wildcat'... The Kittyhawk was an extremely rugged aeroplane with what would now be termed a great deal of structural redundancy. In other words, your enemy could blast a lot of big holes in it but it would still get you home. The Japanese aircraft of that time, for all their superiority in range, speed, manoeuvrability and armament, could not survive much combat damage and their highly experienced crews usually went down with them.

Geoff Fisken, top-scoring RNZAF fighter pilot in the Pacific[27]

In March 1943 No 1 (Islands) Group RNZAF established itself on Espiritu Santo, administering all the New Zealand units in the area. By now there were two fighter squadrons, Nos 14 and 15 Squadron, forward on Guadalcanal flying Kittyhawks, or Warhawks as they were also known, and one squadron on Espiritu Santo. From August 1943 these squadrons were resupplied by Dakotas of No 40 (Transport) Squadron operating from Whenuapai. By August 1943 we had four fighter squadrons in the Solomons and rotated two forward at Henderson and two in reserve at Espiritu Santo.

New Zealand fighters shot down seven Japanese dive bombers trying to attack shipping carrying 3 Division off Vella Lavella on 1 October, and in the same month Nos 15 and 18 Squadrons moved to Ondonga Airbase on New Georgia and formed the RNZAF Fighter Wing. They gave air cover to the New Zealand landings on Sterling and Mono Islands, and were involved in air support to the Bougainville landings, destroying a total of 18 aircraft in sweeps over Rabaul in December 1943. They were the first to use the fighter strip developed on Nissan Island on 6 March 1944, the day it was completed, when 20 New Zealand fighters landed there to refuel en route to Rabaul.

Members of the New Zealand Catalina Flying Boat Squadron, Solomon Islands, 1944. *AUCKLAND WEEKLY NEWS*, AIM

Sidelined but still a job to do

The end of the Solomon Islands campaign saw a sidelining of the RNZAF air effort, as would have happened to 3 Division had it not been withdrawn from combat. The United States had no plans to involve the RNZAF in active operations in the thrust on Japan, instead it was proposed that it be involved in garrison duties only. This was opposed by our government and as a compromise it was agreed that seven of our squadrons be given an active role in MacArthur's South-West Pacific Command in the advance upon the Philippines. A New Zealand Air Task Force was established but we found ourselves relegated to supporting the Australians in operations to clear Bougainville, New Ireland and other by-passed centres of Japanese resistance while the Americans fought the 'real war' on the way to Japan. We provided valuable close support and supply dropping missions to the men of the Australian Corps in their operations against Rabaul, operating from air bases on Green Islands group, Emirau, Los Negros and Jacquinot Bay.

By now Japanese aircraft and ships had been driven from the seas. In February 1945 we reached our peak RNZAF strength in the Pacific with 7929 personnel. A total of 24 New Zealand squadrons served at some time in the Pacific. This included Nos 5 and 6 RNZAF Flying Boat Squadrons flying Catalinas, Nos 14, 15, 16, 17, 18, 19, 20, 21, 22, 23 and 24 Fighter Squadrons, that gradually replaced their sturdy but aged Kittyhawks with Corsair fighter bombers; Nos 1, 2, 3, 4, 8 and 9 Bomber-reconnaissance Squadrons flying Lockheed Venturas that replaced the Hudsons; and Nos 25, 30 and 31 Dive-bomber Squadrons flying Douglas Dauntless and Grumman Avenger aircraft. This was supported by Nos 40 and 41 Transport Squadrons flying Douglas Dakota DC-3 aircraft. At the war's end we had shot down and destroyed 100 Japanese aircraft, although our fighter squadrons only acknowledge 99 as one had been shot down by No 3 Bomber-reconnaissance Squadron.

Giving medical treatment to a young child on Bougainville. As far as the natives were concerned we were miracle workers. AIM

A fire crew struggle to save a burning Corsair at Green Island. CLARKE COLLECTION, AIM

They are a cheerful, hard-working, laconic, well-nigh anonymous lot of men, but American bomber pilots agree that there is absolutely no escort giving them a feeling of confidence like the Warhawk-flying New Zealanders.

New York Times [28]

Never the same again

This was our first time to see motor cars. At first we were afraid of them because we had never seen anything move at such speed. We didn't walk along the roads. But after a while we became used to them and it wasn't long before we were riding in them.

Pole O'Brien, Nurse, Funafuti, Tuvalu [29]

When our coast-watchers arrived in the outer islands of the Gilbert and Ellice Islands they found that the young women still went around topless, but this changed once these strange *palagi* men arrived. And the change was permanent. The war brought a knowledge of the outside world to the Pacific that was irreversible. Motor cars, planes, shipping, radio communications, chewing gum, Coca Cola, ice cream, the movies and money. All the trappings of civilisation that would change their lives forever. Self-sufficiency was replaced by a permanent dependence that for many islands continues to the present day. This is one of the lasting legacies of the Pacific war. [30]

Nakoia Mataniwa ni Kawa
Kam tuangaki ba kam na kaongoia raoi kain ami kawa ni kabaneia, ma irouia ataei ni karokoa aika ikawai,ba ana akea ae e na manga butere ni ioioa bukina, a na bon ti tei ni batere, ni aki kakamakuri bukia...

To all Village Chiefs
You are requested to let everyone in your village both young and old to know that they must not wriggle their bottoms when dancing. They can stand up to dance but they must not move their bottoms about...

Miyoshi, District Officer, 24 January 1943 [31]

Tasting the fruits of 'civilisation'. AIM

Being on time and obeying strange rules from both *palagi* and Japanese was suddenly important. There was also the killing.

> When we got to the cliff the soldier released the strings and told us to line up on the edge of the cliff and squat down close together. Then our eyes were tied up with cloth. The same man who tied our hands tied the blindfold on us. Then I could hear movements behind and felt as though the soldiers were behind us. I was the second man to have my eyes tied up.
>
> Falailiva was the first man to be tied up and was on my left. He said to me 'Are you ready?' and I replied 'Yes, I am ready to die'. Then Falailiva asked 'You remember God?' and I replied 'Yes I remember'.
>
> Then everything was quiet for a moment. Then I fell over the cliff. I did not try to but just fell. Almost at the same time I heard a scream and someone fell on top of me. I think it was Falailiva. I heard others fall but no more screams. Then I heard a lot of shots fired. Falailiva was still on top of me and some of the bullets I could hear were close to me.[32]

Kabunare was the only survivor of the hundred or so Banabans that were kept on Banabas after the remainder had been removed to other islands, and who were executed by the Japanese on 20 August 1945, the day after the Japanese garrison was told that the war had ended.

Slogging up Italy

1943–1945

Italy is about twice as hilly as N.Z., so you will realise it is a very difficult country to conquer quickly.

Stan May, Bandsman, 6 New Zealand Infantry Brigade[1]

As the veteran division in the British Eighth Army we New Zealanders slogged up the Italian Peninsula from landing at the port of Taranto in October 1943 until Freyberg's 'circus' reached Trieste in May 1945. It was a very different war from the African deserts, and we were now a very different division, consisting of 4 Armoured Brigade, with its three armoured regiments — 18, 19 and 20 — each with Sherman tanks, 22 Motorised Battalion and 5 and 6 Infantry Brigades. Vehicles, tanks and Bren carriers in the Division totalled over 4500.[2] The Division was now ideally equipped and balanced for desert warfare, but Italy did not offer the same opportunities for armoured movement. Indeed, what we needed most of all in Italy — infantrymen — were in short supply, the Division having been reduced to two brigades.

Crossing the Sangro until stalemated at Orsogna

I met the battalion trudging slowly out to its billets after daylight, and thought I had not seen men so exhausted since Flanders. Every man was plastered with wet mud up to his neck and their faces were grey.

Howard Kippenberger, Infantry Brigadier[3]

The confidence of the New Zealanders in the hoped-for rapid advance up the eastern Adriatic coast was heightened by their success in crossing the Sangro and capturing Castelfrentano in late November 1943. Winter was approaching and the Division tried to gate crash into Orsogna and failed. It was followed by three further New Zealand attempts, each failing with heavy casualties. It had been a long time since we had failed and it was hard to take. It was also obvious that we had still much to learn in co-ordinating and communicating between our infantry and armour in this type of country. It was a foretaste of things to come.

Our first winter in Italy. New Zealand Sherman tanks of 4 Armoured Brigade, which had anticipated fighting in the open spaces of the desert, found it difficult to adapt to the towns and hills of the Italian Peninsula. AIM

A Sherman tank of 18 Armoured Regiment snowed in on New Year's Day 1944. WAR HISTORY COLLECTION, ALEXANDER TURNBULL LIBRARY

Hell at Cassino

We soon learned what it was like to form part of the American Fifth Army. Everything was expendable, including, I am sad to say, men… As regards material things, we found that the Americans were using cartons of cigarettes (Chesterfield, Camel, Philip Morris, Lucky Strike — take your pick) to fill the shell holes in the walls of the houses they occupied. This was great, as our supplies were meagre.

C W Hollies, 21 Battalion[4]

The four battles for Monte Cassino took place between January and May 1944. The heights of Monte Cassino blocked the road north to Rome through the Liri Valley to the American General Mark Clark's Fifth United States Army. Rome was the goal, but giving urgency to the battle was the Allied forces bottled up and threatened in the Anzio beach head. In the first battle American GIs were cut to pieces in repeated attempts to cross the Rapido River, or 'Bloody River' as they called it.

New Zealanders go over the top following the bombing of Cassino. A M LOWSON COLLECTION, AIM

The sixth-century Benedictine abbey on Monastery Hill, Cassino. WICKHAM COLLECTION, AIM

We came across a pocket-book lying among the rocks, stained notes for a few lire spilling out of it and snapshots of girls and family groups, one taken at Yellowstone Park, according to lines on the back. Noticing the now familiar smell of rottenness, we looked up to see the late owner of the pocket-book not three yards from us, a Yank, and not much left of him, not surprising as he must have been there five weeks at least. He was a rarity in this country, a corpse with his boots still on, but they were in such a condition that even the poorest of unshod Italian peasants might have felt a bit squeamish about taking them.

Lawrie Birks, NZ Artillery[5]

The next attempt was made by Freyberg's newly formed New Zealand Corps consisting of 4 Indian Division and the New Zealanders. This had been formed for the specific task of taking Cassino. The second battle was fought on 15–18 February 1944 and was preceded by the bombing of the sixth-century Benedictine abbey that crowned Monastery Hill. Although it was not occupied by the Germans, it was believed to be so. Certainly every Allied soldier below the heights was convinced it was defended. Freyberg asked that it be bombed and General Alexander, the Army Group Commander, supported him against Clark's doubts.

The monastery was bombed on 15 February 1944, killing many civilians who were sheltering in it. However Freyberg's co-ordination between the bombing and his corps' attack was faulty and the German 1 Parachute Division, 'reputed the best Division in the German Army', had time to occupy the ruins.[6]

Two companies of 28 (Maori) Battalion were committed to capture the Cassino railway station, while engineers bridged gaps along the railway line to allow the tank support to come forward. The Indians attacked Monastery Hill. Both attacks failed with heavy casualties, including 128 men of 28 (Maori) Battalion.

The ruins of Cassino town, flooded by the waters of the Rapido River and devastated by air and artillery bombardment. AIM.

28 (Maori) Battalion about to go forward at Cassino on the attack of 15 March 1944. Lawrence McRae is in the foreground facing the camera. QEII ARMY MEMORIAL MUSEUM

Brothers at war: 28 (Maori) Battalion at Cassino

We were scared. All through the war we were scared... The Rapido River was in flood and to get to the railway station we had to follow the railway line... it was very dark — our artillery had been landing smoke screens so you couldn't see who you were shooting at...

Rawson Wright, 28 (Maori) Battalion[7]

The 28 (Maori) Battalion remained the only volunteer unit in 2NZEF for the duration of the war. Its initial standards had been set by its first Commanding Officer Lieutenant Colonel George Dittmer. It was on this foundation that the Battalion built its reputation in Greece, Crete and North Africa. By 1943 it was tired and desperately in need of reinforcements. Italy was to see it suffer heavy casualties. It lost heavily at Orsogna and again in the Cassino battles. Like every other battalion, its performance reflected the calibre of its commanding officers.

'never a chance of victory'

Everything in the town is smashed to bits, in most cases not even walls standing, just a chaos of rubble, steel reinforcing bars, shattered timbers, rubbish of all sorts. Among this were dud shells, fragments of bombs, ammunition used and otherwise, boxes of all types used by both sides, battered tin hats, torn clothing, broken rifles, all the refuse of war among the ruins of the town that was made a battlefield.

Lawrie Birks, NZ Artillery[8]

Wet weather delayed the third battle until 15 March 1944. Both we and 4 Indian Division attacked together after aircraft bombed the town and there had been an artillery barrage from 600 guns. Vicious house-to-house fighting ensued, with often the same building being occupied by both sides.

Our four days and nights were absolute hell; mortar bombs continued to rain down; we had a nebelwerfer rocket through our roof; and the never-ending smoke shells meant that we were living in a world where there was

The Battle for Cassino. A Tommy gunner takes cover behind the wall of a demolished house. A M LOWSON COLLECTION, AIM

In the shadow of Monte Cassino, German crosses mark the graves of the soldiers who fell for Hitler. McCORQUINDALE COLLECTION, AIM

no day. Our nerves were stretched to breaking point, hands shaking so much that cigarettes were hard to light. Hot meals were impossible, as was washing and shaving. My diary notes, 'it takes all our nerve to move from our position to Company Headquarters 25 yards away.'

C W Hollies, 21 Battalion[9]

Tenacious defence by the German paratroopers meant that this attack also failed. We were withdrawn and the New Zealand Corps disbanded. It was not until May that the German Gustav Line was breached, and it was only then that the German paratroopers reluctantly withdrew from Monastery Hill. It was occupied by 2 Polish Corps. Two of our armoured regiments, 18 and 19 Regiments, took part in this final offensive, and it was 19 Armoured that entered the town on 18 May. The road to Rome was finally open. But this had been won at too heavy a price. Cassino cost 460 New Zealand dead, 1801 wounded (seven captured), and a further 43 prisoners.

The road to Florence

We were soon involved in the fight for Florence and took part in the action to capture San Michele, one of the hottest battles of the New Zealand Division's Italian campaign. By the time we got into the big stone mansion in the hill-top village, the Jerries had bombed it full of holes, like ship's portholes, with their 88-mm guns and there were corpses all about – smell was getting powerful.

Norm Hornibrook, 24 Battalion[10]

After a rest our Division was again involved in hard fighting against German delaying defences north of Rome. Kesselring was intent on tying down the Allied advance while he prepared a major defensive line on the northern Apennines stretching from the Mediterranean to Adriatic.

... the Maori Battalion took Florence but for propaganda reasons was pulled back to let in the newly arrived South African Division. Over the BBC radio we heard the 'news' that the South Africans had taken Florence.

Norm Hornibrook, 24 Battalion[11]

New Zealanders using a captured 75-mm gun at Cassino. AIM

238

Breaching the Gothic Line

> *It was like Guy Fawkes night. Jerry was sending streams of machine gun tracer back at us and putting up planes and we were struggling through those bloody grapevines.... Then I was hit by what felt like the Auckland Limited Express going full speed down the slope to Ohakune. I had collected a bullet... which smashed my arm and ribs, penetrated my diaphragm and lower intestine and lodged in the left lumbar region. I went down like a fallen log and the boys slapped a field dressing on me and continued their advance. I managed to get up and tried to go back in the dark but fell into a Jerry weapon pit. I was unable to climb out and couldn't breathe for my sore ribs...*
>
> Norm Hornibrook, 24 Battalion[12]

It was in this fighting that the Sherman tanks of our armoured regiments met with the heavily armoured Tiger tanks of the Germans. It became a battle of attrition. The heavy Tiger tank usually accounted for a number of Shermans before it withdrew or was destroyed. It was hard fighting and there was a constant stream of casualties. By October, however, the Gothic Line had been breached and we were north of Rimini fighting to secure the Savio River.

Winter in Romagna

By the end of 1944 there was a critical shortage of infantrymen in our Division. Freyberg did what he could to increase infantry numbers by disbanding 14 Light Anti-Aircraft Regiment and some of the small support units. He also converted the Divisional Cavalry into an infantry battalion and 22 (Motor) Battalion became a standard infantry unit. In this way he was able to build up 5 and 6 Brigades from three to four battalions in each.

In December we were back in action in the Romagna, on the line of the Lamone River. As part of 5 British Corps we followed up the successful crossing of the Lamone by 46 British Division (commanded by the New Zealander Major General Stephen Weir) and advanced towards the Senio River. The Germans were driven out of Faenza, and the New Zealanders occupied the line of the Senio River.

Winter was spent along the line of the Senio and units were rotated back into billets in Faenza. We were a tired and weary division and had come close to losing our fighting edge. Freyberg and his brigadiers knew this. The billeting of soldiers among local families, and the food shortages among the civilian population, meant that the black market was widespread. Women could be bought for cigarettes and food. Morale was low, drunkenness common and discipline lax.

> *The house is a big typical farm house with a big kitchen and a huge open fire. In the kitchen we spend most of our spare time. Shooting on and off all day and half the night. The gun line being about one hundred yards from the house. The scene after dark in the kitchen. Blackout shutters closed, lamps lit and a good fire blazing. A semi-circle of chairs round the fire indiscriminately mixed with the Itis and our chaps and a babel of voices in English and Iti — and one of our chaps and an Iti talking in French. At the big table the rest of the boys reading, smoking, playing cards etc. 'Righto prepare for a shoot' and half a dozen chaps struggle into overcoats — the gas cape is a corker mackintosh — and through the mud to the guns and soon the guns are firing — the combined sound being*

Not barrels of wine but 'Ti-Ti' or mutton birds for Christmas for the men of 28 (Maori) Battalion. G F KAYE, QEII ARMY MEMORIAL MUSEUM

A New Zealand Bren gunner at Faenza.
QEII ARMY MEMORIAL MUSEUM

like the swish swish of falling water. In the kitchen things are normal. Dimly one hears the mortars and the 25s firing — and louder — the crump of Jerry's landing...

Clarence Moss, 27 (Machine Gun) Battalion[13]

Freyberg re-organised his division for what he hoped would be its last major offensive. The 27 (Machine Gun) Battalion was converted to infantry and with Divisional Cavalry and 22 Battalion, 9 Brigade was formed. This gave us three infantry brigades, as well as 4 Armoured Brigade, which made the New Zealanders the most powerful division in Italy. Most of the original echelons had returned to New Zealand and the majority of the Division were recent reinforcements, including many from 3 Division in the Pacific. So it was a revitalised division that trained for the 1945 spring offensive in which we would play an essential role.

Many rivers to cross

... streets lined with people who gave us a great ovation. Rather good but rather embarrassing. Have been all day passing through villages and feel now something like the ex-Prince of Wales must have felt. One's wave of the hand and smile becomes mechanical.... The Huns overwhelmed and on again. Infantry are making a fortune over-running Jerry field cashiers and all kinds of things. Shit. We the support don't do so well. Infantry leave a terrific amount of stuff but the bloody partisans are in like Wogs... However we are making wages! Loot is the big thing these days.

Clarence Moss, 27 (Machine Gun) Battalion[14]

The last offensive over the river plains of north-east Italy showed Freyberg and his New Zealanders at our professional best. In April 1945 we were like a rolling wave; engineers laid Bailey bridges over rivers secured by infantry covered by artillery and fighter-bombers, over which the Sherman tanks rolled to continue the advance. The Senio, Santerno, Gaiana, Idice, Po and Adige Rivers were crossed in turn. Staunch German defence crumbled and dis-

Members of 28 (Maori) Battalion preparing hand grenades in the Faenza sector in January 1945. QEII ARMY MEMORIAL MUSEUM

integrated as 2 New Zealand Division led the Eighth Army to Trieste.

By May 1945 we were the longest serving division in the Eighth Army. New Zealand losses in 2 New Zealand Division over six years of war totalled 6581 dead, 16,237 wounded and 6637 prisoners of war.[15]

Debate still continues about whether we should have remained in Europe after the surrender of the German and Italian forces in Tunisia in 1943. Those that say we should have come back to the Pacific ignore the fact that we were responsive to the advice of both Britain and the United States. By 1942 it was American advice that was most important to us because it was they who guaranteed our security in the Pacific. As the Australian experience shows, we would not have had the same opportunities in the Pacific after 1943 that we had in Italy; like the Australians our single division would have been sidelined. We must always remember that it was at Roosevelt's request that we remained in Europe, and because of this New Zealand continued to play a significant ground role in a major theatre of war.

The end of a dictator. Mussolini and his mistress Clare Petacci lie in Milan's square. AIM

Welcome for New Zealand armour in Trieste. AIM

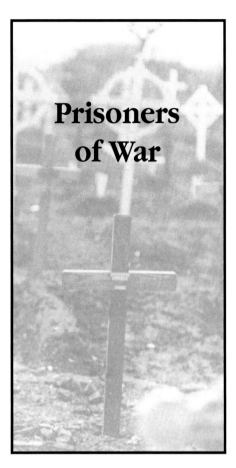

Prisoners of War

Prisoners of the Germans and Italians

The morning dawned cold, the Jerry paratroopers came up in groups along the road, we watched carefully to see what happened to other people and out of the drains, from ditches, culverts, etc. odd groups of our own people stood up and put up their hands... [S]o on the 27th of April, which was a Sunday, we had the ignominious business of being captured.

Ted Everton, No 1 New Zealand General Hospital[1]

Ted Everton was taken prisoner in Greece in April 1941 and like many New Zealanders captured on Greece and Crete was a prisoner of war for four years, until released by Patton's Army just south of Regensberg about 24/25 April 1945. The number of New Zealanders taken prisoner during the Second World War was far greater than experienced in the First World War.[2] This was due to the initial losses on Greece and Crete, and the mobile nature of war in the desert, where large numbers of New Zealanders were captured in 1941 and 1942. Prisoners in 2NZEF totalled 6637 men, and in addition 568 New Zealanders in or attached to the RAF were taken prisoner.[3] It was often months before their families knew whether they were dead or alive. They lived with the guilt of having been taken prisoner, and with the restrictions and frustrations of prison life. They saw and experienced the worst and best of human behaviour, and that experience stayed with them for the rest of their lives.

A padre at war and in prison

Sad to see lonely graves in desert, one with bugle on it... Some lads... had seen many dead. Decided to go and bury some. Took four others including Paddy and went out along escarpment. German dead, numerous unburied, 3 together, 5 together, two, 5 single and one Englishman buried in slit trenches, 4 in 1, 3 in 1, two in one. Had to take out pocket books with photos of children and wife, one with head blown right off — several decomposing, only 8 had discs. Listed stuff taken from prisoners and later handed it with discs to German doctor in hospital area.

Chaplain Major Bob McDowell, 2NZEF[4]

Chaplain Major Bob McDowell conducting a funeral service at Stalag IVB. *Had funeral at 8, they were all late except the French and Italians and myself. We walked on a clear frosty morning… to the low walled cemetery outside Neuburgsdorf… Our funeral was first and after a photograph was taken I conducted and then the shots were fired and then the last post and reveille.*[5] McDOWELL COLLECTION, AIM

Chaplain Major Robert McDowell was a Presbyterian padre with 2 New Zealand Division in North Africa during the 'Crusader' offensive in November 1941. During the battle, with Paddy his driver, he went from dressing station to dressing station, narrowly avoiding German armoured columns, to assist with the wounded and bury the dead, regardless of nationality, until they were taken prisoner, the fate of many hundreds of New Zealanders in the desert campaign. McDowell was imprisoned at Udine in Italy. It was a time of frustration in adjusting to prison life, hoping his letters were getting through to his wife Pat and daughter Mary and being unable to help other prisoners as much as he wanted to.

On the surrender of the Italian forces in September, McDowell was sent to Germany where he was imprisoned at Stalag IVB at Muhlburg. He remained there for the rest of the war, except for a brief stay at Stalag VIIA at Eichstatt. Muhlburg was built for 13,000 but held 33,000 mainly Russian and Italian prisoners; there was also a separate compound for the RAF and Allied prisoners. McDowell ran classes, conducted services, visited the sick and buried the dead.

Finally, in late April 1945, Muhlberg was liberated by the advancing Russian armies.

L J Read was captured at Sidi Rezegh in 1941 and was on board the *Jantzen* en route to Italy when it was torpedoed and ran aground with the loss of some 500 prisoners. Read was in a number of prison camps in Italy before escaping. This photograph was taken in Switzerland in 1941. AIM

> *The Russians have had their land overrun and their men killed ruthlessly, hence they too are ruthless.... In Muhlburg the Russians shot immediately all who had treated their prisoners badly.*
>
> Chaplain Major Bob McDowell, 2NZEF[6]

Prisoners of the Rising Sun

There were relatively few New Zealanders taken prisoner by the Japanese. They were mainly in the RAF stationed in Malaya and Singapore at the outbreak of the war with Japan, civilians working in Malaya, where many New Zealanders were employed on the tin-mining dredges, and merchant seamen. Experiences

'Our victory over the Americans'. A propaganda painting by order of the Japanese Air Ministry. NZ HERALD, AIM

of New Zealand prisoners of war varied from camp to camp, depending on the personalities of the camp commandant or of individual guards. Each area and camp had its own interpretation on how prisoners were to be treated.

Generally speaking, civilian internees were treated far worse than prisoners of war, mainly because they were not 'military', and therefore had no standing in the eyes of the Japanese.

Flight Lieutenant R D Millar, DFM[7]

Working for the Japanese

... there were too few P.O.W. working on the aerodrome for the liking of the Japanese. So they ordered more men be sent out whether they were fit or not... So the doctors had to weed out the sick from the very sick and send them out to work.... And so it went from bad to worse, and then worse still.... As far as we could ascertain, the position of the native labour-gangs brought from Java was even worse. They were dying like flies... Subsequent to my departure from this camp in August 1944, some of the men were catching the maggots in the latrines, bathing them well, fattening them on rice, and eating them to get the extra protein.

Flight Lieutenant R D Millar, DFM[8]

Flight Lieutenant R D Millar was a navigator on a Blenheim in No 84 Squadron RAF on Singapore in its last days in early 1942. Millar was captured at Palembang and at first imprisoned at Bandoeng. The camp was under the internal control of an Australian Medical Officer, Lieutenant Colonel E E 'Weary' Dunlop, FRCS, AAMC, who took a firm stand in his approach to the Japanese and as a result achieved standards that made it one of the best POW camps.[9] In November 1943 Millar was shifted to One Aerodrome Camp at Palembang, where the lack of food and water and terrible working conditions with little or no medical supplies meant that half the camp were in hospital. Millar ended the war in Changi POW Camp in Singapore.

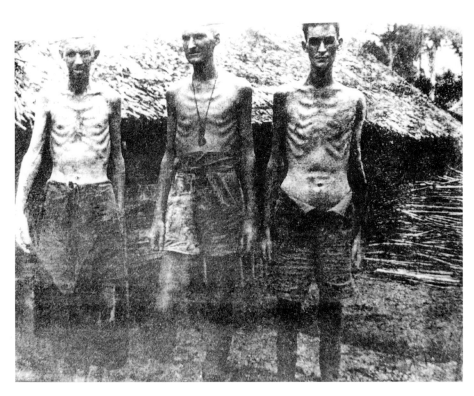

Emaciated prisoners from a Japanese prison camp. NZ HERALD, AIM

'conditions not so hot'

Claude Thompson was a Sergeant Pilot in the RNZAF, who, after graduating as a pilot in New Zealand, was posted to Singapore in April 1941. When the Japanese attacked Singapore he was flying obsolete Vildebeestes, or 'Pigs' as they were known. Thompson was taken prisoner in Java in March 1942 and was a prisoner of the Japanese for the next three and a half years. Initially he was transferred from prison camp to prison camp before being sent to Pekanbaru in Sumatra, where he was employed with thousands of Indonesian forced labourers and hundreds of prisoners constructing a railroad from Pekanbaru to Logas. The daily requirement was to lay two kilometres of track and the men worked until it was completed. It was dangerous, exhausting work for sick, starving men suffering from jungle ulcers, beri beri and dysentery.

> *We had for clothing two G-strings and one sack blanket each. I still had my Australian fur felt hat but Mac had none and we shared a straw mat which was placed over the planks on our sleeping space. For spoons we each had a piece of aluminium beaten into the shape of a spoon and for holding our food a half gourd cut longitudinally. For drink we had a coconut with the top half cut off.*
>
> *When we had our evening wash we washed the G-string that we had worn that day and wore it back to camp wet. At camp we changed to the one that had been hanging drying and put the wet one in its place. When reveille sounded in the early morning we just got off our beds and were ready for tenko or work. When our food was finished we usually poured most of our tea into the gourd, rinsed it round thoroughly and drank the tea. The gourds were then cleaned and we had not wasted a particle of food.*
>
> *Our food was poor and inadequate but never again in my life will I enjoy meals more. We relished every grain of rice — Food and the anticipation of it was our chief concern and because of this great urge we forgot other troubles that would have been intolerable if we had been well fed.*

Claude Thompson, RNZAF[10]

Japanese prisoners of war in Featherston.
AIM

Ripples from Featherston

For a long time I was the only New Zealander in Jaarmarkt. One day the boys came in and said, 'You are for it Tommy, it's been good to know you. So long.' I asked why the concern and they told me to look on the notice board outside the hut. On the board was a story of the appalling cruelty of the New Zealand people who had mercilessly shot down hundreds of Jap P.O.W.s for no other reason than to exterminate them. This was the Jap version of the trouble in a P.O.W. Camp in Featherston, N.Z. I afterwards learned that the Jap prisoners tried to break out and were machine gunned when they attacked the guards. The story on the notice board at Jaarmarkt finished up by describing how the natives of New Zealand, the Maoris, had been forced into slavery and were now the white man's slaves. As a postscript the notice said that reprisals would be carried out against New Zealanders held in Japanese camps. I wondered what would happen. Knowing the Japs I knew that it was quite likely that they would single out New Zealanders for some special punishment, and I must confess I was quite a bit worried. However, nothing happened but for some time I tried to avoid letting the Japs read the identity card which I, like every other man, always had to wear.

Claude Thompson, RNZAF[11]

Former Allied prisoners of the Japanese returning home in the aircraft hold of a United States aircraft carrier. *NZ HERALD*, AIM

Claude Thompson meets with a fellow worker (left) on the Sumatra 'death' railway. CLAUDE THOMPSON

The best and worst in men

I had one spell in hospital for about a week.... On one side of me I had a Presbyterian Padre... I could see nothing organically wrong with him and he went to and from the latrine and moved about outside the hospital freely. I decided he was just living in the hospital because of the extra food and because it gave him an excuse to loaf. All the while he was lying about the Roman Catholic padre, Father O'Rorke, was conducting the services and burying all the dead be they Roman Catholics or Protestants.... When I saw him in Base Camp he was as thin as possible and looked like a walking skeleton... I am not a Catholic but I must say that of the number of padres I saw in the prison camps, Padre O'Rorke was the only one who did his job....

In a lot of ways our officers failed also to do their jobs. An officer is supposed to put the welfare of his men before his own and because he is an officer and is paid at a far higher rate and has great privileges he is supposed to accept responsibility. In all my work on the rail job the responsibility of being hancho [in charge] was borne by N.C.O.s with the exception of the first few days. After that the officers remained in the camp and did camp duties, chiefly in the cookhouse. A great deal of trouble and punishment would have been avoided had there been one officer out at work with us for though at times the Japs would beat up an officer they did respect a commission.

Claude Thompson, RNZAF[12]

Freedom at last

It is impossible to describe my feelings when we were put to bed and efficient, good-looking nurses took charge. The change from squalor had been too abrupt and tears came flooding to my eyes whenever one of the nurses did anything for me... To be treated once again as a civilized human being was just too much to take.

Claude Thompson, RNZAF[13]

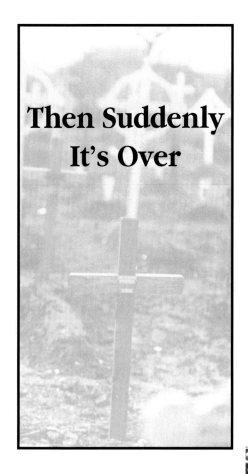

Then Suddenly It's Over

VE and VJ Day

I thoroughly enjoyed being a soldier and one of the sad days to me was the day that the war stopped and I suddenly thought, 'Well it's over now. What am I going to do?' I think many people who were soldiers had that feeling. VE Day was celebrated in Italy. We had a sports day and it was more like a wake as far as I was concerned.

D'Arcy Whiting, 24 Battalion[1]

I had put in for a bee-keeping course with army education and I waited for nine months. I was outside the education hut at the hospital when all of a sudden everybody stopped dead as Churchill's voice rings out over the loudspeakers and says that the war is over. Nobody said anything or did anything. Then out comes this stupid corporal: 'Sister, I've got your bee-keeping course.' I said, 'You know what, you can keep it. It's over...'

We were in Cairo for VJ Day. We were all vastly relieved because, whatever our grandchildren may think about the Japanese, we've got other ideas. It was sort of almost disbelief to think the whole thing was over. It's quite strange to suddenly find you've got a life again.

Nan Simcox, Nursing Sister, 2 New Zealand General Hospital, Caserta[2]

The face of ravaged Europe: Cologne's ruins represented the reality of many European cities. LOWSON COLLECTION, AIM

248

The news of Germany's unconditional surrender reached Freyberg's New Zealanders at the same time as they faced Tito's Yugoslav forces in what was an increasingly tense situation over Trieste. As one war finished, it seemed another was about to start. Fortunately it was defused, but our forces played a major role in this first confrontation of the Cold War between the Western powers and the Soviet Union. By mid May 1945, when the tension had eased, Trieste was a time for 'swimming, good company with our comrades and many beautiful women.'[3] It was also the period when the Division had the highest number of road accidents and highest rate of venereal disease in its history.

Amongst the New Zealand soldiers there was little elation at the news of victory in Europe (VE), as the only prospect was a shift to the Pacific. It was intended that our role would be as the fourth division alongside one each from Australia, Canada and the United Kingdom as part of a Commonwealth Corps under General MacArthur's command for operations on the Japanese mainland.[4]

'Thank God for the Atom Bomb'

> *Suddenly a brilliant white light fills every corner of the hold. Blinded by the dazzle we stagger backward then sprawl on the deck as the ship is sucked downward. It rocks and shakes and shudders in the grip of some mighty force, then rises again to lurch violently to starboard with a loud grinding as the sides scrape against the concrete wharf.*
>
> Edward Sawyer, British Prisoner of War, Hiroshima[5]

At 8.15 a.m. on 6 August 1945 the B-29 Bomber *Enola Gay*, commanded by Colonel Paul W Tibbets, opened its bomb-bay doors and dropped a single bomb suspended by parachute on the Japanese city of Hiroshima. Fifty-one seconds later, at a height of 600 metres, 'Little Boy', the code name for the atomic bomb, exploded above the central city. The bomb weighed 3636 kilograms, contained 5.5 kilograms of uranium 235 and set off an explosion the equivilant of 12,000–15,000 tons of TNT. A gigantic mushroom cloud rose more than 14,900 metres into the sky.[6]

Field Marshal Montgomery signing surrender documents, Lüneberg Heath, Germany. ALEC BEVERIDGE COLLECTION, AIM

Fire storm Nagasaki. 'For the first time I feel pity and sorrow for the Japanese.'[7] AIM

The aiming point or 'ground zero' was just south of an army headquarters, at the northern tip of the island containing Hiroshima's airport. It was a densely built-up area with a mix of residential, commercial, military and small industrial buildings. Hiroshima had escaped the mass-bombing raids suffered by other Japanese cities, and its citizens, used to small numbers of enemy planes in the skies overhead, tended to ignore air-raid precautions. Most factory workers were already at work, while school children were in the open, clearing firebreaks against the feared firestorms of the massed bombing raids. These were the immediate casualties in the blast of the atomic bomb, which blew down buildings and set off innumerable fires fanned by the violent 'fire wind' caused by the intense heat. Practically every building in the city was damaged and the wooden Japanese residential buildings were totally destroyed. The death toll was equally severe; 70,000–80,000 people were instantly killed and the same number injured. This death toll would rise to 130,000 with deaths from radiation sickness.

Prisoners working on the deck of the ship where Sawyer was working were instantly killed, while the shelter of the hold saved Sawyer and his fellow captives from the cyclonic wind that followed and the black rain that burnt its way into exposed skin leaving a grey mark.

Mother and child at Nagasaki. AIM

Looking up river, we see what had been the city of Hiroshima. For about three square kilometres nearly every building has been pulverised into piles of rubble. The river was full of floating bodies and temporary medical stations on the city's outskirts were crowded with people waiting in queues, many of them burnt and bleeding with long strips of skin hanging from their swollen naked bodies. There is no hysteria or panic, only the quiet desperation of the first-aid teams working on the injured and the shocked, dazed stares of the onlookers. For the first time I feel pity and sorrow for the Japanese.

Edward Sawyer, British Prisoner of War, Hiroshima[8]

The US Third Fleet manoeuvres off the coast of Japan. ISITT COLLECTION, AIM

New Zealand's reaction

As far as we were concerned, the abrupt end of the war with Japan on 15 August 1945 after the dropping of the atomic bombs finally allowed our soldiers to dream of going home.

I was on Bougainville when the war finished. I can't remember the day, but I thought the bomb finished the war quicker for us.

Tom Mason, RNZAF[9]

Well, when we heard the news about the atom bomb I don't think we knew much about atomic power in those days. I wasn't sorry when I heard they'd all got killed. They should have dropped it all through Japan. I think it was a relief to know that the whole thing was over really.

Estelle Rolfe[10]

There was great relief at the news of the atom bomb. Because we thought we were in for a year or two fighting out here and the Japs weren't renowned for chucking the towel in. I think the atom bomb saved more Japs than it killed.

Heath Simcox, RNZN[11]

The war officially ended with the signing of the Japanese instruments of surrender on 2 September 1945 on board Admiral William F Halsey's flagship the battleship USS *Missouri*. The Chief of Air Staff, Air Vice Marshal Leonard Isitt, flew from New Zealand to witness the surrender on behalf of New Zealand.

The representative of the Japanese Government signs the instrument of surrender on the deck of the USS *Missouri* on 2 September 1945. ISITT COLLECTION, AIM

New Zealand celebrates

The news of Germany's surrender reached New Zealand in time for the morning papers of 8 May 1945. It had been anticipated for weeks and celebrations began immediately, although 9 May was declared as the official VE Day in New Zealand. It began with bells and sirens, and was a day of civic gatherings and thanksgiving services, parades and partying.

Dancing in Queen Street, Auckland, on VJ Day. *NZ HERALD*, AIM

The speed with which Japan surrendered was less expected. On 15 August the formal announcement meant that the Pacific war was finally over and New Zealand went mad with celebrations through the streets as a two-day public holiday was declared.

Coming home

Flying Officer M Hewitson is met by his twin sons, October 1945. *NZ HERALD*, AIM

We landed at Wellington. They had a dressing station and reception station on Lambton Quay. Because I had to have the end of the stump trimmed up they weren't able to fit me with a leg quickly. So my first leg was a homemade peg leg which the local blacksmith made with a shovel handle. I arrived back here in August 1944 and I was on army pay to about March 1946 when I was discharged and given a war pension.

George O'Leary, New Zealand Engineers[12]

I had met George at a dance studio. He was just a dance partner for a long time. When George came home he was worried I would not accept him as an amputee. However he was still George to me.

Joyce O'Leary[13]

When we arrived back home we were given a leave pass to travel round New Zealand. I went through the North Island calling on members of my platoon. Unfortunately most of them had been killed so it was a bit of a sad time. Then it was out of uniform and back to work. That was a bit of a shock because many of us had grown up in the war. We had virtually left home as boys and had come back as men and it was a different world. I couldn't work for a boss. I tried that and I got a job as a painter on state houses and then I formed my own company...

D'Arcy Whiting, 24 Battalion[14]

It was strange coming back after all those years. Joan was expecting Cynthia, and it was hard to settle down. I wanted to study accountancy, but I couldn't keep that up. I couldn't even read a newspaper properly at night and when I went to bed my nerves were very jumpy. It took me fifteen or twenty years to get adjusted back to civilian life.

Colin Apperley, 25 Battalion[15]

Sergeant C Mutch, August 1945.
NZ HERALD, AIM

In hindsight

In 1945, despite the signing of the United Nations Charter in San Francisco, we held little hope for a world future without war. The cities and economies of Europe and Asia were in ruins and there was fighting in former colonies throughout the world as the European powers attempted to impose the pre-war status quo and claim back their colonial empires. Unlike the situation at the end of the First World War, we had to face an uncertain future in an uncertain world. The fall of Singapore and the inability of Britain to assist us in the Pacific made us aware that despite comfortable ties with Britain our future security in Asia was also dependent upon the United States.

During the Second World War New Zealand for the first time in our history mobilised our resources and fought a total war. Out of a population in 1939 of 1,632,000 it is estimated that the greatest number of personnel overseas at anyone time numbered 75,000, and at its peak in September 1942 we had 157,000 (including some 8500 women) mobilised. This does not count the volunteer services or Home Guard, who reached a peak of 124,194 in April 1943. In addition, merchant seamen serving on New Zealand registered ships numbered 2990 in 1940.[16]

The Maori people sustained the numbers of volunteers to man 28 (Maori) Battalion throughout the war, and matched it with a parallel welfare effort in New Zealand. The Second Maori Battalion was also raised as a Territorial battalion for war service in New Zealand. All this was at enormous long-term cost to the Maori people, and the impact on New Zealand of those leaders who did not come back has its influence to this day.

Casualty figures vary from source to source but our total casualty figures numbered some 36,038, which as the table on page 256 shows were mainly in the army. However, the most chilling figure is that of the Air Force casualties, where there were 4149 deaths out of a total casualty figure of 4979. Most of those dead were New Zealanders in Bomber Command and the figures reveal all too clearly the terrible attrition suffered by our young men in this service.[17]

Private A Stevenson, January 1945. NZ HERALD, AIM

> *Let them in, Peter, they are very tired;*
> *Give them couches where the angels sleep.*
> *Let them wake whole again to new dawns fired*
> *With sun, not war. And may their peace be deep.*
> *Remember where the broken bodies lie...*
> *And give them things they like. Let them make noise.*
> *God knows how young they were to have to die!*
> *Give swing bands, not gold harps, to these our boys.*
> *Let them love, Peter — they have had no time —*
> *Girls sweet as meadow wind, with flowering hair...*
> *They should have trees and bird song, hills to climb —*
> *The taste of summer in a ripened pear.*
> *Tell them how they are missed. Say not to fear;*
> *It's going to be all right with us down here.*
>
> Elma Dean, *Letter to St Peter*[18]

After the war an extensive rehabilitation and resettlement scheme was put into place by the government. This was matched by a war pension scheme. War time controls flowed on into the post-war period and state control continued to be a feature of New Zealand life. The war years affected everyone. For those who went overseas, both men and women, there are positive things that they remember, and the comradeship outweighed the bad times. This is

Fifty years on, veterans remember the cost of the Second World War. *NZ HERALD*, AIM

not the case for the women who stayed at home, made do, raised the family, and lived for the mail but feared the casualty telegram. They hated the war and what it did to them and the ones they loved.

Everyone from those years carries scars; some are visible, some are not. We who are their children are often only seeing for the first time the impact that the Second World War had on our parents' lives and inevitably our own.

The First World War chaps, they did a lot of the groundwork. They made things a lot easier for us. Both on the war pensions side of it and the supply of artificial limbs, they had worked hard and put pressure on the New Zealand Government... — they put people like us in touch with people in our own age group who were amputees, so they would swap ideas on the use of artificial limbs. They were able to forecast the likely problems we would meet and offer advice on how to overcome them. I found the comradeship and friendliness of the war amputees has been wonderful.

George O'Leary, New Zealand Engineers [19]

You don't talk about the war. I don't think anybody does. I think it was such a sad time and it was six years out of people's lives. Those that went away didn't live the lives of young people and they came back old men.

Patricia Connew, clerk, Navy Office, Wellington [20]

J Force

I can remember... when we were getting fairly close to Kure, and it was exactly like sailing into Wellington. I can still see it. And the contour of the land. You would have sworn you were coming back to New Zealand.... My first impression when we walked into Kure where we landed... was just the sheer filth and stench. All the gutters down the side of the street were used as public toilets.

New Zealand soldier, J Force [21]

Our government agreed to provide a brigade group for the British Commonwealth Occupation Force in Japan. It was to be made up of single officers and men from the last reinforcements and volunteers from those who had served longer. They were to serve in Japan for six months before being replaced by volunteers from New Zealand. J Force, or Jayforce as it was called, was formed from Headquarters 9 Infantry Brigade and commanded by Brigadier K L Stewart. It was a fully self-contained force of 4000 personnel, including three battalions, an artillery battery, engineers, signals, transport, ordnance, provost, medical services including a general hospital, a band and a port detachment for the loading and unloading of ships. It sailed from Naples on the *Strathmore* on 21 February and reached Kure on 19 March 1946.[22] No 14 Fighter Squadron RNZAF was also based in Japan from March 1946 until the final elements pulled out in March 1949.[23]

An EnZed of Jayforce writes home. J FORCE ALBUM, AIM

> *We were still more or less told that they were the enemies. That we were over there to control them... and don't whatever you do fraternize... because they were treacherous little buggers.... I can remember when I first went there one of the favourite tricks was to be riding along in the back of an army truck and push some old bloke off his bike as we were passing him on the road. You'd give him a shove and he would go hurtling off the side of the road... When I look back it was barbaric. But we had had that propaganda pumped into us through the war, the Japs were animals... You really went over there hating them until you met them and saw they're just people. There were good ones and bad ones just like we had.*
>
> New Zealand soldier, J Force[24]

The Brigade was based around the old university town of Yamaguchi on the south west tip of the island of Honshu, and was given the task of supervising the repatriation of Japanese service personnel and checking for illegal immigrants from Korea. It was not a happy time for New Zealanders there; accommodation was poor, food bad, and vehicles and equipment showed the wear of six years of war. The routine soon bored our veterans. Discipline was slack, and this was reflected in the high rate of venereal disease, motor accidents, and cases of drunkenness and absence without leave. We simply wanted to go home.

It was only after the initial members of Jayforce were replaced by the first relief of volunteers in June 1947 that the situation improved. Having missed out on the war, going to Japan was the next best option and there was no shortage of volunteers. We remained a fiercely independent national element within the Occupation Force, and there was much more mixing with the local population than occurred with the other Commonwealth forces. Despite requests for us to remain, our government was keen to withdraw us as soon as it was politically expedient to do so. This they did in September 1948.

The mail was more important than being on guard. J FORCE ALBUM, AIM

> *We had an ex-Kamikaze pilot working for us... he was very young, he would only have been 19 or 20. He spoke very good English. I got very, very friendly with him. He was trained as a Kamikaze pilot and I can always remember we were having a conversation one night and I passed the comment. 'You must have been pretty brave sort of guys to do what you do, it's a wonder you weren't scared.' And he said, 'Man we were shit scared.' He said 'we are human beings.' He said, 'we were scared but... the penalty for not doing their job was worse... You were disgraced... but your family was totally disgraced... we had Hobson's choice.' He was a great little guy.*
>
> New Zealand soldier, J Force[25]

National Mobilisation

Population at the outbreak of war	1,632,000
Men of military age (18-45)	355,000
Men and women who served overseas	135,000
Men and women who joined the forces during the war	205,000
Women in the forces during the war	9,700
Peak number in the Home Guard	124,000
Peak number in Emergency Precaution Schemes	150,000

Peak Mobilisation

Army	127,000
Navy	6,000
Air force	24,000
TOTAL	157,000

Casualties

Deaths

Navy	573
Army	6,793
Air Force	4,149
Mercantile Marine	110

Missing

Army	46
TOTAL	11,671

Wounded

Navy	170
Army	15,324
Air Force	255
TOTAL	15,749

Prisoners & Interned

Navy	57
Army	7,863
Air Force	575
Mercantile Marine	123
TOTAL	8,618
TOTAL CASUALTIES	36,038

New Zealand's casualty rate of 24 per 1000 of population compares with 9 per 1000 for Canada and 13 per 1000 for Australia.

War Expenditure

From 1939 to 1944 war expenditure in New Zealand was 31% of the national income. This compared with: UK 43%, Australia and Canada 29%, US 24%, USSR 37%. In 1943 war expenditure reached 53% in Britain, Canada and New Zealand.

Munitions and Equipment

The value of war equipment and munitions produced was £42,000,00.

Wartime Food Shipments

To Britain

1,800,000 tons of meat
685,000 tons of butter
625,000 tons of cheese

To United States forces

190,000 tons of meat
23,000 tons of butter
137,000 tons of vegetables

In addition 5,400,000 bales of wool were appraised for shipment to Britain.

PART 5
Searching for Security

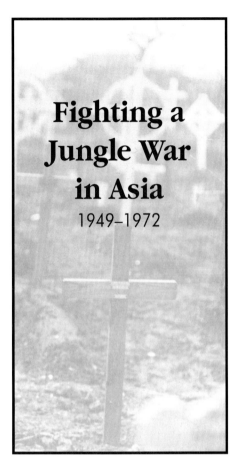

Fighting a Jungle War in Asia
1949–1972

Preparing for a global war with the Soviet Union

New Zealand emerged from the Second World War conscious of the need to ally itself with other powers to ensure its own security in an uncertain world.

Our immediate concerns were the growing power of the Soviet Union and its expansion into Europe. In the event of war we agreed to provide an infantry division and an armoured brigade to defend Egypt and the Suez Canal. After a public referendum in 1949 New Zealand instituted Compulsory Military Training for all males when they reached 18 years to ensure that we had a trained force ready to mobilise if war was declared.

The Kiwis in South East Asia

The Kiwis seem to be really infiltrating into this part of the world.
Unit Diary, No 41 Squadron RNZAF[1]

Following our experiences in the Pacific war, New Zealand carefully set out to ensure its security, and established an arrangement with Britain and Australia over the protection of the vital sea lanes and air space around Australia, New Zealand and Malaya, which was the principal British economic interest in South East Asia. This Australia, New Zealand and Malaya Arrangement (ANZAM) became the cornerstone of New Zealand defence planning in Asia. The ANZUS agreement between the United States, Australia and ourselves was also a key part of our international policy. This and the establishment of the South East Asian Treaty Organisation (SEATO) in 1954 gave us the security arrangements we were looking for. By 1955 our focus had changed from the Middle East and after this we were convinced that our defence efforts should be in Asia.

Previous page:
A V Company patrol moving north of the Horseshoe, Phuoc Tuy Province, Vietnam, 1967. NZ DEFENCE OFFICIAL PHOTOGRAPH, AIM

Sergeant Dave Ogilvie of 1 Troop, and his patrols, with the aborigines of the Central Highlands, Malaya. COOPER ALBUM, AIM

The Emergency in Malaya, 1949–1960

Our commitment to South East Asia began with the outbreak of insurgency in Malaya in 1949. This coincided with the Communist Chinese takeover of China from the United States-supported Nationalist Government of Chiang Kai Chek in 1949 and we sent a flight of Douglas Dakota DC-3 aircraft to provide assistance to Hong Kong. These were based in Singapore at Changi Air Base and inevitably got involved dropping supplies by parachute to British and Commonwealth forces fighting the insurgents in Malaya.

Bristol Freighters over the jungle

> *[It was always] extremely hilly, lots of cloud hanging around them. Most of our dropping zones were in rather tricky places. Fort Brooke was one of these. It was a little area with a little airstrip with hills all around. You had to go in, drop and pour on the power and climb out. This made it extremely difficult. But nevertheless it was all gratifying particularly when you hit the target and that they got their food, clothing, medical supplies, ammunition and whatever they needed.*
>
> Ron Manners, No 41 Squadron RNZAF[2]

An SAS Trooper on patrol, Malaya.
COOPER ALBUM, AIM

The first New Zealanders to be stationed in South East Asia were the men of A Flight No 41 (Transport) Squadron who were based at Changi Air Base in Singapore from 1949–1951 and flew DC-3 Dakotas on supply drops over the Malayan jungle as well as courier runs throughout Asia. The Flight returned to New Zealand in 1951 but was back in 1955 as No 41 Squadron flying the twin-engined Bristol Freighter. With its distinctive, nose-opening cargo doors and its fixed undercarriage, the Bristol Freighter was capable of transporting a large payload of freight or passengers over comparatively short distances.[3] It was an ugly machine which for the next 22 years would become the ubiquitous symbol of New Zealand's defence effort in South East Asia.[4]

A Bristol Freighter — 30,000 rivets flying in close formation. COOPER ALBUM, AIM

A Dakota DC-3 of No 41 Squadron readying to parachute supplies over the Malayan jungle. *NZ HERALD*, AIM

With the Fijians in Malaya

He was quite at home [in the Malayan Jungle]. The jungle was slightly less demanding than the jungle he knew. Most of the Fijians were villagers. Very hardened people and used to frugal living. The idea that the Queen would pay you to go out in the jungle to patrol with a firearm was magic. To be a soldier was a great ambition of most Fijian boys. They looked with great respect on all the veterans from the Solomons who came home. And to this day if you go to a Fijian village you meet the Chiefs, the next thing you meet is a guard of honor of veterans with their medals. They have a status as commoners that they could never earn in any other way. In those days these boys' elder brothers had been to the Solomons and it was a great honour to be chosen for the Battalion.

Ian Thorpe, Adjutant, 1 Battalion Fiji Infantry Regiment[5]

In 1952 Fiji offered a battalion for service in Malaya to assist in the Emergency. New Zealand was responsible for assisting in the training of the Fiji Military Forces, and it was a handful of New Zealand officers and non-commissioned officers that had the task of raising, training and administering 1 Battalion Fiji Infantry Regiment.

The Battalion was barely trained when it went to Malaya in 1952, but by trial and error, initially under the leadership of the New Zealander Lieutenant Colonel Ron Tinker, it became the outstanding battalion on operations in the swamps and jungle around Yong Peng in Northern Johore.

Gradually Fijians replaced New Zealanders in the battalion appointments, but our experience with the Fijians in Malaya established the basis for New Zealand's expertise at jungle warfare. The Battalion returned to Fiji in 1956.

Jets over the jungle

I would take off from Singapore and fly out into Malaya at perhaps 20,000'. You would make contact with the operator and he would take control, and come down to bombing height, normally 10,000'. He would vector you onto his screen and then you rode along the beam. He would give you distance to target, tell you to open bomb doors. We would resettle the aeroplane again because when the doors opened all the trim would change. We would get the aeroplane settled down and then just do exactly as we were told... and eventually he would say 'drop now' and once we pressed the button, the old aeroplane would leap in the air, and away the bombs would go.

Ian Gilliard, Pilot, No 75 (Canberra Bomber) Squadron RNZAF[6]

No 14 (Fighter) Squadron RNZAF, flying Venom jet fighter-bombers leased from Great Britain, transferred from Cyprus to Tengah Air Base on Singapore Island in 1955. Its main job was to be part of the air defence of Singapore, but New Zealand Venoms also carried out rocket and bombing attacks against suspected guerilla positions in the jungle as part of New Zealand's assistance to the Federation of Malaya. In 1958 No 14 Squadron returned to New Zealand and was replaced by No 75 Squadron RNZAF flying leased Canberra bombers. The actual effectiveness of the bombing and rocket attacks against jungle bases was questionable, but the operational flying was valuable experience for our young pilots.

A Fijian patrol in the swamps around Yong Peng. The reaction to seeing the enemy was to run him down until they caught and shot him. COOPER COLLECTION, AIM

You would then call the bombs falling, because you can see them falling away from the aircraft. And then you would stay there and see the impact, with 1000 pounders you could feel the impact of the blast against the

The 14-day ration scale for one man.
NZ HERALD, QEII ARMY MEMORIAL MUSEUM

aircraft... You could actually see the shock wave of the bomb... There would be a deep orangey-red colouring under the jungle canopy, so you could actually see the impact point.

Pat Neville, Navigator, No 75 (Canberra Bomber) Squadron RNZAF[7]

The Kiwi soldier in the jungle

The New Zealand Special Air Service in Malaya

We worked as a squadron and the normal operations was about three months. We would take 14 day rations, which is a very heavy pack. We were dropped off by helicopter or by road... the idea was to walk for 3 or 4 days so that you got beyond where the enemy thought you were. The troops [of about 18 strong] were separated right from the beginning and it was very rare for one troop to see another, and certainly they were so far apart they could not help each other. Each troop would set up a firm base and it could well occupy that base for three months — perhaps move once or twice... the base might be hidden or it might be next door to an Aborigine settlement... to give them confidence to bring you information...

Lance Corporal Doug Mackintosh, 1 NZ SAS Squadron[8]

In 1955 we sent our first Regular Army unit on operations overseas in peace time. This was 1 New Zealand Special Air Service Squadron commanded by Major Frank Rennie. It was specially raised and trained to serve with 22 British Special Air Service Regiment in Malaya. It became the ground element of New Zealand's contribution to the British Commonwealth Far East Strategic Reserve, which also included the jets of No 14 Squadron, the Bristol Freighters of No 41 Squadron, and the regular attachment of a New Zealand frigate. Because of Frank Rennie's leadership the Squadron was superbly fit and trained before it got to Malaya. It built on that foundation and carried out deep jungle patrol operations as part of 22 British SAS Regiment, and became

Lieutenant Lindsay Williams, Commander of NZ 5 Troop. COOPER ALBUM, AIM

the most effective squadron in the regiment. In 1956 it worked in the Fort Brooke area of the Central Highlands in North Malaya and destroyed the Communist guerillas' grip over the aborigine tribes in its area of operations. It was equally successful in the so-called Mountainous Area of Negri Sembilan in 1957.

We proved to be outstanding jungle soldiers with the temperament to withstand the stresses of long operations. We also displayed that instinctive New Zealand trait, drawn from our blend of Maori and Pakeha, for getting on with the locals. This was essential to our success among the aborigines in the Fort Brooke operations. Success was also built on good intelligence and sound planning. We knew the job and we did it well under the leadership of young officers and non-commissioned officers who would graduate from leading patrols in Malaya in the 1950s to platoons and companies in Borneo and Vietnam in the 1960s and 1970s.

The New Zealand SAS Squadron established a reputation for performance that our professional infantry battalions, which replaced them, were determined to maintain. It was an important beginning to 44 years' service in South East Asia for New Zealand Regular Army units.

A New Zealand Battalion in Malaya

I was in front... There were only five of us in the patrol and as I came out to where the main track was, I couldn't believe my eyes because I saw this guy walking towards me in a khaki uniform and he had a khaki hat on and 'Good God! This must be what one of them looks like.' I just stood there, put my rifle up and looked down the sight straight at him and he wasn't actually looking at me. He hadn't heard me... and he had no idea the other guys were behind me and nobody had made any noise and anyway when he was about five yards away... I said 'Halt!' And straight away he dived to one side and he had a really big pistol and he tried to drag that out and I let him have it.

Peter Rutledge, 1 NZ Regiment[9]

A patrol of the New Zealand SAS Squadron in Malaya in 1957. From left: N Pepene, G Otene, A J Allen, P N Hurst, S C Watene and T A Stevens. *NZ HERALD*, QEII ARMY MEMORIAL MUSEUM

In 1957 the New Zealand SAS Squadron was replaced by the First Battalion New Zealand Regiment commanded by Lieutenant Colonel Kim Morrison. It joined 28 Commonwealth Brigade and operated as company groups in the Ipoh area of Perak. It was the closing stages of the Emergency, with the guerilla organisation beaten back into the jungle fastness, avoiding contact, and simply trying to survive.

Once again we showed the same strengths that had made the New Zealand SAS so successful. 'Wild Man' Morrison's Battalion was succeeded by Lieutenant Colonel Jock Aitken's Second Battalion New Zealand Regiment in 1959. The Emergency officially ended on 31 July 1960 with the remaining insurgents holed up in jungle bases across the border in Southern Thailand. Aitken's battalion continued to do jungle operations, as did Les Pearce's battalion that followed it from 1961–1963. But the emphasis now was on training the battalion for its SEATO role in the event of it being deployed on operations in Thailand, Laos or Vietnam.

Soldiers of the First Battalion New Zealand Regiment sail for Malaya in 1957.
NZ HERALD, QEII ARMY MEMORIAL MUSEUM

> *I think the thing that the Kiwi had over everybody else, they were more adaptable to bush life... He could adapt to anything...We had blokes carrying gunny sacks, old sugar bags tied top and bottom, and that was it. And that's how they operated... about 4 o'clock phase when you were on patrol you started to look for somewhere to settle. You made sure you had water, you made sure you were on good ground, you could get to the water easy but you were concealed enough to be comfortable... You'd cut little lanes that you could see and you'd put the vine around, cooked your kai and as soon as it got dark you'd climb into your pit and kept quiet... The Kiwi was good in the bush.*
>
> Buster Hornbrook, 1 NZ Regiment, Malaya[10]

Garrison life in Malaya

Joining the Army as a Regular Soldier

> *I was working on the Matahini Dam in Whakatane, and all of a sudden 20 of my mates decided to join the Army, and that just left me working there. That was Friday, come Monday I was there speaking to Charlie Howard, the Recruiting Sergeant in the Drill Hall in Whakatane. It was 1963. When I retired in 1983 there was only Dick Gibbons and myself in the army of those 20. Just the two of us.*
>
> *The Army was really what I expected. It suited us as well. Outdoor stuff, plenty of activity and we were moving around the country. I suppose the big factor was the friendships that you established. You got to know so many different guys.*
>
> *All those relationships from way, way back, they're still there.*
>
> Dan Heke, New Zealand SAS, Borneo[11]

Young men joined for the same reason young men had joined the New Zealand forces since the Boer War. It was a chance to get away and see the world and do interesting things. Few looked to the army as a long-term career, but for many that is what it became. For Maori in the 1950s the establishment of the Army, Navy and Air Force as professional regular organisations offered a means of advancement on merit that was lacking anywhere else in New Zealand society.

Private R Cook of Avondale, Auckland, on patrol with the First Battalion New Zealand Regiment in 1958. NZ HERALD, QEII ARMY MEMORIAL MUSEUM

An SAS patrol prepares to chopper out from an aborigine camp. COOPER ALBUM, AIM

Kiwi pay night in Ipoh

> *Thursday night was pay night for the Kiwi boys. Anchor Beer was 65 cents a big bottle, and there was broken glass on the floor that thick, and the guitars and the singing. Wild men but happy times.*
>
> Cheam Yeom Toon, FMS Bar, Ipoh[12]

It was the first time that we had large groups of New Zealanders overseas in a peacetime garrison environment, even if it did mean a lot of time jungle bashing. Battalions adopted their own bars. In Taiping the Springtide Night Club was popular, and in Ipoh the Boston Milk Bar in Cockman Street near the Lido Cinema was one of a number of bars that gave the New Zealanders a chance to let off steam.[13]

Things became a lot more formal once the Emergency was over and the New Zealand battalions moved into the 28 Commonwealth Brigade Camp at Terendak outside of Malacca in 1961. Dress for soldiers going on leave was white shirt, regimental tie, grey slacks and black shoes.

New Zealand families in South East Asia

> *It was interesting again from being overseas for the first time and having no knowledge of the East or of how people there lived. We did some terribly insensitive things simply because we knew no better, like thinking we were wearing a [straw] hat when in fact it was a meat-cover. We thought we were frightfully smart and we were laughed at quite a lot by the locals.*
>
> Pru Meldrum, Malaya[14]

This was the first time that we had Regular Air Force and Army units that took their families with them to a foreign country with different cultures. They put their familes into furnished houses while they went off to fly over the jungle

Second Lieutenant Huia Woods, Tracking Platoon Commander, checks a local's ID card. *NZ HERALD*, QEII ARMY MEMORIAL MUSEUM

or fight in it for the next two or three months. For most New Zealanders it was our first contact with Asia.

> *We are also supplied with an Amah, who does all the housework except the cooking, which Bett does herself. The Amah lives out, although there is a room provided for her, and works from 9 am to 5 pm, and for a few dollars will look after the kids if we want to go out... It's a bit awkward though. Her English is very limited and what there is is almost unintelligible. And although I can make myself understood in Malay, she speaks only a little and that with a Chinese accent. So when I'm away, Bett really has a picnic... The Amah's name is NEE MOOI... A good worker, though not above putting the clock forward an hour to knock off early, and likes to pinch my cigarettes.*
>
> Wally White, Company Sergeant Major, 1 NZ Regiment[15]

It was difficult for some families to adjust to the climate and the different culture and life style. Nothing had prepared New Zealand families for garrison life, because there was nothing equivalent in New Zealand, even in the married quarters of our military camps. The ripples of that experience spread throughout the community to a far greater extent than it had with Jayforce or Kayforce because they were made up only of single men seeing the world. Now it was our families and children living among and absorbing a different society. We became conscious of differences, and accepted it as normal, something we New Zealanders have traditionally found difficult to do. It was the continuation of the breakdown of our New Zealand insularity that had started in 1914, but now for the first time involved our families.

In South East Asia, New Zealand trade and diplomatic posts followed our military and their families. Our ambassadors in Asia were the 1 Battalion Royal New Zealand Infantry Regiment Band, our visiting RNZN ships' crews, our Bristol Freighter crews, our unit sports teams, and the Maori Concert parties made up of servicemen and their wives.

Kiwi soldiers of 1 Royal New Zealand Infantry Regiment patrolling for 'Indons' in the Pontian swamps, Malayan Peninsula, 1964. QEII ARMY MEMORIAL MUSEUM

Confrontation over Borneo

Target Jakarta

After a long flight down the Malacca Strait the squadron landed at Tengah after dark to find an air of tense expectation. Our aircraft were armed immediately. Aircraft including Vulcan bombers were dispersed as best they could be, vital points on the airfield were sandbagged and guarded and anti-aircraft gun regiments were deployed around the perimeter. The all-weather Javelin interceptor fighters stood at quick alert at the end of the runway. Only days before the Indonesians had made incursions with paratroop drops 100 miles to our north in the Labis area and Tengah stood ready in case the Indonesians should dare to attack this vital strike base using their Russian-built Badger bombers or older wartime Mitchell bombers. Within the past week the Far East Air Force (FEAF) had bolstered its strike force to 96 aircraft with the arrival of the Vulcan V-Bomber detachment, three Canberra (strike) squadrons, one Canberra (Photo Reconnaissance) squadron, and a Javelin (all weather) squadron to counter the Indonesian threat... for the next few months our training revolved around practice of the phases of attack required against Halim airfield and other secondary targets in Sumatra and offshore islands. The Squadron refined its tactical formations and adopted a level rocket release from 50 feet [15 metres] above the ground. We practised ever mindful of Sukarno's vow that he would crush Malaysia by the time the cock crowed on New Year's Day. But 1965 came and went.

Geoff Wallingford, Commanding No 14 (Canberra) Squadron, RNZAF [16]

In September 1964 we found ourselves involved in what was an undeclared border war between the recently established Federation of Malaysia and Indonesia. It was over the two former colonies of Sabah and Sarawak which shared a common land border with Indonesian Kalimantan on the island of Borneo. President Sukarno of Indonesia saw Malaysia as a threat to his expansionist plans. He believed that the island of Borneo should be part of Indonesia. Following the proclamation of the Federation of Malaysia on 16 September 1963 Sukarno refused to recognise it saying, 'We will fight and destroy it.'

Soldiers of Bob Gurr's battalion laying out sharpened bamboo stakes around their company base. QEII ARMY MEMORIAL MUSEUM

This Confrontation, as this border war in Borneo is now called, had begun with a revolt in the Sultanate of Brunei in 1962, which had been crushed by British forces. But Indonesia had trained Brunei dissidents in Kalimantan and sent them back on raids over the border. A series of coastal landings in Malaya by Indonesian military in August 1964 and the dropping of over 100 Indonesian paratroopers at Labis, North Johore, on 2 September 1964 prompted our government to release our battalion for operations on the Malayan Peninsula, and to send No 14 (Canberra) Squadron to Tengah Air Base on Singapore Island.

Our aircraft never bombed Jakarta, but our Bristol Freighters dropped supplies to British Commonwealth forces in Sabah and Sarawak. Our ships patrolled the seas around Borneo, and our sailors manned two small minesweepers which patrolled the coastline. Our First Battalion Royal New Zealand Infantry Regiment hunted Indonesian paratroopers on the Malayan Peninsula in September and October 1964 and then served in Borneo for six months in 1965 under Lieutenant Colonel Bob Gurr, and in 1966 for six months under Lieutenant Colonel Brian Poananga.

Claret operations in Borneo

A patrol could perform to optimum level for up to 28 days carrying what they could. On the proviso that you had unlimited access to water. Meals rotated around one meal a day with a brew for breakfast and one of those hard biscuits that you dunked in and imagined they were something else. Then the main meal, could be say, at lunch and it could be a tin of sardines, and a pack of noodles (which weighs bugger all), and if you mix sardines and noodles, I know it's hard to visualise, but it can be quite tasty. And then in the evening would be another brew with a second hard biscuit.... So we had to measure time and distance and weight and the fact that when you first go in you're strong, you're capable, and then after a period of some days you could actually have a peak, then without consciously being aware of it you actually taper off. Then you know when you're scraping the bottom, when what is actually a tiny wee hill suddenly looks like a bloody mountain. And you think, 'I think I'm about to hit the wall.'

Eru Manuera, New Zealand SAS, Borneo[17]

Firing the 105-mm field gun from a New Zealand Rifle Company base in Borneo.
QEII ARMY MEMORIAL MUSEUM

Jungle patrol during the Confrontation in Borneo, 1964. QEII ARMY MEMORIAL MUSEUM

In February 1965 we committed a 40-strong detachment of New Zealand SAS to Borneo and once again they worked with squadrons of the British 22 SAS Regiment. The SAS had the job of patrolling the vast jungle-covered mountainous border of Sarawak and Sabah with Indonesian Kalimantan. British and Malaysian resources were stretched wafer thin, and the Iban tribes that lived in the jungle were vulnerable to Indonesian raids. The SAS were there to give early warning of Indonesian raids across the border. This involved 'Claret' patrols, which was the code name for cross-border incursions deep into Indonesian territory to reconnoitre Indonesian bases and river supply routes. Our SAS patrols took part in these Claret operations knowing that if they were killed or captured their presence in enemy territory would be disowned. We sent four SAS Detachments to Borneo and as this border war escalated we slipped patrols across the border deep into Kalimantan, where they watched and ambushed Indonesian camps and river craft, forcing them back from the border.

The Battalion in Borneo

In May 1965, the same month in which our government announced that it was sending an artillery battery to South Vietnam, Lieutenant Colonel Bob Gurr's First Battalion Royal New Zealand Infantry Regiment sailed for Borneo for a six months' tour of duty on the Sarawak border. We took over from a Gurkha Battalion and established a series of border forts, often up to 30 kilometres apart, linked by helicopter with Gurr's headquarters at Simmanggang. We patrolled our 130-kilometre stretch of border looking for crossing places. Like the SAS, our infantry also carried out Claret raids into Indonesian territory, attacking camps and ambushing tracks. It was a secret war that the public were never aware of. By now the New Zealand professional experience of over 10 years of jungle warfare was very evident with jungle veterans at each level of command within the Battalion, from a 10-man section to a 120-strong company. We were very good at what we did and dominated both sides of the border until returning to Terendak Camp in September 1965.

> As we progressed up the axis of the track, one of our right hand clearing parties spotted two Indonesians hiding under some lilies. I deployed troops around them and then moved forward to disarm them shouting out in my best bazaar Malay not to shoot or they would be shot. They didn't seem to understand my language skills as one of them opened up with a Madsen submachine gun and the other threw a grenade at me. Our machine gunner, Roy Kaaka, from up Te Kao way, opened up, shouting: 'They moved boss, they moved.' I didn't know whether to laugh or cry. The grenade hadn't gone off and there I was staring at it, while others in the group were trying to dig a hole with their bare hands. When it was clear the grenade was not going to explode, I said so and they looked at me in amazement. And no, it wasn't just a case of my being cool under fire, my reactions just hadn't been as fast as theirs as I hadn't even thought of diving for cover.
>
> Brian Marshall, Platoon Commander, A Company, First Battalion
> Royal New Zealand Infantry Regiment, Borneo[18]

In May 1966 the Battalion, now commanded by Lieutenant Brian Poananga, did a second tour in Borneo. In Jakarta, Sukarno had been deposed and the Confrontation was coming to an end. There were no more Claret operations, and our soldiers improved their border forts and hoped against hope that the Indonesians would make a raid. It ended in September 1966 when we handed over to a Malaysian battalion.

The names of 66 New Zealanders are inscribed on the walls of the Memorial Hall at the Auckland Museum. They are the names of those who died during New Zealand's commitment to Malaysia from 1949 to 1989, including seven New Zealanders killed in action during the Malayan Emergency.

Thirty-five New Zealanders were to be killed in action during the Vietnam War and 187 wounded.

Reluctantly into South Vietnam

This has to be the best war I've ever been to — it's set in a tropical paradise, free food and lodgings, duty-free grog and tobacco, wonderful company, and non-stop entertainment.
Joe Rutherford, Royal New Zealand Artillery, 161 Battery, Vietnam[19]

New Zealand's involvement in Vietnam in the 1960s was a reluctant one by Holyoake's National government. The deteriorating situation in Vietnam between 1961 and 1963 paralleled the growing confrontation with Indonesia. Our defence forces were at full stretch, and we were keen to meet a commitment to both Britain and the United States. Our only operational infantry battalion, the First Battalion Royal New Zealand Infantry Regiment, was stationed at Terendak as part of the Commonwealth Strategic Reserve, and No 14 (Canberra Bomber) Squadron, which was our only operational RNZAF combat squadron, was committed to the Confrontation in Borneo in September 1964. Other than engineers and possibly medical assistance, there was little left to offer in response to growing American pressure to commit New Zealand resources to Vietnam. Holyoake was aware that it was not the size of the commitment that was important — it was being seen to be there alongside the Americans. He was also aware that once made, there would be inevitable pressure to increase the size of New Zealand's contribution. Our government had no doubts about the importance of supporting both the British and American defence efforts in Asia. The question was what to send?

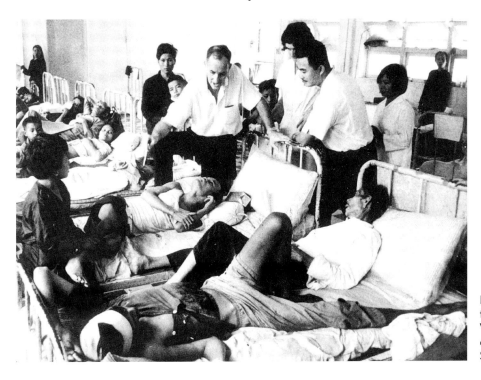

Dr Douglas Short of Tauranga, leader of the New Zealand medical team to Vietnam, on his rounds through the crowded wards of Qui Nhon hospital in September 1966. GEORGE KOHLAP, AIM

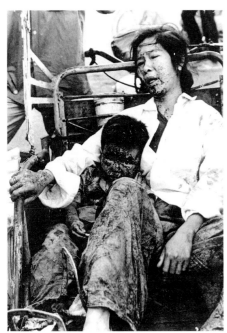

Vietnamese civilians caught in the crossfire of war, 1968. AIM

A medical team to Vietnam

The wards are always full and overflowing. There are thirty-bed wards, but have up to sixty patients in them. There is no separation of the sexes, men and women share the same wards, and often the same beds, and there are always patients being nursed on stretchers down the middle of the wards. From the wards I go back to the operating rooms, and just get stuck into whatever has to be done. This may be some cold cases, or new stuff or we may be inundated with casualties.

Peter Eccles Smith, *Letters From A Viet Nam Hospital*[20]

Our first tangible commitment was a civilian surgical team to a provincial hospital at Qui Nhon in South Vietnam. This was bolstered in 1967 by a Services Medical Team which later shifted to a hospital in the provincial capital of Bong Son. The teams saw at first hand how the Vietnamese civilians were paying for this war. Their purpose was to assist and train the Vietnamese to look after their own people, but training took second place to the ongoing requirement of coping with civilian casualties.

A gunner in Vietnam

I was 23 years old, newly married to Heather my 20-year-old bride, with a 10-month-old daughter Teresa and another (Josephine) in the breech; we lived in an Army married quarter in Papakura furnished with items on hire purchase, and we owned a 1963 light green Ford Cortina. I stole away to Vietnam, like a thief in the night, at 4 o'clock on a frosty late-August Papakura morning. I wore brand new jungle greens, and carried all the belongings I needed for war in one kit bag. Our Hercules flight left Whenuapai early in the morning, in the dark and out of the public gaze. This was not (as the protest movement had it) to avoid unfavourable publicity, but to enable the aircraft to fulfil its complex flight-plan over the long journey to Vung Tau, Vietnam, via Alice Springs and Singapore in daylight.

I served my eight-month tour in a variety of roles; gun line Section Commander (September–November 1970) (for which I was most qualified); artillery liaison officer with the adjacent (Thai) formation in Bien Hoa

New Zealand infantry in Vietnam.
NZ HERALD, AIM

Province to the North (December 1970–January 1971) (for which, only through my inherited personal cunning and guile, I was partially qualified) and Gun Position Officer (GPO) February–April 1971 (for which I was most certainly not qualified).

Bill Barnes, Royal New Zealand Artillery, 161 Battery, Vietnam[21]

Bill Barnes went to Vietnam at the tail-end of our commitment. The Battery that he served with was our first combat force commitment to Vietnam in June 1965 — a four-gun field battery deployed in support of the First Battalion Royal Australian Regiment, which would be part of the United States 173 Airborne Brigade at Bien Hoa. The Battery replaced our first military contribution to Vietnam which was a 25-strong engineer detachment deployed on non-combat engineering work in June 1964. This was withdrawn when the guns were deployed. Our government sent the minimum possible; four guns instead of the standard six guns in a battery, and in our parsimonious New Zealand way trimmed everything else to the bone:

> *This did not prevent the Battery celebrating Guy Fawkes Night by firing coloured smoke, illumination, and white phosphorous rounds into the sky above War Zone D. Some US units, ignorant of the significance of Guy Fawkes Night, asked Brigade Headquarters what was going on to be told that the Kiwis were celebrating some 'Guy' called 'Fox'.*
>
> Bob Breen, *First to Fight*[22]

In June 1966 the Battery was increased to six guns and transferred to 1 Australian Task Force at Nui Dat in Phuoc Tuy Province, south east of Saigon. Working with the Americans was a learning experience for us, and even with the Australians our small Army found it difficult to man the battery and drew from other corps within the Army to provide gun numbers. We served with 1 Australian Task Force in Phuoc Tuy until we were withdrawn in May 1971.

> *My clearest memory of this is the way the artillery was knocking out the reserve line that was forming up. I think it was one of the primary reasons that we didn't get bowled over, because you'd see them move off and the assault line would be getting to the stage where we would consider firing on them, and, wham, down would come the artillery and the whole reserve looked like it got completely wiped out.*
>
> Geoff Kendall, Platoon Commander, D Company, 6 Royal Australian Regiment,
> describing the Battle of Long Tan, 18 August 1966[23]

Captain Morrie Stanley, Royal New Zealand Artillery, the artillery fire controller with D Company 6 Royal Australian Regiment at the Battle of Long Tan, looks at the battlefield the next morning. *NZ HERALD*, AIM

The command post of 161 Battery, Vietnam. AIM

Flying helicopters with the Americans

I did, I think, about two or three weeks flying the UHIB, which was the helicopter gunship that they had. It was a much older aircraft which was loaded up with all these rockets and grenade launchers and the rest of it. It was grossly underpowered and on a hot day you couldn't get it off the ground in a hover enough to fly.... With an assault you'd fly down either side of the formation of troop-carrying aircraft and the artillery would go in first, and then the jet aircraft would go in and strafe and drop CBUs [Cluster Bomb Units], and as the troop lift aircraft came in you'd fly down beside them slightly ahead and you'd strafe the perimeter of the landing zone. So anybody there would keep their head down to give enough time for the troop-carrying aircraft to get their troops on the ground and take off, and then you'd cover them on the way home.

Roger Pearce, Royal New Zealand Artillery, Helicopter Pilot Vietnam[24]

Roger Pearce was the first New Zealander to fly helicopters on operations in Vietnam. In July 1967 RNZAF pilots were deployed with the 9 Royal Australian Air Force Helicopter Squadron supporting the Australian Task Force. In December 1968 our pilots were formally attached to work as Forward Air Controllers with the United States Air Force.

Serving in the ANZAC Battalion: NZ Infantry in Vietnam

I was a section commander in Vietnam and I was lucky enough to have a guy who was my lead scout that I considered to be the best scout in our company at that time, that was Whisky 2 Company, and all the section commanders wanted him. [He could] pick up sign and in places like Vietnam where there are all sorts of bloody signs that the VC [Viet Cong] used to leave around in terms of things like booby traps or bloody mines and that sort of thing, you've got to have people who can pick that up. Normal scouts wouldn't be looking for that sort of thing. They'd be looking for people or buildings. But I found that the scout I had... even a turned leaf, even a broken twig would tell him something.

Dick Smith, Royal New Zealand Infantry Regiment, Section Commander Whisky 2 Company, Vietnam[25]

A Sioux helicopter pilot provides observation as New Zealand infantry leave their armoured personnel carriers below. NZ HERALD, AIM

A V Company patrol moving in the Horseshoe (a company defensive position located eight kilometres south east of the Australian Task Force base at Nui Dat), Phuoc Tuy Province, 1967. NZ DEFENCE OFFICIAL PHOTOGRAPH, AIM

Our government drip-fed increases in our combat commitment to Vietnam. Our involvement in Malaya and Borneo had met with little public response. There was general acceptance, even apathy. Not so with the announcement of combat military support to Vietnam. Holyoake's government was surprised by the depth of public reaction and antipathy and was very careful in how it eked out each addition to the American war in Vietnam. In March 1967 it announced that a rifle company would be sent to Vietnam. Our Battalion had hoped for an ANZAC Battalion, with New Zealand providing the headquarters and two companies. By December 1967 we had two companies, V for Victor and W for Whisky, in Vietnam and in March 1968 an ANZAC Battalion was formally established with Australia providing the headquarters and command staff. We were submerged in the much larger Australian effort.

Our rifle companies were the best that we had. They were commanded by veterans who had served in Malaya and Borneo, and were manned by volunteers who had to compete to get there. By contrast the Australian battalions were manned by conscripted National Servicemen. In January 1969 a Troop of New Zealand SAS was deployed, and New Zealanders in Vietnam totalled 550. This was the peak of our commitment. The 1968 Tet offensive had been a military disaster for the Viet Cong and the North Vietnamese, but it was also their political victory. Television showed pictures of fighting in downtown Saigon, and of summary executions in the streets. It convinced the American public that this was a war that could not be won, and one they should not be fighting. It had similar echoes in New Zealand.

While Vietnam was a dirty war, it is important to remember that in Phuoc Tuy Province, which was the Australian area of operations, we achieved a semblance of normalcy for the population before withdrawing in 1971. By then it was obvious that this was not a war we could win. We crept away under the excuse of 'Vietnamization' and left two training teams to cover our departure.

Facing up to Vietnam

> *I was teaching at Selwyn College. I just thought that the war was a calamity and that there was no cause for American interference and that there was no cause for our government to take New Zealand into a war of dubious origin and outcome.*
>
> Jeny Curnow[26]

The Expeditionary Force that we sent overseas to fight the Second World War didn't come home until 1972, when New Zealand withdrew our forces from Vietnam. During that time we kept small forces overseas in support of Britain and the United States to ensure that the threat we faced from Japan in 1941 never came as close again. It was something that the New Zealand public took for granted; Jayforce in Japan, was replaced by Kayforce in Korea, which overlapped our RNZAF squadrons and Special Air Service Squadron in Malaya fighting in the Emergency. Our SAS Squadron was replaced by an infantry battalion, and was involved in turn in the Confrontation in Borneo from 1964–1966, and then in Vietnam. It was our involvement in Vietnam that finally prompted the New Zealand public to question what we were fighting for. The Second World War, in a sense, ended for New Zealand in 1972.

Anti-Vietnam war protestors in Auckland's Civic Square during a march through the city of SAS troops bound for duty in Vietnam, 1971. *NZ HERALD*, AIM

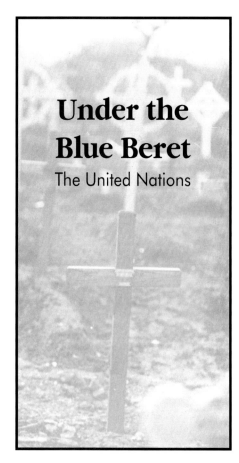

Under the Blue Beret

The United Nations

...a world organisation for peace and security and social and economic justice is a great achievement in cooperation and unity.

Peter Fraser, Prime Minister of New Zealand, 1945[1]

During the Second World War, the Allied nations fighting the Axis powers of Germany, Italy (until 1943) and Japan decided that they had to work together to ensure that there would never be another world war. This had been the aim of the League of Nations in the 1920s and 1930s, but without the support of the United States this organisation did not have the authority nor the will to achieve that aim. At San Francisco on 26 June 1945, even before the Second World War had ended, the 51 countries on the Allied side signed the Charter of the United Nations. The United Nations (UN) became a legal international body on 24 October 1945.

As we had been with the League of Nations, New Zealand was, and continues to be, a keen supporter of the United Nations. In 1945 our Prime Minister, Peter Fraser, was whole-heartedly behind the UN, and it was his hope that it would support small countries in the international arena when larger countries were using their power to get their own way.

While there has not been another world war, perhaps due to the work and influence of the UN, the organisation was not successful in ensuring that wars did not happen again; conflicts between nations have been a feature of the last fifty years of the twentieth century.

Among the many additional roles and responsibilities that the UN has taken on, its key aim is still to work for a peaceful solution to disputes between countries and within countries. If a situation or crisis arises this may be investigated by the Security Council, which is always in session, and it can recommend imposing sanctions or the implementation of peacekeeping action. The Security Council consists of five permanent members, who were the major powers at the end of the Second World War; the United States, Russia, the United Kingdom, France and China, and ten others elected every two years which are grouped according to region. New Zealand is eligible for election from the 'Western Europe and others' group of states. We were a member of the Security Council in 1954–55, 1966 and from 1993 to 1994, playing an important role in the United Nations' involvement in the former Yugoslavia.

The Korean War: Our first UN involvement

Our navy first

North Korea's invasion of South Korea on 24 June 1950 led to the decision by the UN Security Council to drive the North Korean People's Army back over the 38 Parallel by force if they did not withdraw voluntarily. New Zealand was one of the first to support the UN in this action. On 29 June Prime Minister Sidney Holland promised naval support and on 3 July two of our frigates, HMNZS *Tutira* and *Pukaki*, sailed for Korea and were part of the convoy escorts during the Inchon landings. This was General Douglas MacArthur's bold counterstroke to cut off the North Korean forces in South Korea by mounting an amphibious landing at the Port of Inchon near the South Korean capital of Seoul. In turn, the New Zealand frigates *Taupo, Hawea, Kaniere* and *Rotoiti* also served. At any one time, two were maintained in Korean waters under UN command for the next four years, until March 1954.

> *We went over and did two patrols off Korea, one down off Pusan and one around on the other side. I remember we really learnt what it had been like in the winter up there.... even at slow speed the spray coming over the foc'sle was icicles by the time it hit the bridge. You were standing up there in a sou'wester and oil skins and a towel around your neck. You would have to duck as you could get badly stung by the ice. Ice all over the 4 inch and over the Squid up forwards. You were watching that you weren't getting top heavy. The ship would be sweating down below, cold as charity. We had heaters in the ship, but trying to keep any warmth in the ship was difficult... It was pretty miserable.*
>
> Lieutenant E C Thorne, RNZN[2]

The Korean War involved all six frigates in eight completed tours of duty involving half of the total Navy; some 1350 personnel in all. By the time the ceasefire talks were agreed, New Zealand ships had steamed 339,584 miles (546,390 kilometres) and fired 71,625 rounds of ammunition. One seaman was killed during *Rotoiti*'s first tour when a raiding party went ashore, and naval personnel were awarded seven Distinguished Service Crosses (DSC), two Distinguished Service Medals (DSM), one Member of the British Empire (MBE), 14 Mentioned in Despatches and one posthumous Mentioned in Despatches. During the Korean War New Zealand ships intercepted pirate attacks on shipping, mounted commando raids, patrolled the coastline of North and South Korea and bombarded shore targets.[3]

A helicopter lowers an intelligence officer onto the decks of HMNZS *Taupo* off the Korean Coast. QEII ARMY MEMORIAL MUSEUM

The Kiwis of Kayforce

> *I had always been dead keen to get away overseas. I had the travel bug. It was the spirit of adventure. I didn't even know where Korea was. When we left New Zealand we thought it was going to be a great holiday. We more or less expected the Korean War to be finished when we got there.*
>
> Ian Mackley, 16 Field Regiment, Royal New Zealand Artillery[4]

A Loch Class frigate, HMNZS *Tutira.*
JORDAN COLLECTION, AIM

The deteriorating situation for the UN in Korea and the withdrawal of the United States and Republic of South Korea's (ROK) forces back into the Pusan perimeter on the south-east toe of the peninsula led to New Zealand's offer of Kayforce (K for Korea), a 1000-strong contingent consisting of 16 Field Regiment, Royal New Zealand Artillery, and other smaller units including a transport platoon.

Gunner George Horsfall. MACKLEY COLLECTION, AIM

> *A lot of them had been in J Force, perhaps 20 per cent had been in the Second World War. The majority had no service experience at all. I was 22.... My first impression of Korea was of absolute horror. The city of Pusan was a whole lot of shacks and huts, with 10 times its normal population with refugees pouring in. It was a freezing morning. The cold was the first thing that hit us. We were so poorly equipped. The guys who had been in Italy said it was nothing like as cold as Korea.*
>
> Ian Mackley, 16 Field Regiment, Royal New Zealand Artillery[5]

While Kayforce assembled in New Zealand, the United States-led UN force had driven the North Koreans beyond the border at the 38 Parallel and decided to reunite the country. This saw China enter the war and equally rapidly drive the UN forces south. Kayforce arrived in Korea during this Chinese offensive. They joined 27 British Commonwealth Brigade, which included two British and one Australian battalion, and on 24 January 1951 fired the first of the 750,000 shells fired by our artillery during the Korean war. Our gunners played an important part in providing fire support in the Battle of Kapyong from 23–25 April 1951, when the Chinese made their last great effort to throw the UN forces back into the sea.

> *By this time the ROKs were going past by the hundred and we commenced firing at 7000 yards and the range got shorter and shorter to 400 yards. At 1900 hours [7 p.m.] came the order 'prepare for open sight shooting — corner 300 yards away'. Almost immediately came the sound I shall never forget — a panicked army [the South Korean] at the double filling the whole road and coming around the corner 300 yards away. Had we opened up on them we could have probably saved the lives of a number of the [27] Brigade as we discovered afterward that the Chinese were coasting along with them…*
>
> Second Lieutenant William Watson, 16 Field Regiment, Royal New Zealand Artillery[6]

Recruits for K Force: *It was the spirit of adventure.* QEII ARMY MEMORIAL MUSEUM

A forward observation post. Fred Frederickson and Graham Thompson with the binoculars. MACKLEY COLLECTION, AIM

After this battle, Kayforce was increased to 1500 with the arrival of the trucks of 10 Transport Company of the Royal New Zealand Army Service Corps. We became part of the newly formed 1 Commonwealth Division and our trucks carried troops and supplies to 28 Commonwealth Brigade. We did all sorts of jobs: driving trucks, being signallers at headquarters, manning a 'Kiwi' tank in a British armoured regiment, and attached as infantry to the Australian battalions.

Jack Spiers: An infantryman in Korea

> *I'd grown up very, very quickly. I'd seen a lot of men killed, a lot of men wounded and at that stage towards the end I was getting scared myself because the odds were getting a bit bloody short... looking back now as an older man it took me many years to come down to earth.*
>
> Jack Spiers, New Zealand infantry attached to 3RAR[7]

From December 1951 a stalemate developed with both sides dug in along the hilly country marking the general line of the 38 Parallel. It was a cold, bloody war, similar in many ways to the trench warfare on the Western Front. Finally an armistice was signed on 27 July 1953, but our artillery regiment was not withdrawn until the end of 1954. The last New Zealanders left Korea in July 1957.

Our involvement in the Korean War received general public support in New Zealand. It was under the UN banner and was seen as necessary, with the Soviet Union consolidating its hold in Europe and Communist China growing increasingly powerful in Asia. Wars of nationalism were being fought in Indo-china and Malaya, and we saw them as Communist-inspired and a threat to our national security.

Korea has become one of our forgotten wars. Some 4700 personnel served in Kayforce, with another 1300 serving on our frigates. Forty-three New Zealanders lost their lives in this seven-year commitment to the UN.

16 Field Regiment in action at the Battle of Kapyong. QEII ARMY MEMORIAL MUSEUM

Peacekeeping operations — tailor-made for New Zealanders?

Peacekeeping is not a job for soldiers, but only soldiers can do it.

Dag Hammarsjkold[8]

Many peacekeeping operations of different types have been carried out by the UN, assisting countries to resolve their differences by providing neutral military observers to monitor ceasefire agreements, to assist in free elections or to protect humanitarian aid. The term 'peacekeeping' is confusing; it implies something other than a military operation, but that is wrong. Peacekeeping is an operation of war demanding all the skills of service personnel in wartime, and something more. It demands the highest self-discipline at every level, particularly when a potentially fatal situation could arise out of an incident that occurs after months of boring routine. It is just these skills that our soldiers displayed in Bosnia, East Timor and Afghanistan.

> *It's… small groups of New Zealanders sorting problems out on the ground, in many cases with people pointing automatic weapons at them. It's discipline and skill that lets them stand impartial even when morally they might feel that one side has a superior position.*
>
> Major General Piers Reid, Chief of General Staff, New Zealand Army[9]

Initially our commitment to peacekeeping operations was secondary to our military commitments with Britain and the United States in South East Asia. Our military observers came principally from the ranks of the Territorial Force, and while that does not reflect at all on the standard of their performance, there was a feeling in the 1960s and 1970s among New Zealand Regular Service personnel that peacekeeping postings were a lesser priority, and somehow not really operational. That ended in the 1980s. Peacekeeping operations are anything but peaceful and the number of operations grow every year with New Zealand actively participating in many of them.

The United Nations Military Observer Group in India and Pakistan (UNMOGIP) 1951–1976

New Zealand's first commitment of military observers was to Kashmir, an area in north-west India that was being fought over by both India and Pakistan after the 1947 partition of British India. UNMOGIP was established to monitor the ceasefire agreement between India and Pakistan. Initially, New Zealand agreed to send three Territorial officers in 1951 and they worked in small teams along the ceasefire line. It was a demanding job in rugged, mountainous country, where a hefty walking stick was obligatory protection against dogs in a land where rabies is endemic. The number of New Zealand observers varied according to the state of tension between India and Pakistan. We ended our commitment to UMOGIP in 1976 as a government cost-cutting measure.

The United Nations Truce Supervision Organisation (UNTSO) 1954–

New Zealand agreed to provide military observers to UNTSO in response to a UN request for additional military observers because of the deteriorating situation along the ceasefire lines between Israel, Egypt, Jordan, Syria and Lebanon. Two Territorial officers were sent in July 1954, and we have maintained a commitment to UNTSO ever since, making it New Zealand's longest ongoing involvement with a UN mission. As in Kashmir, the number of New Zealand military observers has varied according to the state of tension in the Middle East, and in response to the outbreak of war in 1956, 1967, 1973 and the invasion of Lebanon in 1982. At present New Zealand has a specialist team of 10 battlefield clearance experts in Lebanon helping clear some of the estimated one million mines that litter the landscape after the fighting between Israel and Hezbollah in July 2006 alone.

Both Regular and Territorial Force officers have served with UNTSO in what at times has been a most dangerous assignment to maintain peace. New Zealanders have been wounded, and beaten up, but as yet none have lost their lives in this the most constant of the world's flashpoints.

> I ended up in Lebanon in the first month of the Israeli invasion. The UN flew in a force on an emergency basis to set up a buffer zone along the Litani River… There were a lot of people being killed in Lebanon at the time… mainly by mines. I drove a lot by myself, and for protection I used to sit on two flak jackets, and if I hit a mine so be it. The mines were the greatest threat, then the PLO. They would ambush you and steal your vehicle. There was nothing you could do, they were armed and you were not. They stole 400 UN vehicles and you would see them being driven around but you could not touch them.
>
> Clive Sinclair, UNTSO and UNIFIL (United Nations Interim Force in Lebanon)[10]

Policing for the United Nations in Cyprus: United Nations Peacekeeping Force in Cyprus (UNFICYP) 1964–1967

Following the independence of Cyprus from Britain in 1960, violence broke out between the Turkish and Greek communities living there. UNFICYP was established in March 1964 to maintain law and order between the two communities, and between 1964 and 1967 79 members of the New Zealand Police served with the United Nations Civil Police (UNCIVPOL) in Cyprus.

Major Pat McDonald and his team at Assembly Area 'Mike'.
NZ DEFENCE OFFICIAL PHOTOGRAPHY

The Commonwealth Monitoring Force (CMF): Zimbabwe 1979–1980

In 1979 New Zealand committed 74 personnel to the British-sponsored CMF that was to monitor the ceasefire agreement between the forces of the Ian Smith's government in Rhodesia, that had unilaterally declared Rhodesian independence in 1964 and which fought a bitter civil war against the forces of the Patriotic Front. The CMF was primarily British with small contingents from Australia, New Zealand, Kenya and Fiji. Our New Zealand Contingent, commanded by Colonel David Maloney, provided a small headquarters in the Rhodesian capital Salisbury (now Harare), a number of teams to monitor Rhodesian Army units. Two teams were also provided to man two assembly areas: Assembly Area Lima for members of Robert Mugabe's Zimbabwe African National Liberation Army (ZANLA), and Assembly Area Mike for Joshua Nkomo's Zimbabwe People's Revolutionary Army (ZIPRA). Our small New Zealand teams were effective in very difficult conditions among hundreds of armed and suspicious men where the wrong look or reaction could have led to bloodshed.

Sergeant Jerry Haiwai driving the 'Kiwi Express'. NZ DEFENCE OFFICIAL PHOTOGRAPHY

I visited the assembly places as often as I could. Brian Hewitt was in the middle of nowhere with a ZIPRA camp. Very professional with East German-type training, who were nice guys and good people except they were savage. You know their discipline was shooting people basically. Pat McDonald had a motley crew of ZANLA guerrillas and he had a lot more of them as well. His circumstances were a bit better, being in an old mission hospital… The only real stand-up I had was down at the border where Gordon Gullery was. We went into the Mess where the Rhodesians and South African officers were, and nobody talked to us, nobody. At the end I stood at the door and told them that I'd been in officers' mess all over the world and that they were the rudest bunch of bastards I had ever met in my life, and that I would be quite delighted if I never saw any of them again. And the British officer with me nearly wet his trousers. I also told them that Gordon Gullery was trying to do a job and you are not making it easy for him, and I find that bloody offensive. Eventually one or two of them actually helped Gordon after that. So it had done some good, but that's the sort of thing we were up against. We were part enemy, part not.

Colonel David Maloney, Commander New Zealand Contingent, CMF, Zimbabwe[11]

Training the monitoring forces in the Sinai: Multinational Force and Observers (MFO) 1982–

I was posted as the Duty Operations Officer to Sinai during the period October 1994 to May 1995 as part of New Zealand's contingent of 25 personnel. My job was to run the MFO Operations Centre which monitored the 31 observation posts and checkpoints throughout 'Zone C' in the Sinai. I would also investigate any alleged violations of the treaty which were reported. My job in Sinai was extremely busy and rewarding... Being posted to Sinai as a peacekeeper meant an awful lot to me. It was a chance to illustrate to the other participating nations the professionalism and dedication of the New Zealand Army. It was also an opportunity to put my years of training into practise.

Captain Karyn Marie Te Moana, RNZ Signals[12]

Captain Karyn Te Moana sitting on some debris of battle in the Sinai. TE MOANA COLLECTION, AIM

The MFO was established independent of the UN at the instigation of the United States to monitor a 164-kilometre wide no-man's-land known as 'Zone C' in the Sinai Desert. Zone C was established after the peace treaty between Egypt and Israel, which saw the evacuation of the Israeli forces in 1982. Initially our contribution was to an ANZAC unit operating 10 Iroquois Helicopters, two of which were operated by RNZAF personnel. Two of these RNZAF personnel became the first New Zealand women posted to a peacekeeping operation, albeit one run outside the auspices of the UN. The ANZAC Helicopter unit disbanded on Australia's withdrawal in 1986, after which New Zealand provided staff for MFO Headquarters and a 12-strong Training and Advisory Team for the training of MFO personnel.

In 1989, a New Zealander and former Chief of General Staff, Major General Don McIvor, was appointed MFO Force Commander in the rank of Lieutenant General and became the first New Zealander to command a major international peacekeeping operation. Appropriately enough it was in a part of the world that had seen a New Zealander, Major General Ted Chaytor, command the Anzac Mounted Division during the First World War, and where Major General Sir Bernard Freyberg commanded 2 New Zealand Division in the Second World War. McIvor's appointment is the highest-ranking operational command held by a New Zealander since Freyberg in the Second World War.

Twenty-five years later, our commitment to MFO continues with ongoing provision of transport drivers, a driver training team and headquarters staff.

Monitoring the Iran–Iraq ceasefire: the UN Iran–Iraq Military Observer Group (UNIIMOG) 1988–1991

I was posted to Northern Iran and Kurdistan. I was the sector commander and took over from a Finnish officer. The sector stretched for 500 kilometres from the Turkish border and the altitude was 3000 metres, so it was like operating at the summit of Ruapehu. It was minus 20 degrees in winter and very hot in summer. I commanded 41 observers of 14 different nationalities and we patrolled that border. It was the first time I had the chance to negotiate peace at a local level and resolve local hot spots.

Lieutenant Colonel Clive Sinclair, UNIIMOG[13]

In 1988 the bloody eight-year Iran–Iraq war ended. At short notice New Zealand provided 10 military observers, commanded by Lieutenant Colonel

An Afghan girl with a butterfly mine – detonator intact – which she found near her hillside home. HEATON COLLECTION

John Fisher, who deployed along the ceasefire line as part of UN observer teams in the days before the ceasefire came into effect. All the New Zealanders were based in Iran. Living conditions were primitive, with extremes of temperature, and teams were isolated among suspicious soldiery or Iranian Revolutionary Guardsmen. Initially, ceasefire violations were common and the duties taxed the most professional – one such duty was arranging the exchange of bodies between the opposing forces. An RNZAF Andover was attached and provided a vital transport link between the UN headquarters in Tehran and its sector headquarters in the field. Iraq's invasion of Kuwait led to the disbanding of the observer group in February 1991.

Operation Salam: training Afghan refugees in Pakistan to clear mines, 1989–1991

Millions of unmarked land-mines – grim reminders of the Soviet occupation of Afghanistan left after their withdrawal in 1989 – continue to take a deadly toll. The UN set up the United Nations Mine Clearance Training Team (UNMCTT) to train Afghan refugees in camps in Pakistan to identify and clear mines so that they could return to their homes and clear the surrounding pasture land and get on with their lives. We committed a five-man team of New Zealand Army engineers to take part in this programme in 1989. Based in Peshawar, in north-western Pakistan, our engineers ran a series of courses and trained several thousand Afghans, including instructors, before being withdrawn in December 1991 for commitment to Cambodia on a similar task.

Assisting Elections in Namibia: the United Nations Transition Assistance Group (UNTAG) 1989–1990

UNTAG was established to supervise the ceasefire between South African Forces and the South-West Africa People's Organization (SWAPO) in Namibia, and to assist in tasks associated with holding the country's first elections. Thirty-two New Zealand police were part of a UN Civilian Police organisation monitoring the Namibian police and ensuring their impartiality. In addition, a team of 14 engineers were attached to an Australian Engineer unit on de-mining duties and destruction of ammunition and explosives. Our team withdrew in 1990.

Our second war for the UN: the Gulf War 1990–1991

The Iraqi invasion of Kuwait on 2 August 1990 led to the creation of a UN force under United States command that assembled in Saudi Arabia to resist any Iraqi invasion. It was the second time that New Zealand had become involved in a war waged by the UN. In this instance, our contribution was minute. Our commitment was to provide two C-130 Hercules transport aircraft and an Army Medical Team to the 500,000-strong multinational forces in Saudi Arabia. Our Air Force worked in with the RAF, and our 32-strong medical team became part of the United States Navy's 6 Naval Fleet Hospital. A further 20-strong medical team from all three services was sent in January 1991 and served with an RAF hospital. The rapid success of Operation Desert Storm by the UN forces and the liberation of Kuwait meant that there was little operational work for our medical teams and the last of our personnel were withdrawn in April 1991.

Destroying Iraq's weapons of mass destruction: the UN Special Commission on Iraq (UNSCOM) 1991–1999

> *When you would cross the road people would throw rocks at you, spit at you and even try to run you down in their cars.*
>
> Major David Le Page, Royal New Zealand Army Medical Corps[14]

After the Gulf War, UNSCOM was established to supervise the destruction of Iraq's long-range missile systems, its chemical and biological weapon stocks, and their means of manufacture. New Zealand initially provided the medical support for this team, then expanded to include administrative and communications support. It was highly dangerous work in a volatile and intensely unfriendly environment.

Monitoring the truce in Angola: the UN Angolan Verification Mission (ANAVEM) II and III, and clearing the minefields, 1991–1999

> *Angola is a beautiful country, rich in resources with a superb climate. The very sad thing is that it was clear that both sides have had a gutsful of war, and demonstrated that they could get on with each other and start to make it work. But now its back to fighting. I think we achieved something, and I still feel satisfaction for what I did there.*
>
> Colonel Trevor McComish, New Zealand Military Observer, UNAVEM II[15]

New Zealand contributed a large number of military observers to UNAVEM, which was tasked with overseeing the carrying out of the peace accord between the two principal warring factions, the UNITA rebel forces and the MPLA forces of the Angolan government. Angola had been a stage for conflict between the great powers, with the United States and South Africa supporting the UNITA rebels of Joseph Savimbi and the Soviet Union using Cuban forces to support the MPLA government. Years of war totally destroyed the economic infrastructure of this resource-rich country. It was to supervise the tenuous peace that saw New Zealand initially committed between 1991 and 1993. Our observers saw the promise of a tentative peace, the beginnings of economic recovery, the

A typical multinational UN group.
From left: Captian Steve Challies, (New Zealand), Major Krishna (India), Major General Shabinda (Zimbabwe), Captain Fencey (Brazil) and Lieutenant Colonel Fal (Senegal).
CHALLIES COLLECTION, AIM

Captain Steve Challies and Captain Ines Bergstram (Sweden) stand in front of an Uruguayan armoured vehicle in Huambo.
CHALLIES COLLECTION, AIM

holding of elections and then, when one side, UNITA, did not like the out-come — a collapse back to anarchy and war. We saw people killed and could do nothing. New Zealand was lucky that we had no casualties, but all our observers carry the mental scars of what they experienced.

New Zealand returned to Angola in 1994 hoping that history would not repeat itself. A new peace agreement was signed in November 1994. A third UN Angola Verification Mission (UNAVEM III) was deployed in 1995, and we committed five military observers and 12 de-mining training instructors and staff similar to programmes that we successfully ran in Pakistan, Cambodia and Mozambique.

In 1997 UNAVEM III ended, but three New Zealand observers and three instructors remained at the Angolan National Institute for the Removal of Explosive Devices to train staff in the skills of planning and carrying out de-mining operations.

Monitoring the elections and clearing the minefields in Cambodia with the UN Transitional Authority Cambodia (UNTAC), the Cambodian Mine Action Centre (CMAC) and Mine Clearance Training Unit (MCTU) 1992–2005

The bridges we build, the wells and accommodation we provide, the roads and airfields we repair, and the minefields we clear mean that whatever government takes over, the communities of Cambodia will inherit an array of practical improvements and a basic infrastructure for reconstructing their nation.

Colonel Neil Bradley, Force Engineer UNTAC[16]

Our New Zealand engineers were the first mine clearance specialists to arrive in Cambodia after the UN-brokered peace settlement. Being first, they developed the training techniques and procedures that became standard in both CMAC and MCTU. It has made our small forces world authorities on teaching de-mining techniques to indigenous peoples. These techniques are still being taught in Cambodia but also in Pakistan, Angola and Mozambique.

Corporal William White gives a mine clearing demonstration to Cambodian military personnel. NZ DEFENCE OFFICIAL PHOTOGRAPHY

We also made a major commitment to the UNTAC, which at its peak consisted of over 20,000 military, police and civilian personnel. We provided communication specialists to work together with the Australians to form an ANZAC signals unit. The New Zealand female signallers were the first New Zealand service women to serve in a UN peacekeeping operation. We also provided naval personnel to assist in monitoring Cambodia's waterways and coastline. A New Zealander, Colonel Neil Bradley, was Force Engineer commanding some 3000 personnel and responsible for all UNTAC military engineering work.

Khmer Rouge resistance made this mission a difficult one. UN observers, including New Zealanders, were detained by the Khmer Rouge, and in Siem Reap Khmer Rouge soldiers attacked a house occupied by New Zealand peacekeepers, retreating only when shots were fired over their heads.

New Zealand support to CMAC ceased in April 2005 when the Centre became completely run by its own nationals.

Supplying UN forces in Somalia: the UN Operations Somalia (UNOSOM) 1993–1995

> *God in whatever form he or she takes, walked away from this country three years ago and hasn't looked back.*
>
> Group Captain Bruce Fergusson, RNZAF[17]

Somalia is a country where the rule of law collapsed in the 1980s, and anarchy and famine reign. New Zealand provided an Army supply detachment to UNOSOM, which was tasked to monitor the 1992 ceasefire between the various factions, work to achieve a political settlement and ensure the secure distribution of humanitarian aid. As far as the Somali gangs were concerned, UNOSOM was just another player in the ongoing gang warfare.

> *Two days of sniper fire from overlooking buildings kept a lot of our guys on edge. They [the snipers] were coming down at nine in the morning*

A victim of the 'killing fields', Cambodia. NZ DEFENCE OFFICIAL PHOTOGRAPHY

A member of the New Zealand Army contingent to UNOSOM at the Mogadishu port-side warehouse behind the comparative safety of the razor-wire fence.

SERGEANT PAUL STEIN, RNZAF OFFICIAL PHOTOGRAPH

and plugging away until early afternoon. Several rounds came in over the camp. The [US] Marines had to go in with Hueys [Gunships] and clean them out.

Sergeant P K Farrant, No.42 Squadron, RNZAF[18]

To provide security, a United States-led Unified Task force (UNITAF) was authorised by the UN to deploy 32,000 personnel into Somalia. In addition to the supply detachment, we provided three Andover transport aircraft from No 42 Squadron RNZAF, which deployed in January 1993 to the airport at Mogadishu, the capital of Somalia. Our aircraft flew 233 missions, carrying 7600 passengers and 155,000 kilograms of cargo throughout Somalia.[19]

In May 1993 UNITAF withdrew and the 22,000-strong UNOSOM II took its place. This was the first UN peacekeeping force charged with the responsibility of restoring law and order, disarming combatants and continuing to provide the distribution of humanitarian assistance. We replaced our supply detachment with a 43-strong supply platoon, providing rations to the UNOSOM II force. Shelling and small arms fire were common, and any movement outside of the UNOSOM camp at Mogadishu airport was in armed convoy due to the threat of ambush. It was a difficult job in an operation where the UN failed to achieve its purpose and withdrew from Somalia in March 1995. As always in war it was the women and children who were the victims.

They all had a story to tell; many had lost husbands or children in the horrible violence of the civil war, and one woman had seen her daughter shot down just that morning. Others had been raped by bandits or warring clansmen. It was terribly sad.

Squadron Leader John Kennelly, Medical Officer, RNZAF[20]

Brigadier Brett Bestic, Commander Land Force Command, visits the New Zealand supply detachment at Taniwha Hill, Magadishu. RNZAF OFFICIAL PHOTOGRAPH

Santici Camp at night. A former tanalising plant, the camp was ringed with razor wire, making it seem like a prison. Rusting machinery lay strewn about the grounds. After patrols and checkpoint duties the New Zealanders returned to accommodation that was little more than converted shipping containers.[21] ANDY RADKA, NZ DEFENCE OFFICIAL PHOTOGRAPH

Protecting the supply of humanitarian aid to Bosnia: the UN Protection Force (UNPROFO) and its successors, 1995–2007

> *You had to recognise that it wasn't a case of being the strongest person in town. The job was to be the most tolerant, the most patient, and it was about building relationships. Force wouldn't work… Our guys washed their uniforms, they brushed their boots, so when they were on checkpoint duty they looked like professionals… The warring factions could look at us and say, 'hey, they're not here for a holiday. We like doing business with them.'*

Lieutenant Colonel Graham Williams, Commanding Officer First New Zealand Contingent[22]

War broke out in what was Yugoslavia in 1991. The country broke up into the states of Serbia and Montenegro, Croatia, Slovenia and Bosnia-Herzegovina. Vicious and bloody fighting occurred between the ethnic groups comprising the Serbs, Croats and Muslims. A ceasefire was agreed in 1995. New Zealand sent three contingents, each 250-strong, to form K (Kiwi) Company as part of a British Battalion in Bosnia. This was our largest overseas deployment since the war in Vietnam finished in 1972, and our first deployment in Europe since the end of the Second World War. The Kiwis occupied Santici Camp in Bosnia and had the task of ensuring that humanitarian aid and supplies got through to villages and towns cut off by opposing ethnic groups.

Bosnia marked a watershed in our involvement in UN peacekeeping operations. When many of the major powers of Europe were not prepared to act, New Zealand made an important gesture and committed combat forces to Bosnia, risking New Zealand lives in the cause for peace. The New Zealand Contingent was withdrawn on the establishment of the NATO Stabilisation Force (SFOR) in 1996 and replaced by staff officers on headquarters and liaison and observation teams that live within the community and monitor the security environment.

This continued under the European Union-led Force that replaced SFOR in December 2004 until the New Zealand contribution withdrew in August 2007. New Zealand has also contributed liaison staff to the UN Mission in Kosovo (UNMIK) since 1999.

Christmas mail from home arrives at Santici Camp. ANDY RADKA, NZ DEFENCE OFFICIAL PHOTOGRAPH

A Peace Monitoring Group convoy in Bougainville, 1998.
© NEW ZEALAND DEFENCE FORCE

Bougainville: Searching for Peace 1990, South Pacific Peacekeeping Force (SPPKF) 1994, Truce Monitoring Group (TMG) 1997–1998, Peace Monitoring Group (PMG) 1998–2003

New Zealand played a leading role in searching for peace to end the conflict on the island of Bougainville in Papua New Guinea. We got involved against the wishes of the Australian government, who saw it as their preserve. In mid 1990 New Zealand deployed three RNZN ships off the coast of Bougainville to act as a venue for peace talks between the Papua New Guinea government and secessionist leaders. In 1994 we provided support to the SPPKF in an unsuccessful attempt to bring peace. After further talks in 1997, New Zealand made a major contribution to the TMG, which was deployed to monitor the ceasefire under command of New Zealander Brigadier Roger Mortlock. New Zealand provided the largest contingent of the multinational force drawn from Australia, New Zealand and Vanuatu, providing three RNZN Ships, RNZAF helicopters, and Army personnel. A permanent ceasefire came into effect on Bougainville at the end of April 1998 and the TMG was replaced by the Australian-led PMG, with a much smaller New Zealand contribution. Positive political developments and improved security led to its conclusion in June 2003.

Bougainville was a major undertaking for New Zealand, and showed that we were prepared to act as it saw fit in security issues in the Pacific and not always in complete concert with Australia.

Timor-Leste: the UN Mission in East Timor (UNAMET) 1999, International Force East Timor (INTERFET) 1999–2000, UN Transitional Authority in East Timor (UNTAET) 2000–2002, UN Mission of Support in East Timor (UNMISET) 2002–2004, UN Office in Timor-Leste (UNOTIL) 2005–2006, UN Integrated Mission in Timor-Leste (UNMIT) 2006–2007

I don't think we should measure our success by the contacts we have had

Dili, capital of Timor Leste, on polling day. Private Ben Hajdu patrols through a village district. © NEW ZEALAND DEFENCE FORCE

with the militia. Apart from the first contact we had, every time we have met groups of militia we have got the better of them. But then so we should, given our training and our levels of professionalism. I think our success is best measured by the condition of the East Timorese people, who at last see the prospect of peace and stability after so much suffering. Their smiles, their gratitude makes us feel really humble. They are now planting crops, putting up buildings, and occupying empty villages where previously they had been too scared to return to them... That's how I measure the success of the Battalion's efforts here over the last six months.

Lieutenant Colonel Martin Dransfield, NZ BATT 2, UNTAET[23]

The rapid descent of East Timor into violence after the referendum voting for independence from Indonesia in 1999 saw the committal of the UN-authorised, Australian-commanded International Force East Timor (INTERFET) in September 1999. It became New Zealand's largest military deployment in 35 years and saw New Zealand commit an infantry battalion on operations for the first time since Borneo in 1966. The initial commitment involved over 1000 personnel of the Defence Forces, a frigate and a helicopter squadron with essential support from RNZAF C-130 Hercules aircraft. The New Zealand battalion's area of operations was around the town of Suai and along the southern border with West Timor. Its role was to maintain border security and help bring order by subduing Indonesian-sponsored militia gangs. The dangerous nature of this mission was made apparent when on 24 July 2000, while following the trail of a group of militia, a New Zealand soldier was killed, the first New Zealander to be killed in action since Vietnam. This was the first of a number of contacts with militia over this period.

In addition, local aid projects were undertaken; army engineers built roads and schools, and set up local water supplies. Soldiers helped teach English and doctors and nurses provided medical treatment. In all, some 6000 New Zealand Defence Force personnel served in Timor-Leste between 1999 and 2002 when the battalion was withdrawn, as well as 30 New Zealand police, corrections and customs officers.

Providing a battalion every six months was a major strain on the New Zealand Defence Force and this over-commitment, particularly of Army personnel, led to an exodus of experienced personnel, which had a long-term impact on New Zealand's defence capabilities.

In May 2006 a strike by members of the Timor-Leste armed forces and rioting led to requests for assistance for the restoration of law and order. New Zealand committed an infantry company and support personnel to the Australian-led mission.

Corporal Willie Apiata VC and veterans at Te Kaha marae.
© NEW ZEALAND DEFENCE FORCE

Afghanistan: Operation Enduring Freedom (OEF) 2001–

> *In total disregard for his own safety, Lance Corporal Apiata stood up and lifted his comrade bodily. He then carried him across the seventy metres of broken, rocky and fire-swept ground, fully exposed in the glare of battle to heavy enemy fire and into the face of returning fire from the main Troop position. That neither he nor his colleague was hit is scarcely possible. Having delivered his wounded companion to relative shelter with the remainder of the patrol, Lance Corporal Apiata re-armed himself and rejoined the fight in counter-attack.*

Extract from Citation for Victoria Cross, Corporal Bill Henry Apiata, 2 July 2007

The attack on the World Trade Centre in New York on 11 September 2001 saw New Zealand make an immediate contribution to Operation Enduring Freedom, the operational name given by the United States to its global war against terror, and in particular the operations of the coalition of countries supporting the United States in its invasion of Afghanistan. The invasion was assisted by RNZAF logistics airlift support and both RNZN frigates, HMNZS *Te Mana* and *Te Kaha*, were deployed to the Arabian Sea and Gulf of Oman on maritime interdiction operations.

Standing guard, Afghanistan, 2006.
© NEW ZEALAND DEFENCE FORCE

New Zealand committed combat forces with the deployment of the SAS on operations in Afghanistan in the hunt for leading members of Al Qaeda, the terrorist organisation behind the destruction of the World Trade Centre and attacks on other western targets. There were a number of contacts with pro-Taliban insurgents and it was during one such engagement in 2004 that Lance Corporal Bill Apiata, NZ SAS, carried a wounded comrade to shelter while under intense fire, a deed for which he was awarded the Victoria Cross in 2007. Apiata was the first New Zealander to receive this honour since Captain Charles Upham VC was awarded the bar to his Victoria Cross in September 1945 for his actions in North Africa in 1942.

New Zealand was also one of the first countries to provide a Provincial Reconstruction Team (PRT) in September 2003, at a time when many Western European countries were reluctant to make a similar commitment. The NZ PRT team, numbering some 122 personnel, operates in Bamyam Province on six-monthly rotations and is tasked with maintaining security. It carries out patrols through the province, provides advice and training to local police and oversees a series of aid projects sponsored by the New Zealand government and employing local workers.

> *Unfortunately there are never enough resources to go round. The key frustration for me is hearing the concerns and problems of the local communities and not being able to help out more. In a country with an ancient heritage and a long history of conflict we must satisfy ourselves with the steady but meaningful progress that we make. For example, things like functioning water wells [which] make a huge difference to struggling village communities.*
>
> WO1 Marcus Fowler, NZPRT[24]

Solomon Islands: Regional Assistance Mission to the Solomon Islands (RAMSI), 2003–

> *Our primary role in the Solomon Islands is to assist RAMSI and local police to maintain security but when the opportunity arises it is great to be able to help communities in need. The response we got from the villages we were able to help was amazing. They really appreciated the work we did.*
>
> Major Nigel Gattsche, RAMSI[25]

The breakdown of law and order in the Solomon Islands and the ongoing volatility of the situation saw New Zealand make a major contribution to the Australian-led RAMSI. The initial deployment from the 11 participating Pacific Island nations totalled some 2000 police and military personnel. New Zealand's contribution was a detachment of four Iroquois helicopters; crews, engineering and support staff, and headquarters staff officers. This was augmented by an infantry platoon, making a total of 222 New Zealand personnel.

An outbreak of violence and the burning down of Honiara's business centre saw New Zealand increase its infantry presence to that of a rifle company totalling 125 soldiers. These numbers have since been reduced back to a platoon supporting the 35 New Zealand police officers serving at any one time in RAMSI's Participating Police Force alongside the Royal Solomon Islands Police.

Private Deborah Kendon helping local children clean up around a village on the island of San Cristobel, Solomon Islands, February 2007. © NEW ZEALAND DEFENCE FORCE

291

Inspecting damage to a shop in the CBD of Nuku'alofa, Tonga, after the riots of 2006.
© NEW ZEALAND DEFENCE FORCE

And so it goes on

Peace is a state of mind. You have got to have something to live for and that is what we as peacekeepers tied to do.

Colonel Dave Gawn, 3LFG[26]

This chapter lists some of the many peacekeeping operations that New Zealand has been involved with. This commitment has grown considerably since the end of the Cold War and the collapse of the Soviet Union. Over recent years, the Pacific Islands have proved anything but peaceful and New Zealand has committed itself to assisting in regional assistance missions under UN mandate to Bougainville, Timor-Leste, Solomon Islands and, more recently, Tonga. While our involvement in the Pacific in on our doorstep, we also make a major contribution to UN and multinational peacekeeping operations world-wide. These do not always succeed, but they are better than standing by and doing nothing. For our size we do more than our share, but that also reflects on the number of times we are asked to assist, because we are seen to be good at what we do.

Small in many peacekeeping operations is, if not beautiful, at least appropriate. Our forces are used to operating in small, flexible units. We fit in small niches. We have skills that can take on the sort of tasks that peacekeeping demands: clearing mines, communications, medical teams.

Colin James, *When Peacekeeping Turns to War*[27]

ENDNOTES

PART 1: NEW ZEALAND WARS

Te Riri Pakeha

1. T Buddle, *The Maori King Movement in New Zealand*, Auckland, 1860, p. 18.
2. George Clarke, *Notes on Early life in New Zealand*, Hobart, 1903.
3. M Rogers (ed), *The Early Journals of Henry Williams, New Zealand, 1826–40*, Christchurch, 1961, p. 217.
4. Ibid, p.235.
5. Ibid.
6. Quoted in J Cowan, *The New Zealand Wars*, Vol 1, Wellington, 1983 (reprint), pp. 67–8.
7. Ibid., p. 87.
8. Pei Te Hurinui, *King Potatau*, Auckland, 1959, p. 228.
9. T Buddle, op.cit., p. 37
10. L S Rickard, *Tamihana the Kingmaker*, Wellington, 1963, p. 189.
11. Ibid., p. 164.
12. R Taylor, *The Past and Present of New Zealand*, London, 1868, p. 235.
13. J Cowan, op.cit., p. 425.
14. G Mair, *The Story of Gate Pa*, Tauranga, 1937, p. 53.
15. Quoted in J A Wilson, *Missionary Life and Work in New Zealand 1833–1862*, Auckland, 1889.

The Settlers' Story

1. Quoted in H Millar, *Race Conflict in New Zealand 1814–1865*, Auckland, 1966, p. 152.
2. F E Maning, *History of the War in the North of New Zealand Against the Chief Heke*, Auckland, 1862, pp. 9–12.
3. In Michael Barthorp, *To Face the Daring Maoris*, London, 1979, p. 26.
4. Quoted in T L Buick, *New Zealand's First War*, Wellington, 1926, p. 95.
5. H T Kemp, Protector of Aborigines, Russell, 8 July 1844 (Great Britain Parliamentary papers 1845, p.89).
6. T L Buick, op.cit., p. 118.
7. Michael Barthorp, op.cit., pp. 102–3.
8. In J Rutherford, *Hone Heke's Rebellion 1844-1846*, Auckland, 1947, pp. 18–19.
9. Octavius Hadfield, *A Sequel to One of England's Little Wars*, London, 1861, pp. 6–7.
10. Gore Browne, *Narrative of the Waitara Purchase and the Taranaki War*, Dunedin, 1965, pp. 9–10.
11. Enclosed in a letter from Grey to the Duke of Newcastle, 1 August 1863 (Great Britain Parliamentary Papers 1862-4, p. 387).
12. E A Williams, Journal, Hocken Library, Dunedin.
13. James Bodell, *A Soldier's View of Empire*, Keith Sinclair (ed), London, 1982.
14. In Rose Young, *G.F. von Tempsky: Artist and Adventurer*, Martinborough, 1981, p. 105.
15. Quoted in James Belich, *The New Zealand Wars*, Auckland, 1986, p. 181.
16. Great Britain Parliamentary Papers 1862–64, p. 602.
17. Quoted in Ormond Wilson, *War in the Tussock*, Wellington, 1961, pp. 16–17.
18. Quoted in J A Mackay, *Historic Poverty Bay*, Gisborne, 1966, p. 269.
19. Quoted in Marilyn Duckworth, 'Captain Gilbert Mair', *New Zealand Heritage*, p. 999.
20. *The Daily Southern Cross*, 14 July 1863.
21. Raewyn Dalziel, *Julius Vogel*, Auckland, 1986, p. 105.

PART 2: FIGHTING THE EMPIRE'S WAR

New Zealanders and the Anglo-Boer War 1899–1902

1. Rudyard Kipling (1865–1936) 'The Absent-Minded Beggar'. This popular poem was used for patriotic purposes in Malcolm Ross, *A Souvenir of New Zealand's Response to the Empire's Call*, Wellington, 1900, p. 14.
2. Eversley Belfield, *The Boer War*, London, 1975, pp. 166–7.
3. W S Gilbert (1865–1911). Gilbert wrote the libretto for Gilbert and Sullivan's *HMS Pinafore* (1878).
4. *New Zealand Herald*, 2 October 1899.
5. 'Theta', 'The Situation in South Africa', Napier, 1900.
6. See Simon Johns, 'Sons of Empire. A Study of New Zealand ideas and public opinion during the Boer War'. Unpublished BA (Hons) research exercise, Massey University, 1974, p. 18.
7. Harrison M Wright, *The 'New Imperialism': An Analysis of Late Nineteenth-Century Expansion*, Lexington, 1961, viii.
8. New Zealand Parliamentary Debates (NZPD), 28 September 1899, p. 75.
9. Ibid., p. 78.
10. Ibid., p. 87.
11. Ibid., p. 89.
12. For a useful account of the development and demise of the New Zealand Volunteer Force see: G Clayton, 'Defence not Defiance: The shaping of new Zealand's Volunteer Force'. Unpublished D Phil thesis, University of Waikato, 1990.
13. 'A New Zealander'. *New Zealanders and the Boer War*, Christchurch, c.1902, pp. 263–4.
14. Thomas Edward Taylor (1862-1911), elected to a Christchurch constituency in 1896 as a radical independent. He insisted that the Anglo-Boer War was a 'capitalist war'. After his 1899 defeat he returned to parliament in 1902.
15. W A Burnaby. Published in *New Zealand Herald* (supplement), 4 November 1899.
16. NZPD, 110, pp. 87–88. For a fair analysis of this debate see Ian McGibbon, *The Path to Gallipoli: Defending New Zealand 1840-1915*, Wellington, 1991, pp. 106–9.
17. *New Zealand Herald*, 13 October 1899.
18. *Tablet*, 28 September 1899.
19. Rutherford Waddell (1850–1932), Presbyterian minister and social radical.
20. *Waikato Argus*, 31 January 1900.
21. Trooper H D Coutts, previously a Taranaki farmer, rescued a Burmese Mounted Infantry NCO, under heavy fire. See Richard Stowers, *Kiwi Versus Boer, The First New Zealand Mounted Rifles and the Anglo-Boer War 1899–1902*, Hamilton, 1992, p. 160.
22. Laurie Barber, *No Easy Riches*, Auckland, 1985, pp. 134–5.
23. Simon Johnson, op,.cit., p. 30.
24. *Press*, 2 February, 1900.
25. Richard Stowers, op.cit., p. 23.
26. Trooper James Madill unpublished manuscript, formerly in Defence Force Library.
27. Field Marshall the Viscount Montgomery of Alamein, *A History of Warfare*, London, 1968, p. 452.
28. Sir Philip Magnus, *Kitchener: Portrait of an Imperialist*, London, 1958, pp. 171–2.
29. Appendices to the Journal of the House of Representatives (AJHR), 1900, 4–6a.
30. Richard Stowers, op.cit.
31. E Kinnear, *To the Modder River with Methuen*, London, 1900, p. 77.
32. See Eversley Belfield, op.cit., pp. 48–66.
33. Major General J P D French (1852–1925), later Field Marshal and Earl of Ypres, Chief of the Imperial General Staff (1914–15) and Commander of the British Expeditionary Force (1914–15).
34. Trooper G R Bradford died in captivity, probably never regaining consciousness after his fatal wounding. A memorial exists to his honour at Primrose Hill, Paeroa.
35. Trooper Alex Wilkie, 'The Battle of New Zealand Hill'. See Richard Stowers, op.cit., pp. 48–50.
36. Field Marshal Lord Roberts (1832–1914) won a Victoria Cross in 1858, and was arguably the best-loved commander in the history of the British Army.
37. General Piet Cronje was a poor strategist who wasted his initial opportunity in the war. See Peter Warwick (ed), *The South African War*, Harlow, Essex, 1980; and Thomas Pakenham, *The Boer War*, London, 1979.
38. Trooper Frank Perham, *The Kimberley Flying Column*, Timaru, nd., p. 18.
39. James G Harle Moore, *With the Fourth New Zealand Rough Riders*, Dunedin, 1906, p. 69.
40. Richard Stowers, op.cit., p. 62. Captain L March Phillips, of Rimington's Guides, confirmed this lack of citizen appreciation. See L March Phillips, *With Rimington*, London, 1902, p. 71.

41. An all too brief account of these actions is given in the official history: D O W Hall, *The New Zealanders in South Africa, 1899-1902*, Wellington, 1949, pp. 22–6.

42. Lieutenant Colonel R S B Baden-Powell, later Lieut-General Baron Baden-Powell (1857–1941). He achieved his greatest military fame as defender of besieged Mafeking.

43. Farrier–Major W J Hardham, 4th Contingent. See Richard Stowers, op.cit., p. 238.

44. Lord Kitchener of Khartoum (1850–1916) was Chief of Staff to F M Roberts 1899–1900 and thereafter Commander-in-Chief in South Africa until the Peace. Between 1914–16 he was British Secretary of State for War.

45. An excellent account of Boer commando tactics is given in Deneys Reitz, *Commando*, London, 1929. See also Hew Strachan, *European Armies and the Conduct of War*, London, 1983, pp. 76–9; and B Viljoen, *My Reminiscences of the Anglo-Boer War*, London, 1902.

46. Rudyard Kipling, 'the Parting of the Columns', Definitive Edition, London, 1912, p. 469.

47. Trooper Frank Perham, op.cit., p. 64.

48. Eighty per cent of all New Zealanders present were casualties. See Stowers, op.cit., p. 6.

49. Correlli Barnett, *Britain and her Army*, 1509–1970, London, 1970, p. 368.

50. 'A New Zealander', *New Zealanders and the Boer War*, op.cit., p. 51.

51. Lt. Col. A D Carbery, *The New Zealand Medical Service in the World War 1914–18*, Christchurch, 1924, p. 4.

52. Thomas Packenham, *The Boer War*, London, 1979, pp. 237–8.

53. 'A New Zealander', *New Zealanders and the Boer War*, op.cit., pp. 227–8.

54. This breakdown is compiled from official casualty reports in the New Zealand Defence Reports to Parliament from 1900–1903.

55. For a clear account of life in these concentration camps see A C Martin, *The Concentration Camps, 1900–1902. Facts, Figures and Fables*, Cape Town, 1957. The best contemporary account is Emily Hobhouse, *The Brunt of War and Where it Fell*, London, 1902.

56. R L Wallace, *The Australians and the Boer War*, Canberra, 1976, p. 303.

57. D O W Hall, *The New Zealanders in South Africa, 1899–1902*, op.cit., p. 97.

58. See G Clayton, *New Zealand Army*, Wellington, 1990, pp. 75–81.

59. Sir Uchter John Mark Knox Ranfurly, Fifth Earl (1856–1933). Governor of the Colony of New Zealand 1897–1904.

60. *Otago Daily Times*, 19 July 1902.

61. R H Bakewell, Mss Diary, 1902, Alexander Turnbull Library, Wellington.

62. R W Brown, *Te Moa: 100 Years History of Inglewood County, 1875–1975*, New Plymouth, 1975, pp. 173–4. See also Laurie Barber, 'Davies, Centurion of Empire'. 1, *The Volunteers* (*Journal of the New Zealand Military History Society*, 15.3), October 1989, pp. 118–19.

63. Corporal F Twisleton, *With the New Zealanders at the Front*, Christchurch, 1902, p. 324.

64. James G Harle Moore, *With the Fourth New Zealand Rough Riders*, op.cit., pp. 174–5.

65. Christopher Pugsley, *Gallipoli: The New Zealand Story*, Auckland, 1984, p. 42.

PART 3: THE GREAT WAR OF 1914–18

The Empire at War

1. Charles James Clark, interview with author. Original tape QE II Army Memorial Museum, and film interview TVNZ Archive. See also Maurice Shadbolt, *Voices of Gallipoli*, Auckland, 1988, and Pugsley, *Gallipoli The New Zealand Story*, Auckland, 1984.

2. OE Burton, *The Silent Division*, Sydney, 1935, p. 121.

3. S Seddon, interview with author. Notes in author's possession.

4. Dan Curham, interview with author. Tape and transcripts QE II Army Memorial Museum, and film interview TVNZ Archive. See also Shadbolt, op.cit., and Pugsley, op.cit.

5. Henry B G Lewis, interview with author. Tape and transcripts QE II Army Memorial Museum, and film interview TVNZ Archive. See also Shadbolt, op.cit, and Pugsley, op.cit.

6. Charles James Clark interview with author. Tape and transcripts QE II Army Memorial Museum, and film interview TVNZ Archive. See also Shadbolt, op.cit., and Pugsley, op.cit.

7. John Alphege 'Tony' Fagan interview with author. Tape and transcripts QE II Army Memorial Museum, and film interview TVNZ Archive.

8. Joseph G Gasparich interview with author. Tape and transcripts QE II Army Memorial Museum, and film interview TVNZ Archive. See also Shadbolt, op.cit., and Pugsley, op.cit.

9. George Albert Tuck, Letters, copy in author's possession, Alexander Turnbull Library and QE II Army Memorial Museum.

10. Cecil Laurence Lovegrove, 'Forty Years Ago Today They Marched Away to Adventure', *Wanganui Chronicle*, August 12, 1954, Lovegrove Papers, Wanganui Public Library.

11. Nancy Coad (ed), *My Dear Home: The Letters of Three Knight Brothers who Gave their Lives During WW1*, Auckland.

12. E C McKay Reminiscences, Kippenberger Library, QE II Army Memorial Museum.

13. E R Norman, Canterbury Infantry, letter dated 18 August 1914, QE II Army Memorial Museum RV1573.

14. N M Ingram, *ANZAC Diary, A Nonentity in Khaki*, Christchurch, p. 18.

15. Eric Millar, *Camps, Tramps and Trenches*, Dunedin, 1939.

16. N M Ingram, op.cit., p. 18.

17. Telegram, Harcourt to Liverpool Governor General of New Zealand, 12.20 a.m., 6 August 1914, *Times Documentary History of the War*, Vol X (Overseas), Part 2 London, 1919, p. 176. See Pugsley, op.cit., p. 52.

18. P M Thompson, Otago Infantry, Diary, Otago Regimental Museum, Dunedin, p. 30. See Pugsley, op.cit., p. 61.

19. 'Tony' Fagan, interview with author, op.cit.

Anzac

1. Auckland Museum Collection.

2. Richard F Ward, Diary and letter 25 April 1915, copy in author's possession, also copy in H H S Westmacott Papers, Westmacott Family and microfilm, Alexander Turnbull Library.

3. Diary Charles Wallace Saunders, NZ Engineers, Otago Regimental Museum, Dunedin. See Pugsley, *Gallipoli: the New Zealand Story*, Auckland, 1984, p. 94.

4. John Alphege 'Tony' Fagan, Auckland Infantry Battalion, interview. See also Shadbolt, *Voices of Gallipoli*, Auckland, 1988.

5. Diary, Lieutenant Herbert Spencer Westmacott, Auckland Infantry Battalion. See Pugsley, op.cit., p. 126.

6. Diary, Lieutenant Colonel Percival Clennell Fenwick, Assistant Director of Medical Services, New Zealand & Australian Division, Auckland Museum Library Collection. See also Pugsley, op.cit., and A D Carbery, *The New Zealand Medical Services in the Great War 1914–1918*, Wellington, 1924.

7. C E W Bean, *Gallipoli Mission*, Crows Nest, 1990, p. 102.

8. Lord Kinross, *Ataturk*, London, p. 76.

9. Diary, Frank E McKenzie, Auckland Infantry, Lawyer, QE II Army Memorial Museum Collection.

10. Diary, Colvin Stewart Algie, Alexander Turnbull Library.

11. Auckland Museum Collection.

12. Major General Godley, Commanding NZ and Australian Division to James Allen, NZ Minister of Defence, Allen Papers, National Archives.

13. Diary, Lieutenant Colonel P C Fenwick, op.cit.

14. Diary of James Robert Ruxton Leys, 7 May 1915, Leys Family. Copy in author's possession.

15. Diary, Lieutenant Herbert Spencer Westmacott, op.cit. See also Pugsley, *Gallipoli: The New Zealand Story*, op.cit., p. 112.

16. J M Downey, NZ Field Artillery, Gallipoli Diary, QE II Army Memorial Museum.

17. Cecil Malthus, *Anzac: A Retrospect*, Wellington, 1965, p. 90.

18. Harvey Johns, interview with author, original tape QE II Army Memorial Museum, film interview TVNZ Archive.

19. James Swan, DCM, Wellington Infantry, letters, QE II Army Memorial Museum.

20. Ion Idriess, *The Desert Column*, Sydney, 1939, p. 52.

21. Cecil Malthus, op.cit., p. 86.

22. Diary, Charles Wallace Saunders, NZ Engineers.

23. Diary, Lieutenant Colonel P C Fenwick, op.cit.

24. James Swan,DCM, op.cit.

25. Ibid.

26. George W Bollinger, Diary and letters, QE II Army Memorial Museum.

27. Lieutenant E G Pilling, *An Anzac Memory*, p. 35.

28. Cecil Malthus, op.cit. p. 93.

29. Joseph G Gasparich interview with author. Tape and transcripts QE II Army Memorial Museum, film interview TVNZ Archive. See also Shadbolt, op.cit., and Pugsley, op.cit.

30. Ion Idriess, op.cit., p. 55.

31. James Cowan, *The Maoris in the Great War*, Wellington, 1926, p. 37. See also Pugsley, *Te Hokowhitu A Tu*, Auckland, 1995, p. 36.

32. Julie Collier, 'Rawene Boys', from her album *The Coming of Age*, Wellington, 1988.
33. Ormond E Burton, 'A Rich Old Man', unpublished MS, p. 108, Alexander Turnbull Library, MS438.59.
34. Diary, Captain Colvin S Algie, Auckland Infantry, Alexander Turnbull Library, MS1374.
35. Major W H Cunningham letter to Lieutenant Colonel R Hughes, L King Collection. See also C L Lovegrove Papers, Wanganui Public Library.
36. Vic Nicolson, interview with author and television transcript, TVNZ *Gallipoli the New Zealand Story*, QE II Army Memorial Museum.
37. O E Burton, *The Silent Division*, Sydney, 1935, p. 120.
38. Letter to Sonnie from Lottie Le Gallais, Malta, dated 13 September 1915, AIM MS94/36.
39. John Duder, Diary of the Hospital Ship *Maheno*, 11 July–31 October 1915, AIM.
40. Cyril Bassett quoted in Pugsley, *Gallipoli The New Zealand Story*, p. 314.
41. Lieutenant Colonel P C Fenwick, Gallipoli Diary, AIM.

Keeping the Home Fires Burning
1. The reminiscences of Laura Mary Hardy as told to her daughter', AIM MS136.
2. L O H Tripp, 'War Relief and Patriotic Societies', in H T B Drew, *The War Effort of New Zealand*, Wellington, 1923, Chapter XI.
3. 'The reminiscences of Laura Mary Hardy as told to her daughter', op.cit.
4. Howard Robinson, *The Post Office in New Zealand*, Wellington, 1964. p. 194.
5. 'The reminiscences of Laura Mary Hardy as told to her daughter'.
6. Ibid.
7. Ibid.
8. Ibid.
9. Indeed the *Truth* got it right and the only case of ballot tampering occurred when one of the female clerks removed her boyfriend's card. Paul Baker, *King and Country Call*, Auckland, 1988, p. 109.
10. Paul Baker, Ibid., Chapter 5. See also Pugsley, *On the Fringe of Hell*, Auckland, 1991, Chapter 14.
11. James K Baxter *Collected Poems*, Wellington, 1979, p. 281.
12. See Paul Baker, op.cit., and Pugsley, op.cit., pp. 214–35.
13. Archibald Baxter, *We will Not Cease*, Marlborough, 1980, p. 123.
14. Pugsley, op.cit., p. 233.
15. Michael King, *Te Puea*, Auckland, 1977, p. 89.
16. 'The reminiscences of Laura Mary Hardy as told to her daughter', op.cit.
17. Pugsley, op.cit., p. 78.
18. *Auckland Weekly News*, 21 October 1915. See also Pugsley, op.cit., p. 78.
19. 'The reminiscences of Laura Mary Hardy as told to her daughter', op.cit.
20. James Allen, acting prime minister and Minister of Defence, to Lieutenant General Sir Alexander Godley, Commander NZEF dated October 1917, Allen Papers, National Archives.

On the Road to Damascus
1. C G Nicol, *The Story of Two Campaigns*, Auckland, 1921, p. 179.
2. E C McKay, *Reminiscences*, Kippenberger Library, QE II Army Memorial Museum, p. 112.
3. Ibid. p. 117.
4. C Guy Powles, *The New Zealanders in Sinai and Palestine*, Wellington, 192, pp. 3–4.
5. Christopher Pugsley, *Gallipoli: The New Zealand Story*, Auckland, 1984, p. 50.
6. Ion Idriess, *The Desert Column*, Sydney, 1951, p. 173. See also C Guy Powles, op.cit., p. 69.
7. John Robertson, *With the Cameliers in Palestine*, Dunedin, 1938, p. 14.
8. A Briscoe Moore, *The Mounted Riflemen in Sinai and Palestine*, Christchurch, 1920, pp. 16–17.
9. E C McKay , op.cit., p. 165.
10. William H Johns, letter to his mother, W H Johns Collection, AIM.
11. Elisabeth Ogilvie, 'Nursing in the First World War', draft in two parts, part one later published in the *Christchurch Press*, 10 November 1979.
12. John Robertson, op.cit., p. 27.
13. E C McKay, op.cit., p. 70.
14. A Briscoe Moore, op.cit., pp. 79–80.
15. J Masterman, Diary, Kippenberger Library, QE II Army Memorial Museum.
16. Ibid.
17. The Rollbook of the Wellington Mounted Rifles is in National Archives, that of the Canterbury Mounted Rifles is in the QE II Army Memorial Museum. Similar Rollbooks, usually of smaller size that could be kept in a haversack by the Squadron Sergeant Major, were held for each Squadron. With rare exceptions, they have not generally survived.
18. A Briscoe Moore, op.cit., p. 78.
19. A J Hill, *Chauvel of the Light Horse*, Melbourne, 1978, p. 71.
20. Ibid., p. 453.
21. E C McKay, op.cit., p. 106.
22. J Masterman, op.cit.
23. E C McKay, op.cit., p. 167.
24. A Briscoe Moore, op.cit., p. 85.
25. C G Nicol, op.cit., p. 119.
26. A D Carbery, *The New Zealand Medical Services in the Great War 1914–1918*, Wellington, 1924, p. 463.
27. E C McKay, op.cit., p. 108.
28. E C McKay, op.cit., p. 98 and p. 109.
29. John Robertson, op.cit., pp. 197–8.
30. Siegfried Sassoon, Collected Poems, London, 1947.
31. E C McKay, op.cit., p. 164.
32. Ibid. p. 177.
33. Ibid.
34. A Briscoe Moore, op. cit., p. 90.
35. Harry Frost, Auckland Mounteds.
36. E C McKay, op.cit., p. 141.
37. A D Carbery, op.cit., p. 481.

Our Women at War
1. Jane Tolerton, *Ettie: A Life of Ettie Rout*, Auckland, 192, p. 122.
2. A quote, 'Nursing Sister Ella Cooke, 1885-1917' from *Kai Tiaki* in AIM MS94/36.
3. Letter from Nurse Ella Cooke, Bernay, France, dated 31 December 1914, published in *Kai Tiaki*, Journal of the NZ Nurses Association, April 1915.
4. Ibid.
5. Ibid.
6. Ibdi.
7. Elizabeth Ogilvie, 'Nursing in the First World War', draft in parts, part one later published in the Christchurch Press, 10 November 1979.
8. Ibid.
9. Letter to Leddra Le Gallais from Lottie Le Gallais, July 1915, AIM MS94/36.
10. Letter to Sonnie from Lottie Le Gallais, Alexandria, dated 17 November 1915, AIM MS94/36.
11. Miss H MacLean, 'New Zealand Army Nurses', in H T B Drew, *The War Effort of New Zealand*, Wellington, 1923, p. 99.
12. Elisabeth Ogilvie, op.cit.
13. H T B Drew, op. cit., pp. 115–26, and A D Carbery, *The New Zealand Medical Services in the Great War 1914–1918*, Wellington, 1924.
14. Catherine Reilly (ed), *Scars Upon the Heart*, London, 1987, p. 108.
15. Gladys Violet Luxford, "How I came to be interested in war and why I went to World War One', AIM MS94/6.
16. Margaret Swarbrick Collection, AIM MS1468.

'On the Fringe of Hell'
1. John Brophy and Eric Partridge, *The Long Trail*, London.
2. Bert Gill to his wife Sophie dated 10/3/18, H H Gill Papers, AIM.
3. Russell Diaries, 21 October 1916, The Russell Family Saga, Volume III, Alexander Turnbull Library.
4. M E Hankins, *Chronicles of the NZEF* Vol IV No 38, 13 March 1918. See also Christopher Pugsley, *On the Fringe of Hell*, Auckland, 1991, p. 7.
5. Diary, Private G C L Clark, Auckland Infantry Regiment, dated 31 July 1917, MS AIM.
6. K L Trent, in *New Zealand at the Front*, quoted in O E Burton *The Silent Division*, Sydney, 1935, p. 188.
7. Owen Le Gallais, Diary, Le Gallais Papers, AIM.
8. W K Wilson Diaries, Wilson Family, copy in the author's possession.
9. Bert Gill to his wife Sophie dated 15/6/18, H H Gill papers, AIM.
10. Ibid., Easter Sunday, France.
11. Ibid., 6/7/18.
12. Ibid., 28/7/18.
13. Ibid., 9/4/18.
14. Ibid., 13/7/18.
15. Ibid., 13/6/18.
16. Ibid. 11/8/18.
17. Ibid., 30/9/18.

18. Ibid., 30/6/18.
19. Quoted in James Gasson, *Travis VC*, Wellington, 1966, p. 12.
20. O E Burton, op. cit., p. 234.
21. F M Twisleton, letter dated 24 April 1917, Alexander Turnbull Library.
22. Bert Gill to his wife Sophie dated 28/4/18., op.cit.
23. Alexander Aitken, *Gallipoli to the Somme*, Oxford, 1963, p. 169.
24. John Brophy and Eric Partridge, op.cit.
25. Ormond E Burton, 'A Rich Old Man', unpublished MS, Alexander Turnbull Library, MS438/59.
26. Bert Stokes, New Zealand Field Artillery, diaries and letters.
27. G A Tuck, letters and diaries, Alexander Turnbull Library.
28. 'My dearest cousin', letters of C S Alexander, Auckland Infantry Regiment, AIM.
29. H Stewart, *The New Zealand Division, 1916–1919*, Wellington, 1921, p. 291.
30. R B Lambert, 'The Stretcher Bearers' from *Chronicles of the NZEF.*
31. O E Burton, *Silent Division*, p. 168.
32. Colin M Gordon, 'Life o a Hospital Orderly in Cairo and England 1915–1916', AIM.
33. C R Baker, 'Blighty', *New Zealand at the Front*, London, 1918.
34. W K Wilson, Diary, Wilson family.
35. G C L Clark Diary, dated 26 March 1918, AIM.
36. R J Richards letter 17 August 1918, Richards Collection, Christs College, Christchurch.
37. Captain G Cory-Wright in a letter to his father dated 23 March 1917, QE II Army Memorial Museum. See Christopher Pugsley, 'Who is Sanders?' *Stout Centre Review*, March 1995, Volume Five, Number One.
38. G A Tuck letters and diaries, letter dated 12 November 1918, Alexander Turnbull Library.
39. Burton, 'A Rich Old Man', op.cit.
40. John Brophy and Eric Partridge, op.cit.

Sea Dogs and Flying Aces

1. See Ian McGibbon, *The Path To Gallipoli*, Wellington, 1991.
2. See Christopher Pugsley, *Gallipoli: the New Zealand Story*, Auckland, 1984, Ian McGibbon, *The Path to Gallipoli*, Wellington, 1991, Paul G Halpern, *A Naval History of World War 1*, UCL Press, pp. 83–6.
3. See Captain Hall-Thompson, 'The Work of the Philomel', in H T B Drew, *The War Effort of New Zealand*, Wellington, 1923, pp. 63–86.
4. This story of HMS *New Zealand* is based on my article 'HMS New Zealand: New Zealand's Gift to the Empire', *New Zealand Defence Quarterly*, No Seven, Summer 1994, p. 22.
5. Alex Boyle Diary, RNZN Navy Museum.
6. Ibid.
7. Ibid.
8. Ibid.
9. Ibid.
10. Ibid.
11. Ibid.
12. Ibid.
13. Ibid.
14. Pelorus Jack papers, AIM. See also Pugsley, op.cit.
15. Ibid.
16. Lieutenant Commander W E Sanders, VC, DSO, letters. Copies AIM.
17. J Bryant Haigh and Alan J Polaschek, *New Zealand and the Distinguished Service Order*, Christchurch, 1993, p. 392.
18. Paul G Halpern, op.cit., p. 343.
19. J Bryant Haigh and Alan J Polaschek, op.cit. p. 390.
20. Ibid., p. 384.
21. Ibid., p. 397.
22. Ibid., p. 382.
23. Roy Alexander, *The Cruise of the Raider 'Wolf'*, Sydney, 1939, p. 61.
24. Paul G Halpern, op.cit., p. 343.
25. *Cumberland*, *Port Kembla* and *Wimmera*, Roy Alexander, op.cit., p. 334.
26. Ibid., p. 78.
27. Carl Ruhën, *The Sea Devil*, Kenthurst, 1988, p. 31.
28. Roy Alexander op. cit., p. 311.
29. Roy Alexander, op. cit., pp. 310–28; Paul G Halpern, op.cit., pp. 373–4.
30. Richard Bickers, *The First Great Air War*, London, 1988, p. 259.
31. The Britannia was returned to the Royal Flying Corps. The research for this article is based on 'Anzac Pilots over Mesopotamia — 1915', an unpublished article by Nick Lee-Frampton commissioned by the *New Zealand Defence Quarterly*. See also T W White, *Guests of the Unspeakable*, Sydney, 1935.
32. H A Jones, *The War in the Air*, Volume V, Oxford, 1935, p. 253.
33. Nick Lee-Frampton, op.cit.
34. Ibid.
35. David Mulgan, *The Kiwi's First Wings*, Wellington, 1960, p. 53.
36. Ibid., p. 42.
37. Ibid.
38. Lieutenant Colonel John Studholme, *Record of Personal Services during the War*, Wellington, 1928, p. 493.
39. 'Auckland from Aloft', filmed by Charles Newham in April 1918. Copy of film AIM and New Zealand Film Archives.
40. A H McLintock, *An Encyclopaedia of New Zealand*, Vol 3, Wellington, 1966, p. 567.
41. J Bryant Haigh and Alan J Polaschek, op.cit., p. 304.
42. Christopher Shores, Norman Franks and Russell Guest, *Above the Trenches*, London, 1990, pp. 94–5.
43. Ibid., p. 62. See also David Mulgan, op.cit., p. 82.
44. Vincent Orange, Sir Keith Park, London, 1984, p. 16.
45. Shores, Frank and Guest op. cit., pp.296-7. See also Vincent Orange, op.cit.
46. Vincent Orange, *Coningham*, London, 1990, p. 28.
47. Haigh and Polaschek, op. cit., p.310; Shores, Franks and Guest, op.cit., p. 118. See also Vincent Orange, op.cit.

Remember

1. Lieutenant Colonel John Studholme, Record of Personal Services During the War, Wellington, 1928, p. 383.
2. Sir Douglas Robb, *Medical Odyssey*, quoted in Keith Sinclair, *A History of the University of Auckland 1883-1983*, Auckland, 1983. p. 74.
3. Henry Lewis, interview with author for TVNZ, *Gallipoli the New Zealand Story*, 1982. See also Shadbolt, *Voices of Gallipoli*, Auckland, 1988.
4. Betty Stewart (née Adams), interview with author Anzac Day at Stokes Valley, 25 April 1996.
5. Sidney M Perry, *Soldiers of the Mangateparu*, 1990, p. 31.
6. John Alphege 'Tony' Fagan interview with author. Tape and transcripts QE II Army Memorial Museum, film interview TVNZ Archive.
7. Cecil Burgess, interview with author, 1985.

PART 4: THE SECOND WORLD WAR 1939–1945

The Road to War

1. Eric Hobsbawm, *Age of Extremes*, London, 1995, p. 36.
2. Meirion & Susie Harries, *Soldiers of the Sun*, London, 1991, p. 101.
3. Prime Minister Michael Joseph Savage in a radio broadcast to New Zealand, 5 September 1939.
4. James Thorn, *Peter Fraser*, London, 1952, p. 170.
5. Sgt L H (Shorty) Lovegrove, MM, *Cavalry! You Mean Horses?*, Glendorran, 1994, p. 15.
6. Robin Kay, *Chronology: New Zealand in the War, 1939–1946*, Wellington, 1968, p. 3.
7. The title 2 New Zealand Division was not adopted officially until 29 June 1942. See Robin Kay, op.cit., p. 3.
8. Clarence J Moss, 27 (Machine Gun) Battalion, Circus Days, War Diaries, Vol 1, p. 20, AIM MS93/134.
9. It would grow to 20,000 by late 1944. See major General W G Stevens, *Problems of 2NZEF*, War History Branch, 1958, p. 188.
10. This summary is largely based on W E Murphy's succinct synthesis of New Zealand in the Second World War in A H McLintock (ed) *An Encyclopaedia of New Zealand*, Vol 3, Wellington, 1966, pp. 568–81.

Keeping the Sea Lanes Open

1. In September 1941 it became the Royal New Zealand Navy. See S D Waters, *Royal New Zealand Navy*, Wellington, 1956, p. 14.
2. S D Waters, *Achilles at the River Plate*, Wellington, 1948, p. 28.
3. S D Waters, *Royal New Zealand Navy*, p. 44.
4. Ibid., p. 60.
5. S D Waters, *Leander*, Wellington, 1950, p. 8.
6. S D Waters, *Royal New Zealand Navy*, pp. 188–94.
7. Ibid., p. 193.
8. Heath Simcox interview. Defence Partners (Pugsley, Rolfe, Missen) *Ordinary People: New Zealanders Remember the Second World War*, Department of Internal Affairs, 1995.

9. S D Waters, *Leander*, p. 29.
10. S D Waters, *Royal New Zealand Navy*, p. 398.
11. Paul Smith, *New Zealand at War*, Auckland, 1995, p. 122.
12. HMNZS *Kiwi* had an additional Oerlikon gun which it is said was obtained from the US Navy at Tulagi in exchange for two bottles of gin.
13. Frank Pugsley interview, 15 March 1995.
14. An aside in Frank Pugsley interview, 15 March 1995.
15. W E Murphy, 'War Against Japan', in A H McLintock (ed) *An Encyclopaedia of New Zealand*, Vol 3, Wellington, 1966, p. 580.

Flying with the Royal Air Force
1. Bill Simpson, discussion with author, June 1996.
2. See W E Murphy, 'The Air Force', in A H McLintock (ed) *An Encyclopaedia of New Zealand*, Vol 3, Wellington, 1966, p. 575.
3. Ibid.
4. John A (Jack) Sherwood, letter dated 18 February 1944, Lynne Curry Family Collection.
5. Sir Arthur Harris quoted in John McCarthy, A Last Call of Empire, Canberra, 1988, p. 119.
6. Newspaper report dated 5 March 1940, *NZ Herald*, Finn Scrapbook, AIM.
7. J D Fletcher, 'My Impressions on Active Service', letter dated 25 September 1988, AIM MS 89/4.
8. Ibid.
9. Ibid.
10. Lloyd M Noble, 'My War', letter to author dated 3 August 1996. AIM.
11. Bill Simpson, discussion with author, June 1996.
12. See W E Murphy, op.cit., p. 575.
13. Admiral H Riiser-Larsen representing the Norwegian Air Force in 1944, quoted in John McCarthy, op.cit. p. 119.
14. Bill Simpson, op.cit.

Baptism of Fire: Greece and Crete
1. Private Vincent J Salmon, West Coast Company, 19 Wellington Battalion, NZEF, letter dated 11 June 1941, AIM MS927.
2. W C McClymont, To Greece, Wellington, 1959, p. 223.
3. Stuart (Buster) Lindsay Snelling, 30 Battery, 6 Field Artillery, RNZA, letter to parents dated 25 May 1941, AIM MS 93/137.
4. Clarence J Moss, 27 (Machine Gun) Battalion, Circus Days, War Diaries, Vol 1, AIM MS 93/134.
5. E Saunders, 'Adventures in Plenty: A diary written by E Saunders on an escape from Greece to Crete', AIM MS 90/66.
6. M E Jackson diary, AIM
7. Ibid.
8. Clarence J Moss, op.cit.
9. See Paul Freyberg, Bernard Freyberg, VC, Auckland, 1991.
10. Private Vincent J Salmon, op.cit.
11. Clarence J Moss, op.cit.
12. Private Vincent J Salmon, op.cit.
13. James Thorn, Peter Fraser, London, 1952, p. 195.
14. Raymond Eaton Riddell, 27 (Machine Gun) Battalion, 'War Experiences in Crete, 1941', AIM MS1537.
15. Ibid.
16. Ibid.

War in the Desert
1. John Mulgan, *Report on Experience*, Auckland, 1947, pp. 14–15,
2. Clarence J Moss, 27 (Machine Gun) Battalion, Circus Day, War Diaries, Vol 1, 24 June 1941, AIM MS93/134.
3. Ibid.
4. Ibid.
5. This was the only thing he mentioned about the war to his son. Casual discussion with son in the Auckland Museum Coffee Shop, 14 February 1996.
6. Gunner Thomas Lawrence (Lawrie) Birks, 42 Battery, 14 LAA Regt, RNZA, letter dated 25 March 1942, 'Letters to his mother', AIM MS1413.
7. Clarence J Moss, op.cit.
8. Kenneth Sandford, *Mark of the Lion*, London, 1962, pp. 150–1.
9. See W David McIntyre, 'New Zealand', I C B Beer and M RD Foot (eds), *The Oxford Companion to the Second World War*, Oxford, 1995, pp. 796–801.
10. C W Hollies, 'Infantry man with the 2nd New Zealand Division in World War II', QE II Army Museum, p. 31.
11. Clarence J Moss, op.cit.

12. Major General W G Stevens, *Problems of 2NZEF*, Wellington, 1958, pp. 107–12.
13. Clarence J. Moss, op.cit.
14. Gunner Thomas Lawrence (Lawrie) Birks, op.cit.
15. C W Hollies, op.cit., p. 34.
16. Gunner Thomas Lawrence (Lawrie) Birks, op.cit.
17. Clarence J Moss, op.cit.
18. Ibid.

The Home Front
1. Newsclipping from 'Papers relating to the New Zealand Coast Guard Service, 1939–1977', AIM MS84/84 (MS1221).
2. Lauris Edmond (ed), *Women in Wartime*, Wellington, 1986, p. 169.
3. Ibid., p. 48.
4. Paul Smith, *New Zealand at War: World War II: The New Zealand Perspective*, Auckland, 1995, p. 102.
5. Anne Else, *Women Together: A History of Women's Organisations in New Zealand: Nga Ropu Wahine o te Motu*, Wellington, 1993, p. 423.
6. EPSO Onehunga District, Paper delivered in the Strand Theatre, Onehunga, on Sunday, 10 August 1941, by J Park, Mayor.
7. Nancy M Taylor, *The New Zealand People at War—The Home Front, Official History of New Zealand in the Second World War 1939–1945*, Vol 2, Wellington, 1986, p. 506.
8. Anna Rogers (ed), *The War Years: New Zealanders Remember 1939–1945*, Wellington, 1989, p. 58.
9. Nancy Taylor, op.cit., p. 779.
10. Ibid., pp. 566–7.
11. Lauris Edmond (ed), op.cit., p. 230.
12. Anne Else, op.cit., pp. 207 and 227.
13. Tony Simpson, 'The Twenty Second Burst', Radio New Zealand, 1971. Quoted in Owen Sanders, *Incident at Featherston*, Auckland, 1990, p. 14.
14. Quoted in Paul Smith, op.cit, p. 147.
15. Quoted in Nancy Taylor, op.cit., p. 954.
16. Michiharu Shinya in *the Path from Guadalcanal*, (trans edition) Auckland, 1979, p. 34.
17. Ibid., p. 154 (translator's notes).
18. A C Barrington, *Trials of a Pacifist*, New Zealand Christian Pacifist Society, [1970s], p. 5.
19. Quoted in Nancy Taylor, op.cit., p. 1165.
20. Ian Hamilton, *Till Human Voices Wake Us*, Auckland, 1984. p. 23.
21. The five detention camps were: Strathmore (near Reporoa), Hautu (near Turangi), Balmoral (near Christchurch), Whitanui and Paiaka (both in the Manawatu).
22. Nancy Taylor, op.cit., p. 893.
23. Quoted in Michael King, *Te Puea — A Biography*, Auckland, 1977, p. 206.
24. Ibid., p. 209.
25. Quoted in Paul Elenio, *Alla Fine de Mondo: To the Ends of the Earth*, Petone Settlers Museum and Club Garibaldi, Wellington, 1995, p. 65.
26. Gregor Riethmaier, unpublished manuscript.
27. Tim Walker, *Margot Phillips — Her Own World*, Te Whare Taonga o Waikato, Waikato Museum of Art and History, Hamilton, 1987, p. 17.
28. Krstyna Skwarko, The Invited, Wellington, 1974, Ch.3 Part 2.
29. Lauris Edmond (ed), op.cit., pp. 168–9.
30. Ibid., p. 169.
31. Harry Bioletti, *The Yanks are Coming: the American Invasion of New Zealand 1942–1944*, Auckland, 1989, p. 37.
32. June and Jack Hinton, *Commemorative Booklet. The Friendly Invasion of New Zealand by American Armed Forces*: June 1942–October 1944, Auckland, 1995, p. 8.
33. Nancy Taylor, op.cit., p. 633.

The Pacific War
1. L J Read, 'My Interesting Four Years 1940–1944', AIM MS 1093, p. 1.
2. Lieutenant Colonel F W Voelcker, DSO, MC, 'Heaven is a Hill', AIM MS1521, p. 233.
3. Translation of a Japanese soldier's diary from Bloody Ridge, Guadacanal, obtained by Mr Ivan Lloyd, wireless operator/gunner, RNZAF, AIM MS90/67.
4. Diary of Peter Kinder, Singapore 1941–1942, dated 28 January 1942, AIM MS93/88.
5. Ibid.
6. Ibid.

7. See p. 202–3.
8. One of the last messages received from a station when the Southern Gilbert Islands were occupied by the Japanese. See D O W Hall, *Coastwatchers*, Wellington, 1951, p. 4.
9. Peter McQuarrie, *Strategic Atolls: Tuvalu and the Second World War*, Christchurch, 1994, pp. 4–5. See also D O W Hill, op.cit.
10. D O W Hill, op.cit., pp. 26–7.
11. Nelson Dyett, interview. Defence Partners (Pugsley, Rolfe, Missen), *Ordinary People: New Zealanders Remember the Second World War*, Wellington, 1995.
12. Lieutenant Colonel F W Voelcker, DSO, MC, op. cit., p. 266.
13. See Lieutenant R A Howlett, *The History of the Fiji Military Forces 1939–1945*, Christchurch, 1948. See also Colin R Larson, *Pacific Commandos*, Wellington, 1946.
14. See Dan van der Vat, *The Pacific Campaign*, London, pp. 199–201.
15. [O A Gillespie], *Pacific Kiwis*, Wellington, 1947, p. 71.
16. That is if one does not count the United States Navy, American air support overhead and the Seabees engineer and construction units that rapidly followed up the initial New Zealand landings!
17. Sergeant W J Pearson, NZ EME. Pearson was mentioned in despatches for his work during the landings. See AIM MS93/147.
18. Ibid.
19. O A Gillespie, *The Pacific*, Wellington, 1952, p. 171.
20. [O A Gillespie], *Pacific Kiwis*, op.cit., p. 118.
21. Leon Missen interview, Defence Partners (Pugsley, Rolfe, Misen), *Ordinary People: New Zealanders Remember the Second World War*, Wellington, 1995.
22. Details of RNZAF aircraft numbers and types are listed in Charles Darby, *RNZAF: The First Decade 1937–1946*, Melbourne, 1978, p. 7.
23. W E Murphy, 'War Against Japan', in A H McLintock (ed), *An Encyclopaedia of New Zealand*, Vol 3, Wellington, 1966, p. 577.
24. Ibid.
25. Squadron Leader J M S Ross, *Royal New Zealand Air Force*, Wellington, 1955, pp. 149–50.
26. John Crawford, *New Zealand's Pacific Frontline*, Wellington, 1992, p. 21.
27. Charles Darby, op. cit., p. 5.
28. Leo White, *Fighters*, Auckland, 1945, p. 43.
29. Peter McQuarrie, op.cit., p. 31.
30. For the impact of this on one island group see Peter McQuarrie, op.cit., pp. 22–42.
31. H C and H E Maude, *The Book of Banaba*, Canberra, 1994, p. 93.
32. Ibid., p. 92.

Slogging Up Italy

1. Stan May, Bandsman, 6 NZ Infantry Brigade, letter to his sister Murial Springall dated 11 May 1944, AIM MS93/157.
2. W E Murphy, 'Second World War,' in A H McLintock (ed), *An Encyclopaedia of New Zealand*, Vol 3, Wellington, 1966, p. 572.
3. Major General Sir Howard Kippenberger, *Infantry Brigadier*, London, 1949, p. 344.
4. C W Hollies, 'Infantry man with the 2nd New Zealand Division in World War II', QE II Army Museum, p. 63.
5. Gunner Thomas Lawrence (Lawrie) Birks, 42 Battery, 14 LAA Regt, RNZA, letter dated 2 July 1944, 'Letters to his mother', AIM MS1413.
6. Major General Sir Howard Kippenberger, op.cit., p. 353.
7. Rawson Wright, 28 (Maori) Battalion, 'War Memoirs of Rawson Wright, OBE, from an interview with Marina Fletcher', AIM MS94/47.
8. Gunner Thomas Lawrence (Lawrie) Birks, op.cit.
9. C W Hollies, op.cit., p. 71.
10. Norcott de Bisson (Norm) Hornibrook, 'Personal Notes of an Autobiographical Nature — Part 2', *Historical Studies Group Newsletter*, No 12, March 1996, Geological Society of New Zealand.
11. Ibid.
12. Ibid.
13. Clarence J Moss, 27 (Machine Gun) Battalion, Circus Days, War Diaries, Vol 1, 1 December 1944, AIM MS93/134.
14. Ibid.
15. Many of these prisoners were also wounded, but do not feature in the wounded numbers. See W E Murphy, op.cit., p. 574.

Prisoners of War

1. E V (Ted) Everton, Prisoner of War Diary 1941-1945, Aug 1–22, 1942, AM MS 968, p. 19.
2. There were 501 New Zealand prisoners of war reported from the NZEF in the First World War. This does not include New Zealanders taken prisoner who served in the Royal Flying Corps or the Royal Navy. Lieutenant Colonel Studholme, *Record of Personal Services During the War*, Wellington, 1928, p. 384.
3. W E Murphy, 'Second World War', in A H McLintock (ed) *An Encyclopaedia of New Zealand*, Vol 3, Wellington, 1966, p. 574 and p. 576.
4. Rt Rev. Major R G McDowell, Diary 12/10/41–28/1/42, Fl of 4, AIM MS874.
5. Ibid.
6. Ibid.
7. Narrative of Prisoners of War Experiences in the Far East', Flight Lieutenant R D Millar, DFM, National Archive, Air 118/50.
8. Ibid.
9. Ibid.
10. Claude G Thompson, 'Into the Sun', AIM MS1102, p. 187.
11. Ibid., p. 62.
12. Ibid., pp. 202–4.
13. Ibid., p. 217.

Then Suddenly It's Over

1. D'arcy Whiting interview, Defence Partners (Pugsley, Rolfe, Missen), *Ordinary People: New Zealanders Remember the Second World War*, Wellington, 1995.
2. Nan Simcox interview, Ibid.
3. Robin Kay, *Italy*, Vol 2, Wellington, 1967, p. 570.
4. New Zealand's involvement was to be subject to MacArthur's approval. See Robin Kay, Ibid., pp. 576–7.
5. See Christopher Pugsley, 'Thank God for the Atom Bomb', *New Zealand Defence Quarterly*, Winter 1995, Issue 10.
6. Based on Christopher Pugsley, Ibid.
7. See Christopher Pugsley, Ibid.
8. Ibid.
9. Tom Mason interview, Defence Partners, op.cit.
10. Estelle Rolfe interview, Defence Partners op.cit.
11. Health Simcox interview, Defence Partners, op.cit.
12. The New Zealand War Amputees Association, *52nd Anniversary History*, November 1992, p. 51.
13. Joyce O'Leary interview, Defence Partners, op.cit.
14. D'Arcy Whiting interview, Defence Partners, op.cit.
15. Colin Apperley interview, Defence Partners, op.cit.
16. See A H McLintock (ed), *An Encyclopaedia of New Zealand*, Vol 3, Wellington, 1966, p. 580.
17. See 'NZ in the Second World War', Defence Partners, op.cit., p. 11; and table in A H McLintock (ed), op.cit., p. 580.
18. Quoted in C W Hollies, 'Infantry man with the 2nd New Zealand Division in World War II', QE II Army Museum.
19. The New Zealand War Amputees Association, op. cit., p. 51.
20. Patricia Connew interview, Defence Partners, op.cit.
21. New Zealand Soldier, Jayforce, interview, RNZAF Museum Wigram.
22. Robin Kay, op.cit., p. 579.
23. See Peter Bates, *Japan and the British Commonwealth Occupation Force 1946–1952*, London, pp. 161–6.
24. New Zealand Soldier Jayforce, interview, RNZAF Museum Wigram.
25. Ibid.

PART 5: SEARCHING FOR SECURITY

Fighting a Jungle War in Asia

1. 41 Squadron Unit History, May 1958.
2. Wing Commander Ron Manners, interview, 27 May 1992.
3. Bristol Type 170B, Mark 31/31E had two 1980 horse-power Bristol Hercules 734 engines. It had a takeoff weight of 44,000 lb (19,958 kg) and a cargo space of 65.2 cubic metres. Seating for 44 passengers could be fitted, which gave it a range of 1658 km (1030 miles). There was provision for a crew of three with a pilot, co-pilot and a radio operator behind the co-pilot. Leonard Bridgman (ed), *Janes All the World's Aircraft 1955-1956*, London, 1956, pp. 60–1.
4. Some 200 freighters were manufactured by 1955 and military versions had been purchased by the Royal Australian Air Force, Royal Canadian Air Force, Royal Pakistan Air Force, Royal Iraqi Air Force and the Burma Air Force, in addition to the RNZAF. Leonard Bridgman (ed), Ibid., pp. 60–1.
5. Brigadier Ian Thorpe, interview, 19 November 1991.
6. Air Commodore Ian Gilliard, interview, 10 June 1993.

7. Air Vice Marshal Pat Neville, interview, 11 June 1993.
8. Captain Doug Mackintosh, interview, 26 September 1991.
9. Peter Rutledge, interview, 27 October 1992.
10. Major G (Buster) Hornbrook, interview, 5 June 1992.
11. Dan Heke, interview, 10 November, 1992.
12. Cheam Yeom Toon, interview, FMS Bar Ipoh, August 1992.
13. Ibid.
14. Pru Meldrum, interview, 6 April 1993.
15. 'Journey to & Early Days in Malaya, Extracts from Letters Home', WO II White, W J, 1NZ Regt, 1 RNZIR Museum.
16. Group Captain Geoff Wallingford, from written notes provided with interview, 18 February 1993.
17. Lieutenant Colonel Eru Manuera, MC, interview, 2 September 1993.
18. Brian Marshall's account later published in Bob Gurr, *Voices of a Border War*, Melbourne, 1964.
19. As quoted by Bill Barnes, RNZA, 'Ho Chi Minh — My Part in His Victory', AIM.
20. Peter Eccles Smith, *Letters from a Viet Nam Hospital*, Wellington, 1969, p. 26.
21. Bill Barnes, op.cit.
22. Bob Breen, *First to Flight*, Sydney, 1988, p. 107.
23. Terry Burstall, *The Soldiers' Story*, St Lucia, 1980, pp. 99–100.
24. Colonel Roger Pearce, interview, 13 November 1992.
25. Dick Smith, interview, 6 November 1992.
26. Jeny Curnow, interview, September 1996.

Under the Blue Beret
1. From 'The UN and US', in Defence Partners (Missen, Rolfe and Pugsley), *Ordinary People: New Zealanders Remember the Second World War*, Wellington, 1995, p. 2.
2. Interview with Rear Admiral E C Thorne, CB, CBE, RNZN, 1992, RNZN Museum, p. 113.
3. 'Royal New Zealand Navy', Report of the New Zealand Naval Board for the Period 1 April 1953 to 31 March 1954, Wellington, 1954.
4. Interview, Ian Mackley, June 1996.
5. Ibid.
6. Ian McGibbon, 'The Guns of Kapyong', *New Zealand Defence Quarterly*, No 13 Winter, 1996, pp. 25–9.
7. Interview, Jack Spiers, 4 June 1992.

8. Gilbert Wong, 'Putting your money where your mouth is', p. 18, *New Zealand Defence Quarterly*, Number 12, Autumn, 1996.
9. Gilbert Wong, 'Where Force Wouldn't Work', p. 14–17, *New Zealand Defence Quarterly*, Number 12, Autumn, 1996.
10. Clive Sinclair interview, 30 August 1996.
11. Interview with author 8 October 1992.
12. Captain Karyn Marie Te Moana, 'The Multinational Force and Observers', Letter to author, AIM.
13. Colonel Clive Sinclair interview with author.
14. Quoted in John Crawford, *In the Field for Peace: New Zealand Defence Force*, 1996, p. 44.
15. Colonel Trevor McComish interview with author.
16. Richard Jackson, 'Making a Mark in the Minefields', *New Zealand Defence Quarterly*, No. One, Winter 1993.
17. Jock Vennell, 'Appointment in Somalia', p. 36–39, *New Zealand Defence Quarterly*, No. One, Winter 1993.
18. Ibid.
19. See John Crawford, *In the Field for Peace: New Zealand Defence Force*, 1996, p. 44.
20. Jock Vennell, op.cit., p. 38.
21. Mark Scott, 'Waging Peace: The New Zealand Army in Bosnia', *New Zealand Geographic*, No 26, April–June 1995, pp. 48–62.
22. Gilbert Wong, 'Where Force Wouldn't Work', p. 14–17, *New Zealand Defence Quarterly*, No 12, Autumn, 1996.
23. John Crawford and Glyn Harper, *Operation East Timor: The New Zealand Defence Forces in East Timor 1999–2001*, Reed, Auckland, 2001, pp. 147–8.
24. WO1 Marcus Fowler, 'Afghanistan: an Army Perspective,' http://www.nzdf.mil.nz/news/feature-stories.
25. 'Father to lead son in the Solomon Islands,' http://www.nzdf.mil.nz/news/feature-stories.
26. Judith Martin, 'Bosnia-Mission Complete,' 10 August 2007, http://www.nzdf.mil.nz/news/feature-stories.
27. Colin James, 'When Peacekeeping Turns to War,' pp. 2–7, *New Zealand Defence Quarterly*, No. One, Winter, 1993.

INDEX

Numerals in *italic type* refer to illustrations.

Acheson Sgt. Maj. William, *34*
Achilles, 167, 170ff
Acland, H D, 212
Admiral Graf Spee, 170
Aerodrome Construction Company, No 1, 220
Afghanistan, 282, 290-1
Afrika Corps, 195
Ahu Ahu, *16*, 29
Aitken, Alexander, 136
Aitken, Lt. Col. Jock 263
Ajax, 170
Albert Barracks, 27, *28*
Alexander, Charles S, 138
Alexander, Gen. Sir Harold, 201, 236
Algie, Colvin, 79, 89
Allen, A J, *262*
Allen, James 79, *99*, 101
Allenby, General, 110
Allum, Sir John, *207*
ambulances, 59, 105-6, 109, 135, 142
American troops, 216, 271, 272
Anderson, Sister C, 105
Andrews, Lt. Col. L W, 190, 191
Angola, 283–4
Anzac Battalion, 275
Anzac Corps, 76ff, 104, 124, 126, 186
Anzac Day, 64, 160-1
Anzac Mounted Division, 281
ANZAM, 258
Anzio, 235
ANZUS, 260
Aotea Home, *105*
Apiata, Corp. Willie VC, 290
Aporo's Book of Dreams, *25*
Apperley, Colin, 252
Arawa, 15, *41*, 42
Armed Constabulary, 27, 37, 39, 41
Armenia, 104
Armentières, 124, *125*, 126
Auckinleck, Lt. Gen. Sir Claude, 195, 201
Auckland Rifle Volunteers, *36*
Auckland, 16, 17, 27, 28, 29, 32, 38, 43
Austin, Bugler, *34*
Australia, 145, 146
Australian Corps, 124
Australian Light Horse, 102, 104, 107, 115

Baden-Powell, Lt. Col. R S, 57
badges, 27, 52, 70, 71, *87*
Baker, C R, 139
Bakewell, R H, 63
Banabas, 233
Bannermann, Capt. Ronald, 156
Barnes, Bill, 271
Barrington, A C, 212
Barrowclough, Maj. Gen., 222
Barton, Charles, 156
Bassett, Cyril, 65, *92*
Bastion Point, 43

baths, 131, 132
battalions, 88, 89, 94, 169, 218, 220, 225, 263, 267, 268, 269
- 20, 191
- 22, 190, 240
- 22 Motorised, 234, 239
- 27 (Machine gun), 169, 240
- 30, 218, 225
- 34, 224
- Anzac, 273
- Auckland, 70, 75, 76, 77, 79, 82, 87, 89
- Canterbury, 72, 86
- 28 (Maori), 168, *169*, 191, *192*, 197, 202, 236, 237, *239*, *240*, 253
- Otago, 86, *161*
- Pioneer, 88, 99, 132, 135
- Wellington, 71, 72, 73, 82, 84, 85, 89, *90*, 92
Battle of Britain, 179, 180
'Battle of Manners Street', 217
Battle of the Atlantic, 175, 177, 179
Baxter, Archibald, 98, 99
Baxter, James K, 98
Bay of Islands, 16-17, 26, 28, 29, 42
Bay of Plenty, 18, 21, 26, 37
Bean, C E W, 78
Beatty, Vice Admiral, 146
Bedouin, 110
Beere, D M, 34
Beersheba, Battle of, 113
Bergstrom, Capt. Ines, *284*
Bestic, Brig. Brett, *286*
Biggs, Maj. Reginald, 40
Birdwood, Maj. Gen. Sir Alexander, 74, 76
Birks, Lawrie, 196, 201, 236, 237
Blamey, General, 186, 195
Bloemfontein, 57, 60
Blucher, 146, 147
Bodell, James, 33
Bollinger, George, 85
Bolsheviks, 104
Bolt, George, 155
Bomber Command, 180, 182
bombs, 154-5, 250
Booth, Lt. Col., 37, 38
Borneo, 266
Bosnia, 278, 287
Bougainville, 224, 231, 288
Boulton, Lt. James, 36
Boyle, Lt. Alex, 146, 147, *150*
Boy Scouts, 207
Bradford, Trooper G R, 55
Bradley, Col. Neil, *284*, 285
Brandon, Lt. A, 156
Breen, Bob, 271
Brewster Buffalo fighter, *220*
Bridson, Lt. Cdr. Gordon, 174
brigades, 169, 189, 190, 191, 197, 198, 222, 223, 224, 225, 234, 239, 240
- 4, 169, 189, 190, 197-8, 240
- 4, Armoured, *234*
- 5, 169, 189, 190, 191, 234, 239
- 6, 169, 234, 239

- 8, 218, 223-4
- 9, 240
- 10, 190
- 14, 220, 223-5
- 15, 223
- Australian, 74, 81
- Naval, 38
- New Zealand Infantry, 81, *90*
- New Zealand Mounted Rifles, 52, 53, 55, 56, 62, 68, 70, 72, 86ff, 101, 102ff
Bristol Freighter, *259*
Britannia, 61
British Pacific Fleet, 173, 177
British Tanker Company, 175
Brown, Ellen, 120
Brown, Officer, 87
Brown, Archdeacon, 37
Browne, Sir Thomas Gore, 17, 32
Buddle, Rev. Thomas, 14
bully beef, *81*, 112, 133
Burdan, David, 208
Burgess, Cecil, 161
Burma, 27, 179
Burn, Lt. Wallace, 154
Burn, Trooper R B, 155
Burton, Ormond, 68, 89, 90, 135, 137, 138, 143, *211*
Burtt's Farm, 21
Bushrangers, 27

Cairo, 199
Cakabau, Capt. Edward, *222*
Caldwell, Keith, 155, 156
Callaway, Trooper, *51*
Callender, Geoffrey, 155, 156
Cambodian Mine Action Centre, 284
Camel Corps, 104
Cameron, Gen. Sir Duncan, 20, 32, 33, 35, 36, 37, 38, *39*
Camerontown, 21
Carbery, A D, 115
Carey, General, 21
Carr, Miss, *123*
Cassino, 235ff
casualties, 57, 59, 61, 62, 65, 78-9, 91, 92, 93, 101, 105, 113, 115ff, 124, 128, 134, 138, 144, 158, 160-2, 167, 171, 172, 173, 177, 183, 185, 189, 193, 196, 198, 199, 202, 206, 236, 238, 239, 241, 250, 253, 256, 268, 275, 177, 283
cavalry, 37, 46, 55, 168, 200
Ceylon, 27
Challies, Capt. Steve, *283, 284*
Changi, 244, 261
Chatham Islands, 24, *25*
Chaytor, Maj. Gen. Ted, *103*, 281
Checketts, Johnny, 180
chemical warfare, 135, 136
China, 166
Christian Pacifist Society, 211, 213
Chunuk Bair, 65, 78, *84*, 88ff, *93*
Churchill, Winston, 167, 195, 220
Claret Patrols, 268

Clark, Charlie, *69*
Clark, G C Latimer, 128, 140
Clark, Gen. Mark, 235
Clarke, George, 15
Cleary, Father Patrick, 51
coast-watchers, 221, 232
Coastal Command, 180
Coastal Defence Searchlight Crew, *205*
'Coconut Bombers', 218
Colenso, 55
Colesberg, 55
Colonial Defence Force, 37
Commonwealth Monitoring Force (CMF), 280
companies:
- 3rd, 70, *77*, *86*
- 15th, 104
- 16th, 77, 104
- K (Kiwi), 287, 289
- New Zealand Rifle, 267
- V (Victor), 273
- W (Whisky), 273
compulsory military training, 258
concentration camps, 61
concerts, 113, 128, 132, 199, 215
Condick, Sister, *105*
Confrontation, 267, 273
Coningham, Arthur, 157, 179
Conor, Capt. O, 172
Connew, Patricia, 254
conscientious objectors, 97-9, 212, 213
conscription, 62, 97-9, 101, 127, 211
contingents, 51, 56
Maori, 49, 50, *75*, 87-8, 99
Naval, 27
- 1st, *46*, *51*, *52*, 55, 56
- 2nd, 51, 56
- 3rd (Rough Riders), 51, 56, *58*, *59*, 64
- 4th (Rough Riders), 51, 56, 58, 59, 65
- 5th, 56, 58, 59
- 7th, 63
- 9th, 59, 63
- 10th, *49*
Cook, Capt., 14, 26
Cook, Pte. R, *265*
Cook, W W, 157
Cooke, Ella, 116, *117*
Cooper, G S, 40
Coral Sea, 219
Cory-Wright, C, 141
Cotton, Sgt. Pilot H, *182*
Courtney's Post, 84, 86
Coutts, Trooper H D, 51
Craddock, Major M, 56
Creswell, W *109*
Crete, 168, 189ff, 237, 242
Crimean War, 27, 47
Cronje, General, 56, 57
Cunningham, William, 89
Curacao, 37, 38
Curham, Dan, *69*, 85
Curnow, Allen, 160
Curnow, Jeny, 273
Cyprus, 279